PACIFIC LINGUISTICS

Series C - No. 51

GURUNG-NEPALI-ENGLISH DICTIONARY

WITH ENGLISH-GURUNG AND NEPALI-GURUNG INDEXES

by

Warren W. Glover
Jessie R. Glover
Deu Bahadur Gurung

Department of Linguistics
Research School of Pacific Studies
THE AUSTRALIAN NATIONAL UNIVERSITY

PACIFIC LINGUISTICS is published through the *Linguistic Circle of Canberra* and consists of four series:

SERIES A - OCCASIONAL PAPERS
SERIES B - MONOGRAPHS
SERIES C - BOOKS
SERIES D - SPECIAL PUBLICATIONS.

ALL CORRESPONDENCE concerning *PACIFIC LINGUISTICS*, including orders and subscriptions, should be addressed to:

The Secretary,
PACIFIC LINGUISTICS,
Department of Linguistics,
School of Pacific Studies,
The Australian National University,
Box 4, P.O.,
Canberra, A.C.T. 2600.
Australia.

First published 1977.

The editors are indebted to the Australian National University for help in the production of this series.

This publication was made possible by an initial grant from the Hunter Douglas Fund.

National Library of Australia Card Number and ISBN 0 85883 147 3

PREFACE

This first Roman edition of a Gurung-Nepali-English dictionary contains about 4000 Gurung words, collected on various field trips between 1967 and 1974 under the agreement of cooperation between the Summer Institute of Linguistics and Tribhuvan University, Kathmandu. We gratefully acknowledge the encouragement, assistance, and active interest of Dr S.B. Shakya, Vice Chancellor of the University, and of Dr P.R. Sharma, Dean of the Institute of Nepal and Asian Studies.

Among our many friends in the village of Ghachok we wish to thank especially Shri Phouda Bahadur Chetri, former Pradhan Panch, and Shri Sher Bahadur Gurung, former Upa Pradhan Panch, of the Lower Chachok Panchayat and Shri Pas Bahadur Gurung, Pradhan Panch of Upper Ghachok Panchayat, for their interest, support, and encouragement on field trips.

A Gurung-Nepali-English Glossary was published in 1976 by the Summer Institute of Linguistics, Kathmandu, in the Devanagari script. We are grateful to the two publishers, of that and of this edition, for agreeing to the use of the same Devanagari Nepali-Gurung index in each volume.

We are grateful to Miss Amrita K. C. of Kathmandu for help in checking the semantics and spelling of the Nepali glosses, and for typing the Devanagari manuscript, and to Mrs Sally Sinisoff of the Department of Linguistics, Australian National University, for her typing of the Roman manuscript, a task made the more exacting by the authors' remoteness from Canberra.

W.W. Glover
J.R. Glover
D.B. Gurung

Pokhara, September 1977.

TABLE OF CONTENTS

INTRODUCTION

Gurung is a Tibeto-Burman language spoken by about 170,000 people, mostly living in Gandaki zone in central west Nepal. With Tamang, Thakali, and Manang, Gurung is a member of the Gurung Family within the Bodish Substock, which includes also the Tibetan Family, Kaike, and Ghale (W. Glover 1974:8-13). The dialect represented here is primarily that of Deu Bahadur Gurung, born and raised in Ghachok village, near Pokhara, in Kaski district. Pronunciation variants shown in the dictionary have all been heard in Ghachok, either from DBG himself or other speakers, some of whom come from other villages up to one day's walk away. Study of Gurung dialects (W. Glover and Landon n.d.) reveals at least three major geographical dialects of Gurung - East, West, and South - with continuous variation within dialects. Ghachok falls within the West Gurung dialect.

1. ORTHOGRAPHY

Gurung and Nepali forms are cited in a Roman transliteration of the Devanagari script. Figures 1 and 2 show the segmental phonemic inventory of Gurung, and symbols used for native Gurung words.

	Labial	Dental	Retroflex	Apico-alveolar affricates	Velar	Glottal
Stops:						
vl. unasp.	p	t	ṭ	c	k	
vl. asp.	ph	th	ṭh	ch	kh	
vd.	b	d	ḍ	j	g	
Fricatives		s				x
Nasals	m	n			ŋ	
Lateral		l				
Flap		r				
Semivowels	w			y		

Fig. 1. Consonants

	Front	*Central*	*Back*
High	i		u
Mid	e	a	o

Fig. 2. Vowels

Although phonemically there is only one sibilant phoneme /s/ in Gurung, as in Nepali, loanwords from Nepali are spelt with the same sibilant symbol as in the Nepali source, whether the 'dental' s, 'retroflexed' ṣ, or 'alveo-palatal' š.

The voiceless glottal fricative x (phonetically [h]) is not a segmental phoneme in native Gurung words but occurs only in loanwords from Nepali, and then only in word initial position. The symbol x is also employed to represent the feature of breathiness on a syllable. The positioning of x in the orthography represents the position of the corresponding Devanagari symbol (transliterated h in Roman Nepali) in the syllable; that is, preceding the vowel, except in the prefix ax-, and preceding the consonants y, r, and w (except that it follows the consonant clusters kr, mr, pr).

In Gurung, aspiration of a voiced stop or affricate is phonemically breathiness on the syllable and is marked by x. The departure from the traditional bh, dh, etc., for voiced aspirates is necessitated by the contrast in Gurung between aspiration and breathiness following voiceless stops: pxi *'carrying basket'*, phi *'bark, peel'*. Once x is used to mark breathiness in this environment, following voiceless stops, consistency dictates use of the same symbol in the environment following voiced stops, and consistency in transliteration from Devanagari requires x for the glottal fricative [h].

Contrastive nasalisation is represented by a superscript tilde (ã, ẽ, ĩ, õ, ũ). Preceding a nasal consonant, Gurung vowels automatically take on a nasal articulation. Should this nasality be written? According to strict phonemic theory, yes, since nasality is a phonemically contrastive feature in the language, and in fact literate Gurungs generally do write the Devanagari nasal diacritic on such vowels, reacting to the phonetic and phonemic nasality. However, many of the words involved are loans from Nepali, and for the sake of orthographic consistency with Nepali, in which language vowel nasalisation is not written before a nasal consonant, and for the sake of orthographic economy in Devanagari (not writing a predictable diacritic), we have in this dictionary written vowels preceding nasal consonants within the same morpheme as oral vowels. Thus taan *'all'*.

Accent, or high tone, is represented by apostrophe (') following the accented syllable. On monosyllabic morphemes (the majority, when loan words are excluded) accent and breathiness intersect to give four tone classes: clear intense (ca' *'he'*); clear relaxed (ca *'vein'*); breathy rising (cxaa' *'tea'*); breathy low (cxa *'son'*). In polysyllabic morphemes, breathiness occurs generally only on the first syllable, but accent may occur on any one syllable or none.

Phonemically long vowels are written geminate. By far the most common is aa. Word finally there is no sharp contrast between -a and -aa. In rapid speech all words written with either the short or long vowel tend to be pronounced with the short, more central, a; in slow, deliberate "spelling pronunciation" speech some words show the lengthened, phonetically lower, aa. The difference is partly conditioned by word tone and shape (as noted for verb suffixes in W. Glover (1974:xxiii)), and an attempt has been made to represent the distinction in the dictionary, but the analysis is not final, nor is the present representation, unfortunately, consistent.

The consonants s, c, and j coalesce with a following y to become lamino-alveolar in pronunciation. The same palatalising process normally occurs before the front vowels i and e, but in a very few words the apico-alveolar pronunciation is retained. These words are marked by a slash through the consonant: ¢xi *'undergrowth'* (contrasting with cxi *'knee'*).

The phonemic sequence /kl/ has different phonetic realisation in different Gurung dialects. In Ghachok it is voiceless lateral fricative with palatal release [ɬʸ], and is represented in the present orthography by a conventional khly (as the symbol cluster in Devanagari approximating as nearly as possible to the phonetic realisation).

Further phonetic description of Gurung, including the tone system, is given in W. Glover (1969).

Nepali words are transliterated using a similar transcription, but without x or ', and with the addition of (nonphonemic) distinctions between 'dental' n and 'retroflex' ṇ, and between 'short' i and u and 'long' ī and ū. The Devanagari script employs a special symbol for the combination /ri/, and the symbol is here transliterated ri+, as in ri+ṇ *'loan'* (*G* che). The primary spelling standard adopted for Nepali words is Singh (1971); words not found in Singh have in some cases been supplied from Meerendonk (1960) or Regmi (n.d.), but many words could not be found in any of these sources.

2. ALPHABETISING ORDER

The Gurung entries are arranged according to the English alphabet, except that the symbols aa and ŋ are treated as units immediately following a and n respectively, and š is a unit immediately preceding ṣ, which in turn precedes s. Thus, words commencing with the long vowel aa appear after *all* the words commencing with a. Retroflexed consonants (indicated by subscript dot, e.g. ṭ, ḍ, ṇ, ṣ) and nasalised vowels (indicated by superscript tilde, e.g. ã, ẽ, ĩ, õ, ũ) precede their counterparts without diacritics; thus, all words with retroflexed ṭ precede words with dental t, and all words with nasalised ã precede words with oral a. Accent, ', is ignored in alphabetising except where words are otherwise identical, when the accented form precedes the unaccented, and a word with accent on the first syllable precedes one with accent on the second syllable. Thus, pa'di, padi', padi.

Entries in the Nepali-Gurung index, being in Devanagari script, are arranged by Devanagari order: a, aa, i, ī, u, ū, ri+, e, ai, o, au, k, kh, g, gh, ŋ, c, ch, j, jh, ṭ, ṭh, ḍ, ḍh, ṇ, t, th, d, dh, n, p, ph, b, bh, m, y, r, l, w, š, ṣ, s, h.

3. STRUCTURE OF AN ENTRY

a) Gurung-Nepali-English entries contain:

1) the Gurung word, followed by superscript numerals if required to distinguish forms with identical segmental phonemes.
2) variant pronunciations, separated by commas.
3) comparative information, in square brackets [ ].
4) grammatical category.
5) Nepali gloss, between pointed brackets < >.
6) English gloss. To facilitate reversal of the entries by computer (in producing a useful English-Gurung index) the word placed first in the English gloss is usually a generic term, with its modifiers following a dash, e.g. 'frog - black, lives in water'. Other information specifying a gloss, including kin specification, is included in parentheses, e.g. 'free fit (of parts)', 'to come (from other than uphill or north)', and 'brother-in-law (ErSiHu)'. Variant glosses are separated by semicolons, e.g. 'bear; put up with; endure'.
7) Gurung citation, with English gloss in *italics*. Where, in order to illustrate use of certain discourse particles, citations cover more than a monologue utterance the words of

different speakers are separated, in both Gurung and English, by double slant lines //.

8) Cross-references to other entries, within square brackets, whether as synonyms, antonyms, or merely comparisons.

Where different senses are discriminated within an entry the senses are numbered, and each sense may contain parts 4) to 8), e.g.

> **khaa'rba**[1]
> 1. *v.i.* **<hallanu>** to shake oneself (of animal shaking water off after rain).
> 2. *v.t.* **<hallaaunu>** to shake (cloth to get rid of dust).

b) English-Gurung entries contain:

1) English word, in *italics*.
2) grammatical category.
3) specification of sense, in parentheses.
4) Gurung gloss, in contrasting type.

Where different senses are discriminated the senses are numbered, and each sense may contain parts 2) to 4). Homonyms in English are listed as separate senses within one entry, not separate entries, e.g.

> *bear*
> 1. n. bxalu'.
> 2. v. *(endure)* khabdiba'.
> 3. v. *(carry)* no'ba.
> 4. v. *(give birth to)* phibaa'.

c) Nepali-Gurung entries contain (in the Devanagari script).

1) Nepali word.
2) specification of sense, in parentheses.
3) Gurung gloss, following a double hyphen.

Nepali homonyms are listed as separate entries, distinguished by the parenthesised sense specification (in Nepali), e.g.

> dhanT (maalik) - khlxye.
>
> dhanT (seṭh) - plxoba.

4. COMPARATIVE INFORMATION

Chepang data is drawn from unpublished early (1969) notes by Ross C. Caughley. (He is currently readying for the press a Chepang-English dictionary.) In the orthography represented here high tone is shown by final q; h is a glottal fricative, ɨ is a mid-central unrounded vocoid, M, N, NG, R, L, W, and Y are voiceless consonants. Chepang examples are prefixed *Cp*.

A few Tibetan forms are cited from Chang and Shefts (1964). The data was supplied to the author by Richard S. Pittman, and in the orthography used here final **h** represents low tone and **c**, **ch** represent [tš], [tšh] respectively. Examples from this source are prefixed *T*.

Reconstructed Proto-Tamang-Gurung-Thakali forms are cited from Pittman and J. Glover (1970), and are prefixed *TaGTh*. The article posits four register classes for monosyllabic words of the proto-language, represented in a four-box array, with the Gurung phonemic features for each class described in the boxes:

Clear Intense KK (q)	*Clear Relaxed* KG ( )
Breathy Rising GK (hq)	*Breathy Low* GG (h)

Where (monosyllabic) reconstructions have initial and final stops, the register class is indicated by the voicing or voicelessness of the stops. A nasal-final word of **KK** or **GK** register has a (silent) homorganic voiceless stop shown final in the reconstruction, e.g. **glink** *'snow'*, **mimp** *'ripe'*. In reconstructions without a final stop or nasal a combination of **q** and **h** represents the register (as shown in the array): "**q** without **h** represents the **KK** pattern (**naq** *'be sick'*), **h** without **q** stands for **GG** (**ngeh** *'milk'*), **hq** marks **GK** (**ngahq** *'five'*), and **KG** has no written prosody symbol" (1970:11). Contrastive vowel length in the reconstruction is shown by reduplication of the vowel (**yuu** *'to pour'*) and **ng** (or **nk**) represents the velar nasal (**mrang** *'see'*, **mrank** *'garden'*).

Benedict's Tibeto-Burman reconstructions (1972) are marked *TB*. Burmese data from Benedict are prefixed *B* and Tibetan forms *T*. Doubtless many of the *TB* forms listed are not in fact related to the Gurung entries where they appear - the listings are very tentative because the detailed philological research needed to establish reliable correspondences between the Gurung Family and larger groupings has not yet been done.

Forms from Benedict are cited as they appear in his index, with references to the text of three types: a simple number (e.g. 179) refers to number 179 in the series of numbered reconstructions throughout the book; n. 484 refers to footnote 484; and p. 317 refers to the text on page 317.

The source of one loan **ispadaa'** *'razor blade'* is cited as the Portuguese **espada** *'sword'* (through Nepali **ispaat** *'steel'*) from Michaelis' *A New Dictionary of Portuguese and English*.

In most cases of loan words the Nepali or English source of the loan is apparent from the gloss. (When Nepali verbs are borrowed into

Gurung medial **-h-** is normally dropped, stem final **-aa** or **-aau** changes to **-i**, certain other vowel changes may occur, and a syllable **-di** is added to the stem, as in **caidi-ba** /caahi-nu/ *'to be needed'*; **khaṭidi-ba** /khaṭaau-nu/ *'to appoint'*; **jugudi-ba** /jogaau-nu/ *'to rescue'*.) In a few cases when the source of the loan is not obvious from the gloss given the loan source is included in the comparative information, from Nepali, English, or Hindi, the latter drawn from Pathak (1966). Sometimes the Nepali source of a loan is also given as the Nepali gloss, but its central meaning in Nepali, as given by Meerendonk (1960) and Singh (1971), is significantly different from the use of the loan in Gurung. In this case the central English gloss of the Nepali word is shown in the comparative information, as in

> **aaṭhapariyaa** [*N* 'bodyguard'] *n.*
> <**aaṭhapahariyaa**> servant in a king's house.

In all cases, comparative data is glossed only where the gloss given in the source is significantly different from the English gloss listed for the Gurung entry.

5. ABBREVIATIONS

Grammatical categories:

a.	adjective
av.	adverb
c.	conjunction
e.	exclamation
i.	interjection
loc.	locative
n.	noun
n.p.	proper noun
num.	numeral
p.	postposition
pa.	particle
pn.	pronoun
s.	suffix
s.n.	noun suffix
s.num.	numeral suffix (as a noun classifier or substitute)
s.v.	verb suffix
t.	temporal
v.	verb
v.i.	intransitive verb
v.t.	transitive verb

Kin specifications:

Br	brother
Ch	child
Da	daughter
Er	elder
Et	eldest
Hu	husband
Ma	man
Mo	mother
Sb	sibling
Si	sister
So	son
Wi	wife
Wo	woman
Yr	younger
Yt	youngest

Language designations:

B	Burmese
Cp	Chepang
E	English
G	Gurung
H	Hindi
N	Nepali
Po	Portuguese
T	Tibetan
Ta	Tamang
TaGTh	Proto-Tamang-Gurung-Thakali (Pittman and J. Glover 1970)
TB	Proto-Tibeto-Burman (Benedict 1972)
Th	Thakali

Other:

Ant.	antonym
cm.	centimetre
Cp.	compare
diam.	diameter
esp.	especially
kg.	kilogram
km.	kilometre
l.	litre
lit.	literally
m.	metre

ml.	millilitre
mm.	millimetre
Syn.	synonym
//	change of speaker

GURUNG-NEPALI-ENGLISH DICTIONARY

A

ãcalaa', ancala *n.* <**ancal**> zone (one of 14 into which Nepal is divided for administrative purposes).

ãgal, angal *n.* <**anikaal**> scarcity; famine.

ãgreji' *n.* <**angrejī**> English language; Englishman, English-speaking foreigner.

ãkhoraa' *n.* <**amkhoraa**> drinking vessel without spout (about 6" high, made of brass or silver).

ãlãã *see* **ããlãã** 'flag'.

ãšaa *see* a'ŋšaa.

a- *see* **ax.**

aba *c.* <**aba**> now, and. [*Syn.* dxero', togo'.]

abbru' *n.* <**ijjat**> honour; self-respect; face; prestige.
abbru' xyaam', pim. *Your self-respect goes, you are embarrassed.*

abgaa'la *a.* <**abagaal**> blame.

abwi' *i.* <**ãbhai**> exclamation of surprise.

acamma *n.* <**acamma**> amazement; astonishment. [*Syn.* chakka.]

acheda' *n.* <**akšetaa**> offering of rice given priests for use in ceremonies, the bulk being kept as part of his payment.

acher, aacher *n.* <**akšar**> letter of alphabet.

acya *i.* <**accyaa**> exclamation of puzzlement.

a'ḍani *n.* <**bandhaki, aḍani**> pawn; mortgage.
khlxyo, gxããnaa, bxããḍo'jaga a'ḍani thẽĩ biri' paisaa' te'ba. *After mortgaging land, or pawning jewellery or vessels you release the money.*

aḍḍaa' *n.* <**aḍḍaa**> office (government). [*Syn.* adlaasa'.]

aḍgal *n.* <**adkal**> estimate of quantity (weight, length, etc.).
aḍgal lai bod. *Take what you think you need.*
[*Syn.* andaaji.]

aḍi *n.* <**ããṭi**> intermediate floor in building.

adikaar *n.* <**adhikaar**> right; authority.
nga'e khlxyo, nxẽ, dxĩ' nga'e adikaar mu. *My land, my house, my ox are (under) my authority.*
[*Syn.* xa'k.]

adlaasa' *n.* <**adaalat**> office (government). [*Syn.* aḍḍaa'.]

aen *n.* <**aen**> law. [*Syn.* kaanun.]

agxaaḍi *l.* <**agaaḍi**> in front.

-ai *s.v.* <**-ta**> emphatic.
to'i lalai axtxu. *Whatever you do it's not right.*

aina' *n.* <**ainaa**> mirror.

akhiri' *m.* <**aakhirī**> last, final. [*Syn.* balla.]

al dxẽba' *v.* <**aali haalnu**> to press mud on paddy wall. [*Cp.* baause.]

a'lachin sũ *a.* <**alaacchin mukh**> rude. [*Syn.* axkho'jyãã.]

alchi' *a.* <**alchī**> lazy; slothful.

ali', al *n.* <**aali (haalnu)**> clod of earth.
al dxẽba'.

ali *n.* <**bhaai**> brother (YrBr, not used in address).

almallaa *n.* <**almalinu, jilla parnu**> perplexed. [*Syn.* bukka.]

a'lmuḍi *n.* <**almaarī, daraaj**>

shelves.

amjyõ *n.* <**kaanchī aamaa**> aunt (FaYtBrWi).

amjyõ aamaa *n.* <**sautaanī aamaa**> stepmother.

ampha *n.* <**aamaako poi (kirīyaa haaldaa bolne ek šabda)**> mother's husband (used in oath).
cu' kxe' phe'ri ladu' biyãã parlo'gar ampha targe'. *If I do this again let me be reborn an animal.*

amrika' *n.* <**amirīkaa**> America.

ancala *n.* *see* **ãcalaa'** 'zone'.

anda'ra *n.* <**antar**> gap between two things (e.g. houses).

anda'rari' *p.* <**kaapamaa, bīcmaa**> within.
sõgaẽ' anda'rari'. *Within three days.*

andare' *a.* <**ṭhikaiko, maadhyam**> moderate; medium-sized.

andaa', annaa' *n.* <**anna**> grain.

andaa' paani' *n.* <**anna paanī**> food and water.

andaaji' *n.* <**andaajī**> estimate [*Syn.* aḍgal.]

ane'ro *n.* <**ãdhyaaro**> darkness.

ani *c.* <**ani**> then; and then (not in wide use).

ani'yaa *n.* <**anyaaya**> unprovoked; without cause (*lit.* unlawfully). [*Syn.* phaa'karna'.]

anjyõ *n.* <**kaanchī**> sister - older than self, but youngest daughter.

anman *n.* <**ali ali maatrai**> impression; semblance; poor copy (in derogatory sense).
yogaaraa mxie anmanba' mu. *A monkey has the semblance of a man.*
[*Syn.* dxuru'sta.]

anthebaa' *n.* <**jethī aamaa, ṭhulīmaa**> aunt (MoEtSi, FaEtBrWi). [*Syn.* aathe.]

anuraadxa *v.* <**kunai nakšatrako naam**> astrological term.

anusaar *p.* <**anusaar, bamojim**> according to.
[*Syn.* xisaab; bamojim.]

anuwaa'r *n.* <**anuhaar**> appearance.

anwaa' *n.* <**haloko samaatne**> handle on plough.
[*Syn.* kxora ḍããḍa.]

aŋaa' [*TB* *na:w 'younger sibling' 271] *n.* <**bahinī**> sister (YoSi).

aŋŋi' [*TB* *ni(y) 'aunt' 316] *n.* <**maaiju**> aunt (MoBrWi).

aŋsabaa' *n.* <**sabhaa**> meeting to plan community projects.

a'ŋšaa, ãšaa *n.* <**ãša**> inheritance; share.

aphis *n.* <**aphis**> office.

aphisar *n.* <**aphisar, hakim, pramukh**> official.

aram *see* **aaram** 'rest'.

arẽ', aarẽ' *n.* <**aaran**> forge.

argo' *see* **aargo'** 'other'.

artha' *n.* <**artha**> meaning; interpretation.
[*Syn.* maldab; maa'ne.]

artha' kholdiba' *v.* <**artha kholnu**> to explain; interpret.
[*Syn.* maldab kholdiba'.]

artha'ba [*H* arthakara 'advantageous; useful'] *a.* <**bisek, raamro, ali arthako**> improved; better.
dwaapar jug bibaa te' artha'. *The age called Dwaapar is a bit better.*
cu' mxi bxanda' ca'de artha'bae mu. *That person is better than this.*

arthi *n.* <**artī**> admonition, advice, instruction (moral).
yuhannaaji chaan lal txum bisi arthijaga lubxīmala.
John used to give them instructions, that they must do thus.

aru *see* **aaru** 'other'.

asami *n.* **<asaami>** debtor.

asauj, asoda' *n.* **<aašwin>** month (6th of Nepali calendar, mid-September to mid-October).

asa'tte *a.* **<asaadhyaa>** unjust; dishonest (as of changing agreed land boundaries, or depriving wife of due property). [*Ant.* satte'.]

aslekha *n.* **<aslekha (kunai nakšetrako naau)>** astrological term.

asnaa' *n.* **<aasan (ḍokaako)>** bottom of container.

asõ', aasõ' *t.* **<agaadi, aghi>** previously, before. [*Syn.* osõ'.]

asoda' *see* **asauj.**

aspataala' *n.* **<aspataal>** hospital.

ašṭamĩ' *n.* **<ašṭami>** Dasera festival - 8th day.

asuni' *n.* **<ašwini (ek nakšetra-ghoḍi)>** astrological term.

asurbi' *n.* **<asarphi>** gold medallion (in necklace).

asyõ *see* **aasyõ** 'brother-in-law'.

athabaa' *c.*
1. **<athabaa>** or.
2. **<arthaat>** namely.

atthu', athu' *i.* **<atha, aatthu>** exclamation of pain when stung, burnt, scalded, pricked. [*Syn.* aya.]

ausi' *n.* **<aaũsī>** new moon.

aũṭhi' *n.* **<aaũṭhi>** ring for finger. [*Syn.* cyaa'.]

au' *i.*
1. **<hai>** emphatic (requiring response if on imperative). chaaba'e calan m-au. *It is indeed that sort of custom.*
2. **<o>** oh (emphatic).

aulo' *n.*
1. **<aule jaro>** malaria. [*Syn.* kwine'.]
2. **<aaglo (dailo waa ḍhikīmaa raakhne)>** axle of rice pounder; bar of door.

aumo *n.* **<bhinaajyū>** brother-in-law (ErSiHu).

autar *n.* **<autar, awataar>** incarnation.

ax- [*Th* a-] **<-daina>** negative prefix on verb.

ax *pa.* **<ho ki>** did you say? (seeking confirmation).

axar *n.* **<ḍakaar>** burp, belch.

axbelle *a.* **<aber>** late. [*Syn.* kxaeba.]

axbxõba' *a.* **<kaccaa, bal nabhaeko>** weak. [*Syn.* kacca', paadulu', pobaa', kamjo'ri, kalilo', kaaphar.]

axccyõ' *n.* **<saanimaa, chyaamaa>** aunt (MoYtSi, address and reference). [*Syn.* axjxyu'.]

axchyãã'ba *a.* **<naraamro>** bad. [*Syn.* axgadilu'.]

axcya *i.* **<accyaa>** exclamation of disgust.

axdxa' barse *a.* **<adhabãĩse>** middle-aged.

axdxa kalsu' *a.* **<adhaakalco>** dumb, idiot, mentally deficient.

axdxari' *p.* **<bīcmaa>** in the middle of, amidst. [*Syn.* mxããjuri, nxõri.]

axdxaa' *n.* **<aadhaa>** half.

axdxe' *n.* **<adhiyãã>** share farming.

axdxe' pi'ba *v.* **<adhiyãã choḍnu>** to let out to share farmers. [*Syn.* nõ jxõba'.]

axgadilu' *a.* **<agatilo>** bad; worthless (of person or of animal which breeds poorly). [*Syn.* axchyãã'ba.]

axgxaẽ', axgxẽ' *n.* <**jeṭhī didī**> sister (EtSi, address by younger siblings, relatively rare). [*Syn.* naa'ni.]

axgxĩ' *m.* <**jeṭho daajyū**> brother (EtBr, address by younger siblings, common). [*Syn.* ṭhaagu.]

axjxai' *t.* <**ajha, ajhai**> yet; even now, still. cxau lxe' cai', axjxai axmrẽ'. *You've eaten that much, and still not satisfied.*

axjxaaraa' *n.* <**acaar**> chutney.

axjxyu' *n.* <**saanimaa, chyaamaa**> aunt (MoYtSi, address and reference). [*Syn.* axccyõ'.]

axkho'jyãã *a.* <**mūrkha**> rude. [*Syn.* a'lachin sũ.]

axmaĩ'la *n.* <**maahilo baabaa**> uncle (Fa2dBr).

axmĩba' *a.*
1. <**kaaco**> sour.
2. <**napaakcko**> unripe.

axmro'ba *a.* <**nadekhine**> invisible.

axmxwĩ' *i.* <**amwi; oho**> exclamation of wonder.

axŋxĩba *i.* <**masur**> fearless, brave. [*Syn.* masur.]

axo *i.* hesitation stutter.

axo- *pa.* emphatic deictic. axo-xa'r ṭiŋŋyũ'. *I lived right there.* [*Syn.* aax-.]

axta'ngadiba *a.* <**natankanu**> inelastic.

axtxuri' *n.* <**hataar, atturī**> haste; urgency; pressing work.

axtxurle *a.* <**hataar garī**> hastily.

axwaa' *n.* <**daai**> elder brother (address for older brothers and cousins, not eldest or youngest in family).

axyãã uĩ' *t.* <**asti bharkhar**> recently a few days ago. [*Syn.* ũĩ'mĩĩ'.]

aya *i.* <**aiyaa**> exclamation of pain when struck (by hand, beam, rock, etc.). [*Syn.* athu.]

AA

ããbaa' *n.* <**ããp**> mango.

ããḍiba' *v.* <**ããṭnu**> to help in starting a project. [*Syn.* madad.]

-ããḍõ', -ããḍõ', -ḍõ', -waaḍõ' *s.num.* <**-waṭaa**> numerical classifier.

ããdi' *n.* <**ããdhī**> gale.

ããdi' pxuri *n.* <**hariyo sarpa**> variety of snake. [*Syn.* pi'bi.]

ããlãã, alãã, ãlãã, aalãã *n.* <**murdaako agaaḍi laane jhanḍaa**> white cloth carried by one man at head of funeral procession (before the gxyãã', and later erected as a flag over the dead man's house during the pae).

ããsi' *n.* <**hãsiyaa**> sickle.

ããṭhidiba' *v.* <**ãceṭnu, thicnu**> press down with foot.

aa *a.* <**ho ki**> question particle seeking confirmation of statement. [*Syn.* xwaa'.]

aabaa *n.* <**baabu; baabaa**> father; uncle (FaBr, MoSiHu).

aabjyõ, abjyõ *n.* <**kaanchaa baabaa**> uncle (FaYtBr).

aabsaĩlaa' *n.* <**sããhilo baabaa**> uncle (Fa3dBr).

aaḍi', aḍi' *n.* <**aaṭi**> intermediate floor in a building; platform. aaḍi'phiri'. *Upstairs.*

aadaa, adaa *n.* <**daajyū**> older brother (ErBr).

aadidiba' *v.* <**aattinu**> to be

nervous; to panic.

aagu *n.*
1. <**mitīnī**> covenanted friend of a woman. [*Syn.* ŋxelsyo.]
2. <**mitīnīko logne**> husband of a woman's covenanted friend. [*Syn.* ŋxelaa.]
3. <**arko, arkaa**> another; the other person. [*Syn.* aargo'.]

aaiba'ji *t.* <**aru belaa**> elsewhere; at other times.

aaitabaara', aitabaara' *t.* <**aaitawaar**> Sunday.

aakhi'ra *n.* <**aakhir**> end. [*Syn.* balla.]

aala'kkale, ala'kkale *v.* <**bistaarai**> carefully, inoffensively.
tixyaaba'e sa'e aala'kkale bxa'l txum. *You have to bring the breakables carefully.*
aala'kkale xrõsa dxī'r syo'le ṭim. *(A mourner) stays separately, scrupulously, in his own house.*

aalu' *n.* <**aalu**> potato.

aamaa [*TaGTh* *ama; *TB* *ma 487] *n.* <**amaa**> mother; aunt (MoSi, FaBrWi).

aamũĩma'ẽ, amuĩma'ẽ *n.* <**puruṣharu**> men, human males.

aamuyũ', aamũyũ', amuyũ' *n.* <**puruṣ**> man, human male; brother of a woman.
ŋxelsyoe' aamuyũ'. *My friend's brother.*

aanaa, anaa [*TB* *na:w 'younger sibling' 271] *n.* <**didī**> elder sister (ErSi).

aanek, anek *a.* <**anek**> various; several.
aanek kisim ba'e. *Various kinds of.*

aaphsos *n.* <**aphsos**> sorrow; sadness. [*Syn.* phikkar.]

aappa'e *n.* <**baabuharū**> paternal uncles (FaBr).

aaram, aram *n.* <**aaraam**> rest; repose.

aaraa'ti *n.* <**aarati**> praise (sung).

aargo'; argo' *a.* <**arko**> other; different, diverse; next.
aargo' bxããḍo'ri. *In the other vessel.*
khlxyebri aargo' aargo' jaad tam. *The* khlxyebri *belong to different castes.*
aargo' jugari' ngxyo' chyããb taxyaam. *In the next age we will become good.*

aa'ridiba *a.* <**ahraaunu**> to order, to command. [*Syn.* hukum pībaa'.]

aarkai' *v.* <**arko, pheri**> again.
sinu' pxaaba'e txiri aarkai' ngxa chyolẽ xraai. *At the time of burying the corpse they played the drums and cymbals again.*

aaru, aru *a.* <**aru**> other. [*Syn.* aargo'.]

aašik *n.* <**aaširwaad**> blessing.

aasam, asam *n.* <**aasaam**> Assam.

aasa'ra *n.* <**asaar**> month (3rd of Nepali calendar, mid-June to mid-July).

aasyõ, asyõ *n.* <**jeṭhaan**> brother-in-law (WiErBr). [*Syn.* jeṭhu.]

aasyõ lxaaba *n.* <**argun garda garne rīti**> ceremony concluding pae (the ritual chasing off of wife's brother).

aasyõ ṭaalu' *n.* <**argun garda maamaaharule dine kapadaa**> cloth given at pae by maternal uncles.

aa'ṭh, aa'ṭha, aa'ḍ *n.* <**aaṭh**> eight. [*Syn.* pxre'.]

aaṭhpariyaa [*N* 'bodyguard'] *n.* <**aaṭhapahariyaa**> *servant in a king's house.*

aaṭek *m.* <**aaṭek, hamala**> attack;

assault (military). [*Syn.* kxaaba.]

aathe *n.* **<aamaako didīharu>** aunt (MoErSi, FaEtBrWi). [*Syn.* anthebaa'.]

aathebaa', atheba' *n.* **<jeṭhaa baabu>** uncle (FaEtBr, MoEtSiHu; loosely FaErBr, MoErSiHu).

aawaj *n.* **<aawaaj>** noise.

aax- *i.* **<-na>** emphatic deictic. õ aax-ca' kidaaba'. *That very book.* [*Syn.* axo-.]

aaxr *n.* **<ḍakaar>** belch.

aaxr labaa' *v.* **<ḍakaarnu>** to belch.

aayu' *n.* **<aayu>** lifetime; age. [*Syn.* cha.]

B

-b *s.v.* **<-ne; -eko>** gerund suffix (occurs usually when closely bound phonologically to following words). khlxyaa' gxri' rẽrib mrõĩ'. *They saw an old ox grazing.* kyar ṭib swaabaa' u kaju'r ṭib swaabaa'. *Is it nice living there, or nice living in Kaju.*

bãgra, baŋra *n.* **<baŋgaaro>** jaw.

-ba, -ba', -baa, -baa' *s.v.* **<-ne; -eko>** gerund (-baa on voiced stop initial, low clear verbs, bobaa; -baa' on other low clear verbs, pĩbaa'; -ba' on rising breathy verbs, jxõba'; -ba on high clear and low breathy verbs, na'ba, kxoba).

bachaardiba *v.* **<muḍkīle haannu>** to punch.

baḍi *a.* **<baḍhī>** enlarged; big. tããn cxamaẽ pri' pri' tamu, gxaḍi' baḍi axta'. *All sons are equal, it's not right for some to get more, others less.* [*Ant.* gxaḍi'.]

baḍiba *v.* **<baḍhnu>** to grow; to enlarge (in numbers or size).

caid mxaĩna tigaẽ baḍiŋŋyũ. *There is one day left in Caid.* gaŋgyu baḍii biri' naa's lawaai. *When the river was swollen it caused damage.*

baḍuli *n.* **<buṭūwaal>** Butwal, a plains town south of Pokhara.

badaba *n.* **<badaam>** peanut.

badaardi xyaaba' *v.* **<baaṭo pahilyaauna nasaknu, biraaunu>** to be lost because of wandering off. gxyãã' ngo axsei biri' badaardi xyaai', khala axyõ'la. *Not knowing the road we wandered off the track, and were unable to come.*

badẽ *av.*
1. **<nira>** near; about (in space). khanir badẽ ṭiŋŋyũ'. *Whereabouts is he living?*
2. **<alikher>** soon, after a little while. togo' badẽ kham. *He will come soon.*

-badi[1] *s.v.* **<hunaale>** since; because. ŋa xyaaba'di ŋalai maẽ pĩĩ'. *Because I went they gave me medicine.* [*Syn.* sero'.]

badi[2] *n.* **<batti>** lamp (used of small kerosene lamp and of small butter lamps used in Buddhist religious rites).

badmaša *a.* **<badmaaš>** wicked; naughty; worthless.

badmaši *n.* **<badmaaši>** wicked person; worthless person.

-baẽ' *s.num.* **<biṭo>** bundles of bamboos, canes, poles (bxaḍaa', mo', saḍaa') carried on shoulder. [*Syn.* pxaẽ.]

-bae, -ba'e *s.v.* **<-eko, -ne>** adjectivising suffix. cu'rbae naa'ni. *The eldest daughter of this house.* xyaaba'e mxi. *The person who went.*

baen *n.* **<bayaan>** report; news; reputation of a man, usually good.

bagaĩcaa *n.* <**bagãĩcaa**> garden. [*Syn.* baari.]

bagal *n.* <**bagal**> flock of sheep.

bagra *n.* <**bagar**> stony ground or soil.

bagyaa *n.* <**boko**> male goat (uncastrated).

baigune' *n.* <**waigunī**> ungrateful man; ingrate.

bainaa *n.* <**bainaa**> downpayment; deposit (pledge).

bairaa *a.* <**bahiro**> deaf. [*Syn.* laḍaa'.]

bairaagi *n.* <**wairaagī**> man bereft of spouse and children; hermit who remains alone. [*Syn.* jogi.]

bairi *n.* <**wairī**> detested person; persona non grata; enemy. ca' dxī'ne baalu ŋa bairi mu. *In the eyes of that household I am a detested person.*

bairu *see* **baairu** 'outside'.

baišaka *n.* <waišaakha> month (1st in Nepali calendar, mid-April to mid-May).

bajaar *n.* <**bajaar**> market; town.

baje *t.* <**baje**> o'clock (used in conjunction with Nepali numerals). [*Syn.* battiba; xraaba.]

bakhu *n.* <**ghum raaḍī**> cloak of goat's wool, water-resistant.

baksa *n.* <**bakas**> tip, gift.

balag balag labaa' *v.* <**balgaaunu, dherai dukhnu**> to throb (of wound).

balchĩ, balsĩ *n.* <**balchi**> fishhook.

balla *n.* <**balla**> finally; at last. [*Syn.* aakhi'ra.]

balo *n.* <**balo**> rafter.

balsĩ *see* **balchĩ** 'fishhook'.

balwaa *n.* <**baaluwaa**> sand.

bam tãã'gaa *n.* <**baam-maacho**> eel.

bamojim *p.* <**bamojim**> according to. ŋad bibae bamojim lad. *Do as I say.* [*Syn.* xisaa'b, anusaar.]

ban[1] *n.* <**wan**> forest; woods; jungle; countryside (slopes surrounding villages).

ban[2] *n.* <**band**> prohibition. [*Syn.* pribaa'.]

banarba'e jantu *n.* <**wanko jantu**> wild animals of the bush.

banḍa patra *n.* <**bããḍ patra**> deed; document recording land ownership.

bandabasta *n.* <**bandobasta**> arrangement; agreement between two persons.

bandaki *n.* <**bandhakī**> mortgage (the money lender pays the land owner a sum, less than the purchase price of the land, and has use of the land until the owner refunds the money and redeems the land) [*Syn.* ujinḍe, raa'ji naa'm, a'ḍani.]

bandaa *a.* <**banda**> stopped; closed.

bandxu' *n.* <**bandūk**> shotgun.

banidiba *v.* <**banaaunu**> to make; to create; to repair. [*Syn.* kyo'ẽba.]

-bar, -ba'r *s.v.* <**-na**> purpose; incentive. caba'r xuim'. *Invites (us) to eat.*

baraa bara *a.* <**baraabar**> equally. [*Syn.* pri' pri'.]

barda *n.* <**baḍhtaa**> more. kxemaẽ barda kĩn, ŋa cyugu'de kĩmũ. *You people take more, I will take (just) a little.*

barenḍi *n.* <**koṭ**> greatcoat.

barkha *n.* <**waršaa**> monsoon; rainy season.

barkhela *p.* <**barkhilaaph**>

against; opposed to; disobeying. kxid bibae tãã barkhela lai. *He disobeyed what you said.*

barša *n.* <warša> year (as unit of time).

barta *n.* <upawaas> ritual fast (for special days - perhaps eating only one meal, fruit only, or only what one has cooked oneself, or perhaps eating in silence); fast - partial. [*Syn.* upaas.]

barta ṭibaa' *n.* <wrat basnu> to fast. [*Syn.* upaas ṭibaa'.]

baru *c.* <baru> instead; rather.

basa *n.* <bas> bus.

bastu *n.* <wastu> domestic animal; cattle. [*Syn.* khyodo.]

baṭṭaa[1] *n.* <baṭṭaa, ḍabba> can; billy; tin container. [*Syn.* syaa'mgo; txu.]

baṭṭaa[2] *n.* <baṭṭa, pyaakeṭ> cane strips (about 100-150 cm. long, used for tying thatch to roof). [*Syn.* bxadaa.]

baṭṭho, baaṭṭho *a.* <baaṭho> cunning, clever. [*Syn.* buddi; dimaag.]

battiba *v.* <bajnu 'time'> to strike (of the clock). jxaale' caa'r battii. *Then it struck four.* [*Syn.* xraaba; baje.]

baunebir *n.* <baaunne> dwarf.

bauridiba *v.* <bauranu> to live again; to be resurrected; to revive from near death; to awake from swoon.

bausa *n.* <boksīko choraa athawaa logne> witch's male relative.

bause *n.* <jyaami> day labourers (assisting in the preparation of the flooded rice paddy for transplanting). bause taan' khaa'gu lai biri' mrõri boi. *Having gathered the labourers he took them to the paddy fields.*

bayaaba' *v.* <laijaanu> to take away; to carry away (of river).

-bãã *s.num.* <bhaag> share; part. cxa ŋxĩ' musero khlxyo ŋxĩbããle kyãã'l txum. *Since there are two sons the fields must be divided in two.*

bããdiba *v.* <bããdhnu>
1. to be clenched (of teeth). xris khasi sa bããdii. *Being angry he clenched his teeth.*
2. to enclose, fence around.

bããgo-ṭeḍo' *a.* <baaŋgo-ṭeḍho> slanting; oblique.

bããgo-ṭĩgo' *a.* <baaŋgo-ṭeḍho> zigzag.

bããgo *a.* <baaŋgo> crooked.

bããju *n.* <bããjho> fallow ground; grassed area.

bããũ *n.* <naap pããc phuṭ jati> fathom (distance between outstretched hands, approximately 180 cm.).

-baa, -baa' *see* -ba 'gerund'.

baabyo *n.* <baabiyo> grass used in making brooms.

baacchaa *n.* <baacaa> oath; promise.

baaḍi *n.* <baaḍhī> flood.

baad *n.* <baatcit> conversation.

baad maardiba', baad sebaa' *v.* <gaph garnu> to chat.

baadaa, baadxa *n.* <baaj> hawk.

baadure *n.* <bahaaduri> bravery. [*Syn.* ããḍiba'.]

baagasa *n.* <baakas> box; trunk.

baagya *n.* <waakya> sentence; utterance.

baagyaa axkho'ldiba *v.* <waakya na.uṭhaaunu> to be speechless.

baahek *a.* <baahek> except. [*Syn.* binaa.]

baairu, bairu *loc.* <baahira> outside.

baajaa *n.* <baajaa> musical instrument (generic).

baaji *n.* <baaji> stake in gambling; game of chance.

baajyu *n.* <baaje> grandfather; male relatives of second ascending generation.
ŋi'e baajyu nero' tarba'e ŋi'e khe baajyu. *Our grandfather and our ancestors above him.*

baaklo *a.* <baaklo> thick - of cloth, paper; strong.
[*Ant.* paadulu'.]

baala *n.* <bhaaḍhaa> rent on house.

baalar pĩbaa' *v.* <bhaaḍhaamaa dinu> to let out a house.

baalecaur *n.* <baalecaur> village near Pokhara.

baali *n.* <tiro-baali> tax (on land).
baal pho'baa. *To pay tax.*
[*Syn.* ṭeksaa', ka'r, bxansaa'r.]

baalu *v.* <saŋa> together; with.
baalu xyaai'. *They went together.*
kxine baalu ŋyu'ii. *I asked you.*
aabaane baalu lumu. *He learns from his father.*

baan *n.* <baan> arrow (especially associated with gods of Hindu mythology); illness caused by curse.

baani *n.* <baani> custom; habit (particularly of negative tendency of character).
ca'e baani kxid se'm. *You know his ways.*

baanu *n.* <gaaro> wall - standing alone, usually of stone.
[*Syn.* gaaraa; bxedaa'; baara.]

baara, baaraa[1] *n.* <baahra> twelve.

baara, baaraa[2] *n.* <waar> day of the week.
sõbaaraa' tam. *Monday is OK.*
saa't baaraa tam. *There are seven days in the week.*

baara, baaraa[3] *n.* <baar> hedge; fence; boundary of a field.
[*Syn.* gaaraa, bxedaa', baanu.]

baareri', baarer *p.* <ko baare> concerning; about.
swaasthaa' baarer to'i thaa' axxre'. *They know nothing about health.*

baari *n.* <baari> garden; field - dry. [*Syn.* mrõ', gxai mrõ'.]

baarkhari' *n.* <baarakhari> syllabary of Devanagari script.
baarkhari' paa's lai. *He passed his ABCs.*

baardali' *n.* <baardali> porch (usually upstairs on end of house, lower caste people given entrance).

baas *n.* <baas> lodging place for one or two nights.
[*Syn.* ḍeraa.]

baasan *n.* <baasnaa> odour.
[*Syn.* thãã.]

bẽḍa *n.* <bĩḍaa> stand for earthern water pot, ring woven of rice straw.

bebasthaa *n.* <bebasthaa> arrangement; organisation.
xrõsalai caidiba'e chenle bebasthaa lal txum. *You have to arrange properly for things you need!*
[*Syn.* banda basta; caal calan.]

bed *a.* <bet> barren; beyond time of bearing children.

bedan *n.* <bedanaa; pascaataap> mourning.

behora *n.* <behora> nature; disposition.
[*Syn.* baani; su'baasaa.]

behordiba *v.* <behornu>
1. to accept.
cu' mrĩd aague' pxasi no'sero' ŋad axbehordi, waam. *Since this wife is carrying another man's child I will not accept*

her, but will throw her out.
2. take possession of.
ca' maenṭolaa' kxid nxõwãã sero' ŋad axbehordi; kxid kyõẽ'i biri' mattre' ŋalaai pĩn. *Since you broke the lantern I will not take it; give it to me only when you have fixed it.*

belaudi', belaaudi' *n.* <belauti, ambaa> guava.

belaa *n.* <belaa> time; occasion (often in astrological usage). [*Syn.* txi, joga.]

belaaid, belaayad *n.* <belaayat> Britain.

belca *n.* <saawel> shovel.

bele *av.* <dherai> very; muchly. [*Syn.* beseri.]

bemaan *n.* <beimaanī> dishonesty.

benca *n.* <benca> bench.

bepaari *n.* <bepaari> trade.

berdiba *v.* <bernu> to roll up (mat, paper); to wind up (bandage around wound); to wrap up; to wrap around; to bind round. [*Syn.* mxuriba.]

besaa *n.* <besaahaa> food grains (bought and sold); articles bought in market.
besaa bele mxããgu'. *Cost of living is very high.*

besaara *n.* <besaar> turmeric.

beseri *av.* <besari> very. [*Syn.* bele.]

beṭari *n.* <byaaṭri> battery. [*Syn.* ges.]

beṭi cxyaa' *n.* tea drunk on first arising (*lit.* bed tea).

bethaa *n.* <rog> illness; disease.

bĩḍi *n.* <bīḍī> cigar; cheroot.

bibaa *v.* <bhannu> to say.

bibaa axŋẽ'ba *a.* <namaannu> disobedient.

bidaa *n.* <bidaa> permission to leave; departure.
xyaal' txui, bidaa pĩn. *I must go, please give me leave.* [*Syn.* chuṭṭi'.]

bideš *n.* <bideš> foreign country.

bideši *n.* <bidešī> foreigner.

bijaar *n.* <bicaar>
1. test; evaluation; plan, design.
mxi na'du biyãã la'mad yo chwii biri' bijaar lam. *If a person is sick the lama feels his pulse and makes an evaluation.*
2. plan; design.
dxĩ' baarerbae bijaar lal txum, khaiba banidim. *You have made a plan about the house, how you will make it.*
3. thought; opinion; consideration of matters.
kxie bijaar to' ja. *What is your opinion?*
kxi prximale' bijaar lam, to' prxim. *When you are writing you think, "What shall I write?"*
kxe' togo' kadi' lxe' mu, pukhru' xyaaba'e phursada mu u axxre', bijaar lal txum. *You have to consider, "How much work is there now? Is there leisure for going to Pokhara or not?"*

bijed *n.* <bicet> extremity.
bijedle ro'i. *Deeply asleep.*

bijed tabaa' *v.* <bicet hunu> to be gravely ill.

bikaas *n.* <wikaas> development; progress.

bikaas ma'la *n.* <wikaas mal> chemical fertiliser (*lit.* development fertiliser).

bikh *n.* <wiṣ (wikh)> poison.

bikri *n.* <bikri> sale.

bilaa *n.* <billaa> emblem of military rank; chevron.

bilidiba *v.* <bilaaunu, paglanu> to melt.

billi *n.* <**billyaaunu**> derision; vocal contempt.
[*Syn.* jxugu'diba.]

bimraa dxũ' *n.* <**bimiroko boṭ**> flora - citron (two kinds - one sweet, one very sour).

binaa *p.* <**binaa**> without.
[*Syn.* baaxek.]

bindi *n.* <**bintī**> request.

bindimu *i.* <**namaskaar**> greeting word. namaste.

biphar *n.* <**biphar**> smallpox.

birgiḍiyar *n.* brigadier.

-biri' *c.* <**ra**>
1. sequential action.
rii biri' kaẽ cai. *He arose and ate rice.*
2. reason.
ŋad lala axkhxãã'n biri' mxijagad axdxe' laŋŋyũ'. *Since I could not do it other people sharefarmed it.*

biridiba *v.* <**biraaunu**>
1. to omit.
sad ŋxĩ' biridibrẽ ciṭhi' pibxĩbrẽ' lala. *I sent letters at two week intervals.*
2. to remove a paddy wall in order to enlarge rice paddy.

bis *n.* <**bīs**> twenty.
[*Syn.* ŋxisyu.]

bisaai bisaai *a.* <**ciranjībī**> long-lived; full.
bisaai bisaai aayu' tad. *May you have a long life.*

biskure' *n.* <**biskure**> locality name in Ghachok.

bišwaas *n.* <**wišwaas**> trust; faith; confidence.
[*Syn.* kwẽ'ba, bxar'.]

bišwaas mxããdiba *v.* <**wišwaas maannu**> to be trustworthy; to deem trustworthy.
[*Syn.* bxa'r pardiba'.]

biṭhẽ *n.* <**biṭhyããĩ**> mischievous, naughty (child or baby animal).

bittaa *n.* <**bittaa**> span of hand.

bittikan *p.* <**bittikai**> immediately after.
[*Syn.* jxwaa'ṭṭan; gxari'nna; todo'n.]

biyaa *see* **byaa** 'wedding'.

-ble *s.num.* <**palṭa, coṭi**> times; turn. [*Syn.* laa.]

-bo *s.num.* <**-waṭaa**> hand-sized, round objects (cups, plates, cyapattis, bracelets, letters, coins, bras).

bobaa [*TB* *ba 'carry' 26; *TB* *buw=*bəw 'carry on back or shoulders' 28; *TB* *s-wa 'go, come' *n.* 447] *v.* <**laijaanu**> to take.

bom *n.* <**bomb**> bomb; explosive charge (as used in killing fish).

bommaẽ *n.* <**braahmaṇ**> Brahmin - highest Hindu caste.
[*Syn.* pxrumaẽ.]

borne *n.* <**borneo**> Borneo.

bra *see* **pxra'** 'hundred'.

-brẽ, -bbrẽ *s.num.* <**payo**> strands twisted together (in rope or plaits).

-brẽ, -bbrẽ, -bbrẽ' *s.v.* <**-dai**> habituative.
saebrẽ' cabrẽ' lam. *They were killing and eating.*
[*Syn.* -ma.]

brĩbrĩ *av.* limply; loosely (of long thin things hanging down, as beans, cucumbers on a vine, wool threads hanging from religious officiants' hats).
xraalbu brĩ brĩ xyaaba'. *The shaman's hat tassels dangle loosely.*

brubrũ, bũbũ *n.* <**jamaraa**> corn shoots (used ceremonially); corn flowers.

bũbũ *n.* <**sim sim paanī**> drizzle.
[*Syn.* nãã' txulaa.]

bũbũle *av.* fluffy; light.
yod pae prẽm bũbũle. *You fluff the wool up lightly by hand.*

bucu *see* **pucu** 'crown of head'.

buḍ judaa *n.* **<buṭ>** boot - military.

budabaar *n.* **<budhawaar>** Wednesday.

buddi *n.* **<buddhi>** intelligence; sense. [*Syn.* dimaag.]

budũ, budu *n.* **<cijharu>** plural marker for things and perhaps cattle.
to' budũ. *What things?*

bugyaani *n.* **<lek>** highlands, beyond tree level but below summer snow line.
[*Syn.* xe, khlyãã', dxusaa', gxaari'.]

buj *n.* **<sallaah, buj>** consultation; advice.
[*Syn.* sa'llaa; kajuri'.]

bukka *n.* **<chakka>** surprise; bewilderment.

bukka mxããdiba *v.* **<chakka, dikka>** to be bewildered, to be amazed, incredulous.

buṭṭa *n.* **<buṭṭaa>** embroidery.

buṭṭa jxõba' *v.* **<buṭṭaa haalnu>** to embroider.

buwaari *n.* **<buhaari>** sister-in-law (YrBrWi).

bxaba' [*TB* *ba 'carry' 26; *TB* *buw=*bəw 'carry on back or shoulders' 28; *TB* *s-wa 'go, come' *n.* 447] to bring - not from up or north.
[*Cp.* bxwiba'.]

bxabi'ṣya *n.* **<bhawiṣya>** future.
bxabi'ṣyar to' tam to' tam? *What will happen in the future, what indeed?*
[*Syn.* pxanxã liũd.]

bxaḍaa' *n.* **<ghar chaauda cahine ek masino saaṭo>** poles (thin, 2-3 cm. diam., used for tying thatch to).
[*Syn.* baṭṭaa.]

bxadu' *n.* **<bhaadra>** month (5th in Nepali year, mid-August to mid-September).

bxaẽba' *v.* **<parkhinu>** to wait.

bxagawaa'n *n.* **<bhagwaan>** god - of senior class (including Ram, Vishnu, Krishna, Lakshman, to whom one offers flowers and grain offerings, but not blood sacrifice).
[*Cp.* parmeswaraa; deudaa; bxayãã'r.]

bxagaa'ri, bxaagaa'ri *n.* **<bhakaarī>**
1. mat of cane, 120x400 cm., finer than **cidra**, often used as roofing on shepherds' huts and cattle sheds.
2. measuring unit for stored grain (if mat is set up as an upright bottomless cylinder).
[*Cp.* cidra; xrããne.]

bxagra' [*N* bhakaaro 'excrement of cattle'] *n.* place of tethering cattle (inside shed).
[*Syn.* pxrõ.]

bxaĩ'kaṭar *n.* **<bhũĩ kaṭahar>** pineapple.

bxailo' *n.* **<bhailo>** recital given during Tiwa festival (late October) for which thank offerings are expected.

bxairu'wa *n.* **<bhairahwa>** Bhairawa (border town south of Pokhara).

bxajan *n.* **<bhajan>** hymn; song of praise.
[*Syn.* aaraa'ti.]

bxakha'r *t.* **<bharkhar>** just now; a moment ago; recently.
bxakha'rbae chami'. *A woman of about 15 to 17 years.*

bxakti' *a.* **<bhakta>** devout; pious; scrupulous about religious regulations (such as washings, diet, etc.).

bxalaa'dmĩ *n.* **<bhalaadmi>** arbitrator; counsellor; persuasive leader.

bxalo' *n.* **<bhalo>** welfare; benefit.

bxalu' *n.* **<bhaalu>** bear.

bxandaa' *p.* **<bhandaa>** than;

compared with.

bxansaar *n.* <bhansaar> customs tax.
[*Syn.* kar, ṭeksaa', baali, masul.]

bxar *n.* <bhar parnu> reliability; trustworthiness.
[*Syn.* bišwaas.]

bxardi' *n.* <bharti> enlistment.
[*Syn.* bxarna'.]

bxarna' *n.* <bharnaa>
1. enrolment.
skular bxarna' labaa'. *To enrol in school.*
2. replacement.
ŋad bxarna' la them. *I will replace it.*

bxaṭṭu' *n.* <bhaṭṭu, bhaat pakaaune silbarko saano bhããḍo> cooking vessel (of white metal, various sizes, similar in shape to bxaagu'na).

bxatwaa' *n.* <bhatuwaa> immigrant from another village (very derogatory term).

bxatyaa'ra *n.* <bhatyaar; bhoj> feast (for wedding, hair cutting ceremony, post-funeral, etc.). [*Syn.* bxoj.]

bxau' *v.* <lyaau> imperative of bxaba 'bring'.

bxaudi'ba *v.* <bhaagnu> to run away. [*Syn.* kxyo xyaaba'.]

bxayãã'r *n.* <bhayẽr> deity to whom a chicken is sacrificed twice a year (April and November), usually at edge of cliff.
[*Syn.* deudaa.]

bxããḍi'diba *v.* <bhaḍaaunu> to entice; to tempt; to exert a bad influence on (as of adulterers, or youths spoilt by bad company).

bxaaḍi' *n.* <hoṭel> inn (providing meals and sleeping arrangements).

bxaagaa' *n.* <bhaakha> tune; pitch; accent.

bxaagaa'ri *see* bxagaa'ri 'mat'.

bxaagu'na *n.* <loṭaa> drinking vessel; container for water.
[*Syn.* ãkhoraa.]

bxaai' *n.* <bhaai> younger brother (YrBr); younger male parallel cousin (FaBrSo, MoSiSo).

bxaale' *n.* <bhaale> rooster.

bxaancha' *n.* <bhaansaa> cooking.
bxaancha' kxrim. *(The castes) may cook together.*

bxaancha're *n.* <bhaanse> cook.

bxaani'ja *n.* <bhaanij> nephew (MoSiSo, WoHuSiSo).

bxaanji', bxaanchi' *n.* <bhaanjī> niece (MaSiDa, WoHuSiDa).

bxaannãã' *n.* <bhanai> statement; story.
cu' bxaannãã' la'mmaẽ kwi' bim. *Some lamas tell this story.*
[*Syn.* tãã.]

bxaara'da *n.* <bhaarat> India.
[*Syn.* iṇḍiyaa'; xindu'sthaa'n.]

bxaara'ti *a.* <bhaarati> Indian.

bxaaraa'[1] *n.* <bahar> bull.
[*Ant.* khlxyaa' kxyoba'.]

bxaaraa'[2] *n.* <bhaaḍhaa> fare; rent.
pukhru' xyaaba'e bas bxaara' kadi' ja? *How much is the bus fare to Pokhara?*

bxaare' *n.* <bhariyaa> carrier; porter.

bxaarse' *n.* <phirtaa aawaaj> echo.
[*Cp.* chyaattiba'; kobaa'.]

bxaasi' *n.* <bhaakaa, bhããsi> accent (manner of speaking).
nãã's nãã'sari kxyui' gxrina' tara bxaasi' syo'na. *In different villages the language is the same but the accent is different.*

bxaasi'diba *v.* <bhaasinu> to sink; to settle (of earth, wall).

bxaau', bxaag, bxaagu' *n.* <bhaag> share; entitlement.
bxaag bxaag chuḍidiba'. *To*

divide into shares.

bxed' *n.* <saraap> curse of witch (causing loss of appetite leading to death).
pumsyoma'ẽdbxed' jxõĩ biri' na'm. *The witch cursed him and he is sick.* [*Cp.* syaa'ba.]

bxedaa' *n.* <bhitto> wall of house - mud plastered.
[*Syn.* gaaraa, baanu.]

bxelgaa' *n.* <bhel> waves.

bxelsĩ' *n.* <balo, bhelsĩ> beam - sloping, of gable roof.

bxeṭi *n.* <bheṭi> offerings to gods or priests (usually money).

-bxĩba' *s.v.* <-dinu>
1. benefactive.
   ca bxĩn'. *Eat it, please.*
2. permissive.
   cala axbxĩn'. *Don't let him eat it.*
   cal bxĩn'. *Let him eat.*

bxiru' *n.* <mugaa> necklace of coral.

bxõ' [*TB* *(d-)baŋ *n.* 325] *n.* <bal> strength.

bxõ' nxaba *v.* <bisaaunu> to rest.

bxõba' *a.* <baliyo> strong.

bxo' *i.* <bho> no.
bxo', ŋa kũ'laa axyõ', yumnaa xyaal' txui. *No, I can't sit down, I have to go quickly.*

bxoba' *see* bobaa 'take'.

bxoḍ' *n.* <bhoṭ> Tibet.

bxoḍe' *n.* <bxoṭe> Tibetan.

bxoḍo' *n.* <bhoṭo> shirt - Nepali style.

bxog *n.* <bhog> sacrifice (of blood).
bxog pĩba'. *To offer sacrifice.*
[*Syn.* khro.]

bxoj *n.* <bhoj> feast; banquet.
[*Syn.* bxatyaa'r.]

bxolaa' *n.* <bhal> stream - seasonal; flood.
[*Syn.* syõ, khola.]

bxryaŋãã' *n.* <bharyaŋ> ladder; steps - portable, wooden.
[*Syn.* li; prẽ.]

bxũḍi' *n.* <bhũḍī> stomach.
[*Syn.* pho'.]

bxudlaa' *n.* <makaiko bokro> wisps of corn ear.

bxudududu *n.* <caraa uḍne šabdaa> fluttering (of a nestling learning to fly).

bxudu'kan *av.* <bhutukka> completely.
amwi', bajaara xyaai', tara pau roṭi kĩba bxudukan mli' xyaai'. *Dear me, I went to the market but completely forgot to buy bread.*

bxugol *n.* <bhūgol> geography.

bxugũ'nḍa *n.* <bhakunḍo> ball.

bxuju'ŋŋa *n.* <bhujuŋgo> cooking vessel (20 cm. diam., 8 cm. depth).

bxujyu' *n.* <bajyai> grandmother.

bxulaa' *n.* <oḍhne khaasṭo> cloak of homespun cloth.
[*Syn.* bakhu.]

bxuldiba *v.*
1. <phasaaunu> to entrap; to beguile; to entangle.
   [*Syn.* bxããḍi'diba; phasidiba'.]
2. <bhulnu> to err; to make a mistake.

bxumi' su'daarar *n.* <bhumi sudhaar> land reform.

bxun *n.* <bhuĩko pwaal> cavity - of earth (due to subterranean caves).
nãã' lxe' yu'du biyãã bxun xyaam. *If there is a lot of rain the earth subsides.*
[*Syn.* bxaasi'diba.]

bxut *n.* <bhūt> spirit - evil.
[*Syn.* mxõ', syaa'gi.]

bxuwaa' *n.* <bhuwaa> wool - fine.

bxwiba' *v.* <lyaaunu> to bring down from higher altitude or from north.
[*Cp.* bxaba'.]

bxyããba' *v.* <phaalnu> to throw away (emphatic).

bxyõba' *v.* <phaalnu> to throw away.
[*Syn.* waabaa'; ple'waabxĩba'; swĩkidi bxĩba'.]

byaa, biyaa *n.* <wiwaaha> wedding; marriage.

byaaja *n.* <byaaj> interest on loan.

byaaulo *n.* <dulahaa> bridegroom.

-byõ, byõ' *s.num.* <paathi> gallons.

byõba *v.* <jasto dekhinu> to resemble.
naa'ni surje dõ' byõba. *Naani resembles Surje.*

C

ca' *pn.* <tyo> that; he; she; it.

ca [*TB* *r-sa 442] *n.* <naso> vein.

cabasa'e *n.* <khaane cij> food (*lit.* eating things).

cabaa' [*TaGTh* *tsa; *TB* *dza 66] *v.* <khaanu> to eat.
[*Syn.* phe'ba.]

cabli *n.* <capal> sandal; thong.

caẽbaa' *v.* <taannu> to pull.
syod caẽm ro. *The ghost pulls you, it is said.*

ca'eba *v.* <bããki> to remain; left over.

caebaa' *v.* <paanī bido hunu> easing off of rain.

ca'ida, ca'id, cai'dra *n.* <caitra> month (12th in Nepalese calendar, mid-March to mid-April).

caidiba' *v.* <caahinu> to be needed.

caj mlẽ' mlẽ' ŋxããba *a.* <nunilo> salty.

caja [*TB* *tsa=*dza 214; *T* tša] *n.* <nūn> salt.

cakku' *n.* <cakkū> knife; pen-knife.

calan, calana, calããn, calaan *n.* <calan> custom; way; manner.

calaakh *a.* <calaak> cunning; smart; clever.

caldiba'[1] *v.* <calaaunu> to be sexually aroused (of male animals).

caldiba'[2] *v.* <calaaunu> to use; to accept and exchange money.
ṭo'xyaaba'e no'ḍa axca'ldi. *Torn notes won't be accepted.*

calidi'ba *v.* <calaaunu> to drive a vehicle.

camĩ', cami' *n.* <chorī> daughter.
[*Syn.* cxamĩ.]

camĩ'ri *n.* <swaasnī maanche> woman. [*Syn.* cxamiri.]

camja' *n.* <camcaa> spoon - big.

cana' *n.* <caana> radishes - sliced and dried.

candramaa' *n.* <candramaa> moon (in astrological context).

carbane' bethaa *n.* <chaare rog> epilepsy.

ca'ri *loc.* <tyahãã> there; over there.

caridiba *n.* <caraaunu> to offer food to spirits.
mxõlaai bxaau caridil txum. *You have to offer a portion to the demon.*

cašmaa' *n.* <cašmaa> spectacles; glasses.

caũthẽ' *n.* <cauthaai> quarter.

caubis *n.* <caubīs> twenty-four.

cauḍaai *n.* <cauḍhaai> width; breadth. [*Syn.* plxi.]

cauḍi' *n.* <cakaṭī> mat - small, round, of maize husks, for sitting on.

cauda *num.* <caudha> fourteen.

caudara *n.* <cautaaro> platform, usually under shady tree.

caulaani' *n.* <caulaani> juices produced in cooking food.

cãã *n.* <sããghū> bridge - temporary, made of bamboo. [*Syn.* pu'la.]

cãã'ba *v.* <jamnu> to be coagulated; frozen.

cããdi' *n.* <cããdi> silver; white of egg.

caa' *see* **cxaa'** 'tea'.

caa'ḍa *n.* <caaḍ> festival.

caakh mxããdiba *a.* <caakh laagnu> curious.

caal calaan *n.* <caalcalaan> organisation; conduct of one's affairs. [*Syn.* bebasthaa.]

caalis *n.* <caalīs> forty.

caana daala *n.* lentil - green. [*Cp.* maa'sa.]

caa'r *n.* <caar> four. [*Syn.* plxi'.]

cẽ *n.* <baagh> tiger.

cẽ lxo *n.* <baagh barkha> year of the tiger (1950,62,74,86).

cẽ'ba *v.* <muchnu> to knead thoroughly. [*Syn.* celaaba', mlobaa'.]

cẽdo', cẽdõ' [*Cp* dyaŋq] *p.* <najik> near; close to.

ce *n.* nickname (not given by astrologer).

ce'na *n.* <caalno> sieve; winnowing tray for small grains.

cewaa *see* **cyowaa** 'supervision'.

cha'¹ *n.* <cihaan> cremation platform on river bank.

cha² *n.* <aayu> life; prosperity; lifetime.
cha ranṭhi' tam. *Life is short.*
[*Syn.* aayu'.]

cha-³ *av.* <tyaso> thus; that way.
chatamaa ŋa axxyaa'. *That being the way it is I'm not going.*

cha'ba [*TB* *tsa 62] *a.* <taato> hot. [*Syn.* laa.]

chabaa' *v.* <caraaunu> to shepherd.

chada' *n.* <chaataa> umbrella. [*Syn.* kxũ.]

chadrã *n.* <paat nabhaeko rukh> tree without leaves.

chadri kule' *n.* <ghaam chekne ṭopi> rainhat; sun helmet.

chaẽ¹ *n.* <heraalo, goṭhaalo> shepherd.

-chaẽ² *s.num.* <kããm> items of work.
ŋad bibae kxe' tichaẽ e' maane axcxuba. *You haven't done a single job I asked you.*

chae [*TaGTh* *tsaay; *Cp* tsyasq] *n.* <coyo> cane strips used in weaving.

chae khlyi *n.* <cuyaako gitra> inside cuts of cane.

chae mĩ' *n.* <cuyaako ããkha> outside cuts of cane.

chaeba *n.* <pasinaa> perspiration.

chagadiba' *v.* <chakinu> to be misled, cheated.

cha'gõ, cho'gõ *n.* <cihaan> cemetery.

cha'kka *n.* <chakka> amazement; surprise.

cha'kka pardiba' *v.* <chak parnu>

to be amazed.
[*Syn.* bukka mxããdibaa.]

chalen *av.* <tyasai>
1. just because; that's the way it is.
2. without special cause.
xindu'sthaa'n xyaa sero'm xindi' kxywi' chalen xram. *Since we had gone to Hindustan we learnt Hindi without special tuition.*
3. free of cost.
chalen pĩĩ. *He gave it to me free.*

chalpha'l *n.* <chalaphala> discussion. [*Syn.* kajuri'; sabxa labaa'; tãã labaa'.]

chamaḍa' *n.* <maukaa> opportunity. chamaḍaa' cxyaasi. *Having taken the opportunity.*

chamĩ', chami' *n.* <tarunī> woman - young, 16 to 30 years.

chammẽ' *n.* <yuwatīharū> plural of chamĩ' 'young woman'.

chapwaa' *a.* <chaapieko> printed - of paadru' (astrological calendar).

charkaali' *n.* <thakaalile buneko kamal> cape of wool worn by Thakalis.
[*Syn.* kaamlo'.]

chature' *n.* <keṭaakeṭī> adolescent human - 12 to 15 years.

chauri *n.* <kukur> adolescent bitch.

chããdiba' *v.* <chããṭnu> to weed out; to prune; to cut down staff; to segregate; to select.
[*Syn.* txããba.]

chaa- *av.* <yaso> thus; that way.
[*Syn.* cha, chu.]

chaa'b *n.* <chaap> imprint.

chaa'ba *v.* <taasnu> to peel.
[*Syn.* pi'ba.]

chaaba'e *a.* <phalan> certain (person or thing).

chaaba'na *av.* <tyastai, yastai> just so; like that.

chaabaa' *av.* <yasto> like this.

chaabdi'ba *v.* <chaapnu> to print; to frank (letters).

chaadan *n.*
1. <gaaro baahiraa samma aaeko chaanu> eaves.
2. <baaradalīko chaanu> roof of verandah.
[*Syn.* paali'.]

chaage' *n.* <chaak> meal.
ek chaage' mattre' cam. *He eats only one meal.*
[*Syn.* cho.]

chaap *n.* <chaap> seal; stamp.

chaa'ra [*TB* *sar 401] *a.* <nayãã> new.

chaare' *v.* <chaharo, jharna> waterfall.

chẽ'raaba *v.* <labaṭaale haannu> to slap with open hand.
[*Syn.* chyaabru'ba.]

che' *n.* <ri+n> loan at interest.

cheba' *v.*
1. <samaatnu> to hold; grasp.
2. <linu> to take.

che'l *n.* <chel, chekaai> obstruction (as interrupting light or of child standing between two people talking).

che'laa ma'li *av.* <misinu> mixed up together.
pxrukxyui' tamukxyui' che'laa ma'lile põ'm. *He speaks Nepali and Gurung all mixed up together.*

chele *see* chyole 'cymbals'.

chen kxyuin labaa' *v.* <raamro garnu> to welcome hospitably.

chenããle *av.* <raamro saŋga> correctly; precisely; well.
[*Syn.* chenle.]

chenle *av.* <raamro saŋga> well.

chĩ, sĩ [*TaGTh* *tšin; *TB* *m-(t)sin=*m-tsyen 74; *Cp* s+n?]

n. <naŋ> claw; nail of toe or finger.

chĩ'ba *v.*
1. <baṭaarnu> to cause to fall.
2. <jhaarnu> shake jungle fibre in sharp downward motion to get water out after boiling.

chĩbaa' *v.* <chĩknu> to sneeze.
naa' chĩ' lad. *Blow your nose.*

chi'[1] [*TaGTh* *tšiq; *TB* *tsil n. 55, n. 449, n. 461; *Cp* tšɨw?] *n.* <boso> fat.

chi[2] [*TaGTh* *tšii] *v.* <ghããs> grass.

chi'baarge' *n.* <chepaaro> lizard.

chi'bula *n.* <muso> wart.

chiḍ *n.* <chiṭo> drop of water sprinkled for ritual cleansing.
chiḍ praa'ba. *To sprinkle water.*

chiḍle' *av.* <chiṭo, cããḍai> quickly.
chiḍle' prxidu biyãã ŋad khe'l axxraa. *If you write quickly I cannot read it.*
[*Syn.* yumnan.]

chi'n *n.* <chin> moment.
chi'n gxri' ṭid. *Wait a moment.*

chi'na phaa'naa *n.* <chinaphaan> settlement; determination of a dispute.
chi'na phaa'naa taxyaai' biri' jxagaḍaa' lala axtu khãã'xyaai'. *When settlement has been reached you must not quarrel. It is finished.*

chi're mi're *n.* <kire mire> cloth - printed with black squares on dark brown background.

chõ *n.* <bepaar> trade.

chõbaa' *n.* <sakinu, turnu> to be finished.
sutkeri tasi ŋi'gaẽri ro chõmu'. *Seven days after childbirth the lying-in is finished.*
[*Syn.* cxiba, khaa'ba, nubaa'.]

-cho [*TB* *tsyow *'cook, bake'* 275] *s.num.* <chaak> meals.
ja'mman kaẽ ticho cal bxĩm'. *You feed everybody rice, one meal each.*

chobaa' [*TB* *tsow 277] *a.* <moṭo> fat; rotund.

choḍo' *n.* <naamlo> tumpline; carrying headstrap (for heavy bundles, made from thread).
[*Syn.* txo'.]

cho'gõ, cha'gõ *n.* <cihaan> grave.

-cho'nõ *n.* <bi-gaarnu> pieces; bits.
kurji'm cuxyaanaa', taan cho'nõ thẽna'. *As for the chair it is broken, all broken to pieces.*

chorõ' *n.* <jhijo> dissatisfaction; disgruntlement; disenchantment.
chorõ' ŋxããba. *To be fed up.*
[*Syn.* kaes; nar.]

chu'[1] [*TaGTh* *tšoop] *n.* <chop> chutney of salt and chillis.

chu[2] *av.* <yaso> this way; this.
pxanxããga cha labaa', chu labaa', bibae tãã. *Orders saying that tomorrow you do this, do that.*
[*Cp.* cha.]

chu[3] *n.* <daamlo> rope.
[*Syn.* xrasi.]

chuḍidiba' *v.t.* <chuṭṭinu> to divide; separate.

chu'iba *v.* <ghusaarnu> to insert; to push through a hole.

chuibaa' *v.* <chunu> to touch - as of touching a defiling caste or animal; to meddle.

chu'ba *v.* <bhuknu> to bark (of a dog).

chubaa' [*TaGTh* *tšuu 'be pleasant'] *v.* <man ramaailo hunu> to feel pleased.

chu'ra *n.* <ek kisimko korkaa> basket - triangular shaped

scoop for collecting dung and dirt.

churbaa' *v.* **<raamro laagnu>** to enjoy.
nxebaalar sxal' churim u, kxemaẽ nãã'sar sxal' churim? *Do you find Nepal pleasant, or your home village?*
[*Syn.* swaaba mxaadiba.]

chuṭṭi' *n.* **<chuṭṭi>** holiday; leave. [*Syn.* bida.]

chutte' *n.* **<icchaa>** wish; desire. [*Syn.* icchyaa'.]

chyããbaa' *a.* **<raamro>** good; pretty; beatiful; good quality.

chyaa'b *n.* **<doṣ>** condemnation, blame. [*Syn.* doṣ.]

chyaabdiba' *v.* **<chaapnu>** to print; to type.

chyaabru'ba *v.* **<laṭṭhīle haannu>** to hit with a stick.
[*Syn.* chẽ'raaba.]

chyaa'n chi'nle *av.* conclusively.
kajuri' chyaa'n chi'nle ṭõwaai'. *The meeting was conclusively resolved.*

chyaar *n.* restraint - moral or social.
rĩ'maẽne baalu kũ'du biyãã aadaa aabaa aamaa muyãã' chyaar tam. *If you sit with girls and your older brother, father, or mother, are there there is restraint.*

chyaa'rba *a.* **<dhaarilo laagnu>** sharp.

chyo' *i.* **<jaaũ>** come on (call to go together).

chyobaa' *v.i.*
1. **<aḍinu>** to halt; stop.
2. **<thaaminu>** to remain; stand still.
[*Syn.* thaamdiba'.]

chyoe *n.* **<pustak>** book used by lama.

chyodo *n.* **<ghaṭṭa>** watermill.
[*Syn.* gxaṭṭe'.]

chyoeba' *v.* **<pitrilaaī caḍhaaunu>** to offer to ancestors.

chyogari', chyogara *loc.* **<cheuma>** off-centre; edge.

chyolẽ, chelẽ *n.*
1. **<jhyaali>** musician's cymbals - medium size.
2. **<jhurma>** cymbals used by lama - large size.

chyolo *n.* **<chelo>** shot-put.

chyu'ḍi xyaaba' *v.* **<gai haalnu>** to run away; to grow uncontrollably; to elope.

chyugu' *n.* **<ghiu>** ghee; clarified butter; oil - cooking.

chyu'iba [*TB* *tsyat 'break' 185] *v.*
1. **<luchnu>** tear with teeth.
2. **<cyaatnu, cũḍaalnu>** rip off; break off.

øi *n.* **<ḍanḍiphor>** pimple.

cib naab *n.* **<naaikeharū>** elders; leaders.

ciba' *n.* **<ṭhulo maanis>** adult; senior important person.

cibmaẽ' *n.* **<prauḍha>** adults.

cible', ciple' *n.* **<niuro>** vegetable (edible fern).

cible' tãã *n.* **<chal>** trick; deception (*lit.* slippery matter).

cidra *n.* **<citra>** matting of thickly woven cane (used as cowshed roofing).

cigõ' *a.*
1. **<chipinu>** mature (of wine, tree, animal, human).
2. **<prauḍha>** adult (of human, animal).

cijidiba' *v.* **<cicyaaunu>** to shriek; to yell.

ci'la *n.* **<cil>** eagle.

cilĩ *n.* **<cilam>** pipe of clay about 5 cm. long for smoking tobacco.

ciliba' *v.i.* <**bigranu, bhããcinu**> to break (into small pieces). **cidra puraano' tadu'biyaa cilii biri phaawaam.** *If matting gets old we break it into small pieces and burn it.*

cili'paaḍe' *n.* <**gãuthalī**> swallow.

ci'llo *a.* <**cillo**> smooth of surface.

cimḍaa' *n.* <**cimṭaa**> tongs for fire.

cini' *n.* <**cinī**> sugar.

ciniyãã' *n.* variety of rice.

cinjina *n.* <**mundro**> earrings - small, worn in ear lobe.

cinu' *n.* <**cinu**> trace; mark; remembrance; memorial. **cinu' ũle' se'm.** *You recognise it by the mark.*

ciṭṭhi' *n.* <**ciṭṭhī**> letter.

ci'ṭṭha *n.* <**ciṭṭhaa**> lottery; raffle.

cituwaa' *n.* <**cituwaa**> leopard.

cõ [*TaGTh* *tsaŋ 'sister-in-law'] *n.* <**bhaaujyū**> sister-in-law (ErBrWi).

cõja *p.* <**waari**> this side; near side. [*Ant.* **kyõja'**.]

co' *n.* <**ḍa**> dot.

cokho' *a.* <**cokho**> pure; ritually clean; undefiled (especially of food but also of people). **cokho'le ṭil txumu, cokho'le cal txumũ.** *He must stay undefiled, eat undefiled.*

cola', colo' *n.* <**colo**> blouse worn by women.

coro', jxoro' *t.* <**aaj kal**> now; nowadays. **tĩĩ'joro'.** *Nowadays.*

cũ'ba *v.* <**becnu**> to sell.

cu'[1] [*TaGTh* *tsuq] *pn.* <**yo**> this.

cu'[2] *n.* <**ḍīl**> edge of flat surface.

cubaa' [*TB* *tsyat 185] *v.* <**bhããcnu**> to break; to fracture; brittle. [*Syn.* **ciliba'; ṭõbaa'; nxõba; tibaa'**.]

cucco' *n.* <**cucco**> bill; beak.

cuduru' *n.* <**cutro**> berry - small, dark blue, ripens in Jesth.

culi' *n.* <**cukli**> slander; calumny.

cunaab *n.* <**cunaau**> election.

curaa *n.* <**curaa**> bangle.

curaaḍaa' *n.* <**curoṭ**> cigarette.

curi *v.* <**pechako suta**> thread (of screw).

curi tho'ba *v.* <**suta kaaṭnu**> to cut thread of a screw.

curnaa' *n.* <**curno**> threadworm.

cwaabaa' *v.* <**khaaidinu**> to consume; to devour.

cwibaa' *v.* <**ghocnu**> to pierce; prick; to stab; to perforate.

cxa [*TaGTh* *dza; *TB* *tsa 'nephew, niece, child' *n.* 86; *TB* *za 'child' 59] *n.* <**choro**> son.

cxacõ *n.* <**choraa buhaarī**> daughter-in-law (SoWi).

cxaẽba *n.* <**dããjnu**> to compare. [*Syn.* **txããba**.]

cxae', cae' *n.* <**ṭikaa**> spot of religious significance placed on forehead after rite, usually of red vermilion.

cxaga *a.* <**yati**> this much (usually a small amount). [*Syn.* **cxaa, cxau, cxo**.]

cxagana *av.* <**tetti nai ho**> that's the way it is; like that.

cxamare' *c.* <**tyo belaa**> so; then; thus.

cxamĩ, cxaamĩ [*TaGTh* *dzame] *n.* <**chori**> daughter. [*Syn.* **camĩ'**.]

cxami'ri *n.* <**swaasnī maanche**> woman.

cxaa' [*T* chah] *n.* <**ciyaa**> tea.

cxau *av.* <**yatti**> so (big, fat); this much.
[*Syn.* cxo, cxaga.]

cxaaba'e, chaba'e *a.* <**yasto**> a certain.
cxaaba'e mxi gxri'. *A certain man.*

cxaablẽ *n.* <**ṭukra**> piece of old canework (as used in thaasũ waaba' ceremony).

cxelo *n.* <**caraa barkha**> year of the bird (1945,57,69,81,etc.).
[*Syn.* nema lxo.]

cxemphar labaa' *v.* <**argunmaa ek riti**> rite conducted in post-funeral ceremony.

cxĩba *v.* <**sakinu**> to be finished.
[*Syn.* nubaa'; khãã'ba; chõbaa'; waabaa'.]

¢xi *n.* <**jhaaḍi (wanko)**> undergrowth; brush - thick, tangled.
[*Syn.* jxyaaḍi'.]

cxi [*TB* *tsik 'joint' 64] *n.* <**ghũḍo**> knee; knuckle; joint.

cxi siri' *a.* <**yati saano**> so small; as small as that.
[*Syn.* cxi thiri'; cyugu' thiri'.]

cxi thiri' *a.* <**yati saano**> this small.

cxiba'[1] *v.* <**kelaaunu**> to winnow from side to side; cull.
[*Syn.* phyurbaa', cyaa'ba, ṭaa'ba.]

cxiba'[2] [*TaGTh* *dzii 'remember'] *v.* <**sãjhanu**> to remember; to consider.

cxiba[3] *v.* <**ṭoknu**> to bite (of dog or snake).

cxijyõ *n.* <**kaanchaa choraa (pyaaro boli)**> youngest son - affectionate diminutive.

cxõ [*TaGTh* *dzaŋ; *Cp* *tyorq] *n.*
1. <**gũḍ**> nest.
2. <**khaaṭ (laas lai jaane)**> bier.
chae e' cxõ ro'i biri' siba'e mxi ca'r jxõm. *Having woven a bier of cane they put the dead person on it.*

cxo[1] *av.* <**yati**> this much.
[*Syn.* cxaga, cxau.]

cxo[2] *n.*
1. <**ṭaakuro**> summit; peak.
ḍaaḍae' cxo. *Summit of a hill.*
2. <**ṭuppo**> top (of tree, pole, statuette).
ka'ĩdue' cxo phiri' chyugu' thẽm. *They put ghee on the tops of the statuettes.*

cxuba', cxũ'ba[1] *v.* <**bããḍnu**> to divide; to distribute.

cxuba'[2] *v.* <**thaapnu**> to prepare; to set up.

cxuba[3] *v.* <**jammaa hunu**> to assemble.
nõgur laba'e mxi cxui biri' kxe' suru' lam. *After the work party members assemble, they begin work.*

cxuba[4] *v.* <**boksi karaaunu**> to howl (of witch at night).

cxuba[5] *v.* <**laagnu (maane)**> to accomplish; achieve.
ca' põ'bae kxe' ŋad lalaa axkhãã'; ŋa to'i maa'ne axcxu. *I can't do that diplomatic work; I would not achieve anything.*

cxuiba *v.* <**nidaaunu**> to go to sleep; to become numb.
nxaru cxwii. *He fell asleep.*

cxyããbu *n.* <**cyaau**> mushroom.

cxyaa' *see* cxaa 'tea'.

cxyaaba *v.* <**taaknu**> to aim at.

cxyaaliba *v.* <**ghicnu**> to overindulge in food, drink.

cxyaarba *v.* <**birko milnu**> matching rim or edge.

cxyoba' [*TaGTh* *dzyaaq; *TB* *r-tsiy 76] *v.* <**gannu**> to count.

cxyogõ *n.* **<khaane samaan raakhne koṭhaa, sṭor>** storeroom for foodstuffs, near cooking area.

cxyurba [*TB* *tsyur 'squeeze, wring' 188] *v.* **<nicornu>** to wring out; to squeeze; screw up.
[*Syn.* jxyũba', khumjidi'ba.]

cya' *i.* **<chyaa>** expression of disgust.

cyãã'ũ cyãã'ũ *av.* **<kacakace>** scoldingly.

cyaa' [*TaGTh* *tsyap] *n.*
1. **<aũṭhi>** ring for finger.
2. **<unko golī>** ball of unspun wool.
pxurlid pxumũ, jxaari' chale cyaa' lam; ca' cyaa' lasiri' raaḍa'r peram. *You tease it with a bow, then in that fashion you make a ball; having made a ball you spin it on a spinning wheel.*

cyaa'ba *v.* **<niphannu>** to winnow, shaking up and down.
[*Syn.* ṭaa'ba, cxība', phyurbaa'.]

cyaabaa' *v.* **<mit lagaaunu>** to covenant as blood brothers.

cyaa'riba *v.* **<baṭaarnu>** to twist (rope, cane).
[*Syn.* pebaa'; khribaa'.]

cyõ[1] *n.* **<kaanchaa bhaai>** youngest born male - calling name.

cyõ[2] *n.* **<khor>** pen; trap - cage-like.

cyõ'ba *v.*
1. **<phĩjnu>** to spread out (of roots).
2. **<aaŋ taannu>** to stretch oneself.

cyõbaa' *a.* **<saano>** youngest - of child or animal; small.

cyõ'ḍi *n.* **<paatī(ek kisimko boṭ)>** chrysanthemum-like plant (used as an antidote to nettle stings and in religious rites).

cyõ'ḍi cituwaa' *n.* **<cituwaa>** panther.

cyõmi' *n.* **<maakho>** fly.

cyõnle ṭibaa' *v.* **<saanu bhaera basnu>** to live humbly.

cyobaa' *v.* **<jhunḍinu>** to hang; to suspend (of lantern, chart on wall, boy clinging to bough).
[*Syn.* mẽ'jyoba'.]

cyoblaa' *n.* tadpole.

cyobraa'lmaẽ *n.* **<bhoṭe>** Tibetans.

cyoe' cyo'e *v.* **<kukur bolaaune šabda>** calling sound for adult dog.

cyowaa, cewaa *n.* **<dekhrekh>** supervision arising from knowledge of bad tendencies (e.g. ensuring sentries don't sleep at post, cattle graze at crops, husbands philander).
[*Syn.* yaad.]

cyũ' laba' [*TB* *ts(y)i·p=*tši·p 'shut' 370] *v.* **<ããkha banda garnu>** to close eyes (of human).

cyu' [*TB* *ts(y)i(y)=*tsyay 404; *TaGTh* *tsyuq] *n.* **<daš>** ten.

cyu'ba *v.* **<thunnu>** to enclose in a pen; to imprison.
[*Syn.* thundiba.']

cyugu' cyugu', cyugu'de *a.* **<alikati>** little amount.

cyugu' thiri' *a.* **<saano>** small in size.
[*Syn.* cxi thiri', cxi siri'.]

cyuība' *v.* **<baannu>** to tether.

cyui lxo *n.* **<musaa barṣa>** year of the rat (1948,60,72,84).
[*Syn.* nimu lxo.]

cyuraa' *n.* **<ciuraa>** rice flakes.

cywaa' cywaa' xyaaba' *v.* **<paaknu (ghaau)>** to discharge, of painful eye.

Ḍ

ḍabal *a.* **<dobar>** double; repeated.

ḍabbaa *n.* <ḍabbaa> box for food; billycan with lid.

ḍaḍu *n.* <ḍaaḍu> ladle for soups.

ḍalla *n.* <ḍallo> lump; clod; ball.

ḍanḍa *n.* <jarīwaanaa> fine; penalty (as if cattle get into fields).

ḍanḍi *n.* <ḍanḍī> beam of scales.

ḍar *n.* <ḍar> fear.
ḍar mxããdiba. *To be afraid.*

ḍããḍa *n.* <ḍããṭha> pole; stem; stalk (of plant such as millet).
pxali ḍããḍa. *Shin.*

ḍããḍa *n.* <ḍããḍo> hill.

ḍããgu *n.* <ḍããku> bandit; robber; brigand.

ḍaaibara *n.* <ḍaaibhar> driver.

ḍaalu *n.* <ḍaalo> basket - closely woven (of varying size, for pounded rice).

ḍer *num.* <ḍeḍh> one and a half.

ḍeraa *n.* <ḍeraa> quarters; accommodation rented for some time. [*Syn.* baas.]

-ḍi *s.v.* <rahanu> protracted action.
kxe' axxre', kũ'ḍiba. *There is no work, I'm just sitting.*

ḍib *n.* leave - military.
pinchina'e ḍib. *Discharge with pension.*

ḍibji *n.* <ḍepcī> pan - handleless, metal.

ḍil[1] *n.* <dil> heart; mind. [*Syn.* saẽ.]

ḍil[2] *n.* <ḍīl> cliff edge; raised portion (of verandah, bank of gully, etc.); ridge.

ḍipeṭ *n.* <ṭuṭṭaa; noksaan; haanī> damage.
ḍipeṭ pardiba. *To suffer damage.*

ḍipṭi *n.* <niyukta kaam> duty; guard duty.

ḍõḍaa *n.* <ḍũḍ> hollowed log (for beehive or feed trough).

ḍoridiba *v.* <ḍoryaaunu> to guide (as a shepherd guides flock).

ḍũḍaa *a.* <ḍũḍe> mutilated; maimed; crippled.

ḍũrune mũ'rule *av.* violently; unrestrainedly (of women fighting).

ḍũwãã *n.* <ḍuŋgaa; naau> boat.

ḍubdiba *v.* <ḍubnu> to sink - of boat.

ḍugu *n.* <thaal (ek kisim, saano)> bowl - brass, 8 cm. high. [*Syn.* thali.]

ḍuldiba *v.* <ḍulnu> to stroll.

ḍxag' *n.* <ḍhak> weight for balances.

ḍxaaḍe' bolo *n.* <balo> beam - longitudinal, in gable roof.

ḍxaagre' *n.* <ḍhaakre> porter (derogatory term); civilian. [*Ant.* laa'ure.]

ḍxoga' *n.* <ḍhokaa>
1. gate.
2. door. [*Syn.* tagara; mraa'.]

ḍxolki *n.* <ḍholak> drum - double-sided, larger than mxããda, played one side with stick, other side with hand.

ḍxolaa' *n.* <ḍhol> drum - large, double-sided, used in military.

ḍxũḍi' *n.* <ḍhuŋgrī> earring worn in centre of ear.

ḍxuḍu' *n.* <ḍhuṭo> husks of rice - very fine, obtained in second pounding.

ḍxuku'ra *n.* <ḍhukur> dove.

ḍxyaa'ppa *av.* <chiṭo chopnu, ḍhokaa laaunu, euṭaa sirakle caar janaalaaī pugnu> suddenly

and completely.
mraa' ḍxyaa'ppa lawaad. *Close the door properly.*

ḍyããgra *a.* **<dublo>** lean (of man, animal, meat); thin.
[*Syn.* kadrãã.]

ḍyaamaa *n.* **<ḍyaaŋ>** row pattern in seedplot; ridge pattern (imprinted on palm by leaning on gundri).

D

-d, -di *s.v.* **<hos>** imperative (with, nonnasal verb stems).
[*Cp.* -n.]

-dã *s.* **<-le>** emphatic.
ŋadã ca'lai ŋo axsxe'. *I certainly don't know him.*

da-, daa- *v.* **<bha->** to elapse; pass - of time.

dabae *c.* **<pheri>** so; then.
dabae phe'ri axla'd. *Therefore don't do it again.*

daẽ *n.* **<daaĩ>** threshing of grain with oxen.
daẽ jxõba'.

dagas *n.* **<ḍar, saram>** awe; nervousness.
mrũne txoyãã ŋxĩsi dagas mxããdim, bil txubae tãã bil axkhãã'. *If you meet the king you are frightened and feel awe; you cannot speak the words you have to say.*

dai *pa.* **<pani>** emphatic particle.
ta'le baairu te'ldi? ŋxeba dai. *Why did you put it outside? It's crying!*

dailo *n.* **<dailo; ḍhokaa>** door,
[*Syn.* mraa'; duwaaraa.]

dakhaastaa *n.* **<darkhaasta>** application of official nature (as for registration of land sale, government employment).

dakhin *loc.* **<dakšiṇ>** south.
[*Syn.* maadi'; kyu'ru.]

dama *n.* **<dama (bajaaune)>** drum covered with cow leather.

dama chyoe *n.* **<dharma saaštraa (bauddha)>** book used by lama.

dana *p.* **<nira>** near; about - in space.
ke' kyar dana xyaal txum. *I have to go to that area over there.*
[*Syn.* badẽ.]

darbaara *n.* **<darbaar>** palace.

darliŋaa *n.* **<dalin (ṭhulo)>** beam - central, supporting upper storey or verandah.

daršan *n.* **<daršan>** vision; view.

daš *num.* **<daš>** ten (in loan phrases).
[*Syn.* cyu'.]

dašaẽ *n.* **<dašaĩ>** festival - major in Hindu-Nepalese calendar (observed for ten days in Asoj (September-October) involving animal sacrifice).

dašmi *n.* **<dašamī>** tenth day (after a given date, especially of dasaẽ festival).

dausure *n.* **<deusure>** custom at Tiwa festival (late October) of asking for gifts around the village in return for singing.

dããti *n.* **<dããtī (kharko)>** edge of thatched roof.

daag thẽbaa' *v.* **<daagaa raakhnu>** to vow revenge.

daaga *n.* **<daag>** crime; evil intent.
daaga labaa'. *To commit a crime.*

daai, daai biri', daasi *c.* **<ani>** then; and.
[*Syn.* jxaale'; jxaale' phe'ri.]

daaigaa *c.* **<tyaso bhaera po>** therefore, I see.
laaḍi dindinu makhaẽ' ḍããḍa bobrẽ lam; khanir bomu? // suryama'e dxi'r bom, daai suryama'e aamaad cxaa' thu'l bxim. // daaigaa khõi' bobrẽ lanaa'. *Every day the dumb girl is taking corn stalks. Where does she take them? // She takes them to Surya's house, and then Surya's mother gives her tea to*

drink. // Oh, I see, so therefore she takes them always.

daajyu bxaai' *n.* <daajyū bhaai> brothers; half brothers; parallel male cousins. [*Syn.* ti'maẽ.]

daakha *n.* <daakha> grape.

daala *n.* <daal> lentils; pulse.

daan punyaa *n.* generosity to poor.

daar baar *n.* <chaanaako kaaṭhharu> beams and rafters (collective term).

daara *n.* <kaaṭh> pole.

daaraa *n.* <battiko phittaa> wick of lamp.

daare, daaraa *n.* <daahro> tusk; fang; tooth which protrudes.

daari *n.* <daahrī> whiskers; beard.

-de¹ *av.* <jati> approximately; about.
thuma'ẽ ŋxĩde' sõ'de. *About two or three friends.*
mxwi' plxide' ŋxade'. *Around four or five rupees.*
caja cxaude kĩbxau'. *Bring about this much salt.*

-de² *av.* <ali> a little.
ca' bxandaa' de chyããb mu. *It's a bit better than that.*

debi *n.* <dewī> goddess. [*Cp.* deudaa.]

deša *n.* <deš>
1. country.
2. India. [*Syn.* inḍiyaa'.]

deši ma'l *n.* <dešī mal> fertilizer - chemical (*lit.* Indian fertilizer).

deudaa *n.* <deutaa> gods of Hindu conception, usually malevolent. [*Syn.* bxagawaan; pramĩsara.]

deuraali *n.* <dyauraalī> shrine for offering religious rites to deudaa - small; memorial or monument on a grave; headstone. [*Syn.* ma'ndir; thaa'naa.]

deuraani *n.* <dewaraanī> sister-in-law (HuYrBrWi).

dewar *n.* <dewar> brother-in-law (HuYrBr).

-dĩ [*TB* *niŋ=*s-niŋ 368] *s.num.* <warṣa> years.

di-¹ *v.* <tyaso bhane> to follow logically. [*Syn.* diyãã; dina.]

-di² *s.v.* suffix marking verb stems borrowed from Nepali. gxumdiba. *To stroll* (from *N* ghumnu).

-di³ *s.v.* <-yo> past tense.

-di⁴ *s.* <ta> emphatic.
ŋalaai di'. *To me, though.*

-di⁵, **-d** *s.n.* <le> agentive.

di'kka *n.* <dika> exasperation; vexation; worried. [*Syn.* chorõ' ŋxããba.]

dile *c.* <tai pani> nevertheless; but; however.
ca' camĩ'ri chyããbaa' mu, dile kxi axyõ'. *That woman is beautiful, but you won't get her.* [*Syn.* dina.]

dimaag *n.* <dimaag> sense; intelligence.
dimaag ṭhi'g axxreba'e. *Mad.* [*Syn.* buddi.]

din *n.* <din> days (suffixed to numerals over 10). [*Cp.* -gaẽ.]

dina, dinaga, dina bile *c.* <tai pani> but; however.
ca' nego' ca' beseri nxena', daai ŋad chuḍidi' waalau. dinaga khim beseri xris khana'. *He and he were fighting a lot, and I separated them indeed. However they themselves are very angry, I see.*

dindinu *t.* <dinkaa din> daily; every day.

dirbin *n.* <durbīn> telescope; binoculars; viewmaster.

dišaa *n.* <dišaa> direction; point

of compass.

diyãã, diyããre' *c.* <**tyaso bhane**> so, then; therefore. kxid ŋalaai khalaa axtu bii xwaa'? // õ. // diyãã ŋa axkha'ri o'? *You said I didn't have to come, didn't you? // Yes. // Then I won't come, OK?*

diyo *n.* <**diyo**> holder for oil lamp (earthern lamp).

-dõ', -dũ' *p.* <**jasto**> like; similar. ca'dõ axta'rge. *May it not be like that.*

-do'[1]**, -do** *s.v.* <**ra**> connective. khru'do' jxaale' chyããbaa' tam. *You wash it and then it is nice.* nõwãã bxal'do khani'xyaai', khani' xyaai? *(We) brought a cat, but where is it? where is it?*

-do'[2] *s.v.* <**ki?**> dubitative. asoda'r phiido', axŋxĩm' munaa'. *He was born in Asoj, wasn't he?*

dobara tebara' *num.* <**dobar tebar**> multiple.

dobaaḍe *n.* <**boksīlaaī dine dosro bhaag**> offering required to placate witch's curse - the second in a series.

dobaaḍe waabaa' *v.* <**boksīlaaī dosro bhog dinu**> rite of placing dobaaḍe offering at fork of road, or crossroads, leading to the house of the accused witch.

-do'n *s.v.* <**-ni**> emphatic past tense. to' to' caidimu', samaanja'u kĩdo'n. *Whatever is needed, we made sure to buy those things.*

doṣ *n.* <**doṣ**> accusation; blame - false. [*Syn.* chyaa'b.]

dosro *a.* <**dosro**> second.

dosti *n.* <**dost**> friend - specially close. [*Syn.* thu.]

dohora saẽ *n.* <**dohoro man**> double-minded; uncertain in decision.

-dũ' *s.t.* <**palṭa (pachillo din)**> after that. pxanxããg dũ'. *The next day.*

-du'[1]**, -du** *s.v.* imperative (non-final in sentence). kaẽ cadu', daai kxe' laba'r xyaa'd. *Eat your rice, then go to do the work.*

-du'[2]**, -gu, -go'** *s.v.* <**-bhane**> if (conditional). cu'r ṭidu' biyãã. *If you stay here.*

du[3] *see* **du·kha**.

dubuje' *n.* <**deupuje**> place name on road from Ghachok to uplands.

dud *n.* <**dūt**> ambassador; envoy.

dui *num.* <**dui**> two (used in loan phrases). [*Syn.* ŋxĩ'.]

dukaan *n.* <**dokaan**> shop. [*Syn.* isṭor.]

du·kha, du *n.* <**du·kha**> trouble; worry. [*Syn.* phikkar; sok.]

dundri *a.* <**dãũtarī**> born in the same year.

dunidiba *v.* <**baṭaarnu**> to twine two strands (of thread together for strength in weaving). [*Syn.* perbaa'; khrĩbaa'; cyaa'riba.]

duniyaa *n.* <**duniyaa**> world. [*Syn.* prithwi.]

durga *n.* <**durga**> god of Hindu mythology honoured during dašaẽ festival (Durga Puja); god of death.

dururule *av.* <**hallaa gardaa**> with great commotion.

dušman *n.* <**dušman**> enemy. [*Syn.* satur.]

duwadaši *n.* <**duwadaši**> twelth day of dašaẽ; second day after dašmi.

duwaali *av.* <**dui paalĪ**> twice.
[*Syn.* ŋxible.]

duwaaraa *n.* <**dailo**> door.
[*Syn.* mraa', dailo.]

dwaapar *n.* <**dwaapar**> era in Hindu chronology - third of four.
[*Cp.* satte', tretaa, kali.]

dxaju'ra *n.* <**dhaturo**> frames of cane bent over to form gable of cattle shed.

dxamaa' dxam' *av.* <**dhamaadham**>
1. in close succession; one after another.
txi' no'bae mxi balla dxama' dxam' khai. *The carriers at last are coming along one after another.*
2. constantly; incessantly.
dxama' dxam' kxe' lad. *Work constantly.*

dxamgi' *n.* <**dhamki**> asthma.

dxami'ro *n.* <**dhamiro**> white ants.

dxan' sampati' *n.* <**dhansampatti**> possessions; wealth.
[*Syn.* dxĩ' naa.]

dxancha'ra *n.* <**dhansaar**> granary, usually room above cattle shed.

dxaradxara *av.* <**dhurudhuru (runu)**> remorsefully.

dxaraa'le *n.* <**dhaai**> nurse for child.

dxarge' *n.* <**dharko**> line; stripe (as on ruled paper, shirt); strip of land - narrow and long, between adjoining fields.

dxari' *av.* <**pani**> even; also.
ŋam ṭusyaa'r dxari' tiblei axxyaaŋŋyũ'. *As for me I haven't gone to Tusya even once.*
cyõd luseyaa phe'ri ŋad dxari' lubxĩl txum. *If Youngest-Brother is teaching you then I also must teach.*
laidi' syõ dxari' baḍibae, gaŋgyum jxan' ta'le axbaḍiba? *Even Laidi River is flooding, so why will not the Seti, all the more, be in flood?*

dxarma *n.* <**dharma**>
1. good deeds.
2. merit acquired by doing good deeds.
dxarmaa' kham. *You get merit.*

dxarma guru *n.* <**dharma guru**> religious teacher.

dxarma labaa' *v.* <**dharma garnu**> to do good works and so gain merit for the after life.

dxarma saastra *n.* <**dharma saastra**> scriptures of a religion.

dxarma pu'tra *n.* <**dharmaputra**> son - adopted.

dxaru' *n.* <**dhaaraa**> water source.
[*Syn.* kyu'waadxũ'; mu'laa.]

dxããja' *n.* <**ḍhããcaa**> fashion.

dxaaire' *see* jxaale' 'then, after that'.

dxaaraa'[1] *n.* <**dhaar**> blade; sharp edge as of axe.

dxaaraa'[2] *n.* <**dhaaraa**> spout of vessel; flow of water.

dxaarne' *n.* <**dhaarni**> measure of weight (approx. 2.4 kg., comprising 8 ser in Pokhara or 12 pau in Kathmandu).

dxeba' *v.*
1. <**laaunu (aali)**> to press mud onto terrace wall.
2. <**kããdhmaa haat raakhnu**> to lean hand on another's shoulder.

dxemyõ' *n.* <**puwaa kaaṭera raakhne bhããḍo**> basket for storing carded yarn.

dxero', te'ro [*Cp* dyahq] *t.* <**aba**> now, henceforth.
dxero' ŋalaai gxoḍaa' tam. *Henceforth I will have a horse.*

dxĩ' [*TaGTh* *dimp] *n.* <**ghar**> house; home.

dxĩ' nxõ *n.* <**ghar bhitra**> ground floor of house (*lit.* inside house).

dxĩ' naa *n.* <**sampatti**> possessions; wealth.
[*Syn.* dxan' sampati'.]

-dxi'š *s.n.* <**-dhiš**> authoritative person; in-charge; official responsible for.
ancalaa'dxi'š. *Zonal commissioner.*
nyaayaadxi'š. *Judge.*

dxõba' [*TB* *tuk 'pound' 387; *TB* *dup∿*dip∿*tup∿*tip 'beat' 399] *v.* <**piṭnu; kuṭnu**> to strike; to pound; to hit.

dxõle' *av.* <**jasari**> just like.
ŋad dxõle' lad. *Do as I do.*

dxodro' *av.* <**dhotro**> hollow - of tree.

dxowo' *t.* <**ahile**> shortly; of the present time; now.
[*Syn.* togo'.]

dxũ' [*T* šiŋ doŋ] *n.* <**boṭ**> plant; bush; tree.

dxũba'[1] *v.* <**ṭeknu**> to stand; to rest upon.
[*Syn.* nxeba; mxaeba.]

dxũba'[2] [*TB* *tu·k 'thick' 356] *a.* <**moṭo**> thick; fat; large.
[*Cp.* plxaaba.]

dxũri' *n.* <**lokharke, nyaulo?**> marten (furry animal, size of a squirrel, eats chickens).

dxũsĩ' *n.* <**dumsī**> porcupine.

dxub *n.* <**dhup**> incense used in offerings.

dxub jxõba' *v.* <**dhup haalnu**> to burn as an offering (strictly of incense, but also butter or oil).

dxubaa'raa *v.* <**dhupauro**> censer; vessel for carrying fire when making offerings.

dxurdi'ba *v.* <**dhuiro parnu**> to crowd in.

dxuri' *n.* <**dhurī**> central gable of house (under which lower caste people may not enter).
[*Cp.* pĩḍi; baartali'.]

dxuri' saeba' *n.* <**dhurī maarnu**> to finish off thatching at ridge pole.

dxuru'staa *a.* <**durusta**> resembling; exact likeness.
ca' mxi dxuru'staa yogaardõ' byõba. *That person looks exactly like a monkey.*
tasbir mxie anuwaa'r dxuru'staa kham. *A photo shows a man's face exactly.*

dxusaa' *n.* <**saano saano rūkh bhaeko wan**> scrubland (about 2000-2500 m. altitude).
[*Cp.* bugyaani.]

dxyaan *n.* <**dhyaan**> attention.
[*Syn.* yaad.]

dxyaan pĩbaa' *v.* <**dhyaan dinu**> to heed; to pay attention.

E

-e[1] *s.v.* <**-la**> dubitative; interrogative.
khani' mue'? *Where can it be?*

-e[2] *s.n.* <**-ko**> of (possessive).

e[3] *n.* <**thaar**> sambhar, Indian elk. [*Syn.* jaraayo.]

eba' *v.* <**pharkinu**> to return.
exyaaba'. *To go back.*

egxaaraa' *num.* <**eghaara**> eleven.

e'k, e'ga *num.* <**ek**> one.

ek kaam dui banda *av.* <**eka pantha dui kaam**> achieving two goals with one effort; killing two birds with one stone.

ekadaši *n.p.* <**ekadaši**> eleventh day of dašaẽ.

ekaraa'de *a.* <**ek raat ko**> lasting one night (of pae).

ekaali' *av.* <**ek pheraa**> once; singly.

ekaantaa' *av.* <**ekaanta**> alone; privately.
[*Syn.* eklaasi'.]

ekkaais *num.* <**ekkaaīs**> twenty-one.

ekkaasi' *av.* **<ekaasi>** suddenly; immediately.

eklaasi' *av.* **<ekaanta>** alone. [*Syn.* ekaantaa'.]

eksre', yosare *n.* **<eksre>** X-ray examination.

ekwaa' *n.* **<melo>** residue; remainder (of uncompleted work). [*Syn.* tõ.]

e'ra *n.* **<malla>** plant (small red berry, ripens in November-December, very bitter).

eriyaa' *n.* **<ilaakaa>** area; surrounds.

eusare', eksare' *n.* **<khusra, ek rupĩyããko noṭ>** change (strictly, single rupee notes).

ewaaba' *v.* **<phirtaa garnu>** to return; give back.

exor doxor *av.* **<ohor dohor, ekohoro-doharo>** to and from; back and forth.

exor doxor põ'ba *v.* **<ekohoro-doharo bolnu>** to converse.

exor saẽ pyaa'ba *v.* **<ekohoro man bhaeko>** to be stubborn; single-minded; undeviating. [*Syn.* gxama'nḍi, yogora saẽ pyaa'ba.]

G

ga^{1} *v.* **<ho>** to be.
gxyãã' mĩ ga khobbre' pakha'. *The name of the road is Khobbre hill.*
daajyu bxaai' satur ga. *(My) brothers are (my) enemies.*

ga^{2}**, go** *pa.* **<ta>** emphatic focus.

gaba *n.* **<pĩḍaaluko gaabo>** new shoot of plants.

gabu *n.* **<gabuwaa; baalṭī>** bucket with lid.

gacche *n.* **<gacche>** wealth. [*Syn.* pũji', plxoba'.]

gaḍabaḍ *n.* **<gaḍabaḍ>** uproar; confusion.

gadaa *n.* **<gadhaa>** donkey.

gadilu' *a.* **<gatilo>** upright; righteous; industrious; good (of man). [*Syn.* chyããbaa'.]

-gaẽ' *s.num.* **<din>** days.
tigaẽ'. *One day.* [*Cp.* din.]

gaĩdiba *v.* **<gããsnu>** to join; to repair; to mend. [*Syn.* jordiba.]

gairo *a.* **<gahiro>** deep (of water or hole).

gaj *n.* **<gaj>** yard (measure of length).

galbandi *n.* **<galebanda>** scarf - long, woollen (worn by men).

galdi *n.* **<galati>** mistake; error. [*Cp.* paa'b.]

galdiba *s.v.* **<galnu>** to be soft; workable (of earth).

galẽja *n.* **<galãĩcaa>** carpet. [*Syn.* xraḍi, kaamlo'.]

gaŋgridiba *v.* **<gaŋgrinu>** to be numb with cold. [*Syn.* ṭhiridiba'; kaaṭhidiba'.]

gaŋgyu *n.* **<seti kholaa>** gorge; Seti river.

gaph sa'b labaa' *v.* **<gaph garnu>** to chat; to converse. [*Syn.* baad maardiba'.]

garaa, garaa gadi *n.* **<garaa (naraamro din)>** inauspicious time.

garbhasṭaa *n.* **<garbha wasṭa>** pregnancy.

garbha ŋxe *n.* **<garbhasṭa dūdh>** milk of pregnant woman.

garib *a.* **<garib>** poor. [*Syn.* khlyaanu.]

garlaane gudlile *av.* wriggling (as of a snake).

garmi *n.* **<garmi>** heat; warmth

(of weather).

gate, gade *n.* <gate> date of the Nepali month.

gaũ[1] *n.* <gaũ> village (used only in loan phrases).
gaũ panjyaida'. *Village council.*

gaũ[2]**, gau** *n.* <gahũ> wheat.

gaucaran *n.* <gaucaran> pasture for cattle (uncultivated).

gauri *n.* <gaagri> vessel - water carrier (metal, 15 litres).

gããḍa *n.* <gããḍa> goitre.

gããṭho *n.* <gããṭho> knot in rope; ankle; loop in making a Devanagari letter.

gaaḍa *n.* <gaaḍaa> cart.

gaaḍi *n.* <gaaḍi> car; vehicle, truck.

gaajar *n.* <gaajar> carrot.

gaal ke'ba *v.* <gaali garnu> to rebuke; to reprimand; to abuse.

gaar *n.* <gaahro> offence; umbrage.

gaar mxããdiba *s.v.* <gaahro maannu> to be offended; to be angry.
gaar axmxããdidu, tara cu'r axṭi'd. [*Syn.* ṭxuba'.]

gaara *a.* <gaaro> wall of stone. [*Syn.* baanu, bxedaa'.]

gaaro *a.* <gaahro> difficult. [*Syn.* muškil.]

gaasa *n.* <gããs> mouthful; small quantity of rice.
gaasa cyugu' thiri' pĩn. *Give me a small helping.*

gẽ *n.* <dailo> threshold; doorway.
mraa' gẽr raa'namu. *They were standing in the doorway.*

-ge' *s.v.* <ho ki; hagi> uncertainty. [*Syn.* -e'.]

gesa *n.* <beṭeri> battery (dry cell).

-gĩ *s.num.* <ghar> households.
dxĩ' ti'gĩr kaẽ camma'ẽlai jaan bim. *We call the people who eat rice in one household a family.*

gi[1] *pa.* <hoki> but; however (clause final).
mxid axŋxĩn' gi, gaŋgyudi. *Not by men, however; by the river.*

gi[2] *c.* <ki> isn't it (interrogative). [*Syn.* u.]

-gi[3] *s.n.* <bhaaṣaa> language.
prxugi. *Nepali language.* [*Syn.* kxyui'.]

gidra *n.* <gidro> cane strips used in basketry and mats. [*Syn.* chae khlyi.]

gilããsa *n.* <gilaas> glass.

-go' *see* **-du'** 'if'.

golbxẽḍaa' *n.* <golbhẽḍaa> tomato.

goli *n.* <golī> bullet; pill; tablet. [*Syn.* phũ.]

golmol *n.* <golmaal> confusion.

-gon *s.v.* <-ni> indeed; emphatic past tense.
tel nẽsa'ri xyoigon ochẽ. *(You) cooked it last night, indeed, poor dear.*

goraama'ẽ *n.* <goraaharu> European; white foreigner; paleface.

gorkhaa *n.p.* <gorkha> Gorkha (town between Kathmandu and Pokhara, origin of present Shah dynasty in Nepal); Gurkha Brigade (comprising Nepali troops in Indian and British armies).
si's gorkhaa. *6th Gurkha Rifles.*

gorkhaali *a.,n.* <gorkhaali> Nepali (person or language).

gosar *n.* <goswaaraa> office of district administration; law court - district.

graaun *n.* <graaun> airstrip.

-gru *s.num.* <haat (naapnu)> cubit. [*Syn.* kru.]

gũḍa *n.* <khurkilaa> wall across path to keep cattle from crops.

-gu' *s.v.* <-hos> imperative on bxagu' 'bring'.

-gu *see* -du' 'if'.

gue *n.* <gohi> crocodile.

guji *n.* <khaltī> pocket.

gulaaph *n.* <gulaaph> rose.

gulaaphi *a.* <gulaaphī> pink; light red.

gun *n.* <guṇ> charity; benevolence.

gunadi' gunan *av.* <guṇle guṇai> gratitude - in (ironically).

gundri *n.* <gundrī> mat about 180x90 cm., woven of rice straw.

gundru *n.* <sinkī> pickle made from radish leaves (pounded in a bamboo cylinder then allowed to stand for a week till fermented. They are then sun dried and stored for later use). [*Syn.* jimbu.]

gur *n.* <dhaamī kaamnu> trance with shaking (of religious officiant).
gur nxeba. *To shake in a trance.*

-guraa *s.num.* <-hal> yoke of oxen.

guraa *n.* <sakhar> sugar - raw.

guru *n.* <guru> teacher (especially religious).

guruŋ, gurũ *n.* <guruŋ> Gurung. [*Syn.* tamũma'ẽ.]

guwaar, guhaar *n.* <guhaar> help.

gxaḍi'[1] *n.* <ghaḍi> clock; watch.

gxaḍi'[2] *a.* <kam> less; smaller.

gxaḍi'ba *v.* <ghaṭnu> to shrink; reduce in size.

gxaĩḍi *n.* <ghãĩṭo, gaagri> earthenware pot.

gxai mrõ' *n.* <ghaiyaa baari> field close to one's house; garden.

gxaji'diba *v.* <ghacghacyaaunu> to rattle; shake (a door).

gxama'nḍi [*N* 'proud, arrogant'] *a.*
1. <jiddī hune> self-willed; unteachable.
2. <agyaani> ignorant; prejudiced.
[*Syn.* jiddi labaa'; igura saẽ.]

gxanḍaa' *n.* <ghanṭaa> hour.

gxanmase *n.* <ḍallẽṭho> mallet (for breaking up clods).

gxa'r jawẽ *n.* <ghar juwaaī> son-in-law of household (who lives in wife's house and, in absence of wife's brothers, inherits through wife).

gxa'r khe'daa *n.* <ghar khet> property; house and land.

gxarchi'n *av.* <chin bhari>
1. instantly. [*Syn.* gxari'nna.]
2. momentarily; briefly. [*Syn.* chi'n gxrirna'; tisyaa.]

gxari' *av.* <ghari ghari> repeatedly; over and over.

gxari'nna *av.* <ek chinmai> quickly; without delay. [*Syn.* ekkaasi.]

gxase'ḍa *n.* <hããgaa (paat nabhaeko)> branches stripped of leaves (by cattle).

gxaṭṭe' *n.* <ghaṭṭaa> mill - water-driven.

gxaudi'ba *v.* <ghoknu> to shout; proclaim (news, announcement).

gxãã' *n.* shell of snail.

gxaa' *n.* <ghaau> wound; cut; sore.

gxaaḍ *n.* <hūl (baaṭoko)> crowd (of people meeting at trail junction).
mardi kholaa gxaaḍ pardiba'e khlxyo mu. *Mardi Khola is a place where people meet.*

gxaaḍaa' *n.* <ghaaṭ> bank of river. [*Syn.* cha'.]

gxaaḍo' *n.* <ghããḍo (purkhako naac)> dance (of old Gurung type).

gxaanaa', gxaanaa' paa'd *n.* <gahaanaa> jewellery.

gxaanaa' gxoḍ' *n.* <ṭhulo paanī parne belaa> time of very heavy rain.

gxaara' *n.* <jel jasto> court-house; cells.
ko'ḍ gxaaraa'r thundiba. *To confine in the courthouse.*

gxaaraa' *n.* <ghaar (mauriko)> bee-hive.

gxaari' *n.* <paakho, ghaari> highland zone around 1300 to 2000 m. altitude with small brush.
[*Cp.* bugyaani, pakha'.]

gxẽba'[1] *v.* to employ other's oxen (having none of own). [*Syn.* paryaali' laba'.]

gxẽba'[2] *v.* <aaḍlaaunu> to lean back; lean on.

gxẽ'xyaaba' *v.* <marnu> to die (vulgar term).
[*Syn.* sixyaaba'.]

gxesaa'rdiba *v.* <ghisranu> to crawl; drag oneself along.

gxisaa'rdiba *v.* <ghisaarnu> to drag.

gxõ' *n.* <ṭhulo kholsaa kholsi> rocky area (hard to make way through).

gxoḍa' *n.* <ghoḍaa> horse.

gxoḍa' lxo *n.* <ghoḍaa warṣa> year of the horse (1942,54,66, etc.) [*Syn.* ta lxo.]

gxodaa' raa'ba *v.* to go to watch funeral or pae of adult.
[*Cp.* ŋxyoba (for a child's funeral).]

gxri', kri' [*TB* *t(y)ik=*(g-)tyik n. 251, n. 271] *num.* <ek, euṭaa> one. [*Syn.* ti-.]

gxri'n *a.* <eklai> alone.

gxrinaa' *a.* <ekai> same; identical.

gxublu'kkale *av.* shrouded completely (of wearing cape).

gxumdi'ba *v.* <ghumnu> to wander; stroll; rise and fall (of voice pitch); go around; detour.
[*Syn.* ḍuldiba.]

gxus *n.* <ghus> bribe.

gxusa' *n.* <ghussaa> fist - clenched.
gxusa'd bachaardiba. *To punch.*

gxusu'l *n.* <nuhaaune calan> ablutions; bathing.

gxyãã' [*TaGTh* *gyam] *n.* <baaṭo>
1. road; path.
2. sheet of white cloth carried ahead of corpse.
3. side (in genealogy).
   aamaae' gxyaa'ũle' ŋõ'lõ phem. *He is a cross-cousin on my mother's side.*

gxyãã' kha'rja *n.* <bhaaḍaa> fare; travel cost.

gxyãã' kxaaba *v.* <baaṭo samaatnu> to set out on journey.

gxyããbri' *n.* <baaṭo muni> locality name in Ghachok (below the road).

gxyõ' *n.* <ghogo> cob of corn.

gxyõsĩ' *n.* <uttisko boṭ> alder-tree.

-gya, -gyaa *s.a.* suffix marking colour adjectives.
olgya. *Red.* mlõgya. *Black.*

gyaa *n.* <solṭi> cross-cousin (FaSiSo, MoBrSo - term of address). [*Syn.* ŋõ'lõ.]

gyaan[1] *n.* <**gyaan**> self-control.
xris axkha'du biyãã, su'baas chyããbaa' mudu' biyãã, gyaan tam. *If you don't get angry, if your temperament is good, you have self-control.*

gyaan[2] *n.* <**gyaan**> wisdom; knowledge.
khe'i biri' to'ndori xram, gyaan tam. *After studying one knows everything, one has wisdom.*

-gyõ *s.num.* <**curoṭko kosaa**> cigarette.
[*Cp.* kosa, khilli'.]

I

ĩṭ *n.* <**ĩṭ**> brick.

-i *s.n.* <**pani**> also.
[*Syn.* -m; -jai.]

icchyaa' *n.* <**icchaa**> wish; desire. [*Syn.* chutte'.]

igura saẽ *av.* <**ekohoro man**> stubborn; single-minded; undeviating.
[*Syn.* gxama'nḍi; jiddi.]

igurle' *av.* <**phirtaa na-aaune (namaagne)**> permanently; irrevocably.

ijed *n.* <**ijjat; khandaan**> reputation; prestige; self-respect; face; honour.
ijed xyaam'. *He loses face.*
ijed muba'e mxi. *A man of prestige.*
[*Syn.* abbru'.]

ikh *n.* <**ĩkh**> jealousy; malice; spite.

ilaam *n.* <**pešaa, ilam**> profession; occupation.
ilaam pi'waaba'. *To leave one's profession.*

ilbaa' *v.* <**saas thunnu**> difficulty in breathing as a result of eating a certain plant.

-ile' *p.* <**baaṭaa; dekhi**> from.
[*Syn.* ule'; le'.]

imaandaari *a.* <**ĩmaandaar**> honest; faithful; hard working.
[*Syn.* saẽ satte' tabaa'.]

imaansaa'th *n.* <**ĩmaan saath**> truthfulness; honesty.

-imu *s.v.* <**-eko**> completed action. [*Syn.* -ŋŋyũ'.]

-inamu *s.v.* <**-daicha**> continuative. [*Syn.* -ri.]

inaama *n.* <**inaama**> reward.

inaar *n.* <**inaar**> well - large.

inḍiyaa' *n.* <**bhaarat**> India.
[*Syn.* bxaara'da; desa; xindu'sthaa'n.]

iskim [*E* 'scheme'] *n.* <**jukti; upaay**> design; plan.

iskrub *n.* <**pecha**> screw; bolt.

iskrub ḍaaĩbxar *n.* <**pecha kas**> screwdriver.

ispadaa' [*Po* espada 'sword'] *n.* <**ispaat**> razor blade.

ispan *n.* <**jhyaau**> sponge; moss.

ispit, isbiṭ *n.* <**ispiṭ**> speed.

iṣṭami'ttra *n.* <**iṣṭamitra**> relatives; fellow villagers.

isṭor *n.* <**dokaan**> store.
[*Syn.* dukaan.]

istri *n.* <**istirĩ**> iron (for ironing clothes).

itixaas *n.* <**itihaasa**> history.

J

jãgal *n.* <**jãgal**> jungle.

ja *v.* <**ho**> to be (interrogative).
[*Cp.* ŋxĩba'.]

jab *n.* <**jab**> recitation of beads.
bxaktiji kxe' axlaa', jab lam ma'ttre. *The ascetic doesn't work, but just recites his beads.*

jabdiba *v.* <**jabnu**> to recite beads.

...jadi ...jadi *p.* <jati> as for X..., Y on the other hand... muyũma'ẽ jadi jxudi' kũ'nũ, rĩ'maẽ jadi jxaadi' kũ'n. *You men sit here; you women, on the other hand, sit there.*

jaer *n.* <naališ> complaint reported officially.

jaga[1] *n.* <jag> foundation.

-jaga[2] *s.n.* <haru> plural. [*Syn.* -maẽ, budũ, -jau.]

-jai *s.* <pani> also. [*Syn.* -yaa, -i, -ai, -laadi.]

jaisi, jasmaẽ, jasi, jyaisi *n.* <jyotiṣi> astrologer. [*Syn.* la'maa; pujyu'.]

jal tha'l, jal thal *av.* splashing; overflowing. mrõ'jare kyu' jal tha'l xyaana'. *The water has overflowed around the paddy field.*

jalgo *n.* <jalgo> fern-like edible plant.

jalgo kxure' *n.* <saaras> crane.

jalidiba *v.* <jalaaunu> to burn oil in a stove. [*Cp.* khrõba'; mroba'; phaabaa'.]

jamin *n.* <jamin> land as opposed to sea.

jammaa, jamman *n.* <jammaa> total; gathering.

jamra *n.* <jamaraa> shoots of barley grown indoors for ceremonial purposes at **dasaẽ**.

janawaar *n.* <janaawar> beasts; wild animals. [*Cp.* khyodo, jantu, jibjantu.]

jane *n.* <janai> sacred thread of Hindu worn on neck or wrist.

janma *n.* <janma> birth.

janma din *n.* <janma din> birthday.

janma thal *n.* <janma thal> birthplace.

janmadiba *v.* <janmanu> to be born. [*Syn.* phibaa', yõbaa'.]

janta *n.* <jantaa> people of a kingdom or country; commoners as opposed to royalty.

jantu *n.* <jantu> animal - four-legged. [*Cp.* khyodo, janawaar, jibjantu.]

jara *n.* <jaro> root.

jaraayo *n.* <jaraayo> elk - Indian; sambhar. [*Syn.* e.]

jare *p.* <tira> near; round about.

jasi, jasmaẽ *see* **jaisi** 'astrologer'.

jasta *n.* <jastaa> zinc; corrugated iron roofing.

jatamanse *n.* nard.

jaũle *n.* <jamlyaahaa> twins (of offspring of normally monogenetic animal); plants shooting close together. [*Syn.* joḍaa.]

-jau *s.n.* <-haru> plural. [*Syn.* jaga; -maẽ.]

jawẽ *n.* <juwaaĩ> son-in-law (only in gxa'r jawẽ).

jay *e.* <jay> long live; victory to... jay nxepaal. *Victory to Nepal.*

-jãã *s.num.* sections; joints of cane.

jããge [*H* jaaghe] *n.* <kaṭṭu> shorts; underpants.

jããj *n.* <jããc> test; examination, inspection. aphisa'r bosi, jããj lasi, chyããba' tãã mu u. *They took him to the office, and cross-examined him, whether the story was correct or not.*

jããj buj *n.* <jããc-bujh> investigation. pulisma'ẽ bosi jããj buj lai. *They took the police and made an investigation.*

jaad *n.* <jaat> caste; kind; sort; species.
[*Syn.* tha'ri.]

jaade *a.* <thari> clan; caste within Gurung society.
ca' mxi caa'r jaade yaa. *That person is of the Four Clans.*

jaagir *n.* <jaagir> employment; salaried position.
[*Syn.* no'kori.]

jaala *n.* <jaala> fishing net.

jaali *n.* <jaali> screen on windows to keep out insects; mantle on pressure lamp.

jaama *n.* <jaama> skirt.

jaan, jaanmaẽ, jaanãã *n.* <jahaan> family - wife and children; wife.

jaari *n.* <jaarī> adultery; damages payable to husband.
aague' mrĩ jaari lasi bxwilaa'. *He took another man's wife adulterously.*

jei *pa.* <jei; huncha> yes; OK.

jeṭha *n.* <jesṭha> month (2nd of Nepali calendar, mid-May to mid-June).

jelaa *n.* <jyaalaa> wages; pay (for a day's work).

jeṭhu *n.* <jeṭhan> brother-in-law (WiErBr).
[*Syn.* aasyõ.]

-ji[1] *s.num.* monosyllables.
tiji ŋxiji bibaa. *To speak shortly.*

-ji[2] *s.n.* <-le> agentive.
[*Syn.* -di.]

-ji[3] *s.v.* <-yo> past tense.
[*Syn.* -i, -di.]

jib *n.* <jip moṭara> jeep.

jibjantu *n.* <jiwjantu> animals - four-footed.
[*Cp.* jantu.]

jiddi labaa' *v.* <jiddhī garnu> to insist on one's own opinion; to be dogmatic.
[*Syn.* gxama'nḍi; igura saẽ.]

jillaa *n.* <jillaa> district - administrative (76 in Nepal, each district including about 50 village panchayats).
[*Cp.* ancalaa'; pancaayat.]

jimbu *n.* <jimbu> sauerkraut of garlic leaves; garlic leaf preparation (made by Tibetans).
nxu'e gundrulaai jimbu bim. *We call garlic pickle* jimbu.
[*Syn.* gundru.]

joḍaa *n.* <joḍaa> pair; partner (as of two friends).
khani' xyaai', kxie joḍaa? *Where has he gone, your friend?*
[*Syn.* jããle.]

joḍdiba *v.* <jornu> to add (in arithmetic).

joga *n.* <joga> time; occasion - astrological.
[*Syn.* belaa.]

jogi, joi *n.* <yogi> ascetic-religious (normally scholar with beard and yellow robes. He is the only Hindu who cuts off topknot lock of hair. Often mendicant); holy man - Hindu, the caste of Giri (even though an individual of the caste may not be ascetic).
[*Cp.* bairaagi.]

-jon, jo'n, ju'n *s.v.* <-yo ni> emphatic past.
talaa'n bijon. *I said it before.*
ŋa lxogõ thẽn taju'nde. *I am a native of Lxogon, indeed.*

-jor *s.num.* classifier for clothes.
kwẽ ŋxijor bolaa axtxu. *It is not necessary to take two sets of clothes.*

jordiba *v.* <jornu> to join; to assemble (machinery, etc.); to add possessions.

-ju *see* -du' 'if'.

juḍa *n.* <juṭho> food contaminated by other's touch; ritual defilement (9-11 days after childbirth, 14 days after contact with corpse).

juda *n.* <juttaa> shoe.

juga *n.* <jug; yug> epoch; age.

jugudiba *v.* <jogaaunu> to protect; to save.

-ju'n *see* -jon' 'emphatic past'.

juni *n.* <juni> life; lot.

juraaba *n.* <juraab; mojaa> sock.

juwaa *n.* <juwaa> gambling.

juwaa khlyõbaa' *v.* <juwaa khelnu> to gamble.

juwaaba, juwaapha *n.* <jawaaph> answer; reply.

juwaaḍe *n.* <juwaare> gambler.

jxaḍĩ'yãã *n.* <jyaadaa ris uṭhne> short-tempered; irritable; violent (of man or animal).

jxagaḍaa', jxaḍa *n.* <jhagaḍaa> argument; quarrel; lawsuit.

jxagu' *n.* <jau> barley.

jxaja' [*TB* *ziy=*źəy 'small' 60; *TB* *tsa 'child' n. 86; *TB* *za 'child' 59] *a.* <bacco> offspring of animal; small. [*Syn.* cyõbaa'.]

jxa'n *pa.* <jhan> the more; rather; contrary to expectation. oho, cu' kurji'm jxa'n, ca' bxandaa', cu' ka'ra axyõ'm munaa'. *Oh, as for this chair though, it is even more uncomfortable than that.*

jxarãã'go *n.* <kokro> basket - large, conical.

jxaṭke'lu cxa *n.* <jhaḍhkelo choro> stepson.

jxããkri' *n.* <jhããkrī> witch-doctor. [*Syn.* pujyu'; la'ma; jaisi, la'm kani'.]

jxaa- *n.* <utaa paṭṭi> thither; over there. [*Ant.* jxu-.]

jxaab jxup *a.* <jhaap jhuppa> quickly; hurriedly. ŋxyo' jxaab jxu'pale ladu' biyãã chi'n gxrirna' khãã'm. *If we do it quickly it will be finished in a moment.*

jxaadi' maadi' *a.* <yataa uti> in all directions.

jxaale', dxaaire', jxaaire *c.* <tyahãã baaṭa> then; after that. [*Syn.* daai; phe'ri.]

jxaale' maale' *a.* <yataa utaa baaṭa> from all directions.

jxaaraa' *n.* <jhaaraa> statutory labour; community projects (such as work on irrigation channels, roads, schools, animal pounds).

jxaasa', jxaaja' *n.* <jahaaj> vehicle (air or sea); boat; plane.

jxĩjyãã' *n.* <jhĩjo (daauraako)> kindling.

jxilge'[1] *n.* <thailī> purse - cloth, women's, for money.

jxilge'[2] *n.* <jhiliŋgo> rice straws. [*Syn.* khyuni'.]

jxili ra mi'li *n.* <jhilimili> city high life; sights; bright lights.

jxõba' *v.* <haalnu> to pour; put in (bolt in place, seeds in ground, sugar in tea, chickens under basket, feed in manger).

jxõju' *n.* <odaan> tripod over fire (for cooking pots).

jxoga' *n.* <kokro - baalakh sutne> basket (baby's crib).

jxu- *a.* <yataa paṭṭi> hither; this side. [*Ant.* jxaa-.]

jxugu'diba *v.* <gijyaaunu> to laugh at; deride; mock.

jxulaa' *n.* <jhul> mosquito net.

jxumsaa' *n.* <jhumsaa> Jomosom (town on road to Mustang).

jxuṭṭaa' *n.* <jxūṭ> lie; falsehood.

jxyaaḍi' *n.* <jhaaḍī> bush; tuft. [*Syn.* ¢xi.]

jxyaalaa', jxyaali' *n.* <jhyaal> window.

jxyaale' maale' *a.* <jhaale maale> variegated in colour; spotted; speckled (of animals or cloth).

jxyaalkha'na, jxyaalga'na *n.* <jelkhaan> jail.

jxyaampha'l *n.* <gal> crowbar. [*Syn.* pwe'e phargu.]

jxyaaure' kxwe' *n.* <jhyaaure gīt> songs; folk songs.

jxyolaa' *n.* <jholaa> bag worn on shoulder.

jxyũba' *v.* <khumcinu> to crumple - cloth, paper; wrinkle - skin. [*Syn.* khumjidi'ba; cxyurba.]

jyaisi *see* jaisi 'astrologer'.

-jyãã *s.* <le> emphatic agentive.

jyããṭha *n.* <jããṭha> abusive term.

jyããṭhisyo *n.* abusive term (addressed to a woman).

jyaaũ jyaaũ *n.* <jhyaaũ jhyaaũ> hubbub; commotion of many talking.

-jyaa *s.num.* <muṭṭho> sheaf (grass or fibres).

jyaadaa, jyaastaa *a.* <jyaastaa> much; a lot of.

jyaamera *n.* <jyaamir> fruit (citrus intermediate in size between lemon and lime).

jyaanmaaraa' *n.* <jyaanmaaraa> murderer.

jyomaẽ lyomaẽ *d.* <gijyaaune šabda - laamaale paḍhda> hocus-pocus; words simulating lama's reading of Tibetan chants.

-jyu, -jyu'[1] *s.num.* tens. sõ'jyu. *Thirty.* ŋxajyu'. *Fifty.*

jyu[2] *n.* <jiu> body (of human).

jyu khru'ba *v.* <nuhaaunu> to bathe.

jyujyu baaje *n.* <jiju baaje> forefathers; ancestors. [*Syn.* khe.]

jyuni *n.* <juni> life; lot in life. xaardi'bae juni. *Wretched lot.*

K

kãgaḍaa' *n.* <tamaakhu> tobacco.

kãgaa', kangaa' *n.* <kanikaa> rice fragments broken during husking.

kãje xaaus *n.* <pašuharūlaaī thunne khor> pound for animals.

kãlã *n.* <labsi> fruit (tart flavour, size of apricot, rough brown skin, large brown stone).

ka kha *n.* <kakhaharaa>
1. Devanagari alphabet (consonant symbols only).
2. elements only (of a skill). ka kha mattre' xram. *She knows only the elements.*

kabae *n.* <bhuwaa; piuri> ball of wool.

kabli *n.* <moṭe> Fatty (nickname).

ka'blo[1] *n.* <ḍauraako gããṭho> knot in wood.

ka'blo[2] *n.* <jorni> joint of knee, ankle, elbow, knuckle. [*Syn.* kudũ', kunjyu'.]

kabol labaa' *v.* <kabul garnu> to promise.

ka'bu *n.* <ciple kiro> slug; snail. [*Cp.* mainaa' ka'bu.]

ka'bu gxãã' *n.* <ciple kiro> snail.

kaburaa' *n.* <kapur> camphor.

kacca', kacci' *a.* <kaccaa (kaam)> weak; crude; second rate. [*Syn.* axbxõba', kalilo, kaaphaar. *Ant.* pakkaa'.]

kachuwaa' *n.* <kachuwaa> turtle.

kaḍa *n.* <-ko laagi> for; purpose. bxakundo khlyõba' kaḍar yu'ba. *He comes to play football.* [*Syn.* -r.]

ka'ḍãḍa labaa' *v.* <daahraa kiṭnu> to grit teeth.

kaḍawaa' *n.* <bhaĩsīko paaṭho> calf of buffalo - up to one year old.

kaḍbaa'ra *n.* <kaṭhabaara> partition - wooden, in house.

kadaa'sũ *n.* <himaal> mountain; snow peak. [*Syn.* kailaas.]

kadi', kati' *a.* <kati> how much; how many.

kadrãã *a.* <dublo> lean; thin. [*Syn.* ḍyããgra.]

kadu' *n.* <okhar> walnut tree.

ka'dura *a.* <kããco> unripe of fruit. [*Syn.* axmxĩba'; kaji.]

kaẽ *n.* <bhaat> rice - cooked.

kaẽ koḍa *n.* <dhaan raakhne bhakaari> container of cane matting for storing rice.

ka'ẽḍu[1] *a.* <ũbho; uttar> upwards; north. cu' sero' ka'ẽḍu. *From here up.*

ka'ẽdu[2] *n.* <bhaatko mūrti> statuette of rice flour used in religious ceremonies, especially funeral and post-funeral.

kae *n.* <aawaaj> voice.

kae te'ba *v.* <karaaunu> to shout; yell.

kaeda' *n.* <bandhan> bond; charge not to repeat an offence. pulisa'd bii biri' kaeda'r jxõm'. *The police spoke, and put him on a bond.*

kael *n.* <kaayal> pledge not to repeat offence the signing of which is a condition for release from prison; confession of guilt.

kaeldiba' *v.* <kaayal garnu> extract confession, often by beating.

kaes *n.* <gaahro laagnu> reluctance; unwillingness. kaes mxããdim. *He is unwilling.* [*Cp.* chorõ' ŋxããba.]

kaga' aaba *n.* <kaakaa> uncle (FaBr, MoSiHu); stepfather.

kagaa' *n.* <kaag> crow.

ka'graa ku'gru *a.* <kakrakka> frozen; stiff; paralysed as in a fit.

kaĩẽdu *see* ka'ẽdu 'statuette of rice'.

kaĩji' *n.* <kaĩci> scissors.

kaĩlaa' *n.* <kaaĩlo> son - fourth; brother - fourth eldest.

kaĩli' *n.* <kããĩli> daughter - fourth; sister - fourth eldest.

kailaas *n.* <kailaas> mountain abode of the gods; snow peak. [*Syn.* kadaa'sũ.]

kaj kaj labaa' *v.* <kic kic garnu> to nag. [*Syn.* xaudiba'.]

kaji *a.* <napaakeko, kããco> unripe (of berries, fruit). [*Syn.* axmxĩba', ka'dura.]

kaju' *n.* <ghaacok> Ghachok (village northwest of Pokhara).

kajuri' *n.* <sabhaa> council; meeting. [*Cp.* sabxa labaa'; tãã labaa'.]

ka'l *n.* <kal>
1. machine; engine.
2. tap; piped water.

kali juga *a.* <kali yuga> era of the present age in Hindu mythology, fourth in series. [*Cp.* satte', dwaapar, tretaa.]

kalilo' *a.* <kalilo> young, tender (of plants and men). [*Syn.* kaaphaar; kacca'; axbxõba'.]

kalkada' *n.* <kalkata> Calcutta.

kallãã' *n.* <aali> wall of terrace field. [*Syn.* ali'.]

kalli' *n.* <kalli> anklet.

kamalo' *a.* <kamalo> tender; soft. [*Syn.* ŋiliba'. *Ant.* kidriba'; saaro'.]

kamdi' *a.* <kamti> less; few; little. [*Syn.* cyugu'de.]

kamẽja' *n.* <kamij> shirt.

kamĩ' *n.* <kaami> blacksmith caste.

kamjo'ri *n.* <kamjori> weakness. [*Syn.* axbxõba'.]

ka'naa *n.* <kaano> blind in one or both eyes.

kanchaa' *p.* <kaancho> son (YtSo); brother - youngest (YtBr). [*Syn.* cyõbaa'.]

kanchi, kãji, kaaji *n.* <kaanchi> daughter (YtDa); sister - youngest (YtSi).

kanda'ni *n.* <kandani> vertical stroke in Nagari script for aa vowel.

kangaa' *see* kãgaa' 'rice fragments'.

kanne' *n.* <kanyaa> virgin (of male or female).

kapṭelu' *n.* <bããsko kapṭero> split wood or bamboo.

kar[1] *n.* <kar> tax on motor vehicles. [*Syn.* ṭeksaa'; bxansaar; baali.]

ka'r[2] *n.* <kar> compulsion; coercion.

ka'ra *n.* <aananda> comfort; ease; convenience.
ka'ra axyõ'm muna'. *It wasn't comfortable, I found.*

karããba' *v.* <baamesarnu> crawl on all fours.

karẽŋa' *n.* <paalīko bhaaṭo> beam of verandah.

karib *a.* <karib> approximately; about.
karib xa'jaar ŋi' pxre'. *About seven or eight thousand.*
[*Syn.* -de.]

karmaudu' *n.* <tite> vegetable like bamboo shoots.

karnal *n.* <karnel> colonel.

karu *n.* <uwaa> a grain (oats?, barley?) planted in November.

karwaa' *n.* <karuwaa> drinking vessel with a spout but no handle, made of brass, copper, or silver.

kasam *n.* <kasam> oath.

kasam cabaa' *v.* <kasam khaanu> swear an oath.

kasam kĩbaa' *v.* <kasam khaanu> to swear an oath (invoking curse on oneself if oath is broken).

kasdiba'[1] *v.* <kasinu; tayaar hunu> prepared; ready to do something.
ca' mxi xyaaba'r kasdii. *That person is ready to go.*
[*Syn.* tayaar.]

kasdiba'[2] *a.* <raamro (maasu)> fat; tasty (of goat meat).

kasdiba'[3] *a.* <kaseko> tight (of rope, belt, binding).

kasĩ' *n.* <kasĩgar> dirt, rubbish.

kaṣṭa *n.* <kaṣṭa> trouble; affliction; calamity - often invited by ignoring advice of astrologers.

kasũḍi' *n.* <kasaũḍī> water vessel - small, round.

kasyaari' *n.* <kaseri> village on eastern bank of Seti.

kaṭara' *n.* <kaṭahar> fruit - jack fruit.

kaṭṭi' *n.* <kammar> waist.

kaṭwaale' *n.* <ghoṣaṇaa garne maanis> town crier; crier.

kathaa' *n.* <kathaa> story - fable or history.

katle' *n.* <katlaa> scale of fish.

ka'tti, katti' *a.* <katti> how (emphatic); not at all.
katti' yumnaa mli'xyaai. *How quickly (you) have forgotten.*

kaũri *n.* <ḍaḍheko dūdh> sediment of burnt milk.

kauḍi' *n.* <kauḍi> game with sixteen shells where players gamble on number falling right way up.

kausi' *n.* <kausi> balcony; roof garden with balustrade.

kawiba' *v.* <bhak bhake> stutter.

kayaa', kxayaa *n.* <khaṭkaulo> cooking pot of copper or brass with ring handles.

kãã'[1] [*TaGTh* *kamp; *TB* *(m-)ka, *(s-)ka 470] *n.* <ciũḍo> chin.

kãã[2] *n.* <pitta> bile; gall bladder.

kãã'ba *v.* <haai aaunu> yawn.
[*Syn.* xa'i labaa'.]

kããbaa' [*TB* *ka 8; *TaGTh* *kam] *a.* <tito> bitter; acidy.

kããchi *n.* <paagur> cud.

kããchi ŋebaa' *v.* <ugraaunu> to chew the cud.

kããḍi' *n.*
1. <kããṭī> nail.
2. <bunne siyo> knitting needle.

kããdaa' *n.* <kum> shoulder - especially towards neck.
[*Cp.* pxaẽdo.]

kããji' *n.* <pote> necklace of beads worn by women other than widows (in Brahmin custom, only by married women with living husbands).

kããju' *n.* ring of iron surrounding bamboo container.

kããsa *n.* <bããgaaro> molar tooth.

kããsi' waale' *a.* <kaasī waale> printed (of astrological calendar) (*lit.* from kaasī, a place near Varanasi).
[*Syn.* chapwaa', paadru'.]

kããsu' *n.* <kããs> pewter; white metal.

kaa'[1] [*TaGTh* *gab 'lid' (but tone mismatches)] *n.* <birko> cover; lid; screw top; second line of couplet.
kaa' jxõba'. *Sing second line of a rhyming couplet.*

kaa[2] *n.* <puwaako bhuslaai phaalne nigaaloko cimṭaa> implement for cleaning naī.

kaa'ba *v.* <chopnu> cover (something with something).

kaabi' *n.* <kaapī> writing paper; notebook.

kaa'bro *n.* <kaapa> split cane or wood used as fork.

kaagadi' *n.* <kaagati> lime (small chartruse citrus fruit).
[*Cp.* mxība.]

kaagaadaa', kaagat *n.* <kaagat> paper.

kaagī' *n.* <ṭhulo baabu> uncle (MoYrSiHu - first born).

kaaidaa' *n.* <kaaidaa> manner; way of pronunciation.

kaal *n.*
1. <kaal> time to die.
kaal khasero' sixyaam. *Since (my) time has come I'm dying.*

2. <mri+tya> death.

kaal raa'di *n.* **<kaalraatri>** night of death. (Many animals die on night of **kaalraadi**. Many people stay awake on this night, the eighth day of **dasaĩ**, called **aṣṭami'**, in order to "cut the death".)

kaamlo', kaammlo' *n.* **<kaamlo>** rug woven of sheep or goat's wool. [*Syn.* **xraḍi, galaĩcaa'**.]

kaanun *n.* **<kaanūn>** law. [*Syn.* **aen.**]

kaaphaar[1] *a.* **<kaatar>** nervous; cowardly; fearful. [*Syn.* **ŋxĩba; txaarba.**]

kaaphaar[2] *a.* **<nirdho>** fragile (of glass); tender; weak; delicate (of animals). [*Syn.* **kalilo; kacca'; axbxõba'.**]

kaar, kaaraa *a.* **<sukeko>** dry (of wood, clothes).

kaaran *n.* **<kaaran>** cause; reason.
ca' kaaran maa'madi' xyaai'. *For that reason Uncle went.*

kaa'rãã mãã'rãã, ka'rãã ma'rãã *n.* **<haat goḍaale ṭekera hĩḍnu>** crawling and toddling; toddling unsurely. [*Syn.* **karããba'.**]

kaarbaa' *v.i.* **<suknu>** dry (to become).

kaa'rgyu [*TB* ***kroy** 'surround' 313] *p.* **<golo bhaera basnu>** surroundings; round about.
kodaa' kaa'rgyun mxi mu. *There are people around the fireplace.*

kaariba' *v.* **<sukeko>** to be dry.

kaarjya *n.* **<kaaryakram>** occasion of importance (marriage, **pae**, house building) which necessitates astrological guidance.

kaarkhanaa' *n.* **<kaarkhaanaa>** factory.

kaartika, kaati' *n.* **<kaartik>** month (7th of Nepali calendar, mid-October to mid-November).

kaa'sa *n.* **<kachaaḍ>** kilt of white cloth worn by men.

kaaṭhidiba' *v.* **<kaaṭhinu>** numb with cold. [*Syn.* **ṭhiridiba'; gaŋgridiba; kõ'ba.**]

kaaṭhmaanḍu *n.* **<kaaṭhmaanḍu>** Kathmandu, capital city of Nepal.

kaati' *see* **kaartika** 'month 7'.

kẽ [*TB* ***kuw=*kəw** 255] *n.* **<sasuro>** father-in-law (WiFa, HuFa).

ke' kyari' *loc.* **<u tyahãã>** there, way over there.

keb *n.* **<kamaaro>** slave.

ke'ba *n.* **<daabilo>** stirrer - wooden.

kebaa' [*TB* ***kut** 383] *v.* **<cilaaunu>** to itch.

ke'ga *n.* cake.

ke'ma *n.* **<kyaamp>** camp - army.

ker txuba *a.* **<kaam laagnu>** useful.

kerdiba' *v.* **<kernu (prašna sodhnu>** to interrogate; cross-examine. [*Syn.* **khyaabdiba'.**]

khab, khaba' *pn.*
1. **<ko>** who (interrogative).
ca' khab jaa? *Who is that?*
2. **<jo>** whoever.
khab aasõ' rimu ca'di ŋxĩ' caba. *Whoever gets up first he will eat two.*
3. **<kun>** which.

khaba'e *pn.* **<kohi>** anyone.
khaba'e axxre'. *No one was there.*

khaba'la *a.* **<kasko>** whose.

khabar *n.* **<khabar>** news; message. [*Syn.* **samjaa'r; tãã.**]

khabaa' *v.* **<aaunu>** to come (from other than uphill or north).

khabdiba' *v.* **<khapnu>**
1. to last.
   bxõba kwẽ kĩdu'biyãã lxe' saal sammaa' khabdim. *If you buy strong cloth it will last many years.*
2. to endure, to bear; put up with.
   beseri na'yãã ŋa khabdila axkhãã'. *If it hurts a lot I cannot bear it.*

kha'dra khu'dru *n.* **<khatra khutru>** odds and ends; sundry articles.

kha'ẽ *n.* **<haawaa>** wind.

kha'ẽba *v.* **<kaaṭnu (dhaan)>** to reap; cut at ground level (rice, grass).

kha'eba *v.* **<puwaa kaaṭnu>** to card thread - not wool. [*Syn.* **pxuba.**]

khaebaa' *v.* **<dherai kuraa bolne>** talkative.

khaen... khaen *pn.* **<kehi... kehi>** one... the other.
mxi gxridna' khoyõ khaen bim, khoyõ khaen bim. *The one person says sometimes one, sometimes the other.*

kha'ga khu'gu *av.* in a massed manner. [*Syn.* **khaa'gule.**]

kha'i [*TB* *m-kal 12] *n.* **<mirgaulo>** kidney.

khaibaa' *a.* **<kasto>** what kind of?

khai *av.* **<kasari>** how?
khai laŋŋyũ'? *How has he done?*

khai'lase *av.* **<kasaigari>** emphatically; definitely.
khai'lase kho'. *Whatever happens, come.*
khai'lase tãã to'i axta. *He did not speak at all.*

khaire' *a.* **<khairo>** brown.

khaire *n.* **<kholaako naam; ṭolko naam>** stream in Ghachok; locality name.

khajij *a.* **<ali bisek>** recovered slightly (from illness).

khalag *n.* **<khalak>** lineage; family - vertically extended.

khalaa' *n.* **<khalo>** threshing floor (area cleared in the rice field for threshing at harvest time).

kha'lbal *n.* **<khalbal>** confusion; uproar.

khani' *pn.*
1. **<kahãã>** where.
   khani' boi? *Where did (he) take it?* [*Syn.* **kho'i.**]
2. **<jahãã>** wherever.
   khani' ṭimu, ca'rna swaaba' mxããdim. *Wherever (I) live (I) find it pleasant there.*

khani' mxani *pn.* **<kahĩ kahĩ>** here and there; in only a few places.

khanji' khanji *loc.* **<jataa sukai>** everywhere.
khanji' khanji'ũle' kham. *They are coming from everywhere.*

khantadan *loc.* **<jataa sukai>** everywhere.

khanwaa' *a.* **<khããdilo>** solid, not hollow (of jewellery); heavy.

kharaa' *n.* **<kharaayo>** hare; rabbit.

khargana' *n.* **<khaṭkãũlo>** cooking vessel for rice - large.

kha'rgũ *n.* **<juwaa>** yoke of oxen. [*Syn.* **-gur.**]

kharguna' *n.* village on east bank of Seti River.

kha'ri *n.* **<ghããṭi>** throat (external); neck; neck of jar. [*Syn.* **gardan, mlõ'gu.**]

kha'rja *n.* **<kharca>** expenditure; expense.

khasi' *n.* **<khasi>** castrated goat.

khasi' labaa' *v.*
1. **<khasi paarnu>** to castrate (goats and sheep).

2. <kalami kaaṭnu> to prune.

khasro' *a.* <khasro> coarse; big; rough.
[*Ant.* masinu'.]

khaṭidiba' *v.* <khaṭaaunu> to appoint (to a task); detail (to do something).

khatam *n.* <khatam> end; finish.

khatraane khutru labaa' *v.* <khatryaaka khutruka garnu> stumble about; upset things.

khãã'ba *v.* <siddhinu; saknu> to finish; to be able.
[*Syn.* nubaa'; cxĩba; chõbaa'.]

khããdiba' *v.* <khããdnu> to press; compress.
gundru banidimale' beseri sĩ'd khããdim. *In making pickle one compresses it hard with wood.*

khããj *n.* <khããco> shortage; need (of goods, money, facilities).

khaa'ba *v.* <nikhannu> to redeem mortgaged property.

khaabaa' [*TB* *ka:p 'draw water' 336] *v.* <bharnu - paanī> to fill (almost always with object kyu' 'water').

khaabdiba' *v.* <khaapnu> to stack one on top of another.
bxããḍo', tõ' khaabdim. *(She) is stacking up the pots and dishes.*

khaa'ḍa *n.* <khaaṭ> bedstead (wooden).

khaa'd *n.* <thupro> heap; pile.

khaa'gae *a.* <ali ali> a little.
[*Syn.* cyugu'de, jxaja', ti'brãde, ti'nade.]

khaa'gu^{1} *a.* <jammaa> all; together.

khaa'gu^{2}, khaau *p.* <wari pari> around; round about.
gxyãã' khaagu ro'mũ. *(They) sleep by the road.*

khaal^{1} *n.* <khaal> kind; variety.
cu' khaalbae. *Of this sort.*

khaal^{2} *n.* <khaal> space between poles in a rack for stacking corn cobs.

khaal^{3} *n.* <khaal> place for dancing or gambling.
naa'j khaal. *Dance floor.*
juwaa khaal. *Gambling den.*

khaal^{4} *n.* <khaal> skin of goat used at pae ceremony.

khaal gxriba' *a.* <ekai naasko> identical.

khaali'^{1} *a.* <kewal, khaali> only.
khaali' sũd mattre' bim. *It is only words.*
[*Syn.* sirib, mattre'.]

khaali'^{2} *a.* <khaalī> empty.
[*Syn.* thedẽ', suŋnen.]

khaa'rba^{1} *v.*
1. <hallanu> to shake oneself (of animal shaking water off after rain).
2. <hallaunu> to shake (cloth to get rid of dust).

khaa'rba^{2} *v.*
1. <utranu> to alight (from plane, boat).
2. <jharnu> drop.
3. <orlanu> descend.
4. <jhaarnu> throw to the ground.

khaa'riba *v.* <jharnu; khasnu> to fall from tree (of fruit).
[*Syn.* khaa'rxyaaba'.]

khaa'rxyaaba' *v.* <khasnu> to fall down.
[*Syn.* kxurixyaaba'; khaa'riba.]

khaa'sgari *a.* <khaas> genuine; correct (of speech).
khaa'sgari tãã. *Correct speech.*

khaau *see* khaagu 'around'.

khẽbaa' *v.* <ṭaalnu> to patch.

khe *see* khi 'he himself'.

khe *n.* <jiju baaje; pūrkha> ancestors; forefathers.

khe'ba [*TaGTh* *khep] *v.* <paḍhnu> to study; read; read aloud sacred writings.

khedi' lxaidiba *v.* <ubjaaunu> to cultivate.

khedi' paadi' *n.* <kheti paati> agriculture; cultivation.

khe'l *n.* <khel> game; races.

khemaẽ *pn.* <aaphuharū> themselves.
khemaẽ dxĩ'r xyaai'. *They have gone to their own home.*

khe'rarale *av.* <jahaa tahĩ pugnu> everywhere (of child walking).
khe'rarale prxaba'. *(He) walks around everywhere.*

khere[1] *n.* <khiraako rukh> tree species (when branch is crushed and soaked in river, fish are poisoned and easy to catch).

khere[2] *n.* <rããḍo> bachelor; divorced male; widower (insulting term).

khere bicche *n.* grub (greenish-yellow, lives in khere dxũ', corn, rice foliage in Srawan, irritates skin on contact).

khi, khe *pn.* <aaphu> he himself; she herself; oneself.
khi'e sudgyaari'lai cal bxĩĩ'. *He fed his wife.*

khi lxo *n.* <kukur barkha> year of the dog in Tibetan 12 year cycle (1946,58,70,82,etc.).
[*Syn.* nagi lxo.]

khi'ba[1] [*TB* *kik 484; *TB* *ki:l 373; *TaGTh* *khiq] *v.* <poṭuka baannu> to bind on a cummerbund.

khi'ba[2] [*TB* *s-kiy 'borrow' 31] *v.* <paĩco garnu> to lend (food or small amount of money, not at interest).
[*Cp.* che' pĩbaa'; ŋaẽba'.]

khiba', khira *n.* <buḍho> old man.

khibaa' *a.* <lagaaunu (lugaa)> to wear clothes or jewellery.

khiidiba' *v.* <khiinu> to wear away; get thin - of metal implements.

khilli' *n.* <curoṭko paaip> cigarette; cigarette holder.
[*Syn.* kosa.]

khiridiba' *v.* <baṭaarnu> to be twined tightly; neatly finished (of rope).
[*Syn.* khrĩbaa'.]

khitt'ba *v.* <khicnu> to take (photos); record (sounds).

khlxyaa', khlyaa *n.* <goru> ox.

khlxyaa' bxaaraa' *n.* <bahaar (sããḍhe)> bull.

khlxyaa' ḍõḍaa *n.* <goruko daanaa khaane kaaṭhko bhããḍo> manger; feed trough.

khlxyaa' kxyoba' *n.* <goru (jotnu)> ox (specifically distinguished from bull).

khlxyaasa'ẽ *n.* <hali> ploughman.

khlxye[1] *n.* <kharka> jungle clearing used for shearing.

khlxye[2] *n.* <dhani, maalik> owner.

khlxyebri, lxebbri *n.* <jhããkrĩ> religious officiant, indigenous Gurung, of shamanistic (Tibetan Bon) tradition.

khlxyõ [*Cp* gloŋq 'top of tibia'] *n.* <nalihaaḍh> shin.

khlxyõba [*TaGTh* *gloŋ] *v.* <nilnu> to swallow.

khlxyõbae *n.* <laamkiro> snake - large.

khlxyo *n.* <ṭhaaũ> place; location; sleeping place.

khlxyo nxẽ *n.* <jagga jamin> lands; fields.

khlxyoba *n.* <phokso> lung.

khlyãã' *n.* <wan (paadal)> forested area - high, 9000 feet.
[*Syn.* bugyaani.]

khlyããbaa' *v.* <ghasranu> to wriggle; to slither on stomach (of infant unable yet to crawl); to glide.

sasaa khlyããbaa'. *To glide on earth (of snake).*

khlyaanu' *n.* **<garib>** poor person.

khlye' *n.* **<ghale gaaũ>** village across Seti from Ghachok.

khlyĩ' [*TaGTh* *glink (but tone mismatches); *TB* *kyam 224; *Cp* yuŋ] *n.* **<hiũ>** snow.

khlyi [*TaGTh* *kli; *TB* *kliy=*kləy 125] *n.* **<gu; disaa>** faeces; waste.
mi khlyi. *Ashes.*

khlyi bebẽ *n.* **<guye kiraa>** beetle - black with a foul smell, around dung; dung-beetle (?); cockroach (?).

khlyi chõmĩ' *n.* **<hariyo maakha>** blowfly.

khlyi txõba *v.* **<disaa garnu>** to defecate.

khlyi'ba *v.* **<cirnu>** to split cane or wood lengthwise. [*Syn.* ku'ba.]

khlyõbaa' [*TaGTh* *klaŋ] *v.* **<khelnu>** to play.

-khlyu *s.num.* **<ek kap>** glasses; cups of liquid. [*Syn.* pxela, gilããs.]

khlyubaa' *v.* **<ghopṭyaaunu>** to upend; invert a vessel (chiefly used of emptying manure out of basket).

khlyunaa' *a.* **<naaŋgo>** naked (of person).

khõ'ba[1] *v.* **<laagnu>** about to.
nãã' yu'bar khõ'i. *It's about to rain.*

kho'ba[2], **xobaa'** [*TB* *hwaŋ 218] *v.* **<pasnu>** to enter.

khõbaa' *v.* **<lobh garnu (khaane belaamaa)>** to be greedy; gluttonous; asking for more (especially food).

khõ'ḍa *n.* **<kanjus>** ungenerous person; selfish person. [*Syn.* saẽ axsxaba'.]

khõĩ, khõyõ yaa *t.* **<sadhaĩ>** always.

khõyõ... khõyõ... *t.* **<kahile... kahile...>** sometimes... other times...
khõyõ xyaamũ', khõyõ axxyaa'. *Sometimes he goes, sometimes he doesn't.*

khõyõ, khoyõ *t.* **<kahile>** when.
kxi kaju'r khõyõ xyaamũ'? *When are you going to Ghachok?*

khõyõ bile *t.* **<jahile pani>** whenever.

khõyõ khõyõ *t.* **<kahile kahĩ>** sometimes.

khõyõm *t.* **<jahile>** whenever.
khõyõm krobdõ'i bimu ni syumu. *Whenever (she) speaks as if weeping (they) laugh.*

kho' [*TaGTh* *khoq] *v.* **<aaija>** come (imperative of khabaa').

kho *n.* **<kããḍho(jauko)>** wisps of barley, rice, wheat.

khobaa' *n.* **<khopaa>** recess in wall to hold lamp so that work can be done at night.

khobaa' *v.* **<man parnu; rucaaunu>** to like; to find something appeals to you.

khoḍi' *n.* **<khoṭ>** physical blemish of man or animal (such as scar, birthmark, crossed eyes, twisted limb, any malproportion).

khogro *a.* **<khokro>** hollow (especially of something which should have things in it, as peanut shell).

kho'i[1] *pa.* **<khoi (jawaaph dine šabda>** exclamation of frustration or evasiveness in response to an awkward request or question. [*Syn.* txasi.]

kho'i[2] *pa.* **<kahãã cha; khoi?>** where (of movable objects or people).
aabaa kho'i? *Where's (your) dad?* [*Syn.* khani'.]

kho'j guwaar labaa' *v.* <upcaar garnu> to treat; to cure (by any means).

khojyãã *n.* <raamro subhaasko maanis> courteous person who keeps on good terms with all. axkho'jyãã mudu' biyãã tããn' mxine pri' pxõm. *If one is not courteous he argues with everybody.*

khol ṭol *n.* <ṭolko waripari> surrounding area; locality around a town.

kho'l *n.* <khaam - ciṭṭhīko> envelope.

kholdiba' *v.* <kholnu> to open (as of road's completion, switching on a radio, opening a box for customs inspection, commencing an army career); to explain meaning of word, proverb, etc.

kholdõ *n.* <khopi> hole in ground.

kholẽba' *a.* <khukulo> loose; free fit (of parts). [*Ant.* kasdiba'.]

khole' *n.* <khole> mash made of corn, fed to cattle. [*Syn.* kũḍo' khole'.]

kholo *n.* <aaru> peach.

kho'mro bxĩba' *v.* <baalnu> to light a lamp (emphatic variant). [*Syn.* mrobaa'.]

khonã [*TB* *ka·k p. 7, n. 482] *n.* <khokne khakaar> phlegm.

khonã waabaa' *v.* <khakaarnu> to clear throat.

khoplẽ *n.* <aadhaa> half.

khoraa *n.* <khor> cage-like trap; trap. [*Syn.* ŋo'.]

khorẽ' *n.* footrot (?) in cattle (treated with camphor); sores on face (of humans).

khore' *n.* <khoriyaa> hillside fields - unterraced.

khorsaani' *n.* <khorsaani> chilli.

khoyaa' *n.* <makaiko khosṭaa (bhutlo)> leaves surrounding corn cob.

khoyõ *see* khõyõ 'when'.

khrẽbaa' *v.* <bhok laagnu> to be hungry (always with pho' 'stomach').

khrĩbaa' *v.* <baaṭnu> to plait; twine rope.

khri'ba *v.* <dããtle makai kopaarnu> to gnaw on (a bone or corn cob, etc.).

khribaa' [*Cp* krohq 'wrist joint'] *v.* <markanu> to sprain; injure joint (usually as a result of a fall).

khrõbaa' *v.* <polnu> to burn; to roast in coals; to singe an animal after killing; to sting (of nettles). [*Syn.* phaabaa'; jalidiba.]

khro pĩbaa' *v.* <bhog dinu> to offer an animal sacrifice (especially to consecrate various parts of new house, such as foundations and rafters).

khru'ba [*TB* *kruw=*krəw 'bathe one's body' 117] *v.* <dhunu> to wash. jyu khru'ba. *Bathe one's body.*

khũ' [*TaGTh* *khuunk] *n.* <pwaal> hole.

khũ'ba [*TB* *kyam 224] *a.* <jaaḍho> to be cold (of day, hence of person).

khu' [*TaGTh* *khuq] *n.* <jhol> soup.

khub *av.* <khub> very. [*Syn.* beseri.]

khubaa' *v.* <jammaa garnu; baṭulnu> to assemble people. [*Syn.* tũ'ba.]

khubi' *n.* <khopi> sleepout; enclosed side verandah often occupied by widowed, adolescent, or divorced members of family.

khudu' [*N* khudo 'molasses'] *n.* **<maha>** honey.

khu'jũ khu'jũ xyaaba' *v.* **<khocyaaunu>** to limp.

khulidiba' *v.* **<khulaaunu>** to provide; spread (a feast).
bxatyaa'r khulidimu. *(They) provide a feast.*

khullaa' *a.* **<khulaa>** open (of ground, road, box).

khu'lu khu'lu labaa' *v.* **<kullaa garnu>** to gargle.

khumjidiba' *v.* **<khumcinu>** to become loose; wrinkled.
se gxaḍi' xyaasero' ṭxubi khumjidi'm. *Since the flesh reduces the skin wrinkles.*
[*Syn.* jxyũba'.]

khu'ndri *n.* **<pwaal>** hole - small (in clothing, wall, rocks); cranny.

khura *n.* **<khur>** hoof; cloven hoof.

khurkudiba' *v.* **<khurkanu>** to scrape bark; whittle; shave wood.

khurunḍa' *a.* **<khuranḍo>** blemished.

khuši' *n.* **<khuši>** happiness, joy. [*Syn.* santok.]

khusra *n.* **<khudraa>** change (strictly, single rupee notes).
[*Syn.* eusare'.]

khwããlãã' *n.* cane - piece of which is carried by women in procession around effigy at puju's pae.

khwaa'l khwaa'l *n.* **<umaalnu>** bubbling; boiling - *onom.*

khwe' *pa.* **<le>** give it to me.

khwe'ba *v.* **<linu (kaakhmaa)>** to hold closely (as of baby).

khwi'ba *v.* **<aaja gaera aajai pharkanu>** to return on the same day from a journey.

khwĩkidi'bxĩba' *v.* **<phaalnu>** to fling down; throw down.
[*Syn.* bxyõba'.]

khyããbaa' *v.* **<tarsanu(saato jaanu)>** to be afraid (with plxa).
[*Syn.* lõba'.]

khyaabaa'[1] [*TaGTh* *khyab] *v.* **<ṭikaa lagaaũnu>** to apply decorative spot to forehead.

khyaabaa'[2] *v.* **<bhirnu>** to wear (a knife in the belt, or feathers in headband).

khyaabdiba' *v.* **<khyaapnu; kernu>** to press an accusation; to pester.

khyodo *n.* **<wastu>** cattle; domestic animal.
[*Syn.* bastu.]

khyolõ' *n.* **<khilaŋ>** village name - Gurung, NE of Pokhara.

khyuni' *n.* **<jhiliŋge>** rice crackers (prepared by extruding boiled mashed rice, drying in sun, and frying in deep fat for eating).
[*Syn.* jxilge'.]

kĩba' [*TaGTh* *kim] *v.* **<linu>** take; get; buy; receive.

ki'... ki'... *c.* **<ki... ta... ki>** either... or...
ki' mlõgyaa jxõmu' ki' pĩgya jxõmu'. *Either you put in black or you put in green.*

ki *pa.* **<ki>** or? (interrogative particle).
xo ki? *Isn't it?*

kidaaba' *n.* **<kitaab>** book - printed.

ki'giba' *a.* **<guliyo>** sweet.

kilããsa', klaas, kilaasa *n.* **<kilaas, šreṇī, kakšaa>** class.

kiliba' *n.* **<kilib(gahanaa)>** hair clip; bobby pin.

killi' *n.* **<kidli>** kettle.

kilo' *n.* **<kilo>** stake; tethering peg.

kiraai *n.* **<kiraayaa>** rent; hire; fee; fare.
[*Syn.* baala.]

kire' *n.* **<kiriyaa>** mourning rites performed up to thirteenth day after death.

kire' kĩbaa' *v.* **<kiriyaa haalnu>** to curse someone or something; to take an oath.

kisim *n.* **<kisam>** kind; variety.
[*Syn.* khaal.]

-kkyo *see* **-kyo** 'blows'.

kõ' *n.* **<bhaau>** price; rate of goods or services.
te'la kõ' khaile tam? *What is the price of oil?*

kõ' kasdiba' *v.* **<bhaau kasnu, baḍhaaunu>** haggle; bargain.

kõ'ba *v.* **<ṭhihirinu>** to be numb with cold.
[*Syn.* gaŋgridiba; ṭhīridiba'; kaaṭhidiba'.]

kõbaa' *v.* **<misaaunu>** to mix; to join or unite of rivers.
la'la kyu'ne sī kõbaa'.
Mixing hot water with cold.

kũju'r xyaaba *v.* **<kunjieko>** to be paralysed.

ko' [*TaGTh* *kaaq] *n.* **<ragat>** blood.

ko' yu'ba *v.*
1. **<ragat aaunu>** to bleed.
2. **<parasarnu>** menstruate.

ko'ba *v.* **<khuwaaunu>** to feed an infant or invalid solids.
[*Cp.* tī'ba.]

kobaa' *v.* **<prati dhwani aaunu>** to echo.

kobaa'ra *n.* **<gobar>** dung of large cattle.
[*Syn.* khlyi; ma'laa.]

kobdiba' *v.* **<khopnu>** to carve a figure; to prick; to vaccinate.

kobre' *n.* **<koparaa>** spitting pan; chamber pot.

ko'ḍ gxaara', ko'ḍ gxaaḍa' *n.* **<koṭhaa(thunne)>** cell; guard house.

koḍeba' *v.* **<koṭṭyaaunu>** to poke; pick at; nudge; finger; scratch.

kodaa' *n.* **<agenu>** fireplace.

kodaali' *n.* **<kotaalo>** hoe - small. [*Cp.* kuḍi.]

kode' *n.* **<gā̃ḍyaulo>** earthworm.

kolaa' *n.* **<mahi>** buttermilk.

koldu, koldo *see* **kuldu** 'hood'.

kolo' *n.* **<baalakh>** child.

kom nesaa' *t.* **<bhare belukaa>** tonight (future).

komãã' *v.* **<bhare>** later (on the same day).

konma'ẽ *n.* **<ghotane>** clan - one of the upper four in Gurung society; caste name.
[*Cp.* plxonmaẽ; paĩgima'ẽ; lemma'ẽ.]

koras *n.* chorus.
[*Syn.* ṭuka.]

koraa' *n.* **<koraa>** cloth - raw, unprocessed.

korbyo' *n.* **<thunse>** basket - large, closely woven, for carrying purposes.

kordiba' *v.* **<kornu>** to score; scratch (as of a pen).

kore' *n.* **<kora; koḍha; kuṣṭa>** leprosy.

korlãã *n.* **<kaanmaa laaune riŋ>** earring with chain.

ko'rmẽ *n.* **<bhãgero>** sparrow.

košiš *n.* **<košiš>** attempt; try; endeavour.
košiš labaa'. *To make an attempt.*

kosa' *n.* **<curoṭ>** cigarette.

[*Syn.* gyõ, khilli', sigres.]

ko'sa prim *n.* **<ragat baarnu>** rest day (work or travel forbidden).

koṭhaa' *n.* **<koṭhaa>** room in house.

kowiba' *see* **kawiba'** 'stutter'.

koyaa' *n.* **<bhaṭmaas>** soy bean.

krišnaa' *n.* **<kri+šnaa>** Krishna (Hindu god).

kra [*TB* *(s-)kra 155; *T* tra 'hair (of head)'; *Cp* kraṇq 'upward'] *n.* **<kapaal>**
1. head.
2. hair of head.

kra khoplẽ *n.* **<khappar>** skull.

kra khru'b tabaa' *v.* **<para sarnu; rajaswalaa hunu>** to menstruate. [*Syn.* phuḍiba'; ko' yu'ba.]

kra lxaaba' *v.* **<munṭo hallaaunu>** to shake head in negation. [*Syn.* kra saliba'.]

kra saliba' *v.* **<ṭaauko hallaaunu>** to shake head in negation. [*Syn.* kra lxaaba'.]

kralũ[1] *n.* **<munḍe ghar>** concrete construction.

kralũ[2] *n.* **<kaaṭeko kapaal>** hair cuttings.

kramĩ' *n.* **<dhaago (kapaalmaa lajaaune)>** plait of black cotton (which is plaited in with woman's own hair).

kramũ' *n.* **<majetro>** scarf worn on woman's head.

krãã'ba *v.* **<kuhunu>** to rot (of vegetation and fruit).

kre[1] *n.* crevices (above beam attached to external wall of house to support verandah roof). paali' krer.

kre[2] *n.* **<ḍhaaḍ>** back - small of; lower back.

krebaa' *v.* **<caḍhnu>** to mount; ride (car or animal); to climb (tree or mountain).

kregũ, krigũ *n.* **<siraani>** pillow; place where one lays head for sleeping (towards fireplace). kregũ khani' lam? *Where will (you) make (your) pillow?*

kri' *num.* **<ek>** one. [*Syn.* gxri'.]

kribaa'[1] *v.* **<khursaani ṭoknu>** to bite on chilli to improve bland meal.

kribaa'[2] *v.* **<baal kaaṭnu>** to cut hair. [*Syn.* waabaa'.]

krigi' *n.* **<pheṭaa>** turban; headgear of white cloth.

krigi' pĩba' *v.* **<naacnelaai bakas dinu>** to give a dancer money in appreciation of good performance.

krišna' caritra *n.* **<puraano naac>** dance (of old Gurung type).

krobaa'[1] [*TB* *groy 'scream, screech, howl' 310; *TB* *krap 'weep' 116] *v.* **<runu>** to cry; weep.

krobaa'[2] [*TaGTh* *kro] *v.* **<ḍaḍhnu>** to be burnt up; to scorch (intransitive).

kromãã' *n.* sword used in weaving apparatus.

krophũ' *n.* **<ãgaar>** charcoal; cinder. [*Syn.* mi phũ; mebro'.]

kru[1] *n.* **<naap>** length; height. [*Ant.* plxi.]

kru[2] [*T* thru] *n.* **<haat (naapne)>** cubit. [*Syn.* -gru.]

kru'ba *v.* **<ota basnu>** to shelter from rain.

krubaa' *v.* **<naapnu>** to measure length in cubits.

krxaamu [*TaGTh* *gram] *n.* **<gaala>** cheek.

krxi [*TB* *kriy=*krəy 460; *Cp* rɨy

'dirty (of skin)'] *n.* <mailopana> dirt.

krxiba *v.* <milnu> to agree; to be compatible; to be similar; to match.

krxiji *n.* <dhamilo> soot above fireplace.

krxõ *n.* <mukhiyaa> headman of village in pre-panchayat time; master of a slave.
[*Syn.* muli'.]

krxo *n.* <puraano anna> grains - old.

krxosena' *a.* <sããccai> true; certain; real.
krxosena'le axlu'mala. *(He) did not learn it properly.*
[*Ant.* syur te'ba.]

kũ *n.* <pisaab> urine.

kũ txõba *v.* <pisaab garnu> to urinate.

kũ'ba, kxũba *v.* <basnu> to sit; relax.
kxe' axxre', kũ'ḍiba ŋami. *There's no work, I'm just sitting, I am.*

kũḍo', kũḍo' khole' *n.* <kũḍo> mash of corn or grains for cattle.

kũdo' *n.* <dhuri khaambaa> uprights (central forked poles of a cattle shed).

kũsyu *n.* <mutwaa> bed wetter.

ku'[1] [*TaGTh* *kuq; *TB* *d-kuw= *d-kəw, *d-gaw 13; *T* quh] *num.* <nau> nine.

ku[2] *n.* <chaatī> chest.

ku'ba[1] [*TB* *ka 'spread' 469] *v.*
1. <saarnu> move (a cowshed); to transfer (shed).
2. <sarnu> to spread (of infection).

ku'ba[2] *v.* <cirnu (nigaalo)> to split cane.
[*Syn.* khlyi'ba.]

ku'ba[3] [*TaGTh* kop 'lift, raise up, support'] *v.* <ukkinu, upakinu>
1. break up; crumble.
ṭxubie juda khii biri' dxī' nxõr prxadu' biyãã dxī' ku'xyaam. *If you walk in the house with leather shoes the floor will crumble.*
2. lift off (of stamp, plaster).
chiṭṭhi' syu tadu' biyãã ṭikaṭ ku'xyaam. *If the letter gets wet the stamp will lift off.*

kubaa'[1] *v.* <doṣ laagnu> to be blamed.

kubaa'[2] *v.* <boknu> to move; carry.
ma'la kubaa'. *To carry compost.*

kubaa'[3] [*TB* *klup 'cover' 479] *v.* <oḍhnu> to cover oneself with a blanket; wear (head covering).

ku'bra *num.* <nau say> nine hundred.

kubinḍa' *n.* <kubinḍa> melon (about 15 cm. diameter, with hairy green skin and white flesh, used in Dasain sacrifices).

kuḍi *n.* <kuṭo> mattock - small.
[*Cp.* kodaali'.]

ku'di *n.* <pīŋ> swing made of bamboo uprights (lain ku'di); ferris wheel (xraa ku'di).

kudi' kudi *i.* <kuti kuti> calling sound for pup.

ku'di mxaeba' *v.* <pīŋ khelnu> to ride on a swing or ferris wheel.

kudruge' *n.* <kaalo nihuro> vegetable of forest - bracken-like.

kudũ' [*B* du 'knee' (but Benedict does not regard this as an inherited *TB* element)] *n.* <kuino; koṇ pareko> elbow; bend in pipe.
[*Syn.* ka'blo; kunjyu'.]

ku'gaaḍa' *n.* <kanjus> selfish; ungenerous person.
[*Syn.* khõ'ḍa, saẽ axsxaba'.]

ku'i *pn.* <kohi> some people.

kuja *n.* <kuco> broom; hand brush.

kuji'[1] *n.* <sããco> key.

kuji'[2] *pa.* <ta ni> emphatic - sentence final.

kujidiba' *v.* <kucyaaunu> dent; crumble; squash. [*Syn.* jxyũba'.]

kujwir *n.* <ṭheulaa> chicken pox.

kujyõ *n.* <ghuccuk> nape of neck.

ku'jyu *num.* <nabbe> ninety.

kukru'ga *a.* <kukruka> hunched up from cold or fear.

kula *n.* <kol> press for extracting oil or sugar juice.

kulbaa', kulbxĩba' *v.* <paṭhaaunu (maanchelaaī)> to send a person on an errand.

kuldu, koldu, koldo *n.* <thailo> hood of sackcloth; sack for holding grains or flour (10 pathi or larger). [*Syn.* nedo'.]

kule' *n.* <ṭopī> cap.

kulu' *n.* <kulo> channel for irrigation.
kulu' bxandaa' pxrĩũba'e khlxyo ci's tam. *The land below the channel is wet.*

kunaa' *n.* <kunaa> corner; angle.

kundiba' *v.* <kũdnu> to hollow out a hole.

kuni *n.* <ḍhiki> rice pounder.

kunjyu' *n.* <ghũḍaa> back or knee; crook of elbow. [*Syn.* kudũ', kuino.]

kunnyo' *n.* <kuniyo> haystack.

kunnyo' jxõba' *v.* <kuniyo lagaaunu> to stack sheaves.

kur [*TB* *koy 'bend' 307, *TB* *kuk 'bend, crooked' *p.* 77] *a.* <nihurinu> bent over; stooping. [*Syn.* kwaar; kurle; kurbaa'; ku. *Ant.* ṭhaar.]

kuraani' *n.* <kurauni> sediment in pan after boiling milk. [*Syn.* kaũri.]

kurbaa' *v.*
1. <nihuranu> stoop.
2. <nihuraaunu> to bend cane after heating. [*Syn.* kur.]

kurji' *n.* <kursi> chair.

kurku' *n.* <korka(kukhuraa chopne)> basket - open weave, used for covering chickens to prevent them from wandering. [*Syn.* jxarãã'go.]

kurli' *n.* <koraalo> cow - adolescent, not having borne young. [*Syn.* kxurima.]

kurraa' *n.* <korraa> whip.

kurus *n.* <ãkuse siyo> crochet hook.

kusyaali' *n.* <koselī> present of food (taken by a woman visiting her relatives).

kuttiba' *v.* <kudaaunu> to speed in motor vehicle.

kuwaa *n.* <kuwaa> pool; water hole - small.

kwãã'ba *v.* <paailo saarnu> to step.

kwaalaba' *v.t.* <tataaunu> to heat (fluids).

kwaar *a.* <kupro; nihurinu> bent; stooped.
kwaarle' pxram'. *To walk stooped.*
[*Syn.* kur; kurle'. *Ant.* ṭhaar.]

kwẽ'[1] *n.* <kaakh> lap.

kwẽ[2] [*TB* *gwa-n∿*kwa-n 'dress' 160; *TB* *wat *n.* 78] *n.* <lugaa, kapaḍaa> clothes.

kwẽ[3] *n.*
1. <naati> grandson (ChSo).
2. <bhatijo> nephew (WoBrSo, MaWiBrSo).
3. <naati> grandnephew (MaSbChSo).

kwẽ ṭaalaa' ṭuli' *n.* <lattaa

kapaḍaa> rags; scraps; fragments of cloth.

kwẽ'ba *v.* <patyaaunu> to believe.

kwẽḍo' saa'daa *n.* <taan bunne kala> loom.

kwẽmĩ' *n.*
1. <naatinī> granddaughter (ChDa).
2. <bhatijī> niece (WoBrDa, MaWiBrDa).
3. <naatinī> grandniece (MaSbChDa).

kwe *n.* <mauri> bee. [*Syn.* kxwe'.]

kwĩbaa' *n.* <kaamnu> to shiver (with fever).

kwĩ'jiri tãã'ga *n.* <jhĩge maachaa> shrimp; prawn; crayfish.

kwi *n.* <koṭ> place of ceremonial killing of animals.

kwi'ba[1] *v.* <hausalaa dinu> to encourage; to support. [*Syn.* xusi'diba, manidiba'.]

kwi'ba[2] [*TB* *ku 'lift' *n.* 281] *n.* <ucaalnu> to lift; to weigh. [*Syn.* tauldiba'; ucaaldiba'.]

kwine' *n.* <aule jaro> malaria. [*Syn.* aulo.]

kwrẽ' [*TB* *d-ka·y 51] *n.* <gãgaṭo> crab.

kxaeba'[1] *v.* <ghaceṭnu> to push.

kxaeba[2] *v.* <ber hunu> to be delayed; late. [*Syn.* axbelle.]

kxalphũ *n.* <gulaa> testicle.

kxar *see* ka'r 'coercion'.

kxarlaa *n.* <garlaŋ> village name (east of Ghachok).

kxau *n.* <paahaa> frog (large, 15 cm., grey with yellow underside, edible, lives under rocks in uplands).

kxayaa *see* kayaa' 'cooking pot'.

kxaaba *v.*
1. <samaatnu> to hold on to.
na'ga bxaale' kxaaibiri' se'm. *He dances holding a rooster.*
gxyãã kxaaba. *To begin a journey to a certain place (lit. to grab the road).*
2. <pakranu> to catch; arrest; seize.
ŋid kxaa bxadi' jxaale' thundii. *We caught it, brought it, and penned it up.*
3. <laagnu> to attain to a certain age; to turn.
ŋa teisa'r kxaai. *I have turned twenty-three.*

kxẽ *n.* <roṭī> bread fried in oil.

kxe' *n.* <kaam> work.

kxeba *v.* <thap maagnu> to ask for more food.

kxegu labaa' *v.* <pheri garnu> to do again work which was done unsatisfactorily.

kxemaẽ *pn.* <tapaaīharū; timīharū> you (plural).

kxi'[1] [*TaGTh* *giq] *n.* <khar> thatch.

kxi[2] *pn.* <tapaaī, timī, tã> you.

kxibru' *n.* <puraano khar> thatch (old, rotten, discarded when renewing roof).

kxo [*TB* *s-ga·l 'back, loins, groin' *n.* 66; *TaGTh* *go; *Cp* kahq] *n.* <piṭhyũ> upper back. [*Syn.* ũsyu'.]

kxoba[1] [*TaGTh* *go] *v.* <bujhnu> to understand.

kxoba[2] *v.* <aljinu; aḍhkanu> to be entangled; snag; catch; jam; get stuck.

kxoẽba *v.* <bharnu> to measure by volume; to buy by measured volume.

kxoe'[1] [*TB* *kwa-y 159; *Cp* wasq] *n.* <maauri> bee.

kxoe'[2] *n.* <git> song.

kxoe' ḍõḍaa, kxoe' la' *n.* **<maauriko ghaar>** beehive.

kxoja *n.* **<khukuri>** dagger (Nepalese, with curved blade).

kxole *n.* **<gilo bhaat>** rice gruel - sticky.

kxone muba'e camĩ'ri *n.* **<garbhawatī strī>** pregnant woman.

kxora *n.* **<halo>** plough.

kxorbae tabaa' *v.* **<para sarnu>** to menstruate. [*Syn.* kra khrub tabaa'.]

kxori *loc.* **<maathi>** above; high in altitude.
kxorbae nãã'sa. *The upper village.*

kxorbae khlxyo *n.* place where woman sits to cook meals.

kxoũ *a.*
1. **<maathi>** above.
2. **<jeṭho, ṭhulī>** elder (of siblings).
   xrõs bxanda' kxoũbae anãmaẽ. *My older sisters.*

kxowãã pxadẽ *loc.* **<maathi nira>** on the upper side of; above.

kxũ *n.* **<syaakhu; ghūm>** umbrella-like protective head cover (made of woven cane interlined with leaves).

kxũba *v.* **<aakaašmaa baadal laagnu>** to be overcast (of sky). [*Ant.* thõbaa'.]

kxuiba[1] *v.* **<jããḍh banaaunu, chããdnu>** to brew beer.

kxuiba[2] *v.* **<namra nibedan garnu>** to beg. [*Syn.* xriba.]

kxuiba[3] *a.* **<kukhurīko phul bikranu>** to be rotten - of eggs.

kxuipaa' *n.* **<jããḍ>** beer. [*Syn.* paa'.]

kxure', kwre *n.* **<giddhaa>** vulture.

kxure' lxo *n.* **<giddhaa barkha>** year of the vulture (1952,64, 76,etc.). [*Syn.* mubru' lxo.]

kxurima[1] *n.* **<koraalo>** cow - adolescent, not having borne young. [*Syn.* kurli'.]

kxurima[2] *n.* **<aaune saal>** next year.

kxurixyaaba', kwri xyaaba' *v.* **<loṭnu; laḍnu; khasnu>** to fall down.
pxro'd kxurixyaai' u? *Has (he) fallen over a cliff, or what?*
[*Syn.* pxyo xyaaba'.]

kxurwaaba' *v.* **<laḍaaunu>** to cause to fall over; trip.

kxyããba *v.* **<ek dar saŋa milnu>** to match; to be uniform.

kxyaalaba *v.* **<ramaailo hunu>** to be pleasant.

kxyoba'[1] *v.* **<jotnu>** to plough.

kxyoba[2] [*TaGTh* *gyoo 'be fast, clever'] *v.* **<dagurnu>** to run.

kxyonõwaaraa *n.* **<ban biraalo>** wild cat.

kxyu', kyu [*TaGTh* *gyuuq; *TB* *ke·l=*kye·l∿*kyi(·)l 'goat' 339] *n.* **<bheḍo>** sheep.

kxyu' khaarbu *n.* ram - young (one to two years).

kxyu' lxo *n.* **<bheḍo barkha>** year of the sheep in 12 year cycle (1943,55,67,etc.). [*Syn.* lxu lxo.]

kxyu' mxalwaa *n.* ewe - adolescent, before bearing. [*Syn.* kxyu' mxodõ'.]

kxyu' mxodõ' *n.* ewe - adolescent, before bearing. [*Syn.* kxyu' mxalwaa.]

kxyu' sãã'ḍe *n.* **<sããḍh>** ram - full grown.

kxyuba *v.* **<ghusaarnu; pasaalnu>** to thrust in; to cause to enter in.

kxyui', kxwi' *n.* **<bhaaṣaa>**

language. [*Syn.* -gi.]

kya, kyaa, ke', kyaadi' *loc.* <utaa> there. [*Syn.* jxaadi'.]

kyãã'ba [*TB* *da·n 22] *v.* <kaaṭnu> to cut (meat, cloth, branch - general term).

kyããmsal *n.* <raddī(garnu); kyããnsal (hunu)> cancellation. nãã' yu'sero' kyããmsal tai'. *Because it rained (the meeting) was cancelled.*

kyõjãã' *p.* <paarī> other side of.

-kyo *s.num.* <paalī (coṭi)> blows (with knife).

kyo'ba *v.* <gaaḍhnu> to drive in stakes.

kyobaa' *v.* <bhijaaunu> to soak; wet.

kyo'ẽba, kywẽ'ba *v.* <maramat garnu> to repair; mend. [*Syn.* banidiba.]

kyogyõ' khabaa' [*TB* *g-ya 'itch' 451] *a.* <phohor cilaaunu> to be itchy because of caked mud and insects in planting season.

kyolõ' *n.* <main> beeswax.

kyolo [*TB* *g-ya∿*g-ra 98] *a.* <daahine> right (body parts).

kyolo paṭṭi' *v.* <daahine paṭṭī> rightward.

kyũbaa' [*TaGTh* *kyuŋ] *a.* <amilo> bitter; sour.

kyũḍaa' *n.* <sinkī> sauerkraut made from radish. [*Syn.* gundru.]

kyu' [*TaGTh* *kyuq; *TB* *s-kyur= *s-kywar 42; *T* chu] *n.* <paanī> water.

kyu' *see* kxyu' 'sheep'.

kyu' aamaa *n.* dragonfly.

kyu' jxaasa' *n.* <paanī jahaaj> boat; ship.

kyu' jxõba' *v.* <paanī haalnu; paanī lagaaunu> to pour water; irrigate (a field).

kyu' pibaa' *v.* <tirkhaaunu> to be thirsty.

kyugyũ' *n.* <gubho> central shoot of plant - grass, millet.

kyu'gyu *n.* <panyaalo; jhol> liquid (especially of thin or weak liquids). cxaa' kyu'gyu. *Weak tea.* [*Syn.* panyaalu'.]

kyuĩbaa'[1] *v.* <calaaunu> to sweep rice back into hole during pounding.

kyuĩbaa'[2] *v.* <paskanu> to serve out (rice from pot); dish out.

kyulbaa' *v.* <chirnu> to pass through; to thread a needle.

kyulu' *n.* <kilo; ghoco> post (some inches in diameter, used particularly for tethering cattle, bigger than phargu or pxre). [*Syn.* mxẽ; phargu; pxre.]

kyuraa' *n.* <taamo> copper.

kyu'ru *loc.*
1. <tallo (tira)?> downwards. [*Syn.* maadi'; oraa'lu.]
2. <dakšiṇ> south. [*Syn.* dakšiṇ.]

kyu'ru prõ' *v.* <ũdho munṭo> upturned (of a vessel holding liquid to tip out the last bit). kyu'ru prõ' ladu' biyãã jamman cxaa' yu'm. *If (you) upturn it all the tea comes down.*

kyu'waa dxũ' *n.* <paanī panero> spring; water tap or source.

kywaaliba' *v.* <pauḍhanu, pauḍhi khelnu> to swim.

kywẽ'ba *see* kyo'ẽba 'repair'.

kywĩbaa' *see* kyuĩbaa'.

L

lãgaḍaa' *n.* **<laŋgaḍo>** crippled or deformed person; maimed person (usually congenital). [*Syn.* ḍuḍa.]

-la^1, -laa *s.n.* <-ko> possessive (on sentence topic); of.
cu' ŋalaa'. *This is mine.*
kxilaa pxasyaa pxasi mu u axxre'? *Do you have children or not?*
[*Syn.* -e; -ba'e; -ma'e.]

-la^2 *s.v.* <-yo> pluperfect.
[*Syn.* -di; -i; -lau.]

la^3 [*TB* *la=*(s-)la 486] *n.* **<paat>** leaf.
[*Syn.* pxo.]

-la^4, -l *s.num.* **<mahinaa>** months.
mxaina sõ'l tai. *It's three months now.*

-la^5, -l *s.v.* <-nu> infinitival.
bajaarar ṭila axyõ'. *You can't stay in the bazaar.*
kaẽ cal bxĩm'. *She feeds him rice.*
kaẽ jxõl khãã'ĩ. *I've finished putting in the rice.*
ŋad kxril lasyo'. *I'll make it match.*
ŋxe pĩl txumu. *You have to give milk.*
xrõsadi cal yõbaa' khil yõbaa' tam ro. *He says (the things) he gets to eat and to wear are o.k.* [*Syn.* -laa^1.]

-la^6, -l *s.n.* <-le> as for; concerning; in the case of.
khab khaba'l khani' tho'e. *As for everybody, where can they chop.*
kwi' kwi'la lam, kwi' kwi'la axlaa'. *As for some people they do it, others don't.*

-la^7, -l *s.n.* emphatic.
khil kanchin ya. *She herself is Youngest-Daughter indeed.*
mxi sõ'de plxide'l mudu' biyãã. *If there are THREE OR FOUR people.*

-la^8, -l *p.* **<-ko>** dative (on sentence topic); for.
lxe' mxila nausan tai. *For many people there was loss.*
[*Syn.* -lai^2.]

laba'r lxaidiba *v.* **<garna laagnu>** to cause someone to do something.

labaa' [*TaGTh* *la] *v.* **<garnu>** to do; to make; to perform; verbaliser (when conjoined with abstract nouns).
byaa labaa'. *To marry.*
dxarma' labaa'. *To do good works in order to gain merit.*
dxĩ' labaa'. *To build a house.*

labji' *n.* <laacok> Lahachok (village west of Ghachok).

labri' *n.* **<argun gardaa jhããkrĩle garne naac>** dance performed by pujyu' at funeral.

labu' *n.* **<mulaa>** radish.

lacchin *a.* <lakšaṇ> lucky; good fortune.
sũ lachin. *Charming.*
xyõ lachin. *Prospering in wealth.*

lacchin yo *a.* **<lakšaṇ haat>** skilful with hands; causing things to prosper.

laḍaa' *n.* <laaṭo> dumb person (male); mute.
[*Cp.* laaḍi.]

laḍẽ' *n.* <laḍaai> war.
[*Cp.* nxeba'.]

-ladi' *see* **-lai** 'to'.

laen *n.* **<garaũlaa>** line of parade; astrological calculation; line of argument.

-lai^1 *s.v.* <holaa> probabilitative.
[*Syn.* -lase'.]

-lai^2 *p.* **<laaĩ>** to (dative and accusative).
ca'lai ããĩãã bim. *(We) call it ããĩãã!*
ŋad kxilai axca'syo. *I won't eat you.*
ŋalai khani' ṭimu, ca'rna swaabaa'. *To me, wherever I live, that place is fine.*

lain ku'di *n.* **<ligai pĩŋ>** swing with bamboo uprights.

lakha'ẽ *n.* <kããkro> cucumber.

la'la *a.* <taato> hot - of fluids.
[*Syn.* laa.]

la'm kamĩ' *n.* <dhaami> diviner from lower caste.
[*Cp.* pujyu'; khlxyebri.]

la'maa, la'mãã, laa'maa *n.* <laamaa> Buddhist priest; lama.

lambaai *n.* <lamaai> length.
[*Syn.* kru^{1}.]

lamgadi'ba *v.* <lamkanu> to stride.

la'mmaẽ *n.*
1. <tamaŋ> Tamang.
2. <laamaaharu> Buddhist priests.

-la'se, -lase' *s.v.* <holaa> probabilitive.
[*Syn.* -lai^{1}.]

lasgadiba' *v.* <laamo banaaunu> to be stretched; lengthened (of foot prints on slick surface, of vowel sounds).

-lasi' *see* **-lai** 'to'.
mximaẽlasi' xrẽgaa' khibxĩmũ'. *(They) give people capes to wear.*
pxrõ ku'b lasi' bibaara barjit tam. *For moving sheds Thursdays are inauspicious.*

lataga', lataak *n.* <lataak> Ladakh (region in north-west India).

la'thaa li'ŋ *n.* <lathaaliŋ> confusion (of papers, goods, furniture).

-lau' *s.v.* <-yo ta> pluperfect (emphatic of -la^{2}.]

lauḍaa' *n.* <ṭhulo nihuro> fern - of which young shoots are eaten.

laugaa' *n.* <laukaa> gourd (with 1 metre long fruit).

lau'ra *see* **laa'khur** 'military service'.

la'ure *see* **laa'khure** 'soldier'.

la'waaj *n.* inarticulate or impedimented speech.
la'waaj matre' põ'i. *Spoke slurringly.*

la'yãã [*TB* *s-la∿*g-la=*s-gla 144; *Cp* lahq] *n.* <jun> moon.

-lãã'^{1}, -lã', -lãã *s.v.* exclamatory; discovery.
kalkadaa'ũle khalãã'. *He had come from Calcutta, I saw!*

-lãã'^{2}, -llãã' *s.* emphatic suffix (occurring on words ending in -l).
kxillãã axŋxĩ'. *It isn't YOURS!*
mxaina pxlila'llãã yõm. *(You) get FOUR months (leave).*

lãã'ḍaa lũ'ḍe *n.* haste causing bungling.

-laa^{1} *s.v.* <-nu> infinitival (with negative auxiliary).
prxalaa' axkhxãã'. *Not able to walk.*
[*Syn.* -la^{5}.]

laa^{2} *n.* <belaa> time.
[*Syn.* txi.]

laa^{3} *a.* <taato> hot (of fluids).
kyu' laad beseri kxyããnle syaa'lamu. *(He) washes it very evenly with hot water.*
[*Syn.* la'la.]

laabaa' *v.* <tataaunu> to heat up (fluids).
[*Syn.* cha'ba.]

laaḍi' *n.* <laaṭi> dumb person (female).
[*Cp.* laḍaa'.]

-laadi' *see* **-lai** 'to'.

-laai *see* **-lai** 'to'.

laa'khure, laa'ure, laaure, lau're, lxaaure *n.* <sipaahi> soldier.

laa'khuri, la'ura *n.* <nokari> military service abroad.
aama laa'khur xyaai. *Mother went abroad with the army.*

laase' *see* **-lai** 'to'.
mlxaasi'laase' cããolan bim. *They call paddy* cããol*!*

laasi' *see* **-lai** 'to'.
ŋalaasi' aargo' gxyãã' tẽdi'. *To me, though, he revealed another way.*

laattaa' *n.* <**laatti**> kick.

-laa'udo *p.* <**-ko suru dekhi**> from the beginning of; from the early part of.
pu'ṣ laa'udo. *From the start of Pauṣ.*

le'[1] [*TaGTh* *leq; *TB* *m-lay∿*s-lay 281; *TB* *(m-)lyak∿*(s-)lyak 211] *n.* <**jibro**> tongue.

-le'[2] *see* **-ũle'** 'from'.

-le'[3], **-lle'** *s.* adverbialiser; in this manner.
axtxurle'. *With urgency.*

-le[4] *s.v.* <**-ũ**> hortatory (1st plural).
xyaale'. *Let's go.*

-le'[5] *s.* emphatic (especially on words ending in le').
jxaale'le. *And THEN!*
khlxyoũle'le. *From that place and all around.*
sõ'ga'ẽmale' ŋxyom. *Within THREE DAYS (he) will look.*

-le'[6] *s.n.* <**-le**> agentive.
mxi ŋxĩle' te'bxwi'm. *It will be brought out by two people.*
[*Syn.* -di.]

-le[7] *s.v.* <**-bhane**> conditional.
laa'khure khale, ḍxaagare' khale, aabaa aamaadi axpĩ'no. *Whether a soldier comes, or whether a civilian comes, O Father, Mother, do not give (me), please!*

lebel *n.* <**lebhel, lain**> surface (of an object).
plenẽ muyãã' lebel krxiba. *If it is a slab the surfaces are parallel.*

lede' *n.* <**jhyau**> moss.

lemma'ẽ *n.* <**lamichane**> clan within Gurung society (of the upper four).
[*Cp.* kon; plxon; paĩgi.]

lepṭen *n.* <**lepṭen**> lieutenant (military rank).

lesṭa' *n.* <**bharpaai**> receipt; card (official).
rajisṭar lesṭa'. *Receipt for registered letter.*

lĩ'ba *a.* <**miṭho**> tasty.

lĩ'bae thãã khabaa' *a.* <**raamro baasan aaune**> fragrant.

li'[1] [*TaGTh* *liiq] *n.* <**mukh**> face.

li[2] [*Cp* lɨy?] *n.* <**lisnu (ek kisimko bharyaaŋ)**> ladder; stepped pole.

li pxali *n.* <**pachaaḍiko khuṭṭaa**> hind leg.
[*Ant.* uĩ pxali.]

li'ba *v.* <**siddhyaaunu**> to finish; to set (of sun, moon).
paĩtis barṣa li'bae camĩ'. *A woman past 35 years old.*
pae li'bae dinari'. *On the closing day of the* pae.

ligũ' *n.* <**piḍaulaa**> calf of leg.

ligyãã' *n.* <**sakoṭṭa**> evil spirit.
See Appendix B.
[*Cp.* mxo', syo', sawa mana, bhut, masana', syaa'ki.]

lili *av.* <**pachi**> behind.
sixyaaba'e mxie lili. *Behind the corpse.*

lili khabaa' *v.* <**pachi pachi aaunu**> to follow.

lili lili bibaa *v.* <**pachi pachi bhannu**> to repeat words after someone.

liũba'e tãã bibaa *v.* <**bhawiṣya bataaunu**> to predict; to foretell.

liũdi' *p.* <**pachi; pachaaḍhi**> after (in time); behind (in space).
[*Syn.* lili.]

-llãã' *see* **-lãã'**.
gxrillãã'. *Separately, alone.*

-lle' *see* **le'** 'adverbialiser'.
syura axtxelle'. *Not telling falsehood.*

lõlo, loŋ lxo *n.* <**gaaĩ barkha**> year of the cow (in Tibetan twelve year cycle, 1949,61,73, 85). [*Syn.* mxe' lxo.]

lõbaa'[1] *v.* <**tarsanu**> to be

afraid; to be startled (of plxa).

lõbaa'[2] *v.* <**bikri hunu**> to sell; to retail.

lo *see* **lxo** 'year'.

lo'ba *v.* <**luknu; lukaaunu**> to hide.

lobx *n.* <**lobh**> greed; covetousness.

lobx labaa' *v.* <**lobh garnu**> to be greedy; to be covetous.

loḍaa' *n.* <**loṭaa**> drinking vessel.

lom khabaa' *v.* <**baaph aaunu**> to steam.

lomãã, lom *n.* <**baaph**> steam.

loŋ lxo *see* **lõlo** 'year of the cow'.

lũ' *see* **miulũ'**.

lũ'ba [*TB* *ploŋ 'burn' 139] *v.* <**balnu; jalnu**> to blaze; burn.

lũbaa' *v.* <**bhããcnu; ṭhunkyaaunu**> to break up long things into pieces (wood, bamboo, fried bread); cut (long things).
yod lũlaa axkhããdu' biyãã ããsi'd lũn. *If you can't break it with your hands cut it with a sickle.*
[*Syn.* kyãã'ba.]

lũ'ḍaa *n.* <**biṭo**> sheaf; bundle (of poles for carrying).
[*Syn.* muṭhaa'; cyaa'.]

lũgi' *n.* <**luŋki**> skirt.

lũṭhe *n.* <**ṭhuṭo**> chips of wood; cane offcuts; fragments of long things; stumps; stubs of cigarettes; cuttings from hair.

lu'[1] *pa.*
1. <**e**> come now.
2. <**la**> take it (somewhat disrespectful).

lu[2] *n.* <**naag**> snake; serpent form of a god.

lubaa' *v.* <**siknu; sikaaunu**> to learn; to teach (usually with causative particle, but not always).
maasṭara'd iskular lub tajo'n. *The teacher IS teaching in the school.*
camaẽd lubxĩ' sero' cyugu' cyugu' xram. *Since they have taught (her) (she) knows a little.*

luccaa' *n.* <**luccaa-phaṭaaha**> swindler; rogue; embezzler.

luḍiba' *v.* <**luṭnu**> to plunder; to loot.

ludu' *n.* <**luto**> itch; scabies (in man); mange (in animals).

lu'ki-cu'ri *n.*
1. <**lucca-phaṭaahaa**> deceit; falsehood; cheat (smaller amounts than luccaa').
ŋa'e baani lu'ki-cu'ri dõ'bae baani axxre'. *It is not my custom to tell lies.*
2. <**lukī-corī**> scheming together to steal.
lu'ki-cu'ri labae mxi cu'r khalaa axtaa'. *It is not permitted for thieves to come here.*

lulaa' *n.*
1. <**lulo (haat, khuṭṭa)**> maimed or crippled person (usually congenital deformity).
2. <**lulo (bal nabhaeko)**> weak (of a limb).
[*Syn.* laŋgaḍaa'; ḍũḍa.]

luŋta *n.* <**baar - ek kisimko gharko**> prayer flag (erected on bamboo poles before Buddhist monasteries and homes).

lxagaidiba *v.* <**lagaaunu (doṣ)**> to affix (blame).

lxagaardiba *v.* <**lakheṭnu**> to chase; to pursue.

lxaidiba[1] *v.* <**lagaaunu (kaam garna)**> to compel; to command.
laba'r lxaidiba. *To make (someone) do (something).*

lxaidiba[2] *v.* <**laagnu (samaya)**> to be required.

ca' khe'bari sõga'ẽ lxaidim. *It requires three days to read that.*

lxajbi' *see* **labji'** 'Lahachok'.

lxam'khuṭṭe' *n.* **<laamkhuṭṭe>** mosquito.

lxataardiba *v.* **<ghisaarnu>** to drag; to haul.
[*Syn.* gxisaa'rdiba.]

lxau' *pa.* **<aau>** come (used affectionately with small children or friends).
lxau', kũ'kho'. *Come on, come and sit.*

lxaudiba *v.* **<laagnu (kharca)>** to cost; to be required; to begin.
ṭikaḍaa' kadi' lxaudim. *How much does a ticket cost?*
pu'ṣari ãgreji'la argo' saa'l lxaudim. *In Paus another year begins for the English (calendar).*

lxauna *n.* **<karkalo>** vegetable - arum colocasia.

lxayo *see* **lxoyo** 'mercy'.

lxããdur *n.* **<lããdur>** village, west of Ghachok, on road to Ghandrung.

lxããlõ *n.* **<kukhuraa (bharkhar hurkeko)>** hen - before laying eggs, 3 or 4 months old.

lxaa *n.* **<laahaa (ciṭṭhīko)>** wax for sealing.

lxaaba'
1. *v.t.* **<hallaaunu>** to rock (a baby).
   kra lxaaba'. *To shake one's head.*
2. *v.i.* **<hallanu>** to shake.
   [*Syn.* txaarba.]

lxaaba *v.*
1. **<khapaaunu>** to drive away; to drive out.
   mxõ' lxaaba. *To drive out a demon.*
2. **<khednu>** to hunt game.
   pho lxaaba. *To hunt a deer.*

lxaagiri *p.* **<-ko laagi>** for the benefit of; on behalf of; for the purpose of.
siba'e mxie lxaagir bxoj banidii. *(They) made a feast for the dead man.*
sadaasya jilla lxaagiri kaaṭhmaanḍur xyaai'. *The member went to Kathmandu on behalf of the district.*
u'jyaalo pĩba'e lxaagiri. *For the purpose of giving light.*

lxaare ããba' *n.* **<lahaare ããp>** passionfruit.

lxaaure *see* **laa'khure** 'soldier'.

lxaawaa *n.* rice - roasted, which is thrown by women relatives at corpse and at plxo at a pae, also offered in pujaa.

lxẽba [*TaGTh* *lehm; *TB* *(m-)lyak∿ *(s-)lyak 'lick'] *v.* **<caaṭnu>** to lap up fluid; to lick.

lxe' [*TB* *lay 'exceed'] *a.* **<dherai>** very; many.
lxe' mxie pae. *Many people's pae.*
pukhru'ri moṭaraa' lxe' axxre'. *In Pokhara there are not many cars.*

lxebbri *see* **khlxyebri** 'shaman'.

lxiba[1] [*TaGTh* *lih] *a.* **<garuŋgo>** heavy.

lxiba[2] *v.* **<haanu>** to fire a rifle.

lxiba'[3] *v.* **<olṭyããŋ polṭyaaŋ garnu>** to shuffle through (in looking for something lost).

lxiba'[4] *see* **ŋxyoba lxiba'** 'divination'.

lxõba' [*TB* *klaw 269] *v.* **<khotalnu (gharko kuraa)>** to dig out things in the house; grabbing done by children.

lxo, lo *n.* **<barga, barkha>** year of birth in Tibetan 12 year cycle (changes each year at 15 Paus, about 30 December).
[*Cp.* pho lo (deer, 1959); cilo' (rat, 1960); lõlo (cow, 1961); tolo (tiger, 1962); xilo (cat, 1963); mubru' (vulture, 1964); sabri' (snake, 1965); talo

(horse, 1966); lxulxo (sheep, 1967); pralo (monkey, 1968); cxelxo (bird, 1969); khilo (dog, 1970).]

lxogõ *n.* <**lwaaŋ**> village - Gurung, 3 hours west of Ghachok.

lxoji *n.* <**kaaṭne hatiyaar**> instruments for cutting.
to'ndori kyãã'bae sa'elai lxoji bim. *(We) call all cutting things* lxoji.

lxowaa *see* **lxaawaa'** 'rice thrown'.

lxoyo, lxayo *n.* <**dayaa**> compassion; pity; mercy; kindness.
[*Syn.* mxaya.]

lxũḍi *n.* scourer - pot (straw, husks, corn cob, etc.).

lxũli *n.* <**lumle**> Lumle - village west of Pokhara.

lxuba'¹ *v.* <**mathnu**> to churn milk into butter.

lxuba² *v.* <**saghaaunu**> to help; assist; aid; support; lend a helping hand.

lxuba³ *v.* <**bharera pokhinu**> to overflow.

lxulxo *n.* <**bheḍa barkha**> year of the sheep (in Tibetan 12 year cycle - 1943,55,67,79, etc.).
[*Syn.* kxyu' lxo.]

lxumḍe *a.* <**bodho, bhutte**> blunt-pointed.

lyomẽ, lyomaẽ *see* **jyomẽ lyomẽ** 'hocus pocus'.

M

-m¹ *s.v.* <**-cha**>
1. future tense.
ŋa aarko' tãã jxõm. *I will record another story.*
2. present specific.
pustaa' bibaa sem aa? *Do you know what* pustaa' *means?*
3. present universal.
ciṭhi' ca'jaren bxyõ' thẽm. *(They) throw down the letters round there.*

-m² *s.* <**-ta**> emphatic suffix on nouns and verbs.
aabaada'm. *FATHER did!*
xindu'sthaa'n xyaa sero'm xindi' baadam chalen xramau. *Since (we) have gone to Hindustan (we) learn HINDI without special tuition.*

-ma ... -m(a) *s.v.* <**-daa**> protracted action.
kxyoma kxyom ŋi muba'e soda'r phekhai. *As (they) kept on running (they) arrived in front of us.*

-ma¹, -ma', -maa', -mãã' *s.v.* <**-daa**> concurrent action.
jããj lama balla ko'e cinu' yõĩ. *Making the investigation they finally found a mark of blood.*

ma², maai *loc.* <**tala**> lower down in altitude.

ma'ḍuli *n.* <**mundra - kaanma laaune**> earrings which hang from pierced lobe.
[*Syn.* ḍxũḍi'; korlãã; cinjina.]

ma'd *n.* <**ṣaḍayantra**> conspiracy.
[*Syn.* sa'ila.]

madad *n.* <**madat**> help.
[*Syn.* saidaa'; ããḍiba'.]

ma'dãã mu'dũ *n.* <**khatra khuttrak**> chores of housework; responsibilities associated with funeral or post-funeral ceremonies.
ŋada'm paee' lxaagiram ma'dãã mu'dũ to'i axlaa'di. kho'i to' boba? *I have done nothing of the work for the* pae. *Dear me, what shall I take?*

-madi'¹ *pa.* emphatic.
taan' madi'lai kaẽ cal bxĩm'. *(You) feed rice to EVERYBODY!*

madi'² *n.* <**oṭh**> lip.

madlaba *see* **maldab** 'meaning; purpose'.

ma'duro *a.* <**madhuro**> low (of pitch or volume of voice).

-ma'ẽ¹, -ma'e, -mae, -maẽ' *s.n.* <**haru**> plural marker (for humans and animals).

maẽ^{2} *n.* <auṣadhi> medicine.

maẽ labaa' *v.* <auṣadhi garnu> to treat medically.

-ma'ẽn *s.v.* uncertainty.

-ma'e^{1} *s.n.* <ko> possessive - inalienable.
surjema'e aabaa. *Surje's father.*

mae^{2} *n.* <caak> buttocks.

-mae^{3} *s.v.* discovery aspect.
axxre'namae. *It isn't there, I see!*

mae kwẽ *n.* underpants. [*Syn.* xab jaŋge; phaasu'.]

ma'ema *loc.* <tala> down below (emphatic of ma).

ma'ga *n.* <mag> mug.

maga'r, mxagaa'ra *n.* <magar> Magar (large ethnic group of west Nepal).

ma'gi, mu'i, mu'gi, ma'i, mai [*TB* *lwa·y 'buffalo' 208] *n.* <bhãĩsĩ> buffalo - female. [*Ant.* rããgu'.]

maidaa' *n.* <maidaa> flour - processed.

maila' *a.* <mailo> dirty of vessels, body, clothes.

mainãã' *n.* <mainaa> bird - myna. [*Syn.* saaru'; suga'.]

mainaa' ka'bu *n.* <ciple kiro> slug. [*Cp.* ka'bu.]

mainṭolaa' *n.* <menṭol> lamp - pressure.

ma'iwẽ' *n.* frog - black, lives in water. [*Cp.* penḍo'; pxadgu.]

majaa' *n.* <majjaa> contentment. [*Syn.* tĩ sĩ'ba; saẽ tõbaa'.]

makha'ẽ *n.* <makai> maize; corn. [*Cp.* muraa; khoyaa'; bxudlaa'.]

makha'ẽ muraa *n.* <makaiko juwãã> wisps of hair growing out of corn cob.

makhan *n.* <makkhan> butter.

-ma'la^{1}**, -maa'la, -mula** *s.v.* <-eko thiyo> past repetitive tense.
pailaa' cyõba'e jaadaa mxo lamaa'la. *Formerly the lower castes used to serve as scapegoat.*

-ma'la^{2} *s.v.* <-thiyo> hypothetical result; intended result (?).
khiba' asõ' riyãã', khiba' ŋxĩ' cama'la, ŋa sõ' cama'la. *If the old man gets up first he will eat two, I will eat three.*

ma'la *n.* <mal> compost; fertilizer (mixture of dead leaves and animal dung).

malaai, malaaya' *n.* <malaya> Malaya.

maldab, madlaba *n.* <matlab> meaning; purpose. [*Syn.* maane'; arthaa'.]

-male', -mari' *v.* <-da kheri>
1. while (concurrent action).
pae lamale' dxĩri' yu'm ro. *They say (the ghost) comes down to the house while (you) do the* pae.
2. for (purpose).
khe'male' sõga'ẽ lxaidim. *Three days are required for reading it.*
dxĩ' lamale' chyããba'e jog ŋxyom. *For making a house one looks for an auspicious occasion.*

malgaja *n.* <golpha (wanko)> egg-plant-like fruit from jungle vine.

-ma'n *s.v.* <-chan> emphatic - non-past.
ĩṭam lxe'n xyaama'n. *Many bricks indeed go (into the job), probably.*

ma'n pardiba' *v.* <man paraaunu> to like.
ca' mxi se'ba ŋalai ma'n pardim. *I like that person's dancing.*

maṇḍali [*N* 'group; special committee'] *n.* <maṇḍal> church; gathering of Christian believers.

ma'ndir *n.* <mandir> temple dedicated to Hindu rites.

mandri' *n.* <mantri> minister of government.

-ma'ne *p.* <sita, saŋga> with.
khemaẽ samdima'ne tãã tadi'. *(He) consulted with his son's in-laws.*
mariyaama'ne ṭim. *(He) lives with Maria.*
[*Syn.* -ne, -nepri.]

manidiba' *v.*
1. <phakaaunu> to soothe (a child).
[*Syn.* kwi'ba.]
2. <manaaunu> persuade.

ma'njur *n.* <manjur> approval; consent; agreement.

ma'njur labaa' *v.* <manjur garnu> to comply with a suggestion; to give approval; to consent to a request; to agree.
[*Syn.* ŋẽl labaa'.]

ma'npari *n.* <manpari> indiscriminately; without considering others; according to one's own pleasure.

mantaraa' *n.* <mantra> incantation.

mare' *see* **ma'ttre'** 'only'.

mari'[1] *loc.* <tallo> down there.

-mari'[2] *see* **-male'** 'concurrent action'.

ma'rija *n.* <maric> pepper.

masala' *n.* <masalaa> spices; condiments.

masala' jxõba' *v.* <masalaa lagaaunu> to season food (with spices).

masana' *n.* <masaan (bhūtpret)> spirit of dead person (who has been unable to reach the village of the dead, dwells around cemeteries).
[*Cp.* bhut; mxõ'; syaa'gi; syo'; thaa; sarwẽ'; bikhaa.]

ma'sããũro *n.* balls of ground yam leaves and lentils.

masi'[1] *n.* <masi> ink.

masi'[2], **musi'** *n.* <musi> rafter - rib-like in gable roof.

masin kaa'le *av.* <masino> finely.
pxro' masin kaa'le pxrod. *Grind the flour finely.*

masinu' *a.* <masino> fine; soft; smooth (of flour, cloth, skin, surfaces).
[*Syn.* pobaa'; paadalu'.]

masul *n.* <mahasūla> customs (tax).

masur *a.* <masur> fearless; brave.

masuri' *n.* <masurko daal> lentil - red gram.
[*Cp.* maa'sa, tããgra.]

ma'ttre, mattre', ma'tde, made', madre', mare' *a.* <maatrai> only.
[*Syn.* sirib, khaali'.]

-mau' *s.v.* <-cha> present tense (emphatic).
[*Syn.* -mu.]

maudu' *n.* <ṭusaa> blade of grass; sprout; shoot.

maugaa' *n.* <maukaa> occasion; opportunity.
[*Syn.* yaa'm; txi.]

mããba' *n.* <būḍhī> woman - old.

mããri', maari' *pa.* exceedingly; without restraint (often sentence initial and often with beseri).
ŋam paisaa' yõyãã'm mããri' paldũ chaa'raa ṭxui' biri' khima'la. *If I GOT money, then for sure I would sew new trousers and wear them.*
mããri' gaŋgyu beseri baḍixyaama' kaseri' thẽmaẽlai beseri nausan lawaai. *Then all the more, the Seti being in great flood, it caused great loss to the people of Kaseri.*

-maa, -aa *s.v.* <-chaki> interrogative on present tense.
togo' xyaammaa'? *(You) are going now, are (you)?*

-maa *p.* <maa> in; at (with time

expressions in days).
kuga'ẽmaa. *Within nine days.*

maaba' *a.* <**ũdhoko**> lower in altitude.
[*Syn.* maai'.]

maa'ḍuli *n.* <**riŋg**> earrings worn in lobe of ear.
[*Syn.* korlãã; ḍhũḍi'; cinjina.]

maai, maad, maadi', ma, mai *loc.* <**tala tira; dakhin**> downwards; south.

maainaa' ka'bu *n.* <**ṭhulo ciple kiro**> slug - large, usually 5 to 8 cm. long.

maa'l *n.* <**maal**> baggage; property; goods.
maa'l aḍḍaa'. *Land tax office.*
[*Syn.* samaan.]

maa'laa *n.* <**maalaa**> garland.

maa'maa *n.* <**maamaa**> uncle (MoBr).

maamuli' *a.* <**maamuli**> inferior in quality or rank; ordinary.

maa'n *n.* <**maan**> honour; courtesy.

maa'n labaa' *v.* <**maan garnu**> to honour; to respect; to be courteous.

maane' *n.*
1. <**maane**> meaning - lexical.
   khlxyebri maane' aargo' jaadaan yaa. khlxyebri *refers to another caste.*
2. <**matlab, udešya**> purpose; goal.
   kxe' tichaẽ e' maa'ne axcxuba. *You haven't accomplished a single item of work.*

maa'ph *n.* <**maaph**> pardon; forgiveness.

maa'r kaa'ṭ *n.* <**maarkaaṭ**> butchering (esp. in ceremonies).

maardi'ba *v.* <**baat maarnu**> to converse (always with object baad or equivalent).
ṭhaṭṭaa' maardi'ba. *To joke.*

maari' *see* **mããri'** 'exceedingly'.

maa'sa, mãã'sa *n.* <**maas**> lentil - black grain.
[*Syn.* masuri'; tããgra.]

maasṭara' *n.* <**maasṭar (gurū)**> teacher of school.

maattiba' *a.* <**maattinu**>
1. snobbish; unfriendly.
   aagune baalu lxe' põ'la axŋĩ'; plxob tai' maattim. *He won't speak with people; having become rich he's snobbish.*
2. insolent; disobedient.
   kxe' laba'e mxilaai paisaa' lxe' pĩdu' biyãã liũdi maattim. *If you pay your workers a lot, later they become insolent.*

maayaa *see* **mxayaa** 'love'.

mẽ'jar *n.* <**mejar**> major (military rank).

mẽ'jyoba' *v.* <**jhuḍyaaunu**> to hang from; suspended (emphatic form of cyobaa').

me *n.* <**kããḍa**> arrow.
[*Syn.* txalĩ.]

mebro' *n.* <**kharaanī**> ashes.
[*Syn.* krophũ'; mi phũ.]

medgaa' *n.* <**cibhe**> bird - black drongo (long tailed, crow-like).

medõ' *n.* <**agulṭo (siṭho, rããko)**> cane - dry (used as kindling or for torches)

megãẽ *n.* <**bikh**> poison.

me'kh *n.* <**megh**> lightning strike.
[*Syn.* nããbri.]

melaa' *n.* <**melaa**> fair; exhibition.

mewaa *n.* <**mewaa**> pawpaw; papaya.

mĩ' [*TaGTh* *miiq; *TB* *mik∿*myak 402] *n.* <**ããkhaa**> eye.
txa' mĩ'. *Eye of needle.*

mĩ [*TaGTh* *min; *TB* *r-miŋ 83] *n.* <**naam**> name.

mĩ' cyũ' labaa' *v.* <**ããkhaa cimlanu**> to shut eyes; blink.

mĩ' saebaa'[1] *v.* <**ããkhaa jhimkaaunu**> to close one eye - as in sighting rifle; to wink.

mĩ' saebaa'[2] *v.* <**ṭeḍho ããkhaa bhasko hunu**> to squint.

mĩ' ṭxuba' *v.* <**ããkhaa jhimkaaunu**> to avert the eyes in anger or disgust.

mĩ'ba [*TB* *s-min 432; *TaGTh* *mimp] *v.* <**paaknu**> to ripen (of fruit and grains).

mĩjyãã [*TB* *tsam 'hair of head' 73] *n.* <**ããkhe raũ**> hair of eyebrow or eyelash.

-mi[1], **mĩ'**, **-mi'** *n.* <**-ta**> emphatic.
khi'e phami dešarna' mu. *Her own HUSBAND is in India.*
ŋaimi' thaai axsxe'. *I indeed don't know.*

mi[2] [*TB* *r-may 282] *n.* <**pucchaar**> tail of animal.

mi[3] [*TaGTh* *me; *TB* *mey 290; *T* meh; *Cp* me?] *n.* <**aago**> fire.

mi phũ *n.* coals - live. [*Syn.* mebro', krophũ', phũ.]

miḍiba' *v.* <**meṭaaunu**> to erase.

miḍil *a.* <**miḍīl; madhyaamīka**> middle (in phrase *'middle school'*).

migu' [*TB* *kuw=*kəw 256] *n.* <**dhuwãã**> smoke.

mijiba' *v.* <**micnu**> to polish; rub hard (as hands together, for warmth). [*Syn.* moldiba'.]

mijyaasi *a.* <**mijaasīlo**> charming; peace-maker. [*Syn.* sũ lacchin.]

milḍeri', mileṭi'n *n.* <**phauji**> military.
milḍeri'di solod pīī'. *The army gave a salute.*

mili *n.* <**ããsu**> tears.

mi'm saabaa' *n.* <**mem saab**> white woman. [*Syn.* goraa.]

misaa' *n.* <**ḍaḍhelo**> fire of forest or bush.

mistri' *n.* <**mistri**> craftsman; workman; mechanic.

mitiŋ *n.* <**saabhaah**> meeting. [*Syn.* kajuri', aŋsabaa'.]

mi'ttra, isṭaa' mi'ttra *n.* <**mitra**> friends. [*Syn.* thu; dosti; ŋxelaa; mxijaga.]

miulũ' *n.* <**aagulṭo**> brand of burning sticks. [*Syn.* lũ'ba.]

miwãã' *n.* <**jũnkīrī**> firefly.

mlãã'ba *v.* <**chutte laagnu**> to crave for a specially tasty food (especially used of sick person).
ŋa mxainaa sõ'l na'i biri' uttille' se caja' ŋxããi mlããŋŋyũ. *After I was sick three months I greatly wanted to eat meat, craving it.*

mlẽ'ḍo xyaaba' *v.* <**bhusukkai sutnu**> to oversleep (because of falling into deep sleep).
nxaru mle'do xyaadu' biyaa kxae xyaam'. *If I oversleep I'll be late.*

mli'ba[1] [*TB* *b-la:p 335] *v.* <**birsanu; bhulnu**> to forget.

mli'ba[2] *v.* <**galaa laagnu**> to choke on food.

mlõ *n.* <**kalcaũḍo**> udder of a cow. [*Syn.* thunaa.]

mlõ ku'ji *a.* <**kaalo - beseri**> black - very.
ca' mxi mlõ ku'ji byõba. *That person looks very black.*

mlõ'gu *n.* <**ghããṭi**> throat (internal). [*Syn.* orgõ'; kha'ri; gardan.]

mlõgyaa *a.* <**kaalo**> black.

mlxa *n.* <**dhaan**> rice - paddy, from seed to husking. [*Syn.* nãã; mlxasi'; kaẽ.]

mlxasi' *n.* <caamal> rice - husked, uncooked.
[*Syn.* mlxa; kaẽ; nãã.]

mlxe [*TB* *li=*li∿*(m-)ley 262] *n.* <puruṣ liŋga> penis (of adult man).

mlxoba' *v.*
1. <umranu> to sprout; to spring up.
2. <jhulkanu> to rise (of sun).

mlxogõ *n.* <bhaat> rice - as opposed to less preferred staple foods.
mlxogõ axxre', paigũ' matre' cai. *There was no rice, (I) ate only mash!*

mlxu[1] *n.* <dumsīko kããḍho> quill of porcupine.

mlxu[2] *n.* <ṭããkaa> point.

mlxuba' *v.* <ghocnu> to prick; to stab.
[*Syn.* cwibaa'.]

-mna, -mnaa, -mnaa' *s.num.* <maanu> pints.
timnaa'. *One pint.*
plximnaa. *Four pints.*
[*Syn.* mxana.]

mõḍaa'[1] *n.* <isṭūl> stool - circular, made of bamboo.

mõḍaa'[2] [*TB* *mu:r 366] *n.* <mukh> face; countenance.
[*Syn.* ru'b; li'.]

mo' [*TaGTh* *maq] *n.* <nigaalo> cane - used for weaving.

mo'ba *a.* <hoco> low in height or pitch; short (of man).

modõ' *see* mxodõ 'young female goat'.

moldiba' *v.* <malnu> to rub hard (tobacco into flakes); to polish by rubbing with a cloth.
[*Syn.* mijiba'.]

moloba' *v.* <misaaunu (puwaa ra dhaanko bhūs usinnu)> to boil jungle fibre with rice husks to facilitate combing.

momãã *a.* <maau> female (of animal).
[*Cp.* yomãã' 'female (of birds)'.]

mora' *n.* <saas> corpse.

mo'so *n.* <bhusunaa> gnat; flying, biting insect, smaller than a fly.

moṭara', moṭora *n.* <moṭar> motor vehicle.

mraa' [*TaGTh* *mrap] *n.* <ḍhokaa> door.
[*Syn.* tagara; ḍhogaa'.]

mrẽ'ba [*TaGTh* *mremp] *v.* <aghaaunu> to be satisfied (usually of food).

mre *n.* <pheṭaa> cloth - white, worn as turban during mourning.

mrĩ [*TaGTh* *mriŋ 'wife, woman'] *n.* <swaasnī> wife.

mrĩ xrããḍi *n.* <widhawaa> widow.

mrĩ labaa' *v.* <maithun garnu> to have sexual intercourse.

mrĩsyo' *n.* <swaasnī maanche (maan nagarne bolī)> woman (disrespectful).

-mri *s.num.* <murī> measure of volume - twenty gallons.
ŋxamri. *Five* muri *(100 gallons).*

mrõ' [*TaGTh* *mrank 'garden'] *n.* <khet> field - irrigated, usually for rice.
[*Syn.* baari; pakh mrõ'; khore'.]

mrõbaa' [*TaGTh* *mraŋ; *TB* *mraŋ 146] *v.*
1. <dekhnu> to see.
2. <dekhinu> to appear, to be visible.

mro'ba *a.* <ḍaaha laagnu> envious (of another's material comfort, good food, nice clothes).

mrobaa' *v.* <baalnu> to light a lamp.
[*Syn.* kho'mro bxĩba'.]

mrũ *n.* <raajaa> king.

mrũsyo *n.* <raani> queen.

mru' *a.* <jammaa> assembled; gathered together (of people, flowers).
[*Syn.* khaa'gu tabaa'; tũ'ba.]

mrxe [*TB* *mruw=*mrəw 150] *n.* <biyãã> seeds of fruit or vegetable (not grains).
[*Cp.* plxu'.]

mrxĩsə *n.* <mirsa> village - Gurung, two hours north of Ghachok.

mrxiba' *v.* <puṣṭinu> to swell; to develop (of grains).

mrxu *n.* <tikho> point.
[*Syn.* mlxu.]

mũ'juraa *n.* <mujūr> peacock.

mu¹, mũ present tense of mubaa' 'exist'.

-mu'², -mũ' *s.v.* <-cha> present tense (discourse medial).
khani' tĩmũ', ca'r swaabaa'. *Wherever you live, it is fine there.*

mu³ [*TB* *r-muw 488; *TB* *mu:k 'foggy' 357; *TaGTh* *mu] *n.* <aakaaš> sky.

mu ŋxeba *v.* <aakaaš garjaanu> to thunder (*lit.* sky roaring).

mu thõŋŋyũ' *v.* sky is clear.

mubaa' *v.*
1. <hunu> to exist.
aabaa dxĩr mũ. *Father is in the house.*
nache'tra aaṭhaaisa' mu. *There are twenty-eight birth signs.*
2. <ho> is (attribution, possession).
cu' khaba'la mu? *Whose is this?*
kaẽ lĩ'ban mu. *The rice is tasty.*

mubru' lxo, mubri' lxo *n.* <giddhaa barkha> year of the vulture (in Tibetan 12 year cycle - 1940,52,64,76,etc.).
[*Syn.* kxure' lxo.]

muḍki' *n.* <muḍki> fist - clenched.

mu'dda *n.* <muddaa> lawsuit; law case.

mu'dda labaa' *v.* <muddaa garnu> to file a lawsuit.

mu'dũ *see* ma'dãã mu'dũ 'chores'.

mu'ji *n.* <muji> anus.

mu'juri *n.* <mujuri (jyaalaako laagi dine anna)> wages paid to ploughmen in kind, viz. rice.

mu'l *a.* <mūl> main; basic; central.

mu'l gxyãã' *n.* <mūl baaṭo> main road.
[*Ant.* po' gxyãã'.]

mu'l kaṭṭa' *n.* <murkaṭṭaa> spirit - evil.
[*Syn.* mxõ'.]

mu'l txo *n.* <mukhkhe khããmaa> pillar of house - central, set first in building a house.

mu'l xããga' *n.* <thambaa; mūl rukh; phed (jamin maathiko)> trunk of tree above branches.
[*Cp.* jara 'root'.]

mu'laa *n.* <mūla> water source; spring.

muli' *n.* <mukhiyaa> head man of village under pre-revolution regime in Nepal.
[*Syn.* kxrõ.]

muluk *n.* <muluk> country.
[*Syn.* deš.]

muluka' *a.* <dherai, bhusukkai> large amount.
mxi muluka'n yu'i. *A large crowd of people came.*

munukhe' *n.* <maanis> man (used in religious incantations).
xer munukhe'. *Look, man!*

muraa *n.* <jũgaa> moustache.

murba' yu'ba *v.* <caḍkane parnu> lightning strike (euphemism used because of belief that if the explicit term "nããbri yu'ba" is uttered lightning will strike again).

murti *n.* **<mūrti>** idol; statue; image.
mxie mu'rti. *Statue of a man.*

murkhaa' *a.* **<mūrkha>** uncontrolled; violent "hit first, speak afterwards" reaction.

murkhaa' caalle *av.* **<mūrkha caal>** boisterously; uncontrollably.

murli' *n.* **<muralī>** recorder; fife.

mursa' *n.* **<mūrchaa>** fainting spell.

musaa'ra *n.* **<taaraa>** star.

musi' *see* **masi'** 'rafter'.

muškil *a.* **<muškil>** difficult.
[*Syn.* gaaro.]

muslũ' *n.* **<ḍhikīko dããt>** head of rice husking pounder.

musre' ŋxyui' *n.* **<chiṭ gunyu>** skirt of dark checked cloth worn by Gurung women.

muṭhaa' *n.* **<muṭṭho>** sheaf of grain.

muṭhi *n.* **<muṭhṭhī>** measure of volume (approx. 60 ml., one-tenth of mxana); handful.

mu'waar *n.* **<muhaar>** recitation - memorised.

mu'waar caḍiba' *v.* **<paaṭh garnu (naherikana)>** to recite from memory.

mu'waar khabaa' *v.* to be able to memorise recitations.
ŋalai mu'waar kham. *I have a good memory.*

muyũma'ẽ, mũ'yũmaẽ, mũĩma'ẽ *n.* **<daaju-bhaaiharu>** brothers.
[*Syn.* bxaima'ẽ.]

mwẽ' labaa' *v.* **<mwaaĩ khaanu>** to kiss.

mwi'[1] *see* **mxui'** 'rupees'.

mwi'[2] [*TB* *mul=*(s-)mul∿*(s-)mil∿*(r-)mul 2] *n.* **<rãũ>** body hair; fur.
[*Cp.* kra 'hair of head'.]

mwi' ti'xyaaba' *v.* **<rãũ khoilinu>** to suffer mange (of animals).

mxaba *n.* **<haraaunu>** to lose (especially of concrete objects).
to' budũ mxaxyaaba'? *What things have you lost?*
[*Syn.* mxoba.]

mxadise *n.* **<madhise>** plains dwellers from Tarai and North India.

mxaẽ *n.* **<chetri>** Chetri (a large Nepalese caste).

mxaẽ' thẽbaa' - saẽr *v.* **<samjhanu>** to memorise; to learn by heart.
[*Syn.* mxaẽba'; mu'waar khabaa'.]

mxaẽba', mxwaĩba' *v.* **<samjhanu>** to recall; reflect; remember.
gxaḍi' mxaxyaadu' biyãã saẽr mxaẽm, ŋadi kaẽ cai, jyu khru'i, khani' waathẽi? *If (you) lose (your) watch (you) recall, 'I ate rice, I bathed, (and) where did I leave it?'*

mxae, mxwe *n.* **<paailo>** footprint.

mxaeba'[1] *v.* **<khelnu (pīŋ)>** to play on swing or ferris wheel.

mxaeba[2] *v.* **<ṭeknu>** to step on; stand on.
[*Syn.* ŋwe'ba; nxeba.]

mxaeba[3] *v.* **<khojnu>** to search; to seek for.
pha mxaeba. *To be on heat (of animals).*

mxaĩla *n.* **<maahilo>** brother - second; son - second; second born.

mxaĩli *n.* **<maahili>** sister - second; daughter - second; second born.

mxaĩsir *n.* **<maŋsir>** month (8th of Nepali year, mid-November to mid-December).

mxaidan *n.* **<maidaan>** level ground; field - open and level.

mxaina *n.* <mahīnaa> month.

mxaja' *n.* <keraa> banana.

mxakhanḍi *a.* <makhanḍi (sīp nabhaeko)> unskilled; half-trained.

mxaliba *v.* <alpinu> to forget; to lose one's bearings (sometimes presumed as a result of a spirit's curse).
[*Syn.* mli' xyaaba'.]

mxana *n.* <maanu> measure of volume (approx. one pint = 570 ml., one-eighth of pyõ'no).

mxaŋlaa baaraa', mxaũlaa baaraa' *n.* <maŋal waar> Tuesday.

mxarda *a.* <mardaanaa> male - of humans.

mxayaa, maayaa *n.* <maayaa> love; enjoyment of a loved one's company.
[*Cp.* tõbaa'; khobaa'; sãã.]

mxayaalu *a.* <maayaalu> lovable; likable.
taanmadi'nna khoba'e kolo'lai mxayaalu bim. *A child everyone likes is called lovable.*

mxããba *v.* <jhabakkaa phalnu> to sprout profusely - of leaves.

mxããda *n.* <maadal> drum (tom tom, 20 cm. diameter, 50 cm. long).
[*Syn.* dama, ŋxa.]

mxããda xraaba *v.* <maadal bajaaunu> to beat a drum.

mxããdiba *v.* <maannu> to observe; to follow a religious system; to react to something; to acknowledge.
gaar mxããdiba. *To take offence.*
khani' ṭimũ ca'rna swaabaa' mxããdim. *Wherever (I) live (I) find it pleasant there.*

mxããgu' *a.* <mahããgo> expensive; scarce.
asaa'rari' kxe' laba'e mxi mxããg tam. *In (the month of) Asar workers are scarce.*

mxããjuri *p.* <bicmaa> between; amidst; middle.
mxããjur badẽ. *Near the middle.*
[*Syn.* axdxari'.]

mxããrãã *see* kaa'rãã mãã'rãã 'crawling'.

mxaaba *v.* <pelnu> to press; to grind through a machine.

mxaaga *n.* <maagh> month (10th of Nepali year, mid-January to mid-February).

mxaaidi'ba *v.* <maasnu> to spend money, resources.
[*Syn.* mxaasdi'ba.]

mxaara' *n.*
1. <sun> gold.
2. <pahẽlo - phulko> yolk of egg.

mxaarba *a.* <gajaabko> perfect in physique.
[*Syn.* swaabaa'rẽ.]

mxaarbobõ *n.* <wanmaa hune ek kisimko bajaaune cij> flora - a tubular plant (2-4 m. high in forest at about 3000 m., used as a horn when dry).

mxaarsi *n.* <dhaan - maarsi> rice variety (better quality than ciniyaa'. Planted early asar, it ripens late kaartik).

mxaalar *n.* <belaa, samaya> time, season.

mxaasdi'ba *v.* <maasnu> to spend; to expend; to use up (usually with reckless connotation).
[*Syn.* mxaaidi'ba.]

mxaaswaa' *n.* <phurmaasi garne maanis> spendthrift; prodigal.

mxẽ *n.* <dããī haaldaa gaaḍne ghocaa> post to which threshing oxen are tethered.

mxe' [*TaGTh* *mehq] *n.* <gaai> cow.

mxĩba *n.* <nibuwaa> lemon.

mxi [*TaGTh* *miih; *TB* *r-mi(y) *n.* 301, *n.* 329] *n.* <maanis> person, human being.
mxijaga. *People; other people.*
mximaẽ. *People.*

xrõsae' mximaẽ. *One's own people, relatives.*

mxi labaa' *v.* <maanche gannu> to respect as a person.
cu'di ŋxyo'lai mxi axlaa'. *He shows us no respect.*

mxilidiba *v.* <milaaunu> to set in order; to check; to call the roll.
pareḍar mxilidibar xyaam'. *We go to have the roll checked on parade.*

mxõ' [*TaGTh* *mahŋ; *Cp* mosq] *n.* <bhūt> ghost; evil spirit.
See Appendix B.
[*Syn.* syaa'gi; masana; syo; thaa; sarwẽ'; bikhaa.]

mxõ' ããlãã *n.* <bhūt (ek kisimko)> evil spirit able to appear as a headless form with eyes or lights in the shoulders (said to be fatal if seen front on. Unlike mxõ', mxõ' ããlãã is not a spirit of a dead person).
[*Cp.* bxut; mxõ', syaa'gi; masana; syo; thaa; sarwẽ'; bikhaa.]

mxõba' [*TB* *maŋ=*r-maŋ 82] *v.* <sapanaa (dekhnu)> to dream while asleep (always with mxõḍa as object).

mxõḍa *n.* <sapanaa> dream.

mxo [*TaGTh* *maah; *TB* *ma·k 'son-in-law' 324] *n.*
1. <bahinī jawããĩ> brother-in-law (YrSiHu).
2. <chorī jawããĩ> son-in-law (DaHu).
3. relative who performs son-in-law's responsibilities at a pae, acting as scape-goat (?).

mxoba'[1] *v.* <ṭhaskanu> to moan with pain; to groan.

mxoba[2] *v.* <haraaunu> to lose.
[*Syn.* mxaba.]

mxodõ', modõ' *n.* <koraalī baakhrī> goat - female, adolescent, before bearing young.

mxoraa *n.* <mohar> coin worth half-rupee.

mxũgi' *n.* spirit - evil, inhabitant of na'rge.
[*Syn.* bhut, mxõ', pijaas, syaa'gi.]

mxũjaa *n.* <maujaa> village - Gurung, NE of Pokhara, below yaagõ', near thosõ.

mxũru *n.* <muŋgro> paddle of wood about 18" long used for beating jungle fibres.

mxũũlu *n.* <muŋlo (goruko mukhmaa laaune)> muzzle for ox, woven from cane.

mxuba *v.* <jhamṭanu> to pounce upon; assault (of dogs, quarrelling people); to shake to and fro (of cat with a mouse).

mxuda, mxude *n.* document used to determine astrologically auspicious days.
[*Syn.* paadru'.]

mxuĩsa [*TB* *mwiy=*(r-)mwəy∿ *(s-)mwəy 'sleep' 196; *TB* *mu·ŋ 'dark' 362] *n.* <raat> night.

mxui', mwi' *n.* <rupiyãã> rupees; money.

mxujuri *see* **mu'juri** 'wages'.

mxuri *n.* <muri> measure of volume (20 gallons).
[*Syn.* -mri.]

mxuriba, mxuruba, mxurba *v.* <bernu> to wrap up in cloth.
thaũnid mxurba. *To wrap in old cloths.*
[*Syn.* berdiba.]

mxwaĩba' *see* **mxaẽba'** 'to remember'.
to' axmxwaĩba'e saẽdi' ŋad lwaadi'. *What unthinking things I have done!*

mxyõba *v.* <caakhnu> to taste; to sample food.

myaa'ba *v.* <maajhnu; udyaaunu> to scour; to scrape dishes clean; to whet a blade with a whet stone.

myõ'ba *v.* <**coṭ laagnu**> to be wounded (always ne' myõ'ba).

myũba' *v.* <**tikhaarnu**> to sharpen a point.
[*Syn.* mlxu labaa'.]

N

-n^{1} *s.v.* <**-e**> gerund construction - with labaa' and sammaa'.
mur mrõn labaa' axtaa'ro. *Looking at the sky is not right they say.*
ca' mxwĩsari' plxa xwiba' khãã'n lamu. *That night they finish the calling of the spirit.*
paĩtis barsa axyu'n sammaa'. *Until reaching 35 years of age.*

-n^{2} *s.v.* <**hunale**> since - reason (used only with neg.).
ŋad lala axkhãã'n biri' mxijagad axdxe' laŋŋyũ'. *Since I could not do it, others have share farmed the land.*
ciṭhi' axkha'n axkhaa' bii. *Since the letter hadn't come he wouldn't come, he said.*

-n^{3} *s.v.* causative infinitive (much less common than -l, and always with auxiliary labaa').
sixyaan labaa'. *He caused him to die.*

-n^{4} *see* **-na** 'emphatic particle'.
lxen' mu. *There are MANY.*
kadi' barsar lalen tam. *In whatever year you do it, that's OK.*
cu'rban. *Of THIS place.*

-n^{5} *s.v.* <**-hos**> imperative (if stem vowel is nasal).
pĩn. *Give (it to me).*
[*Syn.* -d.]

-n^{6} *s.v.* <**gayo**> to go and... (auxiliary verb).
khõ'ndi. *Go and enter, then.*
[*Syn.* -ne.]

-na'... -na', nãã'... nãã'... *c.* <**ki... ki**> perhaps... perhaps.
na' sarkhaari' ciṭhi' mui xo na' jxuile' saabma'ẽle' kho' bii ciṭhi' axpĩ'. *Perhaps it was a government letter, or perhaps they didn't give him a letter saying, from the officials here, 'Come'.*

nã', nãã' *v.* <**lau**> take it.

-na'^{1}**, -naa, -naa'** *s.num.* <**-ai janaa**> associative.
sõ'na sõ'na xyaai'. *They went, the three together.*

-na'^{2}**, -naa, -naa', -nãã'** *s.n.* <**-ta**> emphatic particle.
ŋadna' axkxwẽ'. *I don't believe it.*

-na^{3} *s.v.* <**-echa**> discovery aspect; perfect.
sixyaana. *(He) has died, I see!*

na^{4} [*TaGTh* *na; *TB* *s-na∿*s-na:r 101; *Cp* nehq] *n.* <**naak**> nose.

-na' bile, -naa' bile *s.v.* <**bhae pani**> even though.

na'b cha'ba *n.* <**biraamī, pīḍaa**> fever and weakness (loosely - illness generally).

na'b sxaba' *v.* <**bisek hunu**> to recover.

na'ba [*TaGTh* *naq; *TB* *na 80] *v.* <**dukhnu**> to hurt or pain; to be sick; to be ill.

na'bbru *n.* <**kamilo**> ant.

na'bbru kuji' *n.* <**baarulo**> wasp.

na'bbru saaraa dxũ' *n.* <**bhim sen paatīko boṭ**> flora - with leaves white underneath.

nabli *n.* <**uḍus**> bed-bug.

nache'tra *n.* <**nachetra**> astrological birth sign (determined by the exact day and hour of birth).
axṭaaisa nachetra tam. *There are 28 birth signs.*

naḍ *see* **nar** 'weariness with a food'.

na'ga, nau', na'u *n.* <**kukhuro**> fowl; chicken.

nagi [*TB* *kwiy∿*kwəy 159; *T* khi] *n.* <**kukur**> dog.

nagi lxo *n.* **<kukurko barkhaa>** year of the dog (1946,58,70, 82).
[*Syn.* khilo.]

nai sa *n.* **<kukur-dããt>** canine tooth.

na·ĩ' *n.* **<puwaa>** thread extracted from a bush plant like a nettle.

naidi'maa *t.* **<paraar>** year before last.
tugyu'm naidi'maa. *In years past.*

nakaḍaa' *a.* **<nadaṭo (laaj namaannu)>** shameless; coarse.
nakaḍaa' taba'e mxid pil txubae kxe' lanaa' bile axpi'. *A shameless person is not embarrassed even if he does things for which one should be embarrassed.*

nakal te'ba, nagal te'ba *v.* **<nakkal paarnu>** to groom oneself; to make up.

nakali' *a.* **<nakkali>** artificial; hypocritical; affected.

nakhũ' *n.* **<naakko pwaal>** nostril.

nakhũ' sũ *n.*
1. **<naakko swar>** nasal pronunciation.
2. **<širbindu>** diacritic - nasal (in Devanagari script a superscribed dot).

na'ksa *n.* **<naksaa>** picture; photo.
[*Syn.* phoṭo'; tasbir.]

na'la *n.* **<nal; naluwaa>** stalks; hay from millet harvest.

nalgadiba' *v.* **<markaaunu(naacnu)>** to move unrestrainedly, recklessly, in dancing.

nalgi' [*H* nalikaa] *n.* **<nalī>** pipe; tube; water-pipe.

nali' *n.* **<nalihaaḍ>** shin.
[*Syn.* pxali nali'.]

namaste *i.* **<namaste>** greeting word and action of folding hands in greeting.
namaste lad. *Do a greeting.*

na'mjyo[1] *n.* **<jholaa (sarkaarī)>** pack - army style, with shoulder straps; rucksack.
[*Syn.* ru'psai, jxyolaa'.]

na'mjyo[2] *n.* **<phaṭyããŋgro>** grasshopper.

-namu *s.v.* **<-echa>** discovery aspect; past continuous.
lxe' xul' muna'mu, gaar tai. *There was a big crowd there, indeed, and it was difficult.*

na'munaa *n.* **<namunaa>** example; illustration; parable; sample.

naphaa', naba' *n.* **<naaphaa>** profit (especially from corrupt practices).
[*Syn.* phaidaa'.]

nar, naḍ *a.* **<naak laaunu>** weariness with a certain food.
ŋalai aalu' naḍ ṭaba'. *I'm fed up with potatoes.*
[*Syn.* chorõ'.]

na'ram *a.* **<naram>** soft, pliable (of cloth, skin).
[*Syn.* ŋiliba'; kamal taba'.]

na'rgalog *n.* **<naraka>** hell.

na'rge *a.* **<phohorī>** dirty; disgusting.

narwaala' *n.* **<nariwal>** coconut.

na'sa *n.* **<naso>** vein; sinew.
[*Syn.* ca.]

naspati *n.* **<naspati>** fruit (of apple family, ripens in Jesth).

nasu' *n.* **<naaso>** present; gift sent (by mail or messenger, not handed in person).

na'u[1] *see* **na'ga** 'chicken'.

na'u[2] *n.* **<nau>** nine (in Nepali loan phrases).
na'u baje. *Nine o'clock.*
[*Syn.* ku'.]

na'u kisim bibaa *u.* **<naanaa prakaar bhannu>** gossip confidences.

na'udima *t.* **<paraagũ>** year after next.
[*Cp.* naidi'maa.]

na'ule *a.* **<naulo>** different; strange; new; foreign.

na'uli *n.* **<naaŋlo>** tray (wicker) about 75 cm. in diameter, used for winnowing; pan for scales.

naumĩ' *n.* ninth day of Dasera festival.

nausan, naa's, noksan *n.* **<noksaan>** loss; damage.

na'utõ *n.* **<mujūr>** peacock.

na'utuna *n.* **<nautanwa>** Nautanwa (Indian rail head on Nepal border, south of Pokhara).

na'yãã, naa'yã *a.* **<nayaa>** new.

na'yãã tãã *n.* **<khabar>** news.

nãã'... nãã' *c.* **<ki... ki...>** either... or...

nãã'^{1} [*TaGTh* *namp] *n.* **<paanī - barṣaa hune>** rain.

nãã'^{2} *see* **nã'** 'take it'.

nãã^{3}, naa *n.* **<baalo>** head of grain; sprig of bush.
cyõ'ḍie' naa. *Sprig of chrysanthemum.*

nãã' bũbũ *n.* **<simsim paanī parnu>** drizzle.

nãã' ri'ba *n.* **<raat huna ããṭnu>** daylight remaining.
nãã' ri'ba dxero' gxanḍa' sõ' mu. *There is now three hours left of daylight.*

nãã' yu'ba *v.* **<jharī parnu, paanī aaunu>** to rain.

nãã'ba, naa'ba [*TB* *m-nam 464] *v.* **<gandha aaunu>** to smell; stink (always with thãã).
thãã nãã'l bxĩba'. *Making it stink.*

nããbli' [*TB* *(m-)li:t 'water leech' 396] *n.* **<juko (paanīko)>** leech-like worm (lives in water and enters nostrils of animals drinking, then living as parasite on animal's blood).

nããbri *n.* **<caḍkene>** lightning - forked.
nããbri yu'ba. *Lightning striking.*

nãã'sa *n.* **<gaaũ>** village.

nãã'sthẽmaẽ *n.* **<gaaũleharu>** villagers.

naa'^{1} [*TaGTh* *nap; *TB* *s-nap 102] *n.* **<sĩghaan>** mucus (nasal); snot.

-naa^{2} *see* **-na'** 'continuous action'.

-naa^{3} *see* **-n** 'emphatic'.

-naa^{4}, -naa' *see* **-na** 'discovery aspect'.

naa^{5} *see* **nãã** 'head of grain'.

-naa' bile *s.v.* **<-e pani>** even if; even though (contrary to expectation condition).

naa' waabaa' *v.* **<sĩghaan paalnu>** to blow one's nose.

naa'b-jaab *n.* **<naap-jããc>** survey (as of damage in accident).

naa'b^{1} *n.* **<naap>** cubit; measurement. [*Syn.* kru.]

naab^{2} *see* **cib naab** 'elders'.

naabdiba', naapdiba' *v.* **<naapnu>** to measure.

naa'ble *n.* **<jyaadaa sĩghaan aaune>** person whose nose is continually runny.

naabri labaa' *v.* to curse another (usually children, by splaying out the fingers of both hands in the direction of the person being cursed).
[*Cp.* nããbri.]

naai' *n.* **<naaik>** corporal (military rank).

naa'ja, naac *n.* **<naac>** dance.

naane *n.* **<raagan (jornī dukhnu)>** pain; stiffness in joints (often due to vitamin deficiency).

naa'ni *n.* **<jeṭhī, ṭhulī>** eldest sister (term of reference or

address.
[*Syn.* axgxaẽ'.]

naare', naari' *n.* <**kodo**> rye-like grain (eleusine corasana).

naari *n.* <**naaḍi, naạri**> wrist.
yo naari bicaardiba. *To feel the pulse.*

naariba' *v.* <**thaaknu**> to tire; to be weary.

naarwaaba' *v.* <**thakaaunu**> to weary; make tired.

naa's *see* **nausan** 'loss, damage'.

naathu' *n.* <**naataa**> relative.

naati *n.* <**naati**> grandson (or great-grandson in some opinion).
[*Syn.* kwẽ.]

naatini *n.* <**naatinī**> granddaughter (or great-granddaughter in some opinion).
[*Syn.* kwẽmĩ'.]

naause *see* **naamjyõ.**

nẽdo' *n.* <**thailo**> sack; bag for carrying grains (up to 2 or 3 gallons in capacity).
[*Cp.* kuldu.]

ne'[1] [*TaGTh* *net] *a.* <**bharieko**> full.

-ne'[2] *s.v.* <**jaanu**>
1. go and.
   kaẽ canem. *I'm going to eat rice.*
2. go and do (imperative).
   thaa pĩne'. *Go and give the word.*

-ne[3] *c.*
1. <**ra**> and.
   saĩli'ne kanchi. *Sainli and Kanchi.*
2. <**laaī**> accusative.
   nagine axchwi'. *(He) doesn't touch dogs.*
3. <**saŋga**> with.
   axtõ'bae mxine xyaala' txuba. *I have to go with a person I don't like.*
   [*Syn.* nego'; nero'; nen... nen.]

-ne baalu *p.* <**saŋga**>
1. with; together with; association with.
   ca'ne baalu yu'laa. *I came with him.*
2. consulting with.
   aamjaune baalu ŋyu'im. *(You) ask (your) aunts.*

ne' myõ'ba *v.* <**coṭ laagnu**> to be injured; wounded.

-ne pri' [*Cp* brɨk 'with'] *p.*
1. <**saŋga**> with; to.
   pumsyo kxine pri' ṭha'ḍa ṭhu'ḍu tanaa'. *A witch has developed, I see, enmity to you.*
2. <**baaṭa**> from.
   ŋxyo'e dxĩne pri' xrẽgo xwaa'? *It is far from our house, is it?*

neba'e, nebo' *see* **nego'** 'and'.

nebaa' *v.* <**sutaaunu**> to put to bed; to lay down.

nego', neba'e, nebo' *c.* <**ra**> and (linking nouns).
[*Syn.* nero', ne, nen... nen.]

nema *n.* <**caraa**> bird.

nema lxo *n.* <**caraa barkhaa**> year of the bird (1945,57,69,81).
[*Syn.* cxe lxo.]

nen... nen *c.* <**ra**> both... and.
mxinen cẽnen baalu xyaai'. *Both man and tiger went together.*
nxebaalnen kaju'nen swaabaa'. *Both Nepal and Ghachok are fine.*

nero' *c.* <**ra**> and (linking nouns).
[*Syn.* nego'; nen... nen.]

nesa' *n.* <**belukaa**> evening.

netaa' *n.* <**mukhiyaa; netaa**> chief; head.

ni [*TB* *m-nwi(y) 191] *n.* <**hããso**> laughter; amusement.

ni khabaa' *v.* <**hããso uṭhnu**> to be amused.

ni syubaa' *v.* <**hããsnu**> to laugh.

ni labaa' *v.* <**hããso garnu**> to

amuse; to cause to laugh.

ni xe'rara labaa' *v.* <muskuraaunu> to smile (in friendliness or mockery).

nibaa' *v.* <rucaaunu> to have an appetite for.

nimũ, nimu *n.* <muso> rat.

nimũ lxo *n.* <muso barkhaa> year of the rat (in Tibetan 12 year cycle, 1946,58,70,82,etc.). [*Syn.* cywilxo.]

nimur *n.* <anna> stye in the eye.

ni'ra *a.* <nilo> blue.

ni'ri *n.* <jumraako likhaa> eggs of head lice.

nirmae *a.* <nirdayi> hard-hearted; unkind; unbending. [*Syn.* saaro' saẽ; nisṭuri.]

ni'rnae labaa' *v.* <nirṇay garnu> to decide on a course of action.

ni'ro'gi *a.* <nirogi> healthy; free from disease.
ca' mxi ni'ro'gi; to' canaa' bile pattiba', pho' axnxa'ba. *That person is healthy. Whatever he eats he thrives, his stomach doesn't suffer.*

nisṭuri *a.* severe; stern; hard. [*Syn.* nir'mae; saaro' saẽ.]

ni'yaa *n.* <nyaaya> justice; judgement. [*Syn.* nyaa'e.]

-nna', -nnãã' *s.* agentive suffix - emphatic.
lxen' axbxwi' ŋannãã'. *I didn't bring much, I didn't.*

nõ¹ *s.num.* <garo> terrace fields. [*Syn.* nxõ'.]

nõ² *n.* <khetaala> labourers for agricultural work (work party).

nõ³ *see* nxõri' 'inside'.

nõ jxõba' *v.* <khetaala haalnu> to employ agricultural labourers. [*Cp.* axdxe' pi'ba.]

nõ'ba¹ *v.* <oṭhaaro basnu> to sit on eggs; to go clucky.

nõ'ba² *v.* <ãṭhyaaũnu> to press down.

nõbaa' *v.* <parma garnu> to exchange labour.

nõgura *n.* <dherai janaa parma garera hĩḍne ṭoli; huri> group of people co-operating for agricultural work. [*Syn.* daphaa; ṭoli'.]

nõwãã *n.* <biraalo> cat.

nõwãã ḍxaaḍe' *n.* <ḍhaaḍe> tomcat.

nõwãã lxo *n.* <biraalo barkhaa> year of the cat (1951,63,75,87, etc.). [*Syn.* xilxo.]

nõwẽ' *n.* <nuwããĩ> first fruits of rice harvest eaten at a special ceremony.

-no'¹ *see* nu' 'imperative'.

no² *n.* <phal maasu> meat - lean; flesh.

no³ *v.* <jhaar> weeds.

no syui'ba *v.* <jhaar ukhelnu> to weed.

no'ba *v.* <boknu> to carry; to lift; to bear.
pxasi no'ba. *To be pregnant.*
juḍ no'ba. *To be ritually defiled.*
txi' no'ba. *To carry a load.*

no'kori *n.* <nokari> service; employment. [*Syn.* jaagir.]

noksan *see* nausan 'loss, damage'.

no'la *n.* <bokne kaaṭha> carrying pole.

nosa *n.* fertile soil.

no'ṭa *n.* <noṭ> note (currency).

nũ'¹ *n.* <syaakhu silaaune siyo> awl (for sewing rainshield together).

nũ'² *n.* <kukhuro thunne kokro> cage for chickens.

nũ'[3] **<nunu gar (sutaaune bolne šabda)>** lullaby word.
nũ' lad. *Go to sleep.*

nũ'ima *t.* **<parsi>** day after tomorrow.

nũ'imdũ' *t.* **<parsi palṭo>** second day after a given date.
ca' nũ'ĩmdũ ekham. *(I) will come back the second day after that.*

nũ'jile *a.* **<bistaarai>** slowly.

-nu' *s.v.* **<-hos>** imperative (on nasal stem verbs, nonfinal in sentence).
[*Cp.* -n, -du.]

nu'ba *a.* **<aglo>** tall; high (in stature or pitch).

nubaa' *v.* **<siddhinu>** to complete; to finish work.
[*Syn.* cxĩba; khãã'ba.]

nu'kuri *see* **no'kori** 'service'.

nuni' *n.* **<nauni>** butter - unclarified.

nxa [*TB* *g-na=*r-na∿*g-na 453] *n.* **<kaan>** ear.

nxa cxo *n.* ear edge, rim.

nxa khlyi *n.* **<kaane guji>** ear wax.

nxa tẽ *n.* **<loti>** ear lobe.

nxaba[1] [*TaGTh* *nah; *TB* *na 414] *v.* **<bisaaunu>** to rest.
txi' nxaba. *To rest a load.*
bxõ' nxaba. *To rest the strength.*

nxaba[2] *v.*
1. **<susaar garnu>** to look after; support; maintain.
2. **<paalnu>** keep (animals).
3. **<paalnu>** to grow (hair, beard).
   kra xrĩŋgyo nxaba. *(She) has (her) hair long.*

nxabre *n.* **<khajuro>** centipede.

nxakhũ pra'ba *a.*
1. **<chiṭo risaaunu>** short tempered; easily offended.
2. **<ṭhussinu>** sulky.

nxakhu *n.* **<mundri>** circular earring worn on outside of lobe.

nxakkarnaa', nxããkkarna', nxããkarna *t.* **<bihaanai>** early in the morning; first thing.

nxalgyõ nxõrĩ' *n.* vine.

nxambar *n.* **<ãka>** number.

nxaraa n. **<naairo>** leather yoke in ox harness.

nxaru *n.* **<nidraa>** weariness; sleepiness.

nxaru cxuiba *v.* **<nidaaunu>** to fall asleep.

nxaru kxuba' *v.* **<nidraa jhulnu>** eyelids drooping in weariness.

nxaru yu'ba *v.* **<nidraa aaunu>** to be weary, tired.

nxausi *a.* **<bahiro>** deaf.

nxããga, nxããgaa *n.* **<bihaana>** morning.

nxããkkarna' *see* **nxakkarnaa'** 'early in morning'.

nxããmjyo [*TB* *nam 'sky' *n.* 405] *n.* **<kuiro; baadal>** mist; fog; cloud.

nxããnũ *n.* **<aandro>** intestines.

nxẽ *n.* **<bisaaune ṭhaaũ>** resting platform on roadside.

nxeba'[1] [*TaGTh* *naihq 'rub, press down'] *v.* **<maaḍnu>** to thresh by treading with feet; knead with feet; to thresh (general term).

nxeba'[2] *v.*
1. **<laḍnu>** to fight.
2. **<jhããṭnu>** to argue.

nxeba[3] *v.* **<bijhaaunu>** to stick into (as of awkward load sticking into one's back).
axchyãã'ba sĩ'jau txi' jxõdu' biyãã kxo nxem. *If you put bad wood in the load it hurts your back.*

nxeba[4] *v.* **<orlanu (jahaaj); basnu (caraa)>** to land; alight (of bird, aircraft).

nxeba[5] *v.* <ṭeknu (khuṭṭaa)> to step on; rest one's foot on.

nxeba[6] *v.* <dhaamī kaamnu> to go into trance for purpose of divination by communion with a spirit.
[*Syn.* gur nxeba.]

nxeba[7] *v.* <maattinu> to be drunk.
paa' nxeba. *To be drunk with wine.*

nxebal *n.* <nepaal> Nepal; Kathmandu Valley.

nxemẽ *n.* <kaan> ear.
sī' nxemẽ. *Fungus.*

nxewaar *n.* <newaar> Newar (a large ethnic group in Nepal, particularly in Kathmandu Valley).

nxiba'[1] *see* **nxeba'** 'to thresh'.

nxiba'[2] *see* **nxeba'** 'to fight'.

nxiba[3] *see* **nxeba** 'to be drunk'.

nxõ'[1] *n.* <garo> terrace of paddy fields. [*Syn.* nõ.]

nxõ[2] *p.* <bhitra> inside; into.
cẽ cyõ nxõr thundi' waai. *The tiger was shut in the cage.*

nxõba *v.* <bikrinu> to break.

nxõnõna *p.* <bhitra, bhitrai> in; amidst.
mlxa nxõnõna axpxrad'. *Don't walk in the paddy.*
nãã' nxõnõna saaikal khe'l lai. *(They) held the bicycle races in the rain.*

nxõrba *n.*
1. <bhitra> inside.
2. <muni> underneath.

nxõũba' *a.*
1. <bhitrako> inside.
2. <muniko> underneath.
3. <pachiko> later born.

nxo *n.* <pip> pus.

nxora, nxura *n.* <sampatti> wealth; riches.
[*Syn.* sampatti; sa'e nxora.]

nxorī' *n.* <laharo> vine.

nxu' *n.* <lasun> garlic.

nxura *see* **nxora.**

nyauri muso *n.* <nyaaurī mūsaa> mongoose.

nyaa'e *n.* <nyaaya> judgement; finding.
[*Syn.* ni'yaa.]

nyaa'e labaa' *v.* <nyaaya garnu> to judge a case.

nyaa'e dxiš *n.* <nyaaya dhiš> judge.

Ŋ

ŋããgora *n.* <ããkhako chaalaa> eyelid - lower.

ŋa, ŋaa [*TaGTh* *ŋaa; *TB* *ŋa 406; *T* ŋah] *pn.* <ma> I; me.

ŋaẽbaa' *v.* <pãĩco dinu> to lend a durable article (esp. clothing or jewellery).
[*Syn.* che' pĩbaa'; khi'ba.]

ŋa'eba *v.* <ubranu> to remain; to be left over.

ŋãã *n.* <biṭ> hem (of garment); selvedge (if cloth); edge (of weaving, thatch, etc.).

ŋãã saebaa' *n.* <biṭ maarnu, banaaunu> to make hem (of garment); to cast off (in knitting); to finish off edge (in weaving).

ŋaa *pn.* <ma> I (form of ŋa used in phrase final position).

ŋaala' *pn.* <mero> mine.

ŋaar, ŋaa, ŋãã, ŋããr *p.* <-kahãã> to the place of.

ŋẽma'ẽ *n.* <kuṭumba> relatives not of same lineal family.
aarko' santaan laasi ŋẽma'ẽ bim. *Other families we call cousins.*

ŋebaa' [*TaGTh* *ŋem 'hear, obey,

be soft'] *v.* <maannu> to obey.

ŋẽŋẽ' *n.* <kancaṭ> temple (of head).

ŋe' *pa.* <huncha> yes; O.K.
lxau', kũ'khõ. // ŋe', mxo.
Come on, come and sit. // O.K., Brother-in-law.

ŋebaa' *v.* <capaaunu> to chew.

-ŋele' *see* -ŋere' 'while'.

-ŋere', ŋere', ŋele *s.v.* <-kheri> while.

ŋĩ yãã' *see* di yãã 'therefore'.

ŋi'[1] [*TaGTh* *ŋis; *TB* *s-nis 5] *n.* <saat> seven.

ŋi[2] *pn.* <haamī (tapaaĩ baahek)> we (exclusive).

ŋi'braa *num.* <saat saya> seven hundred.

ŋi'e *pn.* <haamro> our (exclusive).

ŋija'ga *n.* <haamīharū> we (emphatic plural - exclusive).

ŋi'jyu *num.* <sattari> seventy.

ŋilaa' *pn.* <haamro> our (exclusive - focus).

ŋiliba' *a.* <kamalo> soft; mild; meek; gentle; flexible.

ŋithru'kale, ŋithru'kan *av.* <nithrukka bhijnu> completely.

-ŋŋyũ' *s.v.* <-eko> perfect aspect.
[*Syn.* -imu.]

ŋo se'ba *v.* <cinnu> to know (a person); to recognise.

ŋõ'lo *n.* <solṭi> cousin - male, cross (MoBrSo, FaSiSo).

ŋõ'lõsyo *n.* <solṭinī> cousin - female, cross (FaSiDa, MoBrDa).

ŋo'[1] *n.* <paaso> trap.

ŋo[2] *see* ŋxo 'forehead'.

ŋo[3] *n.* <kunaa> corner of cloth or mat.

ŋo axcxyoba' *v.* <jhyaamminu (jo saŋga pani)> fearless of strangers.

ŋobaa' *v.* <phuknu (biraamīlaaī)> to blow upon sick person (usually done by religious officiant).

ŋo'eba *v.* <naaghnu> to step over; to jump over.

ŋri *n.* <hããso> laughter.
[*Syn.* ni.]

ŋri'ba ŋri'ba *a.* uneven; wrinkled; serrated.

ŋrxuba' *v.* <gharnu> to snore; to purr.

ŋxa'[1] [*TaGTh* *ŋahq; *TB* *b-ŋa~ *l-ŋa 78] *num.* <pããc> five.

ŋxa[2] *n.* <ḍhyããgro> drum used by lamas (in religious rituals, made with goat's skin).

ŋxabraa' *num.* <pããc say> five hundred.

ŋxaẽ sẽ'ba *v.* rite (third) often necessary to perform in order to neutralise witch's curse.
[*Syn.* paaldu' waabaa'; dobaaḍe waabaa'.]

ŋxaẽba *v.* <baarnu (kunai dišaa)> to be forbidden by astrology; inauspicious.

ŋxajyu' *num.* <pacaas> fifty.

ŋxããba *v.* <man laagnu> to adhere to; to want to (with reduplication of monosyllabic verb stem).
caja' ŋxããm. *Wants to eat.*

ŋxaarba *v.*
1. <suknu (pokharimaa paanī)> to dry up; evaporate.
2. <thaaknu (dūdh)> to dry up (of a buffalo).

ŋxẽba *v.* <suhaaunu> to suit well (usually of clothes).
ca' kamij kxilai ŋxẽŋŋyũ. *That shirt suits you well.*
[*Syn.* krxiba.]

ŋxe[1], ŋxẽ, ŋe *v.* <ta> is (affirmative of ŋxība').
ta'le ŋxe? *Why is it so?*

ŋxe[2], ŋe *i.* <ee> oh (now I understand).

ŋxe[3] [*TB* *nəw=*nuw 419; *TaGTh* *ŋeeh] *n.* <dūdh> milk; breast.

ŋxekra *n.* <dūdhko munṭo> nipple of breast.

ŋxeb ṭxuba *n.* <chimeki> neighbour.

ŋxeba'[1] *v.* <pokhinu> to spill.

ŋxeba[2] *v.* <cuĩ cuĩ aawaaj garnu> to squeak; scrape (of door, etc.).
mraa' ŋxeba. *The door squeaks.*

ŋxeba[3] *v.* <bajnu> to chime (of clock, drum, or gong).
ŋxa ŋxem. *The drum sounds.*

ŋxeba[4] *v.* <gaḍaaŋ guḍuŋ garnu> to thunder.

ŋxeba[5] [*TB* *ŋuw∿*ŋəw 'cry' 79] *v.* <karaaunu> to howl; cry (of animals); to meow; to cheep; to hiss; to neigh.

ŋxeba[6] [*TaGTh* *ŋeh] *v.* <duhunu> to milk - a cow or buffalo.

ŋxelaa *n.* <mīt> covenanted friend (usually of different caste).
[*Syn.* aagu.]

ŋxelsyo *n.* <mītīnī> covenanted friend of a woman; wife of a man's covenanted friend.

ŋxĩ' [*TaGTh* *ŋiihq; *TB* *g-nis= *g-ni-s 4; *Cp* nisq] *num.* <dui> two.

ŋxĩããḍo', ŋxyaũlõ' *n.* <duiṭaa> two (emphatic); both.

ŋxĩba'[1], ŋxe, ŋe', ŋe, ŋxẽ *v.* <ho> to be (equative).
[*Syn.* ga; ya; ja.]

ŋxĩba[2] *v.* <ḍaraaunu> to be frightened.

ŋxĩji *n.* <ḍar> fright; fear.
ŋxĩji mattre' lai. *He could do nothing for fear.*

ŋxĩnaa' ŋxĩ'n *pn.* <duwai> both; two together.

ŋxible *num.* <dui coṭi> twice.

ŋxibraa *num.* <dui say> two hundred.

ŋxisyu *num.* <bīs> twenty.

ŋxoba *v.* <bhuṭnu> to roast; pop grains.

ŋxururu labaa' *v.* <ŋyaar ŋyaar garnu> to growl (of dog).

ŋxyãã *a.* <raamro hunu (swaasthaa)> good physical condition.
beseri ŋxyãã chyããŋŋyũ'. *He is in very good health.*

ŋxyo'[1] *pn.* <haamī (tapaaĩ haamī)> we (inclusive).

ŋxyo[2] *n.* <aahaal; pokharī> ditch; pond.
ma'gi ŋxyor ro'ba. *The buffalo is lying in the ditch.*

ŋxyoba *v.* <hernu> to look at; to look after; to care for; to seek (an auspicious day); to divine supernatural cause of illness.

ŋxyoba lxiba' *n.* <her kor garnu> divination of supernatural cause of illness.
ŋxyoba lxiba' lai axsxa'. *(He) did the divination (but the patient) didn't get better.*

ŋxyo'e *pn.* <haamro> our (inclusive).
ŋxyo'e cxa ŋxĩ' paa's tai. *Our two sons have passed.*

ŋxyolaa' *pn.* <haamro> our (inclusive - focal).
ŋxyolaa' cxa ŋxĩ' paa's tai. *We have two sons who have passed.*

ŋxyo'jaga *pn.* <haamīharū> we (emphatic plural - inclusive).

ŋxyui' *n.* <gunyũ> apron-like garment - black, worn at back by married women.

ŋyaũli' [*TB* *g-li 'armpit' 265] *n.* <kaakhī> armpit.

ŋyããũ *n.* <biraalo karaaune šabda> cry of cat; meow.

ŋyu'ba *a.* <ciso> to be cold (of

fluids).

ŋyu'iba [*TB* *r-yu(w)] *v.* **<sodhnu>** to ask.

ŋyu'mãã *n.* **<ḍhuŋgaa>** stone; rock. [*Syn.* yu'mãã.]

ŋyumnaa *see* **yumanaa** 'quickly'.

O

õ *p.* **<õ>** yes (acknowledging statement or expressing approval). [*Syn.* xajur.]

o'[1]**, o** *i.* **<tyasari>** just (deictic used ostensively). kolma'ẽ o chale kaa'rãã mãã'rãã xyaa'maẽ'. *Children, just the ones who go thus unsteadily.* [*Syn.* xo.]

o'[2] *i.* **<e>** O (vocative).

o[3]**, o'** *pa.* **<na; ta>** please (courteous, polite particle sentence final on requests). dxe'rom ro'lle o'. *Let's sleep now please.* [*Syn.* xai.]

o'baano *a.* **<obaano>** dry (of ground); unirrigated (field).

-oḍa *s.num.* **<oṭaa>** nonpersonal (suffix on loan numeral). baaroḍa lxo nxõri. *Within the twelve years.*

oḍaa'l xyaaba' *v.* **<poila jaanu>** to elope.

ogaldiba' *v.* **<okaalnu>** to vomit.

o'gyãã *n.* **<siũdo>** part in hair.

oilidi'ba, oilidiba' *v.* **<oilaaunu>** to wither; fade (of plants).

okhaldiba' *v.* **<chaadnu>** to spill; flood ink (of faulty pen).

o'lãã *n.* **<bharkhar janmeko baalakh>** infant; baby (up to a few months).

olcae *n.* **<candan>** flora - a timber occurring in both red and white varieties.

oleba'
1. *v.t.* **<calaaunu>** to stir. kaẽ oleba'. *Stirring the rice.*
2. *v.i.* **<calmalaaunu>** to wriggle; stir; move. axo'led, aala'kkale ṭid. *Don't move, sit still.*
3. *v.i.* **<laḍi baḍi khelnu>** to roll over.

olgyaa' *a.* **<raato>** red.

o'lmẽ *n.* **<kilkile; ligalige>** uvula.

oraa'lu *loc.* **<oraalo>** down. [*Syn.* kyu'ru; ka'ẽḍu.]

orgõ' *n.* **<ghããṭī>** throat (rarer than mlõ'gu).

osõ' [*T* sŋa 'before' *p.* 141] *t.* **<aghi>** previously; before (in time or space). [*Syn.* asõ'.]

o'ttiba *v.* **<otnu>** to shelter; cover oneself from rain. [*Syn.* kru'ba.]

oxo *e.* **<oho>** oh (expression of surprise).

P

pãcayat *see* **pancaayat** 'council'.

pãgale' *n.* rug used for sitting upon.

pãgyo' *see* **panyo'** 'ladle'.

pachaaḍi *loc.* **<pachaaḍi>** behind; backward.

pachaardiba' *v.* **<pachaarnu>** to knock down (in fighting).

pachid *n.* **<pachutaau>** regret; remorse. liũdi' pachid mxaẽm'. *Later (he) feels remorse.*

pachyauraa' *n.* **<tauliyaa>** towel.

paḍa[1] *n.* **<paaṭaa>** disc.

paḍa[2] *n.* <paaṭan> Patan - locality within Ghachok.

paḍgadiba' *v.i.* <paḍkanu> to explode.

padamcaalaa *n.* <padamcaal> a root from high grassland, eaten for fevers, smeared on body for aches and pains.

pa'daa pu'dule *av.* <ṭukura ṭukuraa> in small pieces. cidra puraano' tadu' biyãã cilii biri' pa'daa pu'dule phaam. *If matting gets old we break it into small pieces and burn it.*

pade' xyaaba' *v.* <khasihaalnu> to fall.

padyaani' *n.* scrubby area on mountain slopes with cyõ'ḍi, dhurse. [*Syn.* dxusaa'.]

pa'di *n.* <kunai strīko naam> name of girl.

padi' *n.* <naaiṭo> navel.

padi *n.* <paathī> a brass vessel measuring eight manas (of grains); measure of volume (approx. one gallon = 4.5 litre, one-twentieth of mxuri). [*Syn.* pyo'no.]

padkhu' *a.* <ghopṭo> inverted; prone.

padlu', padulu, paadulu' *a.* <paatalo> thin (of cloth, paper); fine; slender; weak. [*Syn.* pobaa' axbxõba'.]

paẽbaa' *v.* <phĩjaaunu> to scatter; separate (paper); spread out.

paẽma'ẽ *n.* <soraa jaat> castes - lower group of "sixteen" in Gurung society.

pae[1] [*TaGTh* *paay] *n.* <ūn> wool.

pae[2] *n.* <argũ> post-funeral ceremony (to conduct a departed spirit to the resting place of the dead).

pa'e[3] *see* **pwe'** 'iron'.

pagḍadiba' *v.* <pakranu> to arrest; to seize. [*Syn.* kxaaba.]

paĩgima'ẽ *n.* clan - one of the upper four Gurung castes. [*Cp.* konma'ẽ; plxonmaẽ.]

paidala' *n.* <paitalaa> sole of foot.

paigũ' *n.* <ḍhĩḍo> mash (of corn or millet flour). [*Syn.* prokhu'.]

paile' *av.* <pahilo> first; at first; once upon a time.

paisaa' *n.* <paisaa> money; pice - one hundredth part of rupee.

pa'jyãã pa'jyããle *av.* thoroughly(?). txĩĩ' txĩmĩ kyu'waadxũr' kaamlo' pa'jyãã pa'jyããle nxel' txum. *(You) have to knead the blanket thoroughly all day long at the water source.*

pajyu' *see* **pujyu'** 'shaman'.

pakh mrõ' *n.* <paakhaa baarī> terraced field (dry). [*Syn.* baari; khore'.]

pakha'r *av.* <paakhaamaa> spilling; splashing of liquid out of a receptacle. [*Syn.* ŋxeba'.]

pakhaa' *n.* <paakho> uncultivated hillside. [*Cp.* gxaari'.]

pakkaa'[1] *a.* <pakkaa (awašya)> certainly. ŋa pakkaa' kham. *I will certainly come.*

pakkaa'[2] *a.* <pakkaa (raamro)> first rate; genuine; strong. [*Ant.* kacca'.]

palãã' *n.* <ãĩselu> berry - yellow, raspberry-like. [*Syn.* cuduru'.]

palḍa'na *n.* <palṭan> regiment; unit (army).

paldũ *n.* <patlun> trousers (long).

pali'diba *v.* <palaaunu> to sprout; to bud.

[*Syn.* mlxoba'; pxuba.]

pa'llaa pa'li *av.* <**jurukkai**> suddenly; hurriedly; instantly. cyẽ ro'rinabile pa'lla pa'lile rii. *Even though Youngest-brother was asleep he got up instantly.*

palo' palle' *av.* <**paalai paalo**> in turns; one by one.

palṭidiba' *v.t.* <**palṭaaunu**> to turn over; to overturn. [*Syn.* oleba'.]

palu' *n.* <**paalo**> time; turn (one in a number). baajyue' palo'ri chaabaa' mulaa. *In the time of (our) grandfather it was like that.*

panaati *n.* <**panaati**> great-grandson (or great-great-grandson in some opinion).

panaatini *n.* <**panaatīn**> great-granddaughter (or great-great-granddaughter in some opinion).

pancaayat, pancaaid, panjyaida' *n.* <**pancaayat**> council - at village, district, or national level.

panḍidma'ẽ *n.* <**panḍit**> pundit (religious scholar).

pani *p.* <**pani**> even. to' dile pani'. *Whatever happens.* [*Syn.* ya.]

panyaalu' *n.* <**panyaalo**> liquid (esp. of thin or weak liquids). [*Syn.* kyu'gyu.]

panyo', pãgyo' *n.* <**panyu**> ladle (flat, round, about 30 cm. long, for serving out rice).

parameśwar *see* **pramīsara** 'God'.

paraa' *n.* <**jahaan; pariwaar**> housewife; household members.

paraala *see* **praalaa** 'straw'.

parda *n.* <**pardaa**> curtain.

pardiba' *v.* <**parnu**> to have to; to become.

pareḍa' *n.* <**kawaaj**> parade drill (military).

parloga' *n.* <**parlog**> Hades (the place or stage following death). [*Syn.* mxi plxamae nãã'sa.]

paru' *n.* <**ṭhekī**> pail (wooden) for storing milk and buttermilk; bucket (of bamboo).

parwaa'[1] *n.* <**pariwaar**> family (wife and children). [*Syn.* paraa'.]

parwaa'[2] *n.* <**parewaa; kaalij**> pigeon (domestic); pheasant.

paryaali' *n.* <**pareli (kaam misaaunu)**> agreement to use another's oxen, having none of own.

pa'saa pa'sai *n.* <**jhismise ujyaalo (bihaanako)**> morning (first light).

pasbana' *n.* <**galebanda**> scarf. [*Syn.* bakhu; kuldu.]

pastugaa' *see* **pustagaa'** 'book'.

paṭṭi'[1] *n.* <**paṭṭī**> bandage.

paṭṭi'[2] *p.*
1. <**tira**> towards; in the direction of. te' jxaaĩpaṭṭi' xyaad. *Go a little that way.*
2. <**paṭṭi**> around; in the area of. telaa' pukhru' paṭṭi' nãã' lxe' yu'i. *Yesterday it rained a lot in Pokhara area.*

patkhu' *a.* <**ghopṭo**> prostrate; lying flat upon the face.

pattu' *n.* <**kurilo**> asparagus-like vegetable.

pauḍara' *a.* <**dhulo (pauḍar)**> powdered. pauḍa'ra ŋxe. *Powdered milk.*

pawitra *a.* <**pawitra**> undefiled; holy.

pãã'ba *v.* <**bhijnu**> to get wet; to be soaked.

pããbaa' *v.* <**bããḍnu**> to distribute; to share out food; to deal out cards.

paa' *n.* <**raksī**> spirits; wine.

paa' kwaalaaba' *v.* <**raksī paarnu**> to distil spirits.

paadru' *n.* <**paatro**> book of astrological information for a certain period giving auspicious days.

paadulu' *see* **padlu'**.

paaeba cilĩ *n.* pipe for hookah.

paai bẽn *n.* pipe band.

paakhru' *n.* <**paakhuro**> arm.

paa'ko *n.* <**jããḍyaahaa**> drunkard; wine-bibber (disrespectful term).

paaldu' *n.* <**boksīlaaī dine bhog**> rite (initial) to neutralise witch's curse.
paaldu' waai axsxayãã' dobaaḍe waadu'. *If (he) doesn't get better after throwing out the first rite, throw out the second rite.*
[*Cp.* dobaaḍe waabaa'; ŋxẽ sẽ'ba.]

paale' *n.* <**sipaahī, paale, caokī**> soldier; guard.

paali' *n.* <**paalī**> roof covering verandah or sleep-out.

paan *n.* <**paan**> betel leaf (eaten with aceca nut).

paanasaa' *n.* <**ṭewaa**> lamp stand for oil wick lamp.

paanaa' *see* **pe'na** 'page'.

paap *n.* <**paap**> sin; defilement.

paa'r *n.* <**paacuke**> divorce.

paa'r labaa' *v.* <**wiwaaha wicched garnu**> to divorce.

paa'raa *n.* <**taraaju**> scales; balances.

paardiba' *v.* <**paarnu**> to have to.
[*Syn.* pardiba, txuba.]

paa's *n.* <**paas**> pass; graduation.
paa's labaa'. *To pass, to qualify.*

paasaagi' *n.* <**saag**> spinach.

paaṭi' *n.* <**paaṭī**> party; group.
[*Syn.* ṭoli.]

paau *n.* <**paau**> foot (of human).
kxie paauri ŋa sewaa lamũ. *I will bow at your feet.*
[*Syn.* pxali.]

pẽ'[1] *n.* <**dhaanko bhus**> chaff of rice; withered ear.

pẽ[2] [*TaGTh* *peŋ] *n.* <**paahaa**> frog - 8 cm., black with white underneath, edible, lives in streams.
[*Syn.* ṭuḍī.]

pẽdo' *n.* <**balẽsi thaam**> stake (forked) which supports eaves of the cattle shed.

pebaa' *v.* <**kapaal baaṭnu**> to plait hair.

pe'da *n.* <**jhaaral**> elk - species of; tahr of Himalayas.
[*Syn.* pho; e.]

pedaalaa' *n.* <**pittal**> brass.

pe'na, paanaa' *n.* <**paanaa**> page.

penḍo' *n.* water frog (reddish in colour, about 3 cm.).

pensal *n.* chalk for blackboard.

perbaa' *v.* <**baaṭnu**> to make thread from fibre.
[*Syn.* dunidiba.]

peški' *n.* <**peškī; bainaa**> advance on salary.

peṭṭi'ko'ḍa *n.* <**peṭikoṭ**> petticoat worn under sari.

pha [*TaGTh* *pha; *TB* *wa=*(p)wa 100] *n.* <**logne**> husband (less respectful term).
[*Cp.* pyũ'.]

pha mxaeba *v.* <**logne khojnu**> to be on heat (of animals, *lit.* husband seeking).

phadi *n.* <**ḍhuŋgro**> blow pipe for

blowing the fire into flame.

pha'di xyaaba' *v.* <ṭuṭnu; phuṭnu> to burst; to crack open (of egg).
phũ' khin pha'di xyaai'. *The egg burst by itself.*

phaebaa' *v.t.* <phukaaunu> to open out (box, parcel).

phaesũ *n.* <culho> kitchen cupboard where clean dishes are placed.

pha'gi *n.* <paṭukaa> cummerbund (about 4 m. long) wound round and round women's waists.

phailidiba' *v.* <phailanu> to spread (of news).

phai'rĩba *v.* <haannu (ḍhuŋgole)> to stone (something or someone).

pha'kkarna' *see* phaa'karna' 'without cause'.

pha'l phu'la *n.* <phal phul> fruit.

phalana' *a.* <phalaano> someone; something; a certain.

phali *n.* <phaalī> plough share (metal).

phalṭu' *a.* <phaalṭu> spare; extra; other.

phar *n.* <phaaro> economising.

phar xyaaba' *v.* <poilaa jaanu> to desert one's husband; run away with another man. [*Cp.* oḍaa'l xyaaba'.]

pha'rak *a.* <pharak> different. [*Syn.* syo'bana.]

pharbu *n.* <ghoco> stake.

phargu *n.* <laṭṭhī> club; stick. [*Syn.* prxe.]

phariyaa' *n.* <phariyaa, saarī> sari.

phasidiba' *v.* <phasaaunu> to entrap. [*Syn.* bxuldi'ba.]

phaṭyããuru' *n.* <phaṭyaaŋgro> grasshopper.

phau raa'ba *v.* <phokaa uṭhnu> to blister.

phaabaa' *v.* <baalnu> to burn (wood as cooking, heating fuel). [*Syn.* khrõbaa'; mrobaa'; jalidiba.]

phaadẽ' *n.* <maĩlī phupū> aunt (Fa2dSi).

phaaga'ẽ, phaanẽ' *n.* <jeṭhī phupū> aunt (FaEtSi). [*Syn.* phubu'.]

phaa'karna', pha'kkarna, phaa'karnaa' *av.* <phaakkaimaa> without cause; just because; unmotivated; unprovoked. [*Syn.* chalen.]

phaanẽ' *see* phaaga'ẽ 'aunt'.

phaasu' *n.* <dhotī> loin cloth; jock strap.

phaawẽ' *n.* <phaalguṇ> month (11th of Nepali calendar, mid-February to mid-March).

phe'ba *v.* <khaanu (makai)> to eat (roast grains, etc.) by tossing into mouth.

phebaa'[1] *v.* <pugnu> to arrive.

phebaa'[2] *v.* <mol parnu> to cost.

phebaa'[3] *v.* <saahinu parne> to be related by kin.

pherdiba' *v.* <phernu> to change; to alter.

phe'ri *c.* <pheri> again; then. [*Syn.* jxaale'.]

phero' *n.* <phero> circumference.

phi[1] [*Cp* pesq, pɨs] *n.* <paad> body gas; flatus.

phi[2] [*TaGTh* *phii] *v.* <bokro> peel of fruit or vegetable; bark.

phibaa' *v.* <janmanu> to be born; to bear a child.

phibi *a.* <maathi maathi> above; overhead.

phikkar *n.* **<phikri>** care; worry; anxiety.
phikkar axmxããdid. *Don't worry.*
[*Syn.* sok; aaphsos.]

phi'l labaa' *v.* **<phel garnu; calaan tyaagnu>** to change one's ways; to forsake.
[*Syn.* pi'ba.]

phi'r phi'ri *n.* toy (stick with propeller of bamboo shoots attached, made in late November).

phirdaa' *a.* **<phirtaa>** returned; back.

phiri' *p.* **<maathi>** upon; above; over; on.

phlebaa' *v.* **<birsinu (baaṭo)>** to lose one's way; to be lost.
sũ phlebaa'. *To make a slip of the tongue.*

pho'[1] [*TaGTh* *phoq] *n.* **<peṭ>** stomach.

pho[2] *n.* **<mri+ga>** deer.

pho' khrẽbaa' *v.* **<bhok laagnu>** to be hungry.

pho lxo *n.* **<mri+ga barkha>** year of the deer (1947,59,etc.).

pho'bõ [*TB* *ba:k 'bat' 325] *n.* **<camero>** bat.

phogo, phau *n.* **<phokaa>** blister.

pho'ja *n.* **<phauj>** army.

phojyõ *n.* **<kaanchī phupū>** aunt (FaYtSi).

phordiba' *v.* **<phoḍnu>** to break open, apart; to cleave; to smash.

phori' *a.* **<phohorī>** obscene; coarse.

phoṭo' *n.* **<naksaa; phoṭo>** picture; photograph.
[*Syn.* tasbir; na'ksa.]

phram tãã *n.* **<khabar haawaa kuro>** rumour; report getting back of words spoken behind one's back.

phrẽ *a.* **<ṭhiṭo; jawaan>** young but full-grown; prime - physically (usually of men, but also of animals).

phrẽsī' *n.* **<ṭhiṭo>** young man - 16-30 years old.

phribaa' *v.* **<chuṭṭinu>** to separate.
[*Syn.* chuḍidiba'.]

phũ'[1] *n.* **<phul>** egg.

phũ[2] *n.*
1. **<geḍaa>** kernels of corn, etc.
[*Syn.* ru'ḍu.]
2. **<kesraa>** segments of fruit (of orange, etc.).
3. **<cokṭaa>** chunk of meat, potato.
4. **<golī>** pill, tablet.

mi phũ. *Coals of fire.*

phu' *n.* **<aago phukne šabda>** pursed lips for blowing up fire.

phu'ba *v.* **<lagaaunu (auṣadhi)>** to apply medicine.

phubaa' *v.* **<bhatkanu>** to collapse (of house or building).

phubu' *n.* **<phupū>** aunt (FaSi).
[*Syn.* phaaga'ẽ, phaadẽ', phojyõ.]

phu'i chu *n.* **<bandhana>** ties; bonds.
[*Syn.* kaeda'.]

phu'iba *v.* **<bããdhnu>** to bind with rope; to swear (an oath).

phuibaa' *v.* **<phuknu>** to blow (a fire into life).

phula *n.* **<buṭṭaa>** embroidery; braid; filigree.

phulḍinaa' *n.* **<kalam>** fountain pen.

phuldiba' *v.* **<phulnu>** to expand; swell; rise (of dough).

phuli' *n.* **<phuli>** ring worn in nose.

phumaali' *n.* **<kamero>** lime; clay - white, used for whitewash.

phurji' [*N* 'note, slip of paper'] *n.* <purjī> permit (as for cutting timber).

phursada' *n.* <phursaat> leisure; spare time.

phutru'kka *a.* <paakeko (besarī)> cooked - very well.

phyo'ba *v.* <baḍhaarnu (kaser)> to sweep up.

phyobaa' *v.* <ḍhoknu> to bow down in respectful greeting.

phyurbaa' *v.* <battaaunu (dhaan)> to winnow rice from above the head, in the wind.

pĩbaa' [*TaGTh* *pim; *TB* *biy=*bəy 427] *v.* <dinu> to give.

pĩḍi *n.* <pĩḍhi> porch; verandah (onto which lower caste people are given entrance).

pĩgyaa *a.* <hariyo> green.

pĩ'na *n.* <šephṭī pin> pin (safety).

pi'ba
1. *v.t.* <choḍaaunu> to shell husks off corn; strip off.
2. *v.i.* <choḍnu> abandon; to stop doing or attending; to give up; to forsake; to release.
aabae' ilam pi'waai. *(He) left (his) father's profession.*

pibaa'[1] *v.* <šarmaaunu> to be shy; embarrassed.

pibaa'[2] *v.* <tirkhaaunu> to be thirsty.
kxilai kyu' pilase'. *You are probably thirsty.*

pi'bi[1] *n.* snake with poor eyesight and painful bite.
[*Syn.* ããdi' pxuri.]

pibi'[2] [*N* 'pus'] *n.* <pīp> froth.

pibxĩba' *v.* <paṭhaaunu (saamaana)> to send (a thing, letter).
[*Cp.* kulbxĩba'.]

picaas *n.* <picaas> spirit; ghost.

pidãã *n.* <phohori šabda> obscenity; coarseness of speech.
[*Syn.* phori'.]

pincis [*E* pincers] *n.* wrench (adjustable); shifter; spanner (shifting).

pir *n.* <pīr> anguish.
[*Syn.* šo'k; phikkar; du.]

pir mubaa' *v.* <pīr hunu> to be sad.

pi'rba[1] *v.* <cepnu> to hold tobacco in cheek.

pi'rba[2] *v.* <paraali (gorūko bhaaḍaa)> to hire oxen and plough, paying with a portion of the crop.
tidĩma ŋa kxine baalu pi'rmu. *This year I want to hire your oxen.*

pi'rba[3] *a.* <ṭããsinu> adjacent; touching.
[*Syn.* xrẽba.]

pirbaa'[1] *v.* <kicnu> to crush; jam (finger in door).

pirbaa'[2] *v.* <soj garī raakhnu> to set aside for later use.
se pirthẽdu' biyãã prxẽmaẽ khamale' ker txum. *If (you) set aside some meat it will be useful if guests come.*

piru *a.* <terso> horizontal; parallel.
dxe'ro piru. *From now on.*

piyããnaa' *n.* <paanīko nikaas> gulley.

piyaaro' *a.* <pyaaro> beloved; cherished; doted on (of a child, with consequent spoiling).
piyaaro' lasero' baani nxõ xyaam'. *Since (they) have doted on (him) (his) character will be spoilt.*

pla'ba *v.* <phukaalnu> untie (shoelaces); loosen (a screw).

plããbaa' *v.* <piṭnu> to hit; to beat.

plaagẽ' *n.* <roṭī> unleavened bread.
[*Cp.* kxẽ.]

plẽ [*TB* *pleŋ 'flat surface' 138] *a.* **<cepṭo; caṭṭaan>** flat; smooth.

plẽbaa' [*TB* *bliŋ∿*pliŋ 142] *v.* **<bharnu>** to be full up.

plenẽ *n.* **<cepṭo; caṭṭaan>** slab (with parallel sides); board.

ple'waabxĩba' *v.* **<huttyaaunu>** to throw down. [*Syn.* bxyõba'.]

plibaa'[1] *v.t.* **<phukaalnu (lugaa)>** to take off (clothes); to strip (leaves off plant).

plibaa'[2] *v.* **<kulchanu>** to tread upon.
mi pliwaa, axpli'd. *(You'll) tread on the fire! Don't tread!*

plo *n.*
1. **<paitaalo>** sole of foot.
2. **<haatkelaa>** palm of hand.

plu'ba [*TB* *pryo 'boil' 250] *v.* **<usinnu>** to steam; stew; simmer; boil.

plxa [*TB* *(m-)hla 475] *n.* **<saato>** soul; senses.
mxi plxamae nãã'sa. *Place of departed spirits (lit. village of men's souls).*
[*Cp.* saẽ, aadmaa'.]

plxa lõba' *v.* **<tarsanu>** to scare; to frighten.

plxari *p.* **<kannaa pachaaḍi>** behind one's back.
ca'e plxari doṣ lagaidim. *Blames him behind his back.*
[*Ant.* ũĩri'.]

plxaaba *a.* **<caaklo>** wide; broad.
cyugu' plxaaba. *Narrow.*

plxi'[1] [*TaGTh* *bliq; *TB* *b-liy= *b-ləy 410] *n.* **<caar>** four.

plxi[2] *n.* **<cauḍaai>** width; breadth.
[*Cp.* kru 'height, length'.]

plxi kru kxriba *a.* **<lambaai cauḍaai milnu>** well-proportioned; right size.

plxoba' *a.* **<dhani>** rich; prosperous.

plxonmaẽ *n.* **<laamichaane>** clan of the four upper clans in Gurung society.
[*Cp.* konma'ẽ; paĩgima'ẽ.]

plxu' *n.* **<biũ>** seed.

põ'ba [*TB* *br(w)ak∿*(s-)br(w)aŋ p. 42] *v.* **<bolnu>** to speak; to talk.
[*Syn.* bibaa.]

põ'bae gxyãã' *n.* **<bolne baaṭo>** right to speak.

põ'sũ *n.* **<bol caal>** conversation.

po' gxyãã' *n.* **<goreṭo baaṭo>** byway; minor road.
[*Ant.* mu'l gxyãã'.]

pobaa' *a.* **<paatalo>** thin (of cloth, paper); weak.
[*Syn.* padlu'; axbxõba'.]

pochyora' *n.* **<pachyauraa>** towel; head covering; shawl.

polo *see* **pulu** 'nettle'.

pošaka' *n.* **<pošaak>** dress - form of; garment.

pra *see* **prxa'** 'hundred'.

pra lxo *n.* **<bããdar warṣa>** year of the monkey (in Tibetan 12-year cycle, 1944,56,68,80).
[*Syn.* yogaara lxo.]

pra'ba [*TB* *pe:r 340] *a.* **<masino>** thin; fine (as of knitting needles).

pracaar labaa' *v.* **<pracaar garnu>** to preach; broadcast publicly.

pramaa *n.* **<marca>** yeast used in making beer.

pramĩsara *n.* **<parameśwar>** God; sky gods - sun and moon (regarded as remote, not requiring animal sacrifice or other offerings); supreme God.
[*Cp.* bxagawaan; deudaa.]

praa'baa[1] *v.* **<bhããcnu>** to break branches of trees.

praa'baa[2] *v.* **<chyaapnu>** to

splash; to sprinkle (as in ritual cleansing).
aargo' jaad chuina' bile chiḍ axpxraa'. *Even if (he) touches another caste (he) doesn't sprinkle water.*

praalaa, paraala *n.* **<paraal>** straw (of rice); hay (of rice harvest).

praarthana' *n.* **<praarthanaa>** prayer.

prẽ *n.* **<bharyaaŋ>** ladder for collecting honey from cliff ledge hives.

prẽ'ba *v.* to demand what has been given to another (esp. of children).

prẽbaa' *v.* **<kelaaunu>** to separate wool, fluffing it with bow after washing process.

pre *see* **prxe'** 'eight'.

pre'ba *v.* **<laagnu ghaam>** to shine (of sun).

prebaa' *v.* **<chuṭyaaunu>** to cause to separate (e.g. quarters of an orange).

prĩ'ba[1] *v.* **<haannu>** to throw (a brick); fire (a rifle); smite (with fist).

prĩ'ba[2] *v.* **<gaaunu>** to sing a song.

priba' *v.* **<baarnu (gaaũ)>** to forbid.

pri'pri *a.* **<baraabar>** equally; alike.

prithwi' *n.* **<pri+thwī>** earth; world.

prõmaẽ *n.* **<pun>** Pun (an ethnic group of Nepal, often regarded as a subgroup of Magars).

pro' *n.* shawl - worn sash-like by mature women.

progyaa *n.*
1. **<ṭhimaahaa>** bastard; illegitimate child.
   progyaa no'ba. *To be pregnant out of wedlock.*
2. **<swaasnīko pahilo wiwahaako choraa-chorī>** stepchild (of a man); child of a woman's previous marriage.

prokhu' *n.* **<phããḍo>** mash - thin (made of flour and water and fed to animals. Formerly drunk by humans with ghee. *Lit.* flour soup); gruel.

promĩ' yogaaraa *n.* **<kaalo bããdar>** baboon.

prũ' prũ' labaa' *v.* to flicker (as of snake's tongue).

pru' [*TaGTh* *prooq 'lunch'] *n.* **<khaajaa>** snack (esp. early morning).

prubaa' *v.* **<chaannu (paakeko kodo)>** to pluck ripe grains only.

prumu' *n.* **<ṭimur>** tree - kind of.

prxa', pra, bra [*TB* *r-gya 164; *T* kah] *n.* **<ek say>** hundred.

prxaba' [*TaGTh* *braq] *v.* **<hĩḍnu>** to walk; to associate with.
aague mrĩne prxaba'. *To consort with another man's wife.*

prxẽ *n.* **<paahunaa>** guest.

prxe'[1]**, pre** [*TaGTh* *bret; *TB* *b-r-gyat=*(b)g-ryat 163] *n.* **<aaṭh>** eight.
[*Syn.* aa'ṭh.]

prxe[2] *n.* **<laṭṭhī>** stick; walking stick; staff.

prxeba *v.* **<bhaĩsī maathi rããgo caḍnu>** to have sexual intercourse (of animals).
[*Syn.* mrĩ laba'; gaĩdiba.]

prxejyu' *n.* **<assī>** eighty.

prxiba'[1] *v.* **<pĩdhnu>** to grind in mortar and pestle.

prxiba[2] [*TaGTh* *bri] *v.* **<lekhnu>** to write.

prxiri *loc.*
1. **<taltira>** downhill.
2. **<muni>** below.

prxiũba' *a.* **<talako>** lower.

prxõ *n.* **<goṭh>** shed (temporary shelter) for cattle.

prxo'[1] *n.* **<bhir>** cliff.

prxo'[2] [*TaGTh* *braaq] *n.* **<piṭho>** flour.

prxoba *v.* **<pĩdhnu (jããtole)>** to grind (grains with a handmill).

prxõsaẽ *n.* **<goṭhaalo>** herdsman.

prxu kxywi' *n.* **<nepaalī bhaaṣaa>** Nepali language.

prxuba' *v.* **<cuṭnu>** to beat sheaves on ground for threshing; to thrash.

prxumaẽ *n.* **<baahunharū>** Brahmins.

pũji' *n.* **<dhansampatti, pũ̄jī>** wealth; capital. [*Syn.* nxor.]

pu[1] *n.* **<haat khuṭṭaako maathillo bhaag>** back of hand or foot.

pu[2] *n.* **<raksi thaapne bhããḍo>** vessel collecting wine in still.

pu'[3] *n.* **<makai - bhuṭeko>** corn - roasted, popped.

pu' ṭxa' dxũ' *n.* **<gurããsko buṭ>** rhododendron (national flower of Nepal).

pucu'[1], **bucu'** *n.* **<taalu>** crown of head.

pucu[2] *see* **pujyu'** 'witchdoctor'.

puḍe *n.* **<culetra>** type of tree.

puḍke *n.* **<puḍko>** short person; dwarf.

pu'du pũdule *av.* **<kuḍko masino>** breaking up into small pieces.

puduba' *v.t.* **<ṭukraa garnu; bhããcnu>** to break (into small pieces, of unleavened bread).

pujaa' *n.* **<pūjaa>** sacrificial rites (generally intended to appease spirits).

pujaare' *n.* **<pūjaarī>** priest of Hindu rites.

pujdiba' *v.* **<pūjaa garnu>** to offer sacrifice to.

puju' *n.* **<kããḍho>** thorn.

pujyu', pajyu' *n.* **<jhããkri (panḍit)>** shaman - who divines supernatural causes of illness. [*Cp.* jaisi; la'ma; pujaare'.]

pukhru' *n.* **<pokharaa>** Pokhara (major market town of central Nepal, 200 km. west of Kathmandu).

pu'la *n.* **<pul>** bridge (permanent). [*Cp.* cãã.]

pulisaa', pulis *n.* **<pulis>** police.

pulu'[1] *n.* **<ṭopī>** hat (Ghandruk dialect). [*Syn.* kule'.]

pulu[2] *n.* **<sisnu>** nettle.

pu'ma *n.* **<hiũd>** cold season (November to February). [*Ant.* uma.]

pumsyo *n.* **<boksī>** witch (a living person who works malice against fellow villagers, either personally or by raising up certain evil forces to do her bidding).

puni' *n.* **<saanu jaat>** lower caste people.

puraa[1] *n.* **<ghaau>** sore.

puraa'[2] *n.* **<puraa>** leavings of a meal.

puraa'[3] *a.* **<pūraa>** whole; total; complete.

pu'rba *loc.* **<pūrwa>** east.

purne' *n.* **<pūrṇimaa>** full moon.

pu'ṣ *n.* **<pauṣ>** month (8th of Nepali calendar, mid-December to mid-January).

pustagaa', pastugaa' *n.* **<pustak; kitaab>** book. [*Syn.* kidaaba'.]

pustaa' *n.* **<pustaa; pīḍhī>** generation (future, not preceding).

pwe', pa'e *n.* **<phalaam>** iron.

pwe'e pharbu *n.* <gal> crowbar. [*Syn.* jxyaampa'l.]

pwi' [*TB* *pwa:y 170] *n.* <bhūs> chaff from husking grains.

pwibaa' *v.* <boknu (baalakha)> to carry child on one's back.

pwiga'ẽ *n.* <caalno> sieve - cane (for winnowing grains).

pxadẽ *see* badẽ 'towards'.

pxadgu *n.* <khasre bhyaaguto> toad.

pxaẽ *n.* <biṭo> bundle of rattan carried as a load. [*Syn.* -baẽ.]

pxaẽba *v.* <dhaak lagaaunu> to be boastful; proud; vain.

pxaẽdo *n.* <kum> shoulder (away from neck). [*Cp.* kããdaa'.]

pxaẽdo pada' *n.* <paato> shoulder blade.

pxagi dxũ' *n.* <kaṭusko boṭ> chestnut tree.

pxal tho'ba *n.* <halant> sign in Devanagari script indicating that no vowel sound follows a consonant (*lit.* foot cutting); halant.

pxalã pxulũ *n.* <kīraaharū> insects.

pxalẽ *n.* <bhala> rivulet; trickle (non-perennial).

pxali [*TaGTh* *bale] *n.* <khuṭṭaa> foot; leg.

pxali ḍããḍa *n.* <nali haaḍ> shin. [*Syn.* nali'.]

pxali ka'blo *n.* <golī gããṭho> ankle.

pxanã liũd *t.* <bholi parsī> later (beyond the immediate future).

pxanxãga *t.* <bholi> tomorrow.

pxanxãgdũ' *t.* <bholi palṭa> following day; next day.

pxanxãlii *t.* <pachi> later (in a few days time).

pxanxãri' *t.* <bholi bihaana> tomorrow morning.

pxasi *n.* <baalakh> infant.

pxasi waabaa' *v.* <tuhaaunu, tuhunu (garbha)> to abort a pregnancy.

pxasxyaa pxasi *n.* <baalak-baalika (choraachorī)> children. [*Syn.* koloma'ẽ.]

pxãã *n.* <sããpro> thigh.

pxaaba' *v.* <gaaḍnu> to bury a person.

pxaagõ *n.* <agenuko tallo bhaag> seating area adjacent to fireplace at the narrow end.

pxaariba *v.* <phulnu> to open out (of flowers); to swell up (of popped corn).

pxẽba *v.* <khosnu> to seize; to snatch away; to grab. cakaleṭ gxri' muyãã' koloma'ẽ pxẽm. *If there is one chocolate the children will snatch (at it).*

pxelaa *n.* <kacauraa> bowl - brass, 10 cm. diam., for cooked vegetables or soup or meat.

pxi *n.* <ḍoko> basket - large, conical, open-weaved for carrying things on back (50 to 100 cm. high). [*Syn.* kurku'; korbyo'; jxarãã'go; swī'di.]

pxiriba [*TB* *pur∿*pir 398; *TB* *byer n. 249, n. 460] *v.* <uḍnu> to fly (of bird, plane).

pxõba *v.* <baajhnu> to abuse; to argue; to quarrel; scold.

pxo [*TaGTh* *baa; *TB* *pak=*pwak 40] *n.* <paat> leaf. [*Syn.* la.]

pxoba' [*TB* *pur 'cover, wrap' 385] *v.* <oḍhnu> to cover oneself with; to wrap oneself with blanket; hold covering over oneself.

pxuba^{1} *v.* <phaṭkaaunu (ūn)> to card wool, usually with bow. [*Syn.* kha'eba.]

pxuba^{2} *v.* <palaaunu> to shoot (of a tree stump, or a cutting). [*Syn.* pali'diba.]

pxulũ *n.* <kīraa> insect (general term including maggots, caterpillars and grubs).

pxuri [*TB* *b-ru:l 447; *TB* *buw= *bəw 27] *n.* <saap, sããp> snake.

pxuri lxo *n.* <sããp warṣa> year of the snake (1941,53,65,77,89). [*Syn.* sabri' lxo.]

pxweba' *v.* <aaljo garnu> to occupy; to engage; to render unavailable.
kxilaai khubi' pxwei' biri' praala thẽl axkhãã'. *Since the storeroom is engaged for you (they) can't put the hay (there).*

pxyaa [*TaGTh* *byab] *n.* <pwããkh> feather; wing.

pxyaagõ *n.* <pakheṭo> wing (less common than pxyaa).

pxyo [*TaGTh* *byo; *Cp* pahq 'bamboo pot'] *n.* <maandro> mat - bamboo, finely woven, 1.5 by 2.5 m. (used mostly for sun drying grains). [*Cp.* gundri; bxagaa'ri; cidra; cauḍĩ'.]

pxyũba [*TaGTh* *byuŋ] *v.* <khoknu> to cough.

pyaa'ba *v.* <hunu> to pertain to; to be attached to.
so' pyaa'bae sa'e. *Living things (lit. things having breath).*
durgala yo baaroḍa pyaa'm. *Durga has twelve arms.*

pyaa'ja *n.* <pyaaj> onion.

pyõ'ba *v.* <phããḍnu> to clear (trees).

pyõ'no *n.* <ek paathī> measure of volume (approx. one gallon = 4.5 litre, one-twentieth of mxuri). [*Syn.* -byõ, padi.]

pyũ' [*TB* *wa=*(p)wa 100] *n.* <logne> husband. [*Cp.* pha.]

pyũba' *v.* <nikaalnu; jhiknu; thutnu> to come loose; come off or out.

pyun *n.* <piūn> messenger (bearer of letter). [*Syn.* sipaai.]

R

-ra^{1} *p.* <maa> in; at.

ra^{2} [*TaGTh* *ra] *n.* <bakhra> goat.

ra ku'di, xraa ku'di *n.* <roṭe piŋ> ferris wheel used only at Dasera festival. [*Cp.* la'ĩ ku'di; ku'di.]

ra'bara' *a.* pliable; plastic.

ra'cche labaa' *v.* <rakšaa garnu> to protect.

ra'li rali labaa' *v.* <laḍī buḍī garnu> to roll over and over.

ra'nḍi *n.* <raṇḍī> prostitute.

ra'nḍi baaji *n.* <raṇḍīwaaja> whore monger; loose liver.

ranṭhi' *a.* <choṭo> short.

ra'ŋa *n.* <raŋ> colour; dye.

ra'sa *n.* <ras> juice of fruits.

ra'silo' *a.* <rasilo> juicy.

rasi *see* xrasi 'rope'.

rããgu' *n.* <rããgo> bull buffalo.

raa'ba [*TaGTh* *rap; *TB* *g-ryap 246] *v.* <ubhinu> to stand; to stand up.
gxodaa' raa'ba. *To attend funeral (or post-funeral).*

raa'da *n.* <raat> night (used mainly in conjunction with Nepali ordinals). [*Syn.* mxuĩsa.]

raa'j gaddi *n.* <raaj gaddī> throne.

raa'j labaa' *v.* <raaj garnu> to reign.

raa'je *n.* <raajya> kingdom.

raa'ji naa'm *n.* <raaji naamaa (mukta hunu)> transfer of land title permanently.
igurle' cũ'waaba'e khlxyolai raa'ji naa'mle cũ'waai bim. *Land sold irrevocably is said to be sold by permanent transfer.*

raa'mid, ra'mid *a.* <ramaailo> pleasant; enjoyable.
mxi lxe' khaa'gu tai biri' raa'mid lam. *When many people gather it is enjoyable.*

raajaa *n.* <raajaa> king.

raar *n.* <jhakkaḍa> persistent begging of a child.

rẽ [*TB* *r-gyap 'stand' 246] *n.* <caaŋ> stack (for wood).
sĩ' rẽ jxõba'. *Stacking wood.*

rẽbaa' *v.* <carnu> to graze.

re' *loc.* <aḍ, niraa> adjacent.
dxĩ' re'rbae baari. *The field adjacent to the house.*

rel gaaḍi *n.* <rel gaaḍī> train.

rĩ'[1] *n.* <bahinī; didī> sisters.

rĩ[2] [*TaGTh* *rin; *TB* *ri:m n. 301] *n.* <bããs> bamboo.

rĩ'maẽ *n.*
1. <didī-bahinīharū> sisters (man's, or woman's husband's).
2. <tarunīharū> women - young.

ri[1] [*Cp* brɨyh 'finger'] *n.* <aũlo> finger; toe.

-ri[2] *s.n.* <-maa> in; at.
[*Syn.* -ra.]

-ri[3] *s.v.* <-dai> continuative; softening negative imperative.
cariŋŋyũ'. *(I) am eating.*
axphorid. *Please don't put it on.*
[*Syn.* -ina, -sen.]

ribaa' *v.* <uṭhnu> to rise; to get up; stand up.

ri'li lili *av.* driftingly.
nxaamjyo ri'lilili xyaai'. *The clouds drifted along.*

ri'ti thiti' *n.* <rīti> religious rules; rites; regulations.

ri'tta *n.* <najikai> closeness; nearness.
ri'tta taxyaai'. *About to die.*
ri'ttale. *Very closely.*

rõ'ba *v.* <suninu> to swell (of flesh by insect bite); to rise (of dough).

rõ'-rõ pi'-pi labaa' *v.* <rogyaaunu; sataaunu> persecute; harass; torment.

ro[1] *pa.* <re> quoted speech marker.

ro[2] *n.* <mūsoko dulo> rat hole.

-ro[3] *s.num.* <raat> nights.
sõ'roba'e pae. *A three-night post-funeral.*

ro'ba[1] [*TaGTh* *raaq] *v.* <bunnu> to weave; to knit.

ro'ba[2] *v.* <sutnu> to lie down.

roḍaa' *n.* <rora> gravel; stones (small).

roebaa' *v.* <kotranu; luchnu (naŋale); kanyaaunu> to scratch (with nails, claws, thorns).

rol *n.* <rol> roll; list.

rũ [*TB* *pren 'boil' p. 143] *n.* <pilo> abscess.

rũ'ba[1] [*TB* *kyoŋ 'tend' 161] *v.* <paharaa dinu> to watch; to guard; to attend (house, grazing animals).

rũ'ba[2], **rũ'du** *a.* <baaklo> thick; stiff (of cloth, stone, timber).
[*Ant.* pobaa'.]

ru'[1] *n.* <dhaago> thread.

ru[2] [*TaGTh* *ru; *TB* *ruŋ=*rwaŋ 85; *TB* *kruw=*krəw 37] *n.* <sīŋ> horns (of cow, deer, etc.); antlers.

ru'b, rup *n.* **<rūp>** appearance (facial, physical). [*Syn.* mõdaa'; anuwaa'r.]

ru'ba *v.* **<phalnu>** to form fruit after flowering.

rubaa' *v.* **<sããghurinu>** to shrink (of cloth or of hole); to narrow (of badly woven mat).

ruḍiba' *v.* **<khaanaamaa du:kha paaunu>** to starve (of men and animals).

ru'ḍu *n.* **<geḍaa>** fruit - pieces of. [*Syn.* phũ.]

ruduba' *v.* **<gholnu; calaaunu; dhulo paarnu>** to stir (liquids).

ruĩbaa' *v.* **<ropnu>** to sow seedlings into prepared fields; to transplant seedlings.

ru'i *n.* **<baantaa>** vomitus.

ru'iba *v.* **<chaadnu; waman garnu>** to vomit.

ru'psai *n.* **<jholaa (sarkaarī)>** pack - army style, with shoulder straps.

Š

šãkaa' *n.* **<šãkaa>** doubt; suspicion.

šahaar *n.* **<šahar>** city.

šakti *n.* **<šakti>** power - spiritual (of gods or religious officiants).

šali' *n.* **<šaalī>** sister-in-law (WiYrSi).

šaturaa' *n.* **<šatru>** enemy. [*Syn.* dušman.]

šaasan *n.* **<šaasan>** law; custom (obsolete word used of Rana period).

šaastra *n.* **<šaastra>** scriptures of a religion.

šiba *n.* **<šiwa>** Shiva (Hindu deity).

šidaa'la *n.* **<šītal>** cool spot; shade.

šigaar khlyõbaa' *v.* **<šikaar khelnu>** to hunt. [*Syn.* pho lxaaba.]

šigaare' *n.* **<šikaarī>** hunter.

ši'lmandri *n.* **<širmundrī>** earrings - small, round, worn on rim of ear.

šilog *n.* **<šlok>** holy books.

ši'r *n.* **<šir>** head (of river or man).

šišaa *n.*
1. **<šīšaa (menṭalko)>** lens of spectacles; glass of pressure lantern.
2. **<šīšaa (bandūkmaa haalne)>** lead (metal).

šiši *n.* **<šišī>** bottle.

ši't *n.* **<šīt>** dew.

šok *n.* **<šok>** worry; anxiety. [*Syn.* pir; phikkar; du:kh.]

šripes *n.* **<šrīpec>** crown (of king).

šuru *n.* **<šuru>** beginning. [*Syn.* laa'udo.]

S

sãgaa'raa, saŋaa'raa *n.* **<sãghaar>** doorway; threshold (esp. bottom member).

sa[1] [*TaGTh* *sa; *T* sa] *n.* **<maaṭo>** soil; earth; floor; ground. sa xil waabaa'. *To finish transplanting rice (lit. leave earth and mud).*

sa[2] [*TB* *s-wa 437] *n.* **<dããt>** tooth.

sa ŋxe [*TB* *r-nil∿*r-ni(y)∿*s-nil 3] *n.* **<gijaa>** gum of teeth.

saba'pati *n.* **<sabhaapati>** chairman.

sabri' lxo *n.* **<sããp warṣa>** year of the snake (in Tibetan 12 year cycle, 1941,53,65,77,etc.). [*Syn.* pxuri lxo.]

sabxaa' *n.* **<sabhaa>** conference; council. [*Syn.* kajuri'.]

saccaa' *n.* **<sããco>** truth.

saccaa' põ'ba *v.* **<sããco bhannu, bolnu>** to tell the truth; to speak truthfully.

sa'ḍãbudã *a.* **<jata tatai charkinu>** dishevelled (thrown all about); scattered (accidentally or intentionally).

saḍaa' *n.* **<saaṭo (bããsako)>** poles of bamboo (used in building cattle sheds, and fences).

saḍu' *n.* **<saaṭo (garnu)>** exchange of goods; reward; return; revenge.

sa'da[1] *n.* **<satītwa>** faithfulness (of wife to husband).

sada'[2], sad *n.* **<saataa, haptaa>** week. [*Syn.* xapta'.]

sadar *n.* **<sadar>** approval; sanction. [*Syn.* sai'.]

sadasi', sadaase' *n.* **<sadasya>** councillor (of village, district or national government).

sa'dẽba' *v.* **<puryaaunu>** to lead; to escort.
banar sa'dẽkhadi. *(They) led (me) to the jungle.*

sadxaaran *a.* **<saadhaaran>** ordinary; plain (of dance). [*Syn.* saadaa'.]

saẽ [*TB* *sam=*səm 'breath, spirit' n. 171, n. 344] *n.* **<man; aatmaa>** mind; soul. [*Syn.* aadmaa'; plxa.]

saẽ bicaara' *n.* **<wicaar>** thought; opinion. [*Syn.* bicaara.]

saẽ bxõlle' ṭibaa' *v.* **<man naḍagḍagaaunu>** to be courageous.

saẽ bxuldi'ba *v.* **<man bhulaaunu>** to be diverted (as from grief).

saẽ cxibaa' *v.* **<jaannu; hoš paaunu>** to be conscious of the consequences of one's actions (as of a child being aware of danger).

saẽ jxõba' *v.* **<dhyaan dinu>** to be attentive.

saẽ krxiba *v.* **<man milnu>** to live harmoniously.

saẽ mrẽ'ba *v.* to be proud of someone, to be pleased.
ṭhaagu chyããba'e kxe' lasi ŋa'e saẽ mrẽ'ĩ. *Eldest son did good work and I am proud of him.*

saẽ na'ba *v.i.* **<du:kh laagnu; du:khi hunu; citta dukhnu>** to grieve; to sorrow; to be sad.

saẽ na'l labaa' *v.t.* **<citta dukhaaunu; du:kh dinu>** to offend; to grieve.

saẽ ŋxĩ' tabaa' *v.* **<dui man hunu>** to be of two minds; to be confused.

saẽ satte' tabaa' *a.* **<cokho man; satya man; imaandaar hunu>** honest; straight of character; faithful. [*Syn.* imaandaari.]

saẽ saaro' tabaa' *a.* **<nirdaya man>** hard hearted; uncompassionate.

saẽ sxaba' *v.* **<daanī>** to be generous; to be unselfish.

saẽ tõbaa' *v.* **<khuš laagnu>** to be happy.

saẽkablo' *n.* **<chaatīko haaḍ>** collar bone.

saẽma *n.* **<wipanaa>** wakefulness (in contrast with sleep).

saẽr mxaẽba' *v.* **<manmaa samjhanu>** to recollect; to discern.

saẽr mxaẽ' thẽbaa' *v.* **<samjhi raakhnu>** to learn by rote.

sa'e[1] *n.* **<cij>** thing.

sa'e[2] *n.* **<mol>** price; cost.

sa'e nxora *n.* <dhan sampatti> wealth; possessions. [*Syn.* sampatti'; nxora; dxī'-naa.]

saebaa' [*TB* *g-sat 58] *v.* <maarnu> to kill (with a knife); to butcher; to finish (hem, edge of thatch).

saebaa' nxeba' *v.* <maarnu laḍnu> to fight with intent to kill.

saed *pa.* <saayad> perhaps.

saer *n.* <syaahaar> care; protection. [*Syn.* sek taa'k labaa'; sayar susaar labaa'.]

saget *n.* <saakkai; sahodar> siblings - full (of same parents); siblings - half (with one parent in common).

saĩlaa' *n.* <sããhilo> brother - third; son - third.

saĩli' *n.* <sããhilī> sister - third; daughter - third.

sai' *n.* <sahī> signature; approval; thumbprint.
sai' jxõba'. *To affix one's thumbprint.*
[*Syn.* sadar.]

saidaa', saaedaa' *n.* <madat; sahaayataa> help; assistance.
saidaa' xrisi kxe' lal khãã'm. *After asking for help (she) is able to do the work.*

sa'idiba *v.* <sahaanu> to endure; to forbear; to accept; to be compatible with.
ŋadi nõwããlai sa'ididu biyãã axnxema'la. *If I accepted the cat it would not meow.*
xa'riyõ makha'ẽ cadu' biyãã axsxaidi'du biyãã na'm. *If (you) eat green corn and it doesn't agree (with you), (you) get sick.*

saidu' *n.* <saait> auspicious time for departing on journey; good omen.

saidu' labaa' *v.* <saait garnu> to set out on a journey.

saikaḍa *a.* <sayakaḍaa> percent.
saikaḍa pããc. *Five percent.*

sail ṭxa' *n.* orchid.

sainu' *n.* <saahinu> kinship relationship; relative.

sajaẽ' *n.* <sajaaya> sentence; punishment designed to reform offender.

sajan *a.* <sajjan> truthful; honest. [*Syn.* satte'; sojo'; sida'.]

sajib *n.* <sacib> secretary.

sajid *n.* <hoš> awareness of surroundings; alertness.

sajid axyõ'ba *a.* <hoš napaaunu> delirious.

sa'jilo *a.* <sajilo> easy.

sakhet *see* saget 'full'.

sa'la *n.* <laas polne belaa> cremation time.

sale' *n.* <salaaī> matches.

salgadiba' *v.* <laskaaunu> to light; to set fire to. [*Syn.* mrobaa'.]

sa'lla *n.* <sallaah> advice; consultation.

sa'maa su'mu *n.* <rim jhim sããj parnu> dusk.
nesa'rbae mĩ' mrõdaa axmrõ'daa xyaaba'e txi sa'maa su'mu bim. *We call the time in the evening when you go along seeing only partially dusk.*

samaaj *n.* <samaaj> society; organisation; community.

samdi' *n.* <samdi> parents-in-law of one's own child.

samet *p.* <samet> even; also; together with.

samjaa'r *n.* <samacaar> news; message.

sa'mjidiba *v.* <samjhaaunu> to admonish; to explain.

sa'mma[1] *p.* <samma (pugnu)>

until; up to.
pae axla'n sammaa' yu'm. *(It) comes down until (you) do the post-funeral.*
ekaaisa' pustaa sammaa' tam. *There are as many as twenty-one books.*

sa'mma[2] *a.* **<samma (maidaan)>** level; flat (of ground or roof).

sampati' *n.* **<sampatti>** possessions; wealth.
[*Syn.* dxĩ' naa, dxan' sampati'.]

samudra *n.* **<samudra>** sea; lake; ocean.
[*Syn.* taa'laa; xraa.]

sanada' *n.* **<sanada>** licence.
ca'maẽd sanada'r ṭhaudiwaai'. *They stamped it on the licence.*

sa'nca, sa'nja *n.* **<sanco>** happiness; health; wellbeing.

sanphres [*E* 'sanforised'?] *n.* cloth printed in various colours.
[*Syn.* nainasu'd.]

sanaatan dxarmaa' *n.* **<sanaatan dharmaa>** religion - traditional (animistic, sacrificial) of the Gurungs.

santanaa', santaan, sanadara' *n.* **<santaan>** descendants.

santok *n.* **<santoṣ>** ease; plenty; contentment; comfort; peace.
garibma'ẽ saẽri bijaar lam plxoblai santok mu. *The poor man thinks the rich have contentment.*

santok tabaa' *v.* **<santoṣ hunu>** to be content; pleased; proud of someone.
ṭhaagu paa's tasi ŋa santok tai'. *Eldest-Son passed and I am proud of him.*
[*Syn.* saẽ mrẽ'ba.]

saŋaa'raa *see* **sãgaa'raa.**

saphphaa' *a.* **<saphaa>** clean; pure.

sa'ra *n.* **<kiran>** ray (narrow, of sun low in sky, or breaking through hole in clouds or roof, or sometimes of moon's rays, or a torch beam).
[*Syn.* xui.]

saraap jxõba' *v.t.* **<saraapnu>** to curse.

sa'raasa'r *av.* **<saraasar>** directly; straight.
ŋa sa'raasa'r dxĩrna' xyaam. *I'm going straight home.*

sarbu' *n.* ball of spun thread; spun yarn.
daai peram, sarbu' phũ cxaa dxũb' tam. *Then (you) spin it, the ball of yarn becomes that fat.*

sardiba' *v.i.* **<sarnu>** to shift; to move; to spread (of infection).
[*Syn.* ku'baa; syo'ba.]

sa'ri *a.* **<ali>** a little.
[*Syn.* te'; cyugu'de.]

sarkha *n.* **<hiũd; jaaḍo mausam>** winter; cold season (November to February).

sarla'kka *a.* **<sarlakka>** bright (of sun shining); attractive (physically).

sastu', sasdu' *a.* **<sasto>** cheap; inexpensive.

saṭṭaa' *p.* **<saṭṭaa>** instead of.
kaaṭhmaanḍu xyaaba'e saṭṭaa' pukhru'rna txonem. *Instead of going to Kathmandu (I) will go to meet (him) in Pokhara.*

satte' *a.*
1. **<satya>** true.
   syur axtxeba'e tãã satte' mu. *A saying which is not a lie is true.*
2. **<sadde>** pure; whole; perfect.
   axnxõba, axṭõ'bae sa'e satte' bim. *We call things not broken or torn whole.*

satte' juga *n.* **<satya yug>** era (first of four) in Hindu mythology.
[*Cp.* dwaapar; tretaa, kali.]

saũlo' *a.* **<saŋlo>** transparent.

sau *see* **say** 'hundred'.

say *num.* <say> hundred.
[*Syn.* prxa'.]

sayar susaar labaa' *v.* <syaahaar samahaar garnu> to care for needs of person (child, old people, etc.).
[*Syn.* sek taak labaa'.]

sayo *n.* <bhũĩcaalo> earthquake.

sãã *n.* <nyaasro> longing for absent friends or relatives.

sãã'be *n.* <sããp ṭhulo> python.

sããdi' *n.* <cheu> boundary; border (of country or property).

sããdiba'[1] *v.t.* <sããcnu> to save up; to store (as opposed to spending or using money or clothes).

sãã'diba[2] *v.t.* <sããghnu> to mix (lemon with spices).

sããgru' *a.* <sããghuro> narrow; confined in space; tight.

sãã'ja *n.* <sããjh> evening.

sããju' *n.* <taalcaa> lock.

sããso *n.* roof of mouth.

sããũli' *n.* <saaŋlo> chain of metal links.
[*Syn.* sigri.]

saabaa', saab *n.* <saaheb> master; sir; prestigious man (usually foreign).

saabaanaa' *n.* <saabun> soap.

saa'ḍe *t.* <saaḍhe> half past certain hour.
saa'ḍe das baje. *Half past ten.*

saada'r *p.* <saathmaa> with; in company with.
ŋa kxie saada'r xyaala'. *I went in your company.*
[*Syn.* -ne; -ne pri; -ne baalu.]

saadaa' *a.* <saadhaa> plain; ordinary; unruled (of paper), unembroidered (of cloth).
[*Syn.* sadxaaran.]

saa'diba *v.t.* bring back from service abroad.
bele saa'di bxwii'. *He brought home a great deal.*

saageta' [*E* 'socket'] *n.* sleeve - threaded, for joining pipe lengths.

saaidu' *see* saidu' 'auspicious time'.

saaika'la *n.* <saaīkal> bicycle.

saaji' *n.* <saakšī> witness (of an act).

saa'l *n.* <saal> year (as unit of time, or in reference to a particular year).
ekkais saa'l nu'kuri lai. *(I) served twenty-one years.*
cauda' saa'lari gãgyu baḍiba. *In '14 the Seti flooded.*

saa'l naa'l *n.* <baahya jananendriyaharū (logne maanisko)> genitals - male.

saaman, samaan *n.* <saamaan> luggage; belongings.

saar *n.* <saahro; sikista> distress; critically ill.

saa'r su'rai *n.* <tayaarī> preparations of seed bed.

saa'raa *n.* <phūl> pollen.

saargi' *n.* <saarkī> cobbler caste.

saa'riba *v.*
1. <phūl phūlnu> to flower (of plants).
2. <kapaal phulnu> to whiten (of hair).

saaro'n *a.* <saahrai> extremely.

saaru' *n.* blackbird.

saaṭṭo' *n.* <saṭṭaa> substitute.
xrõsae saaṭṭo'ri ca' mxi kulbxĩĩ'. *In place of himself he sent that person.*

saa't *num.* <saat> seven (in loan phrases).
[*Syn.* ŋi'.]

saathaa'ri *p.* <saathmaa> together.

saau' *n.* <saahū> creditor.

saa'wẽ *t.* <šraawaṇ> month (4th in Nepali calendar, mid-July to mid-August).

sẽ'ba[1] *v.* <pharkaaunu; waapas dinu> to return goods; to restore; to send back; to turn round.

sẽ'ba[2] [*TB* *sam=*səm 'breath' n. 171, n. 344] *v.* <saas phernu> to breathe.

se[1] [*TB* *sya 181] *n.* <maasu> meat.

-se'[2] *c.* <ra> and (in numeral phrases only).
mxui' gxrise' pandra' paisaa'. *One rupee and fifteen pice.*

-se[3] *s.v.* <bhae pani> even if; even though.
khai' lase ca'maẽ khibne' mããba'e tãã to'i axta'. *Whatever (they) did that old man and old woman's words came to nothing.*

se'[4] [*TaGTh* *syet; *TB* *sar∿*syar n. 251] *n.* <jumro> louse (head and body).

se'ba[1] [*TaGTh* *syeeq; *TB* *syey 182] *v.* <cinnu, thaaha paaunu> to know; to recognise.

se'ba[2] *v.* <naacnu> to dance.

sebaa' *v.* <baat maarnu, gaph garnu> to chat; to tell (a story, narrative).
[*Syn.* baad maardiba'.]

se'k taak labaa' *v.* <sek taak garnu> to care for needs of another.
[*Syn.* sayar susaar labaa'.]

selaa' *n.* <syaal> jackal; hyena.

-sen *s.v.* <-dai> continuative.
[*Syn.* -ri; -ina.]

senimaa *n.* <sinemaa> cinema; films.

ser *n.* <ser> measure of weight (approximately 300 gm. in Pokhara).

se'rãã dxĩ' *n.* <kaṭero> stable for oxen.
[*Syn.* sinĩ'; syo'rããni.]

-sero' *p.* <dekhi> from (in time); since; because.

sewaa, seu *n.*
1. <sewaa> service; homage; obeisance.
2. <aaraadhana> worship.
[*Syn.* phyobaa'.]

sĩ'[1] [*TaGTh* *syink; *TB* *siŋ 233] *n.* <daauraa> wood; firewood.

sĩ[2] *a.* <baasī> stale.

sĩ[3] *see* **chĩ** 'claw, nail'.

sĩ' karmi' *n.* <sikarmi> carpenter (*lit.* wood craftsman).

sĩ' nemãã *n.* <laahããce> woodpecker.

sĩ'ba *v.* <ramaaunu> to be content; pleased; happy.
iṣta mi'ttra sixyaai' biri' kxi tĩ axsxĩ'. *(You) are not happy when a friend dies.*

sĩbaa' [*TaGTh* *syim] *v.* <ciso hunu> cold; wet; to become cold or wet.

sĩbi' buḍi *n.* <sĩmi> beam.

sĩdur *n.* <sĩdūr> red powder used for tika.

sĩgaa *n.* <sĩha> lion.

-si[1] *s.v.* <-nos> imperative - polite.
syuraa axtxelle' bisi. *Please tell me truthfully.*
[*Syn.* -d.]

si[2] *n.* <bhaat - napaakeko> rice - insufficiently cooked.

-si[3] *s.v.* <-era> completive.
ca'd bijaar lasi, khiba baaṭṭho tab lasi, khibad bidi... *Having thought, the old man having become cunning, the old man said...*

sibaa' [*TaGTh* *syi; *TB* *siy=*səy 232] *v.* <marnu; mrityu hunu> to die.

si'baalu' *a.* **<sipaalu>** skilful; clever.

sibi' seb *a.* **<paataalo, dublo>** thinness; skinniness.

s̸ibil *a.* civilian.
kalkada'ri s̸ibil nu'kuri labaa'. *Doing civilian service in Calcutta.*

sida *a.* **<sīdhaa, sojho>** straight.
[*Syn.* sojo; sajan; satte'. *Ant.* bããgo.]

-sidi' *s.v.* **<ta ni>** emphatic.
tam sidi'. *OK, indeed.*

sigreḍ, sigres *n.* **<curoṭ>** cigarette.

sigri *n.* **<sikrī, saaŋlo>** chain.
[*Syn.* sããũli'.]

sigri, sigiri *n.* **<sikri; dhūp>** incense.

sikki' *n.* **<ghamanḍ; sekhī; garwa>** pride.
[*Syn.* pxaẽba.]

silbaḍaa' [*E* silver] *n.* **<silibar>** aluminium.

silidi'ba *v.* **<selaaunu, sakinu>** to finish.
sõga'ẽ sammaa' ca' khe'i daai silidi'i, ca' paelai. *For three days, (they) read that, and then it was finished, that post-funeral.*

si'ldo thi'ba *v.* **<kunai dewataako pūjaa>** to offer a particular sacrifice in the jungle.

simãã *n.* **<daldal; sīm>** swamp; marsh.

simããlaa' *n.* **<naal>** umbilical cord - animal.

simããlaa' *n.* **<simal>** silk-cotton tree.

simenḍi', simanḍi', simãḍa' *n.* **<simenṭī>** concrete.

simi *n.* **<simi>** Franch beans.

sinĩ' *n.* **<kaṭero>** shed; stall (usually for cows).

sinu' *n.* **<sinu; laas>** corpse.

siŋããrdiba' *v.* **<sĩgaarnu>** to decorate; adorn.

sirããũlu' *n.* **<sirãũlaa>** rice - boiled (or freshly harvested) and husked.

sipaai *n.*
1. **<sipaahī>** soldier of lowest rank.
   mxaĩla sipaai pinchin yu'i. *Second-Brother came back with a private soldier's pension.*
2. **<piūn; pulis>** messenger - official.
   jxagaḍaa' laba'e baareri' sipaai ciṭṭhi' bhai' khai'. *A messenger came bringing a letter about the quarrel.*

-siri' *s.v.* **<-era>** completive.
cyaa' lasiri' raaḍa'r peram. *Having made a ball (you) spin it on a spinning wheel.*

sirib *a.* **<sirib; khaali>** only; exclusively.
sirib kxyu' nero' khasi' se mare' cam. *(She) eats exclusively sheep and goat meat.*

sirega *n.* **<sirak>** padded quilt.

skula' *n.* **<skūla; paaṭhašaalaa>** school.

sõ' [*TaGTh* *somp; *TB* *g-sum 409] *num.* **<tīn>** three.

sõ'ba [*TaGTh* *sank 'dry'] *v.* **<sukaaunu>** to dry in the sun.

sõ'gyaa *n.* **<bisan>** grains drying in the sun.

sõ'jyu *num.* **<tīs>** thirty.

so'¹ [*TB* *sak 485; *TaGTh* *saaq] *n.* **<saas>** breath; life.

so² *n.* **<cilaaune cij>** irritation caused by bites of small insects or secretion of plants.

so'ba *v.* **<bããcnu, jīunu>** to live; to survive from disaster or disease.

sobaa' *a.* **<piro>** hot (in taste);

peppery; spicy.

sobaala *n.* **<baulaahaa>** madness (as of religious sadhus, mentally unbalanced people who don't live in a socially acceptable manner); rabies.

sobaardiba' *v.* **<sapranu>** to thrive (of plants).

sobaa'rgi *n.* **<ḍheḍhu bããdar>** monkey - white-faced.

soblaa' *n.* **<buŋgo>** part of banana plant.

soḍa' *n.* **<soḍaa>** soda - baking (a rising agent).

soda'n *t.* **<sadhaĩ>** always; every day. [*Syn.* khõi.]

sodaa' *p.* **<agaaḍi>** facing.
ṭũḍikhe'l sodaa' aspatal mu. *Facing the parade ground is a hospital.*
[*Syn.* ũĩ.]

so'ga *n.* **<aaphsos>** sadness.

so'gõ *a.* **<jīwīt>** living.
[*Cp.* so'.]

sojo', sojaa' *a.* **<sojho>** straight; honest; direct.
[*Syn.* satte'; sida'; sajan. *Ant.* bããgo.]

soloḍ *n.* **<salaam>** salute.

so'raa jaad *n.* **<sohra jaat>** moiety of lower clans among the Gurungs (*lit.* sixteen castes).
[*See Appendix A.*]

sora'di *n.* **<puraano naac>** dance (of old Gurung type).

so'rmaẽ *n.* **<rughaa>** cold - ailment.

sũ [*TaGTh* *suŋ 'mouth'] *n.* **<mukh>** mouth; threshold.
khaali' sũd mattre' bim. *Words without deeds.*
mraa'gẽ sũũle' kxurixyaaĩ'. *He fell from the threshold.*

sũ lacchin *a.* **<mijaasīlo>** charming; peace-maker.

sũ phlebaa' *v.* **<mukh biraaunu>** to slip (of the tongue).

su'ba *v.* **<ulṭo garnu>** to turn inside out.

su *see* **suka** '25 pice'.

subaari' *n.* **<supaarī>** betel nut (hard brown and white flesh); areca.

su'baasaa *n.* **<baanī, swabhaaw>** nature; disposition; habit.
[*Syn.* baani; behora.]

subdaaraa' *n.* **<subedaar>** captain (army rank).

su'cana *n.* **<sūcanaa>** proclamation; notice; warning.

sudgyaari' *n.* **<sutkerī>** woman in childbirth or period of confinement following.

sudgyaari' tabaa' *v.* **<sutkerī hunu>** to give birth.

sugaa' *n.* **<sugaa>** parrot.

suka *n.* **<sukaa>** suka (25 pice, ¼ rupee).

sukha *n.* **<sukh>** comfort; ease.

sukhaa' *a.* **<sukhaa>** dry.
sukhaa' kxẽ. *Dry bread.*

sukri bikri *n.* **<sukrībikro; beca bikhana>** trade; buying and selling.
[*Syn.* chõ.]

sukul *n.* **<sukul>** mat - thick, woven of rice straw (used as floor covering).

sulḍu' *a.* **<sulṭo>** right way up (as of woven mat).
[*Ant.* ulḍu'.]

suli' *n.* **<suli>** frame for stacking corn cobs; corn stack frame.

sumdiba' *v.* **<sumpanu>** to hand over to someone else (things, or responsibility).

sunaara' *n.* **<sunaar>** goldsmith caste.

sundalaa *n.* **<suntalaa>** mandarin; tangerine.

sunidiba' *v.* <sunaaunu> to make known; proclaim.

susaar *n.* <susaar; syaahaa> care; service; attendance. [*Syn.* sek taak labaa'. sayar susaar labaa'.]

susaare' *n.* <susaare> nurse (medical); maidservant.

swa'rga *n.* <swarga> heaven. [*Ant.* na'rga.]

swaaŋ *n.* <swaaŋ> hypocrisy; pretence.

swaaŋ te'ba *v.* <swaaŋ garnu> to be hypocritical.

swaa'l swaa'l xyaaba' *v.* <swaala jaanu> to move body by contraction and shooting out (as of snake's motion, or boy shinning up a pole).

swaabaa' *a.* <asal> good; pleasant; excellent.
swaalle' chyãã ba'e kwẽ khil yõmũ. *(One) gets to wear exceedingly nice clothes.*

swaad *n.* <swaad> taste; savour.

swaalbaa' *v.* <thuknu; nikaalnu> to spew out of the mouth.

swẽ' *n.* <aahaara> bird's food.

swĩ'di *n.* <thunse> basket - large, closely woven, conical, for carrying loads on back (usually harvested grains).

swĩkidibxĩba' *v.* <phaalnu> to throw down.
[*Syn.* bxyõba'.]

swi *n.* <sui> injection.
swi jxõba'. *To give an injection.*

swibaa'¹ *v.* <kornu - kapaal> to comb (hair).

swibaa'² *v.* <kelaaunu> to prepare vegetables for cooking (washing, cutting out waste).

swiṭara' *n.* <swiṭar> jumper; sweater.

sxaba' *v.i.* <niko hunu> to heal.

sxaba'n *a.* <sanco> well (of person).
kxi sxaba'n mu u? *Are you well?*
nxebaal sxa'l churim u? *Do you enjoy Kathmandu a lot?*

sxa'l labaa' *v.t.* <niko paarnu> to cure; to heal.

-syãã *s.v.* <bhane> conditional; if.
krxisyãã baalun, axkrxiyãã syo' tal txum. *If (they) match, then together; if (they) don't, (they) have to be separate.*

syãã *n.* <naulo> stranger; newcomer.

syaa'ba *v.t.*
1. <bheṭnu> to reach.
2. <samaatnu> to catch (friend on road, thief on run).
3. <bheṭṭaaunu> to curse; to afflict; to possess (as of evil spirit).
   pumsyod syaa'i. *The witch cursed him.*
   mxõd syaa'bae mxi. *The person possessed by the evil spirit.*

syaabaas *e.* <syaabaas> bravo; well done! (not used to one's superiors).

syaa'gi *n.* <picaas; waayu> ghost; spirit of a person who has suffered a violent death (can be aroused by witch to hurt people).

syaa'laba *v.* <lipnu> to smooth mud (mixed with cowdung) on walls and floor.

syaamãã' *n.* <syaamaa (tamaaŋnĩharũko aaphno lugaa> skirt worn by Tamang women.

syaa'mgo *n.* <gabuwaa> billy; pot with handle (aluminium, for ghee, milk, etc.).

syaatti syõ *n.* <syaatti kholaa> river joining Seti east of Ghachok.

syõ¹ [*TaGTh* *syaŋ] *n.* <ghaṇṭa> bell.

syõ² [*TaGTh* *syoŋ] *n.* <kholo> river.

[*Syn.* khola; bxolaa'.]

syõbaa' *v.* **<pasaarnu>** to stretch out arm.

syõ'bu *n.* **<saalo>** brother-in-law (WiYrBr).

syõ'di *n.* **<sihũḍī>** cactus.

syõ'raani *n.* **<kaṭero>** shelter above rice husking place. [*Syn.* se'rãã dxĩ'; sinĩ'.]

-syo[1] *s.v.* future, emphatic (on 1st person singular). ŋad kxilaai axca'syo. *I certainly won't eat you.*

-syo[2] *s.n.* **<-nī (strīliŋg)>** feminine. tamũsyo'. *Gurungsini, a female Gurung.*

syo'[3] *n.* **<waayu (kohi maanisako)>** spirit of a person or animal who has died as a result of falling from a cliff.

syo'ba[1] *a.* **<arko kisimko>** a different kind.

syo'ba[2] *v.t.*
1. **<panchaaunu>** to move (something) to a different place to make room.
2. **<saarnu>** to get rid of. [*Syn.* kubaa'; sardiba'.]

syobaa' *v.* **<baḍhaaunu>** to increase; to enlarge; to multiply.

syomãã, syomna *t.* **<uhile>** previously; originally; once upon a time.

syomãã syomãã *t.* **<uhile nai>** long long ago; once upon a time.

syo'wẽ *n.* **<dawa dabe>** type of shrub.

syu[1] *a.* **<kããco>**
1. wet (of firewood or clothes).
2. uncooked (of meat or vegetables, not rice).

syu[2] [*TaGTh* *syib] *n.* **<daaba>** sheath of Nepali dagger.

syu'ba *v.* **<unnu>** to thread.

syubaa' *v.* **<paadnu>** to pass wind rectally.

syu'guba' *v.* **<osaarnu, boknu>** to carry (goods).

syui'ba *v.* **<ukhelnu>** to uproot; to lift.

syuibaa'[1] *v.* **<jhikidinu (ligaa)>** to unveil; uncover.

syuibaa'[2] *v.* **<chaaunu>** to roof; to cover.

syumi, syumĩ *n.* **<saasũ>** mother-in-law.

syura *n.* **<ḍhããṭnu>** lie; deceit. syur te'ba. *To utter a lie.*

syurbaa' *v.* **<ṭaauko maathi ghumaaunu, ghumnu giddhaa>** to wave around. ṭu'lĩ dxubaa'rar jxõĩ' biri', krar syuram, thaasũ waaba'ri. *(He) puts incense in the censer and waves it around (his) head, to drive out the evil.*

syurbi *n.* berry (small, red, bitter, ripens in Mangsir).

syurgu' *n.* **<jhuṭo kuraa bolne>** liar.

syutaa'le *a.* **<tyasai, phaakaimaa>** deceitfully.

Ṭ

ṭaba' *v.* **<laagnu (golī, saraap)>** to strike (of projectile, curse).

ṭaḍe' *n.* **<ṭaaṭo, daag>** scar.

ṭa'ima *see* ṭyaa'ma.

ṭalgadiba' *v.* **<ṭalkanu>** to shine with brightness (of polished boots or sun).

ṭãã'gu *n.* **<laamo laṭṭhī>** pole - long, slender (for knocking down fruit, etc.).

ṭããĩdiba' *v.t.*
1. **<ṭããgnu>** to hang up; suspend. kwẽ ka'ĩdu liũĩ ṭããĩdiba'. *To hang a cloth behind the rice statuettes.*
2. **<ṭããsnu>** attach. phirda' xrasid ṭããĩdi' biri' pibxĩŋŋyũ'. *Having attached*

the acknowledgement card I sent it.

ṭãã'ṭẽ labaa' *v.* <sukaaunu> to set out to dry.

ṭaa'ba *v.* <niphannu> to winnow (shaking tray up and down).

ṭaaldiba' *v.* <ṭaalnu> to mend.

ṭaalu' *n.* <ṭaalo> remnant of cloth; scrap; patch.

ṭẽbaa' *v.* <sukaaunu> to dry wool; set out to cool (boiled millet).

ṭebrikoḍ, ṭebrika' *n.* <ṭeprikorḍ> taperecorder.

ṭeḍo' *a.* <ṭeḍho> zigzag.

ṭeksaa' *n.* <bhansaar> tax (on land, imports, or vehicles). [*Cp.* baali, kar, bhansaar.]

ṭeksi' *see* **ṭyaaksi'** 'taxi'.

ṭha'ḍa ṭhu'ḍu[1] *n.* <dallaa phornu> breaking clods of earth into loose soil.
tha'da thu'du lathen. *Break up the big lumps.*

ṭha'ḍa ṭhu'ḍu[2] *n.* <ṭhaakṭhuk> altercation; dispute; controversy; enmity.
pumsyo kxine pri' ṭha'ḍa ṭhu'ḍu tanaa'. *A witch has developed, I see, enmity to you.*

ṭhagdiba' *v.* <ṭhagnu> to cheat.

ṭhaṭṭaa' *n.* <ṭhaṭṭaa> joke.

ṭhaṭṭaa' maardiba' *v.* <ṭhaṭṭaa maarnu> to joke.

ṭhaudiba' *v.* <ṭhoknu> to affix thumbprint; knock; strike.
ca'maẽd sanada'r ṭhaudi'waai. *They stamped the licence.*

ṭhããḍaa ṭhũḍe *n.* <ṭhuṭo, ṭhunko> left-overs.

ṭhããḍi *n.*
1. <chaapro; pauwaa> shelter - temporary (built in fields distant from home where workers stay overnight).
2. <paaṭī; ṭhããṭī> rest house (built for travellers as a meritorious work).

ṭhãã'ĩ ṭhu'ĩ *a.* <ṭhããṭinu, ṭhããṭī> fashionably dressed. [*Cp.* nakal te'ba.]

ṭhaaḍe[1] *a.* <ṭhaaḍo (maanis)> unaware of work to be done.
thaade' tasero' lxaidibae kxe' mattre' lam. aru kxe' jaga axmrõ'. *Because he is unaware he does only the work he has to, he doesn't see other work.*

ṭhaaḍe'[2] *a.* <ṭhaaḍo> long and narrow (of bucket, cylinder).

ṭhaaḍo' *a.* <ṭhaaḍo> upright; vertical; perpendicular.
pudli' saḍak xyaaba'e ṭhaaḍo' gxyãã'ũ khai. *(I) came up the road going perpendicular to Putali Sadak.*

ṭhaagu *n.* <jeṭho> brother - eldest; son - first. [*Syn.* axgxĩ'.]

ṭhaaldiba' *v.* <thaalnu> to begin.

ṭhaaldũ' *n.* <ṭaaḍno> cattle stall where hay is placed.

ṭhaar *a.* <ṭhaaḍo> upright; erect.
ṭhaarle'n pxram'. *(He) walks erect.*

ṭhegana' *n.* <ṭhegaanaa> address.

ṭheṭaraa' [*E* theatre] *n.* <naac> modern dancing style.
to' naa'j se'm? // ṭheṭaraa' se'm. *What are they dancing? // They are dancing modern.*

ṭhi'ba *v.*
1. <paarnu> to strike a match.
2. <choḍaaunu> to strike corn cobs against each other to get grains off.

ṭhi'k, ṭhig *a.* <ṭhīk> right; correct.

ṭhi'kan *a.* <majhaulaa, ṭhīkkai> fair; satisfactory.

ṭhi'kkale *a.* <ṭhīk saŋga> medium; average.

ṭhiridi'ba *v.* <ṭhihirinu> to be

numb with cold.
[*Syn.* kaaṭhidiba'; gaŋgridiba.]

ṭhũḍe *n.* <ṭhunko> left-overs of food.

ṭhu'ba *v.* <kaaṭnu(ḍallaa)> to break up clods of earth.

ṭhu'ḍu *see* ṭha'ḍa ṭhu'ḍu.

ṭhuḍu' [*N* 'tree stump, denuded branch'] *n.* <ṭhuṭo> stubble of grain.

ṭhyaa'kka, ṭhyakka *a.* <ṭhyaakka, ṭhyaak> exact; careful; precise.
ti'dĩ ṭhyaa'kka yu'na. *It is exactly one year.*
ubaa' nero' kaa' jxõba'e liũdi' tãã ṭhyaa'kkan krxil txum. *The final words of the first line and the response must match (i.e. rhyme) exactly.*

ṭhyaa'm ṭhi'm *n.*
1. <bandobasta> arrangements.
2. <garnu parne kaam> chores.

ṭhyaa'mmaa *a.* <bharī> full to the brim.
bxããḍo'ri kyu' ṭhyaa'mmaa. *The water is up to the brim in the vessel.*

ṭhyaa'ppa¹ *av.* clearly, unmistakably.
pxali pĩḍiri ṭhyaa'ppa lathẽna' ro. *They said her foot had left (a print) unmistakably on the verandah.*

ṭhyaa'ppa² *av.* <chiṭo> immediately, quickly.
mããbad kxe' pi'waai biri' aarko' mxi ṭhyaappa yõĩ'. *After the old woman abandoned the work another person was quickly available.*
[*Syn.* yumna.]

ṭhyaa'ppa³ *a.* well-fitting.
mraa' chenle ṭhyaa'ppa axtaa'. *The door is not fitted well.*

ṭĩbaa' *v.* <ṭhaṭaaunu> to strike; beat; hammer.

ṭibaṭe' *a.* <ṭībaten> Tibetan.
ṭibaṭe' ke'mar xyaai. *(We) went to the Tibetan camp.*
ṭibaṭe'maẽ põ'bae calan. *The Tibetan manner of speech.*

ṭibaa' *v.* <basnu; rahanu> to stay; remain; dwell; continue.
mããba' tadi, bed ṭidi. *(I) have become old, and continue barren.*
bajaarar ṭil axyõ'. *(He) doesn't get to stay in town.*
chyããba'e dxĩr' ṭil yõmu. *(You) get to live in a nice house.*

ṭigaṭ *n.* <ṭikaṭ> ticket; postage stamp.

ṭigisa' *n.* <strīko ek pošak; ṭikīs> woman's skirt.

ṭii' *n.* <siura> comb of cock.

ṭi'na *n.* <jastaa; ṭīn> iron sheets (tinned or galvanised, for roofing).
ṭi'nad syuibaa'. *Tin-roofed.*

ṭõ *n.* <maasī (haaḍ bhitrako)> marrow of bone.

ṭõbaa'¹ *v.* <phaisalaa garnu; niščaya garnu> to resolve (a dispute).
kajuri' axṭõ', khaba'dai ṭxola axkhãã'. *The meeting was not resolved, nobody could win (the case).*

ṭõbaa'² *v.* <chinaalnu; luchnu> to pull apart; cut through; break (in hands).
belaaudi' ṭõb u? *For cutting guavas?*

ṭo'ba *v.* <cyaatnu; phaaṭnu> to tear (clothes, paper).

ṭobaa' *v.* <nidaaunu (bhusukkai)> to be completely asleep; to be numb.

ṭobi' *n.* <naamlo> strap for carrying load on back.
[*Syn.* ṭxo'.]

ṭoḍol *v.* <jammaa> total (of pay entitlement).
chuṭṭi' rol te'sero' paisaa' jau ṭoḍol lam, paisaa' yõm. *After (they) release (you) on the leave list (they) total (your) money, and (you) get the money.*

ṭola *n.* <ṭol> quarter; ward (of village or town).

ṭoli' *n.* <ṭolī, daphaa> group of people; party.
[*Syn.* paaṭi'.]

ṭonḍaa' *n.* <banbaḍe> an edible fern.

ṭowaa *n.* <paraalko ṭauwaa (kuniyo)> rack for stacking rice straw.

ṭũḍikhe'la, ṭũ'ḍikhela *n.* <ṭũḍikhel> parade ground.

ṭuba *see* **ṭxuba'** 'sew'.

ṭuḍī *n.* <paahaa (kholaamaa)> frog - 8 cm., edible, lives in streams, black.
[*Cp.* pẽ.]

ṭuḍi' xyaaba' *v.* <ṭūṭnu, banda hunu> to be used up; expended.

ṭuibaa'[1], ṭxuiba' *v.* <ṭakryaaunu> to collapse; landslide; fall (of large landslip).

ṭuibaa'[2] *v.* <pachyaaunu> to want to follow (of child after parent).

ṭuka, ṭukkaa' *n.* <ṭukkaa (gītko khanḍa)> couplet sung by soloist.
[*Cp.* koras, ubaa', kaa' jxõba'.]

ṭusyaa' *n.* <upallo ghaacok> village name - upper Ghachok.

ṭxa', ṭa *n.* <phūl> flower.

ṭxaa *n.* <tihun; tarkaari> vegetable; curry (rice accompaniment).
kaẽ xyoba, ṭxaa txeba'. *Boiling rice, frying vegetables.*

ṭxaa-ṭxu *n.* <tihun-tarkaari> vegetables - green.

ṭxowãã *n.* <sarãg> rack; shelf above fireplace (to hold wood, wool, meat for drying).

ṭxo' [*TaGTh* *draaq] *n.* <naamlo> strap for carrying load on back; tumpline.
[*Syn.* ṭobi'.]

ṭxoba'[1] *a.* <nyaano> warm (of clothes).

ṭxoba[2] *v.* <jitnu; wijaya hunu> to win.
ãgrej sarkaardi ṭxowaadi. *The English Government won.*

ṭxoḍẽ *n.* ceremony on Tuesdays in Caitra and Shrawan when boys come with incense and banging tins and drums.

ṭxu'[1] [*TaGTh* *druuq] *n.* <cha> six.

ṭxu[2] *see* **ṭxaa ṭxu** 'green vegetables'.

ṭxuba'[1] *v.* <taarnu (ããkhaa)> to glare (in anger).
xris khaibiri' mĩ' ṭxuba', mĩ' axchyãã'b ŋxyoba, mĩ' thebrẽ' ŋxyoba. *Being angry one glares, looks with angry eyes, looks with big eyes.*

ṭxuba'[2], ṭuba [*TB* *d-rup=*drup 456] *v.* <silaaunu> to sew.

ṭxuba[3] *see* **ŋxeb ṭxuba** 'neighbours'.

ṭxubi [*TaGTh* *dri 'skin'] *n.* <chaalaa> skin; hide; leather.

ṭxuiba'[1] *see* **ṭuibaa'** 'collapse'.

ṭxuiba[2] *v.* <nikaalnu> to pull out.

ṭxujyu' *n.* <saaṭhī> sixty.

ṭyaaksi', ṭeksi' *n.* <moṭar> taxi.

ṭyaa'ma, ṭaa'ima *n.* <samaya> time; hour.
cxau baje ṭyaa'mar xyaal' txum. *At that time on the clock you must go.*

T

ta'[1] *n.* <bancaro> axe.

ta[2] *n.* <ghoḍaa (warṣa)> horse (only in ta lxo).

ta[3] *loc.* <upallo> up; above.
[*Syn.* taai'.]

ta' kra *n.* <bancorako paaso> axe

head - back of.

ta lxo, taa lxo *n.* <ghoḍaa warṣa> year of the horse (in Tibetan 12-year cycle, 1942,54, 66,78).
[*Syn.* gxoḍaa' lxo.]

tab *c.* <tab> then.
tab balla kxi sxam'. *Then at last you will get better.*

ta'ba¹ *v.* <kamaaunu> to work for hire in fields.

ta'ba² *v.* <oraalnu> to descend; come down.
[*Syn.* yu'ba; khaa'rba.]

tabaa' [*TaGTh* *ta 'all right'; *TB* *ta:p 'fit' 337] *v.*
1. <pugnu> suffice.
cu' tam u axta'? *Is this sufficient or not?*
2. <huncha> be right, fitting.
nagine chwila axta'. *It's not right to touch a dog.*
3. <huncha> be.
chyããbaa' tam. *It is good.*
4. <hunu> become; happen.
to' tai? *What happened?*

ta'e taadi' *loc.* <ũbho (dherai ṭaaḍhaa)> uphill; above (emphatic).

tagara *n.* <tagaaro> gatepost (of stone, usually) for bar-gate.
[*Syn.* mraa'; ḍhogaa'.]

takhada' *n.* <takhataa> shelf for big pots and water jars.

tal *a.* <aaja (bihaana); agaaḍi> earlier on same day.
tal nxããgari. *This morning.*

talaba' *n.* <talab> salary.
[*Syn.* tanakha'.]

talaa' *av.* <aghinai> earlier; before.

ta'le¹ *av.* <kina?> why?

tale'² *n.* <talaa> storey (of house).
e'k tale' dxĩ'. *A one-storey house.*

ta'lebiyãã *c.* <kinabhane> because.

tamaakhu', tamaa'khu *n.* <tamaakhu> tobacco.

tamsug *n.* <tamsūk> IOU.

tamũ' *n.* <ṭupī> topknot; lock of hair on crown of head.

tamũ *a.* <guruŋ> Gurung.
tamũma'ẽ. *Gurungs.*
tamũsyo'. *Gurung woman.*

tanakha' *n.* <tanakhaah; talab; kistaa> pay.
[*Syn.* talaba'.]

tani' *n.* <phittaa> lace (of boot).

tan.gadiba' *v.* <tankinu> to stretch; to be elastic.

tara *c.* <tara> but.

tardiba' *v.* <tarnu> to cross a lake or river.

tarigaa' *n.* <tarīkaa> way; method.
khaiba'e tarigaa'le banidim? *What way do (you) make it?*

tarwaali' *n.* <tarwaar> sword.

tasala' *n.* <tasalaa> saucepan; pan - brass.

tasbir *n.* <taswīr> photo; picture.
[*Syn.* phoṭo'; na'ksa.]

tauldiba' *v.* <taulanu> to weigh in balances.

tauliyaa *n.* <tauliyaa> towel.

tayaar *a.* <tayaar> ready; prepared.

tãã [*TaGTh* *tam] *n.* <kuraa> conversation; chat; word; matter.

tãã'ga [*TB* *ŋya 189; *T* nyah] *n.* <maacho> fish.

tããgra *n.* <keraau> pea.

taabge' *n.* <taapke> pan - long-handled, for frying food.
[*Syn.* bxujũ'ŋãã; ḍibji.]

taaī', taadi' [*TB* *(l-)tak 'above'

n. 176] *loc.* <**maathi; uttar**> up; above; north.
[*Ant.* maai.]

taa'laa *n.* <**taal**> lake.

taan' *a.* <**sabai**> all; every.

taan' bxandaa' *av.* <**sabai bhandaa**> the most; supremely.
taan' bxandaa' thebaa'. *Biggest.*

taa'ne maa'ne *n.* chores; all the work.
ŋam cu' khaagun taa'ne maa'ne laba' di. *As for me, I have been doing all the chores around here.*

taan.gaja *n.* <**gol kããkri**> a fruit from the jungle.

taa'raa *n.* <**taar**> wire.

taargyaa, taarki', taarki'ti [*TaGTh* *tar] *a.* <**seto**> white.

taarik *n.* <**taarīkh**> date (of English month).
[*Cp.* gate.]

taaš *n.* <**taaš**> cards - playing.
taaš khlyõbaa'. *To play cards.*

tẽ'[1] *n.* <**ḍhisko**> ledge of cliff.

tẽ[2] *n.* <**lotī**> lobe of ear.

tẽ'ba *v.* <**swaagat garnu**> to welcome.

tẽbaa' *v.* <**dekhaaunu**> to show.

te', de' [*Cp* tyunq 'short'] *a.* <**ali**> a little.

te' kwãã'ba *v.* <**lamkanu**> to stride.
[*Syn.* lamgadi'ba.]

te'ba *v.* <**nikaalnu**> to utter; release.
kae te'ba. *To shout.*
swããŋ te'ba. *To be hypocritical.*
syur te'ba. *To lie.*
nakal te'ba. *To dress fashionably.*

tebaa'[1] *v.* <**khanyaaunu**> to empty (a vessel, or a room).
khubi' te'bxĩn. *Please clear out the sleepout.*

tebaa'[2] *v.* <**khasnu**> to fall.
prxo'ũd texyaai'. *(He) fell over a cliff.*

tebaardiba' *a.* <**tesro paṭak**> third time.

te'j *n.* <**tej**>
1. power, strength, pressure.
2. (rarely) brightness.

te'jle *av.* <**tejilo**> brightly; powerfully; strongly.

te'la *n.* <**tel**> oil.

telaa', tel *t.* <**hijo**> yesterday.

te'lẽ *a.*
1. <**ali**> a little.
   chyugu' te'lẽ de' pĩn. *Give me just a little.*
2. <**najik**> close.
   pxror' te'lẽ te'lẽle axxyaad'. *Don't go close to the cliff edge.*
   [*Syn.* te'.]

-teri *e.* <**-terī**> really!
xe'dterī. *Oh, really!*

te'roḍa *num.* <**tehra**> thirteen.

tesro' *a.* <**tesro**> third.

thabdiba' *a.* <**thapnu**>
1. to add; increase.
   paisaa' thabdiyãã' ŋere' kaagada' kham. *If you add more money (to the letter) a card comes back.*
2. extend.
   axdxaa' gxanḍaa' thabdid. *Extend it half an hour.*
   [*Syn.* xrin labaa'.]

thablo' *n.* <**thopo**> drop of liquid.

thaidu', thaaidu' *i.* <**parkhanos, parkhanu**> wait; hold on.

thaili' *n.* <**kharca**> outlay; expenditure.
mrõ'e thaili' togo' pĩl txum. *(I) have to make the outlay for the field now.*

tha'l *see* **jal tha'l** 'splashing'.

thali *n.* <**thaal, thaalī**> dish; plate - for rice, about 25 cm. diam.

thamnãã' *n.* <**khããdarjuŋ**> village name.

thara *n.* <**thaarī**> adolescent female buffalo.

tha'rararale *av.* <**tharaharī**> fearfully; tremblingly.

tha'ri *n.* <**tharī; prakaar**> kind; species.
aanek tha'ribae raŋ. *Various kinds of colours.*
[*Syn.* kisim.]

thauni *n.* <**jhutro; thaaŋno**> ragged; old (of cloth); swaddling clothes.

thãã *n.* <**gandha; waasa**> odour; smell; aroma; fragrance.

thãã naa'ba, thãã nãã'ba *v.* <**ganaaunu**> to smell; to be smelly; stink.

thaa[1] *n.* evil influence (causes disharmony in the home).

thaa[2] *see* **thaaxa.**

thaa kxaeba' *v.* to dispel evil influence.
[*Syn.* thaa waabaa'.]

thaa' numa *av.* <**aakhirī samaya**> eventually; finally.

thaabaa'[1] *v.* <**banaaunu; thaapnu; haalnu**> to build.
nemad cxõ thaabaa'. *The bird is building a nest.*

thaabaa'[2] *v.* <**haannu (bhããisī aadile)**> to butt; gore (of an animal).

thaaxaa *n.* <**thaahaa**> knowledge; information.
nãã'sar thaa pĩne'. *Go and inform the village.*

thaaidu' *see* **thaidu'** 'wait!'.

thaak khola' *n.* <**thaak kholaa**> Thak Khola - river valley in north of Nepal.

thaa'maa *n.* <**thaam**> pillar; column.
[*Syn.* txo.]

thaamdiba' *v.* <**thaamnu**> to halt; to stop.
[*Syn.* chyobaa'.]

thaa'naa, thãã'naa *n.* <**thaan**> shrine to a god (smaller than ma'ndir).

thaasũ *n.* evil influence; spirit - bad.
thaasũ waaba'. *Throwing out the evil.*

thaauni *see* **thauni.**

-thẽ *s.n.* <**kunai gaaũko**> native of.
ŋi aamaa tomnẽ'thẽsyo' yaa. *Our mother was a native of* tomnẽ'.

-thẽbaa'[1] *s.v.* <**-raakhnu**>
1. durative aspect.
   na'ga nxathẽbaa'. *Raising chickens.*
2. perfective (leaving an abiding state).
   telaa' kaẽ xyothẽi. *Yesterday (I) cooked the rice and set it aside.*
   cẽe' ŋo' cxu'thẽla *He had set ready a tiger trap.*

thẽbaa'[2] [*TaGTh* *them; *TB* *ta 19] *v.* <**raakhnu**> to put; place; apply.
kxid yaa'd axthẽ'? *Don't you remember?*

thebaa' [*TB* *tay 'big' 298] *a.* <**ṭhūlo; jeṭho**> big; important - of person; elder (of brothers).
[*Ant.* cyugu'; cyõbaa'.]

thebrẽ', thebbrẽ' *a.* <**ṭhūlo**> big.

thebsyo' *n.* <**jeṭhī**> eldest daughter.
[*Syn.* naa'ni.]

thedẽ' *a.* <**ritto**> empty (of vessel); unladen (porter).

theebaa' [*TaGTh* *thee] *v.* <**sunnu**> to hear; listen.

thĩbaa' *v.* <**milnu; milaap hunu**>

to be compatible; to be in agreement; collaborate.
paargaa thĩdu' biyãã balla din ŋxyol txum. *If the birth signs are compatible finally (you) have to seek an auspicious day.*

thi labaa' *v.* <**soc garnu; jammaa garnu (paisaa)**> to save (esp. money).

thi'ba[1] *v.* <**ḍaḍhnu (lugaa)**> to scorch; burn (cloth).

thi'ba[2] *see* **si'ldo thi'ba.**

-thiri' *a.* small in size - only after cyugu', cxi.
[*Syn.* -siri.]

thõ *n.* <**pahilo pasne koṭha**> vestibule of house.

thõbaa' *v.*
1. <**ḍhokaa kholnu**> to open (door).
2. **pwaal paarnu** to punch (hole).
mu thõŋŋyũ'. *The sky is clear.*

tho'ba[1] [*TaGTh* *thaaq] *v.* <**kaaṭnu**>
1. to chop down; cut (trees, canes).
[*Cp.* thubaa' 'to cut dry wood'.]
2. to slaughter (animal).
kubinḍaa' tho'm, jxaale' ra jxaja' tho'm. *They cut the melon, then they slaughter the goat.*
3. to reduce (pay, army).
ŋiga'ẽbae tanakhaa' tho'waai. *He docked me seven days' pay.*

tho'ba[2] *v.t.* <**kinnu (ṭikaṭ)**> to get (tickets).
ṭigaḍ tho'bar yu'i. *(I) came down to get the tickets.*

tho'ba[3] *v.t.* <**bitaaunu**> to pass; spend (day, life).
din tho'ba axŋxĩ', juga tho'la txumu. *It's not just spending the day, one must spend an age.*

thobaa' *v.* <**jhikaaunu**> to order goods from a distant place (esp. from someone coming from overseas).

thosõ *n.* <**thaak (euṭaa gaaũko naam)**> village name - Thak.

thũ'ba *v.*
1. <**piunu (paanī, dūdh)**> to drink.
bxakha'r ŋxe thũ'bae kolo'ma'ẽ. *Infants (lit. children who have just been drinking milk).*
2. <**piunu (curoṭ)**> to smoke.
sigreḍ tamaakhu' thũ'i. *He smoked cigarettes and a pipe.*

thu *n.* <**saathī**> friend; companion.

thu'ba *v.* <**baarnu**> to erect (fence); enclose (with fence).

thubaa'[1] *v.*
1. <**pugnu (bhaag)**> to suffice.
mxi lxe' khadu' biyãã cu' caba'e sa'e axthu'. *If many people come this food will not suffice.*
2. <**khapnu (baliyo hunu)**> endure; last.
[*Syn.* yu'ba; khabdiba'.]

thubaa'[2] *v.*
1. <**ṭipnu**> to pluck; reap (heads of grain).
2. <**kaaṭnu**> to cut (dry wood); chop up.
sĩ' tho'ba tara sĩ' kaar thubaa'. *We chop down trees, but chop up dry wood.*

thublõ' *n.* <**thunse**> basket - small, closely woven, for harvesting millet.

thundiba' *v.* <**thunnu**> to close; shut up; restrain (in pen or trap); imprison.
ca' gaŋgyu gxanṭaa' ŋxĩ' sammaa' thundi' xyaai'. *That river was blocked for two hours.*
[*Syn.* cyu'ba.]

thupro' *n.* <**thupro**> crowd; heap.
ca' mraa'ri aamũyũ' jau thupro'n mu. *At that door men were standing in a crowd.*
[*Syn.* xul.]

thu'rba *v.* <**bheḍaa judhaai-jutnu**> to butt (of animals in fight).

thurbaa' *v.t.* <**ṭhes laagnu**> to bump into; collide with; stub (toe).

thuri *n.* <**kilo (bhũĩmaa gaaḍne)**> peg in verandah floor to hold loom; spike; stake.

thuttiba' *v.* <**thutnu**> to card thread; pull out; extract.

tĩ [*TaGTh* *tiŋ] *n.* <**muṭū**> heart - human.
tĩ sĩ'ba. *To be pleased, content.*

tĩ'ba *v.*
1. <**khwaaunu (piune kuraa)**> to feed liquid to a child or invalid.
2. <**khwaaunu (dūdh)**> to suckle. [*Cp.* ko'ba.]

tĩĩ'joro' *t.* <**aajkal**> nowadays. [*Syn.* ti'nxããga.]

tĩjyu' *n.* <**kurkuccaa**> heel.

ti-^{1} [*TB* *t(y)ik=*(g-)tyik n. 251, n. 271] *num.* <**ek**> one.
tigaẽ'. *One day.*
tigur. *One yoke of oxen.*
ti'dĩ. *One year.*
ti'na de'. *A little portion of cooked vegetable.*
ti'syaa. *One moment.*
[*Syn.* gxri'.]

ti'^{2} *n.* <**daajyū-bhaai**> sibling of same sex as self.
aab ti' pxasimaẽ. *Father's brothers' children.*
aam ti' pxasimaẽ. *Mother's sisters' children.*

-ti^{3} *see* **-di** 'emphatic'.

ti^{4} *n.* <**kunaa**> corner; angle (of rice field).

ti'ba *v.* <**saaṭnu**> to exchange; barter.

tibaa' *v.*
1. <**ochyaaunu**> to spread out.
prxemaẽ khaibiri' kaamlo' til txum. *When guests come you must lay out a blanket.*
2. <**phuṭnu**> to split; break; crack.
na'ga phũ' tixyaam'. *The eggs will break.*
curoḍ jyaadaa thũ'ĩ biri' madi' tim. *If you smoke a lot of cigarettes your lips crack.*

tibe' [*TB* *r-pat 45] *n.* <**jūkaa (wanko)**> leech in grass, leaves.
[*Syn.* nããbli'.]

ti'brãã de' *a.* <**ek thopo**> a little (fluid); a drop of.

ticyaarna' *av.* <**ekai coṭĩ**> simultaneously.

tidĩma *t.* <**ahile saal**> this year.

ti'la^{1} *n.* <**ek mahĩnaa**> one (of month).

ti'la^{2}, **tila** *p.* <**bharĩ**> throughout.
sarkha ti'la. *Throughout the winter.*

ti'le *see* **ti'nale** 'closely'.

tili' *n.* <**sũgūr**> pig - domestic.
tili' txoba. *Boar.*
tili' momãã. *Sow.*

ti'maẽ *see* **ti'** 'sibling'.

ti'mi *n.* <**tarul**> yam.

timli' kaamli' *n.* <**bijulī (camakane)**> lightning.

timmru' *n.* <**guhẽlĩ**> berry (in jungle, pink, 10 mm. x 5 mm., ripens in Jesth).

ti'nale, ti'le *av.* <**najīk**> closely.
ti'nale ŋxyodu. *Watch closely.*
ma'gine ti'nale axxyaad'. *Don't go near the buffalo.*

ti'ntiri *n.* <**titraa-titro**> pheasant.

tintiyaali *a.* <**tīn pheraa**> thrice.

ti'nxããga *t.* <**aajkal**> nowadays. [*Syn.* tĩĩ' joro'.]

ti'phũde' *a.* <**ek cokṭo**> a little (meat or potato); a chunk of.

ti'ra *n.* <**tīr-kinaaraa**> bank of stream; coast of sea.

tiri' *n.* <**salaha**> locust.

tirthaa *see* **tretaa** 'third era'.

ti'syaa[1] *n.* <chīn (ek); ek dui din> a moment; a short while.

tisyaa'[2] *n.* <cari amilo> berry (very bitter, 10 mm. x 3 mm., black, ripens in Mangsir).

tiyãã' *t.* <aaja> today.

tõ'[1] *n.* <bhããḍo> vessel (for eating or cooking).

tõ[2] *n.* <melo> work incomplete, to be resumed.
telba'e tõ lab xwaa'? *Shall I continue on with yesterday's work?*

tõphyaa'r *a.* <mesai saŋga> unceasing; continuous.

tõbaa' [*TaGTh* *taŋ] *v.* <ramaaunu> to be happy.

to'[1] *i.* <ho ki?> you follow, you know?

to'[2] [*TaGTh* *taaq; *Cp* dohq] *pn.* <ke?> what?

to[3] *n.* <banel> pig - wild.

to' budũ tãã *n.* <kehi kuraa> something.

to lo *n.* <baagh warṣa> year of the tiger (in Tibetan 12-year cycle = 1950,62,74,86).
[*Syn.* cẽ lxo.]

to'ba *v.* <thaapnu> to hold out (a vessel to receive something).

todon *av.* <bittikai> immediately.
[*Syn.* cwaa'ṭṭan; gxari'nnaa; bittikan.]

togo' *t.* <ahile> now; presently; shortly; in a little while.
[*Syn.* dxero'; aba.]

to'i ax... *n.* <kehi pani> nothing.
to'i axyõ'la. *Nothing was available.*

to'laa *a.* <keko> what sort of?

tomĩ' *n.* <upiyãã> flea.

to'ndori, to'nto'ri *a.* <sab (wastu)> everything; all.

toyo' *n.* <pĩḍaalu> flora; a root vegetable, calladium arumacise.

tretaa, tirthaa *a.* <tretaa> second of four eras of Hindu mythology.
[*Cp.* satte'; dwaapar; kali.]

tũ'ba, tu'ba
1. *v.t.* <baṭulnu; jammaa garnu> to gather; collect; glean; harvest.
2. *v.i.* to gather.
mxi lxe' ca'r tũ'i. *Many people gathered there.*

tu'[1] [*TB* *(m-)tuk∿*(s-)tu:k∿ (s-)du:k n. 190, n. 231; *TB* *(m-)twa∿*(s-)twa n. 190; *TB* *twiy=*twəy 168; *Cp* dyurq] *n.* <thūk> spittle.

tu'[2] *n.* <baauso> mallet - flat, heavy, for breaking previously unused ground.

tu' waabaa' *v.* <thūk phaalnu> to spit.

tu'ba *see* tũ'ba 'harvest'.

tubaa'[1] [*TB* *tuk 'cut' 387] *v.* <kaaṭnu (maasu)> to cut (meat).

tubaa'[2] *v.* <banda garnu (ḍhokaa)> to shut (a door); close.

tubaa'[3] *v.* <ṭipnu> to pluck (flowers, heads of grain); to pick up (hot coals with tongs).
[*Syn.* thubaa'.]

tu'd praa'baa *v.* <thuknu> to spit at (usually contemptuously).

tudu' *n.* <mugaamaa raakhne cij> turquoise.

tugyu'm naidi'ma *t.* <pohor-paraar> in years past.

tuĩ' pxuri, twĩ' pxuri *n.* <arĩgoṭhe> millipede.

tundiba' *v.* <tunnu> to mend.

turi *n.* <torī> mustard.

tu'si, tu'sidi' *i.* <kunni> particle expressing ignorance.

tusyu' *n.* <asinaa> hail.

twĩ' pxuri *see* **tuĩ' pxuri** 'millipede'.

txa'[1] [*TaGTh* *dap] *n.* **<siyo>** needle.

txa[2] *n.* **<daajyū-bhaai>** kin of same exogamous clan.

txa' mĩ' *n.* **<siyoko nathri>** eye of needle.

txajyõ *n.* **<daajyū (kaanchaa)>** elder, not eldest, brother (term of address); respectful address for any older man. [*Syn.* axwaa'.]

txalĩ *n.* **<dhanuṣ>** bow for hunting; bow used in carding wool.
txalĩd pae pxuba. *(You) card wool with a bow.*

txargyo *a.* **<debre>** left hand. [*Syn.* txebbre.]

txasi *i.* hesitation word (often initial to discourse in which delicate subject is to be discussed).

txããba *v.* **<rojnu>** to choose; select; prefer; pick out; cull.

txaaba' [*TB* *tu=*du 258] *v.* **<khannu>** to hoe; dig.

txaamlo, txaammlo *n.* **<putaalī>** butterfly.

txaarba *v.* **<kaamnu>** to tremble; shiver; shake (in chill, fright, shaman's trance).

txẽ-chyaa *n.* portents used by shaman in divination.
txẽ-chyaa ṭuimũ, ca' gur nxemu. *He casts(?) the portents, he shakes in a trance.*

txeba'[1] *v.* **<pakaaunu>** to cook vegetables by browning initially in oil, then simmering in own juice or small amount of water.

txeba[2] *v.* **<aṭaaunu, aḍnu>** to fit into a given space.

txebbre *a.* **<baayãã, debre>** left (opposite of right). [*Syn.* txargyo.]

txebbre paale' *n.* **<debre (haat calne)>** left-handed person.

txĩĩ *n.* **<din, diũso>** daytime; days (as opposed to nights).

txĩĩ tximĩ *t.* **<dinbhari>** all day long.

txi'[1] *n.* **<bhaarī>** load; burden; bundle carried by porter.

txi[2] *n.* **<samaya>** time; occasion.
caba'e txi tai. *It's time to eat.*

txiba'[1] *v.* **<uṭhaaunu (dhaan)>** to gather into sheaves.

txiba[2] *v.* **<taapnu>** to warm oneself (at a fire).

tximru, tximmru *n.* **<maakuro>** spider.
tximmru jaalaa. *Spider web.*

tximmru-bicche *n.* **<bicchī>** scorpion.

tximrõ *n.* **<dhipraŋ (gaaũko naam)>** village name, one hour north of Ghachok.

txiyãã, txĩĩ' *n.* **<ghaam, sūrya (diũso)>** sun; broad day (roughly 9 a.m. to 3 p.m.).

txiyãã axdxaa' *n.* **<madhyaahna>** noon; midday.

txiyããe' jyoti *n.* **<prakaaš>** sunlight.

txiyããri' *t.* **<diũso>** by daytime; in the afternoon.

txõba [*TB* *don∿*ton 'go out, come out' p. 125; *TB* *twak 'emerge' n. 63] *v.* **<niskanu>**
1. to emerge; to come out.
2. to leave; to depart on a journey.
   kadi' baje txõ khai. *What time did (you) leave?*
3. to pass (urine, bowel motion).

txo' *n.* **<thaam>** pillar; post.

txoba[1] *a.* **<bhaale>** male (of animal). [*Ant.* momãã.]

txoba[2] *v.* **<bheṭnu>** to meet.

txoba^{3} *see* **txuba** 'must'.

txu *n.* **<ḍhuŋgro>** cylindrical container of bamboo for storing liquids (about 12 cm. diam. x 45 cm. long).

txuba, txoba *v.* **<parnu(jaanu)>** must; ought; to have to.

txula *n.* **<dhūlo>** dust.
nãã' txulaa. *Drizzle (lit. rain dust).*

txuli *n.* **<damaaī>** tailor caste.
txulsyo. *Tailoress; wife of tailor.*

txura *n.* **<saano rukh>** sapling.

tya'te' *n.* **<alikataa>** morsel; small portion eaten by convalescent.
[*Syn.* khaa'gae.]

U

-ũ *s.* **<ṭa..>** locative.
ca' dinaaũ sero' khãã'xyaai'. *After that day it is finished.*
ca' khlxyoũle' rela'r xõĩ'. *From that place (we) boarded a train.*

ũ'ba *v.* **<ghopṭanu; ghopṭyaaunu>** to empty.

ũ'ḍa *n.* **<ū̃ṭ>** camel.

-ũdi', -ẽdi *p.* **<paṭṭi, tira, tarpha>** towards; in the direction of.
[*Syn.* paṭṭi; samma'; -xari'.]

ũĩ, ui, uĩ, ũĩ' *loc.* **<agaaḍi, saamunne, aghi>** in front; before; forward.
ca' ũĩri' tãã axlaa. *(They) don't say it to his face.*
[*Syn.* uyãã'. *Ant.* plxari.]

ũi pxali *n.* **<agaaḍiko khuṭṭaa>** foreleg.
[*Ant.* li pxali.]

ũ'iba *v.* **<dekhaaunu>** to show.

ũĩ'miĩ' *t.* **<asti>** some days ago; day before yesterday.

-ũle' *p.* **<baaṭa>** from (in space).

-ũlõ' *see* **-ulõ'** 'classifier'.

ũsya, ũĩsya *n.* **<pharsī>** pumpkin.

ũsyu'^{1} *n.* **<piṭhyū̃>** back - upper.
[*Syn.* kxo.]

ũsyu^{2} *n.* **<ukhū>** sugar-cane.

-u^{1} *s.* **<u-..>** imperative on bxaau' 'bring'.
[*Syn.* -gu.]

u^{2} [*TB* *pu·k∿*buk 358] *n.* **<oḍhaar>** cave.

u^{3} *c.* **<ki?>** or; interrogative particle.
kxi kanchi mu? u to'? *Are you the youngest daughter? Or what?*

ubaa' *v.* **<šuru garnu gīt gaaunu>** to sing first line of a solo couplet.
[*Cp.* ṭuka.]

u'bjani *n.* **<ubjanī>** produce; crop.

ubxaapradxaan *n.* **<ubhapradhaan pancaa>** deputy mayor.

u'ḍidiba *v.* **<uḍaaunu>** to cause to fly; fly (of kite, bird).

udridiba *v.* **<utranu>** to alight (of a bird; of a person from a vehicle).
[*Syn.* nxeba.]

ugaasdibaa' *v.* **<pharkaaunu (khet)>** to plough after spreading manure, plough repeatedly.

ui *see* **ũĩ**.

u'iḍaa *n.* **<kalejo>** liver.

ujinḍe' *see* **bandaki**.

u'jyaalo *n.* **<ujyaalo>** light; illumination.
[*Ant.* ane'ro.]

ukhaalu' *a.* **<ukaalo>** uphill.
[*Syn.* ka'ẽḍu; taadi'.]

ukhaan *n.* **<ukhaan>** proverb.

u'lḍu' *a.* **<ulṭaa>** upside down; idiotic.
[*Ant.* sulḍu'.]

-ule' *p.* **<-baaṭa>** from.

ŋa pukhru'ule' cha' baje txõyu'lau. *I left Pokhara at 6 o'clock.*

-ulõ', -ũlõ' *s.num.* <oṭaa, goṭaa> classifier - carpets, birds. galẽja' pliulõ'. *Four carpets.*

ulṭaa' pulṭaa' *a.* <ulṭaa pulṭaa> topsy-turvy. ŋad bibjau ulṭaa' pulṭaa' tai. *The things I said have got all mixed up.*

um, umãã *n.* <garam mausam> hot season; summer. [*Ant.* pu'maa.]

umer *n.* <umer> age (of a person).

umgadi'ba [*N* 'to escape, get away'] *v.* <umkanu> to complete (a task, period of service or mourning, etc.). to'ndori umgadi'l khãã'ĩ. *Everything is completed now.*

unes *n.* <unnais> nineteen.

untis, unantis *n.* <uanantīs> twenty-nine.

upaas *n.* <upawaas> fast. [*Syn.* barjit.]

upaas ṭibaa' *v.* <upawaas basnu> to fast. [*Syn.* barta ṭibaa'.]

uphridibaa' *v.* <uphranu> to jump up.

u'rba *v.* <baasnu (bhaale)> to crow (of a cock).

urgyaa *a.* <pahẽlo> yellow.

usidiba' *v.* <osinu> to become wet.

utaardiba' *v.* <utaarnu> to cause to alight; land (aircraft).

utille', uttille, uttile' *a.* <besarī> much; greatly. ŋalai tõba'e saab gxri' mula, utille'. *There was a gentleman who liked me, very much.*

uttar *loc.* <uttar> north. [*Syn.* ka'ẽḍu; taadi'.]

uwaabaa' *v.* <upkaaunu> to lever out of the way.

uyãã', ũĩ, ũiyãã' *t.* <asti> formerly; some time ago; previously. jaisimaẽdl uyãã'n din ŋxyona. *The astrologers looked for an auspicious day some time before.*

W

waa', waa *see* **xwaa'** 'question particle'.

waabaa' *v.* <phaalnu; phyããknu> to discard, throw away. pxasi waabaa'. *To abort a pregnancy.* khõna waabaa'. *To clear one's throat.* tu' waabaa'. *To spit.*

waaphas, waapas *av.* <phirtaa> back.

waastaa *n.* <waastaa> attention.

wochẽ *i.* <bicaro> poor thing; expression of sympathy. tel nẽsa'ri xyoi gon, wochẽ. *You cooked last evening indeed, you poor thing.*

wono', wonõ' *p.* <dekhi, baaṭa> since; from. paile' wono'. *Since the beginning.* mo' dxũ' wonõ'. *All the way from the rattan tree.*

X

xab jããge *n.* <lagaũṭī> underpants.

xaba, xaawaa *n.* <haawaa> air; climate. xaba caba'r xyaaba'. *To take the air, go for a stroll.*

xa'ger xa'ger *n.* <saas phulnu; dam baḍhnu; swãã swãã hunu> panting.

xai *p.* <ni, hai> courteous particle on request. binti mu xai. *(I) have a request, please.*

xa'i labaa', xaiba *v.* <haaī garnu>

to yawn.
[*Syn.* kãã'ba.]

xaid, xer *i.* <hatterī> exclamation (really! indeed!).

xa'jaar *num.* <hajaar> thousand.

xajur *i.* <hajur> response (respectful) to greeting; yes.
[*Syn.* õ.]

xa'k *n.* <hak> orders; right; authority delegated by a sovereign; area of responsibility.
mrũd xa'k pĩdu' biyãã ladẽ' lal txum. *If the king gives the order one must make war.*
kxie menṭola ŋid pĩl txum biba xa'k axlxaudi. *Regarding your pressure lantern we do not have the right to say, '(You) must give it'.*
ancalaa' dxiš ancalaa'e xa'k lxaidim, mrũdi ancalaa' dxišlai xa'k pĩĩ. *The zonal commissioner exercises authority over the zone, (for) the king gave him the responsibility.*

xa'la *n.* <hal> yoke of oxen; plough.
[*Syn.* gura.]

xalla' *n.* <hallaa> uproar; commotion.

xalwaa' *n.* <manbhog> confection made of coconut, sugar, ghee.

xaŋka'ŋ *n.* <haŋkaŋ> Hong Kong.

xaptaa' *n.* <haptaa> week.
[*Syn.* sada'.]

xa'ra xu'ri *n.* <paanī aaunalaaī chinbhari aakaašmaa baadaal laagnu> sudden change from sunshine to threatening rain.

xarbi'na *n.* <haarmoniyam> harmonium; piano accordion.

-xari *p.* <tira; paṭṭi> towards; near; to the area of.
[*Syn.* paṭṭi'; -ũdi'.]

xa'riyo pariyo *n.* <hariyo pariyo> greens (of vegetables).
xa'riyo pariyo ṭxaa ti'nade' pĩn o'. *Please give (me) a little green vegetable.*

xa'ta pata' *a.* <hattapatta (turuntaa)> immediately; hurriedly; instantly.
[*Syn.* turu'nta; gxari'nna.]

xaudi'ba *v.* <hapkaaunu> to rebuke; to scold.

xãã¹ *n.* <hãã (baaghako šabda)> snarl of tiger.

xãã'² *e.* <hãã? (nabujhda sodhne šabda)> expression of puzzlement.
xãã? kxi to' lxo ja? *What? (But) what year are you?*

xããga' *n.* <hããgo> branch of tree.

xããji'ri *n.* <hããjirī> roll call; parade.

xããji'r *a.* <hããjir> present; reporting for duty.
xããji'r taba'r xyaam. *I'm going (down) to report for duty.*

xããsa' *n.* <hããs> duck.

xaani' *n.* <haani> evil; harm.
naa's lawaai, athaba xaani' lawaai. *Caused loss, that is, caused harm.*
[*Syn.* naa's.]

xaaraa' *n.* <daamlo (daaĩ haalne)> rope round neck of threshing oxen.

xaardi'ba, xardiba *v.* <haarnu> to lose; to be defeated.
xaardi'bae juni. *A hard life.*
[*Ant.* ṭxoba.]

xaari'yo *a.* <hariyo> green.
[*Syn.* pĩgyaa.]

xaastaa' *n.* <išaaraa> movement of hands; gesture.

xaati, xaatti *n.* <haatti> elephant.

xaawa' jxaasa' *n.* <hawaai jahaaj; wimaan> aircraft.

xaawaa' nxõxyaaba' *a.* <haawaa bigranu (baulaaunu)> mad.

xaawoldaa'ra *n.* <hawaldaar> sergeant (in Indian or Nepalese army).

xẽba *v.* <usinnu> to boil (trans).

xe[1] *n.* <lek> grazing ground (high, above villages, with sparse trees).

xe[2] *e.* <e> oh, I see (signifying that one has now understood).

xe'[3] *e.* <e?> eh (= do you understand?).
kxen' lari sero'm tõphyaa'r taxyaam' xe'? *When you work and work, it becomes unceasing, you see?*

xegaa'r *n.* <hekaa> alertness; attention.
chenle xegaa'r thẽĩ biri' prxal' txum. *You must walk being fully alert.*

xel' *n.*
1. <waastaa nagarnu> neglect.
2. <helaa> hate.

xepaa *n.* <paahaa (banmaa)> frog - large (15 cm.), grey with yellow underneath, edible, lives in uplands (Thamna dialect).
[*Syn.* kxau.]

xesaẽ *n.* <wanko bhūt> spirit which dwells in forest areas.
[*Syn.* mxõ'; syaa'gi; masana; syo'; sarwẽ'; bIkhaa; bxut; thaa.]

xe't *e.* <hatterī> exclamation (=really!).

xi lxo *see* **xui lxo** 'year of the cat'.

xilaa' *n.* <hilo> mud.

xi'na bina *n.* <hinaamina> harm; damage.

xinbe'g *n.* <haate jholaa> hand luggage; carpet bag.

xindi' kxyui' *n.* <hindī bhaašaa> Hindi language.

xindu'sthaa'n *n.* <bhaarat> India.
[*Syn.* inḍiyaa'; bxaara'da.]

xisaa'b[1] [*N* hisaab 'account'] *n.* <anusaar> according to; proportionate to.
pũji' xisaab pĩm. *(They) give according to their means.*
[*Syn.* anusaar; bamojim.]

xisaab[2] *n.* <hisaab> arithmetic; reckoning; account.

xissa' *n.* <hissa> section; part; share.

xõ *n.* <khaalṭo, khaaḍal> hole.

xõba' *see* **khõ'ba** 'enter'.

xo[1] *e.* <ho> oh; really?

xo-[2] *av.* <-nai> just (deictic used ostensively); precisely.
xo chale raa'd tho'i biri' ṭim. *(They) continue, spending the night in just that way.*

xoba' *v.* <cuṭnu (dhaan aadi)> to beat (grain) with a stick; dash against the ground; thresh.

xoẽba *v.*
1. <jhamṭanu> to pounce.
2. <bhyaauna khojnu> to strive.

xoe' *e.* <hai; hoi> response to call.

xoldõ, xõ'ldõ *n.* <khaaḍal (khaalṭo)> hole.
[*Syn.* kholdõ.]

xoš *n.* <hoš> caution; care.
[*Syn.* yaa'd; cyowaa.]

xošyaa'r *a.* <hošiyaara> careful; cautious.
xyo' khamu, xošyaa'r chenle lad. *A thief will come, keep careful watch.*

xoṭe'l *n.* <hoṭal> inn; restaurant.

xrab se'bamaẽ *n.* <jaanne-sunne, jaana-kaar> wise men; qualified people (either referring to arbitration of quarrels, or to divination).

xraba [*TaGTh* *rah] *v.* <jaannu> to know a skill; to be competent.
tamũkxyui' põ'ba xraba si'baalu mu. *(He) is skilful in (his) speaking knowledge of Gurung.*

xraḍi *n.* <kaamlo> rug for floor

(used for sitting and sleeping upon); woollen blanket. [*Syn.* kaammlo'.]

xramĩ *n.* <ribaaŋ> village, west of Ghachok on Mardi River.

xrasi [*H* rassī] *n.* <ḍorī> rope. [*Syn.* chu.]

xrasid *n.* <rasīd> receipt; acknowledgement.

xrasidiba *v.* <rasaaunu> to solder; to seal a hole; to stop a leak.

xrããḍi *n.* <widhawaa> widow (offensive term - *see* mrĩ xrããḍī).

xraa *n.* <pokhari; talaau> pond. [*Cp.* taa'laa; samudra.]

xraa ku'di, ra ku'di *n.* <roṭe piŋ; carkhe pīŋ> ferris wheel made of rough timber.

xraaba [*TB* *k(h)rap 'beat, thresh' n. 382; *TaGTh* *rab 'beat drum] *v.* bajaaunu to ring; to play; to strike (bell, instrument).

xraaḍa' *n.* <carkhaa> spinning wheel.

xraalbu *n.* headgear worn in ceremonies by pujyu', made of wool with tassels hanging down back.

xraane *n.* <nigaala baaṭa banne ek prakaarko baar baarne (wastu-yantra)> fencing woven from cane (about 10 cm. mesh). [*Cp.* baaraa; baannu.]

xraar *n.* <rahar> desire; wish; liking; envy.
lxe' thuma'ẽne baalu prxaba' xraar kham. *One likes to walk with many friends.*
kxe' lal axtxubae mxi mrõĩ biri' xraar kham. *Seeing a person who doesn't have to work one feels envy.*

xrẽba *v.* <ṭaasnu> to adhere to; to stick.

xrẽdo *n.* <jããto (anna pīdhne yantra)> mill stone for home grinding.

xrẽga' *n.* <bhaaŋgro> mantle woven of jungle thread or cotton, worn by men.

xrẽgo *a.* <ṭaaḍhaa> distant; far away.

xrẽgo prxaba' *v.* <yaatraa jaanu> to go on pilgrimage.

-xreba'[1] *v.* <nabhaeko, sittieko> to not be (negative allomorph of mu).

xreba[2] *v.* <aašaa garnu> to hope; to expect.

xrekha *a.* <dharso, dharko> ruled; striped.

xrĩgyo [*TB* *s-riŋ 433] *a.* <laamo> long (of distance or pronunciation).

xri khabaa' *v.* <gotaa jaanu> to resemble.

xriba[1] [*TaGTh* *rib] *v.* <maagnu> to beg; to ask.

xriba[2] [*TB* *rus 6; *Cp* ṛusq] *n.* <haaḍa> bone.

xrin labaa' *v.* <laamo paarnu> to lengthen; to increase.

xris *n.* <risa> anger.

xris khabaa' *v.* <risaaunu> to be angry; annoyed. [*Syn.* ṭxuba'; gaar mxããdiba.]

xrõsa *pn.* <aaphū> self; own (reflexive pronoun).

xroja *n.* <paanī raakhne ghyaapo> water vessel (copper, 1 m. high).

xrumaala *n.* <rumaal> handkerchief.

xruwaa *n.* <kapaas> cotton.

xũ *e.* eh; interjection of puzzlement.

xuba [*TB* *up 107] *v.* <ḍhaaknu> to cover up; to cover over a hole.

xugaa' xraabae nemãã *n.* <laahããce> wood pecker.

xui[1] *n.* <kiraṇ> ray (of light,

narrow).
[*Syn.* sa'ra.]

xui labaa' *v.* <khui garnu> to sigh.

xui lxo *n.* <biraalo warṣa> year of the cat in Tibetan 12-year cycle (=1951,63,75,87).

xuiba' *v.* <bolaaunu> to call out to someone.

xuku'm, xu'ma *n.* <hukum> law; order - governmental; orders; permission.
ca' txiri xindu'sthaa'n xyaaba'e xu'ma axla'. *At that time they did not give permission to go to India.*

xul' *n.* <hūl> crowd; commotion of people.

xunbyãã'si *n.* <hyaaŋjaa> village on road from Ghachok to Pokhara.

xuski' *n.* whisky.

xu'tta labaa' *v.t.* <huttyaaunu> to fling down.

xwããba' *v.*
1. <phakaaunu> to soothe (a child).
2. <phakaaunu> to court.
3. <phuslyaaunu> to entice; cajole; tempt (by words).

xwaa', waa' *pa.* <ho ki; hagi> question particle (sentence final).
[*Syn.* aa.]

xyaaba'^{1} *v.* <jaanu> to go.

-xyaaba'^{2} *s.v.* completive; passive.
sixyaaba'. *To die.*
lxen' xraxyaam'. *One will learn a lot.*
kxurixyaaba'. *To fall.*
kxi nu'xyaai. *You have grown tall.*

xyaagõ *n.* <indrenī> rainbow.

xyõ *n.* <pitri> ancestors; forefathers.
[*Syn.* xe; khe.]

xyõ baajyu *n.* <pūrkha baaje; jiju; pitri> great-grandfather.

xyõ bxujyu' *n.* <pitri; hajur maa> great-grandmother.

xyõ lachin *a.* <lakšmī baas; lakšīṇ> prosperous; wealthy.

xyõbaa' *v.* <jhuṇḍinu> to hang; hang from; cling.

xyo' [*TaGTh* *yohq] *n.* <cor> thief.

xyoba'^{1} *v.* <cornu> to steal.

xyoba^{2} [*TaGTh* *yoh] *v.* <pakaaunu> to cook.

xyu' *n.* <ããgan> yard of a house.

Y

ya, yaa, yãã *v.* <ho> is.
[*Syn.* ŋxība'.]

yam *n.* <mog> leisure; time.

yaa... yaa... *c.* <ki ta... ki...; waa... waa...> either... or...

-yãã *s.* <bhane> conditional; if.
paisaa' muyãã' pīm. *If (I) have money (I) will give.*

yaa^{1} *pa.* <pani> also.

yaa^{2} *c.* <yaa> or.

-yaa^{3} *s.v.* completive.
bayaai. *Carried it away.*
ca' saeyaaba'e cami'ri ne baalu ca'e bxaani'j ro'l ro. *With the murdered woman was sleeping her nephew, they say.*
[*Syn.* -xyaaba'.]

yaa'd *n.*
1. <dhyaan> concern; thought; care; supervision necessitated by knowledge of weakness.
ŋalai to'i yaa'd axla'. *(They) show no concern for me.*
2. <yaad> memory.
kxid yaa'd axthẽ'. *You don't remember.*

yaa'd axxreba' *a.* <yaad nabhaeko>

forgetful.

yaagõ' *n.* <moriyaa> village name (east of Pokhara).

yaalimaa' *n.* <yaarlin> earring.

-yen *s.v.* <holaa> probabilitative.
liũd phuiyen. *(She) will probably blow it later.*

yõbaa' [*TaGTh* *yaŋ; *TB* *r-ya:ŋ 328] *v.* <paaunu> to get; to find; to be available; to be able.
kxe' lalaa axyõ'. *(I) didn't get to do any work.*

yõ'ba [*TaGTh* *yank] *a.* <haluko> light in weight.

yo [*TaGTh* *yaa; *TB* *(m-)yuŋ 'finger' 355; *Cp* yal 'measure (forearm)'] *n.* <haat> hand; arm.

yo aabaa *n.* <ãũṭho> thumb.

yo aamaa *n.* <cor ãũlo> index finger.

yo cxi *n.* <ãũlaako jornī> finger joint; knuckle.

yo kanchi *n.* <kaanchī ãũlaa> little finger.

yo mxaĩli *n.* <maahilī ãũlaa> third finger.

yo naa'ni *n.* <cor ãũlaa> middle finger.

yogaara *n.* <bããdar> monkey.

yogaara lxo *n.* <bããdar warṣa> year of the monkey (in Tibetan 12 year cycle, 1944,56,68,80 etc.).
[*Syn.* pralo.]

yogõba' *v.* <hallinu> to shake; to move; to shift.
[*Syn.* khaa'rba.]

yogora saẽ pyaa'baa *v.* <ekohoro man hunu> to be single-minded; undeviating; stubborn.
[*Syn.* exor saẽ pyaa'ba, gxama'nḍi.]

yomãã' *n.* <pothī> hen; female of birds.
[*Cp.* momãã 'female of animal'.]

yori *n.* <ãũlo> finger.

yosare' *see* eusare' 'small change'.

yu'[1] *v.* <aau> come down (imperative of yu'ba).
[*Syn.* kho'; lxau'.]

yu[2] [*TaGTh* *yu; *Cp* tsyulq] *n.* <bīḍ> handle.

yu'ba[1] [*TaGTh* *yuq; *TB* *yu(w) n. 289] *v.* <aaunu (maathibaaṭa); orlhanu> to descend.

yu'ba[2] [*TaGTh* *yooq] *v.* <pugnu; daakhil hunu; prašasta hunu> to suffice.
[*Syn.* thubaa'.]

yu'ba[3] [*TB* *yuw=*yəw 430] *v.* <pwaal parnu; cuhinu> to leak.

yuguba' *v.* <hikkaa laagnu; baaḍuli laagnu> to hiccup.

yu'maa *n.* <ḍhuŋgo> stone; rock.
[*Syn.* ŋyu'mãã.]

yumanaa, ŋyumanaa *av.* <chiṭo> quickly.

yunaa *t.* <cããḍo> earlier; before.

yurbaa' *v.* <riŋgaṭaa laagnu> to spin; to turn.
kra yursi prxala' axkhãã'. *(My) head is spinning, so (I) can't walk.*

yuubaa' [*TaGTh* *yuu] *v.* <khanyaaunu> to pour.

ENGLISH-GURUNG INDEX

A

a certain a.
chaba'e, phalana.

a different kind a.
syo'ba.

a little av.
de, khaa'gae, sa'ri.

a little a.
1. te', te'lẽ.
2. *(cooked vegetable)* ti'na de'.
3. *(meat, potato)* ti'phũ de'.
4. *(milk, fluid)* ti'brã de'.

a lot of a.
jyaadaa.

a moment ago t.
bxakha'r.

abandon v.
pi'ba.

able v.
1. *(capable)* khãã'ba.
2. *(have opportunity)* yõbaa'.

able to memorise recitations v.
mu'waar khabaa'.

able to reproduce (of plants) v.
cigõ'.

ablutions n.
gxusul.

abort a pregnancy v.
pxasi waabaa'.

about
1. p. *(concerning)* baareri'.
2. av. *(approximately)* de, karib.
3. p. *(in space)* dana, badẽ.
4. p. *(in time)* badẽ.

about to v.
khõ'ba.

above loc.
kxori, kxoũ, phibi, phiri', ta, taai'.

above (emphatic) loc.
tae'taadi.

abscess n.
rũ.

abuse v.
gaal ke'ba, pxõba.

abusive appellation n.
jyããṭha.

accent n.
bxaagaa'.

accept v.
1. *(suffering)* sa'idiba.
2. *(money as legal tender)* caldiba.

accident n.
eksi'ḍen.

accommodation rented for a considerable time n.
ḍeraa.

according to p.
bamojim, anusaar, xisaab.

account n.
xisaab.

accusation n.
doṣ.

accusative c.
-ne.

accuse v.
lxagaidiba.

add v.
1. *(give in addition)* thabdiba'.
2. *(in arithmetic)* jordiba.
3. *(possessions)* jordiba.

address n.
ṭhegana.

adhere v.
ŋxweba'.

adhere to v.
lxaidiba, ŋxããba, xrẽba.

adjacent loc.
re', pirba.

adjectivising suffix
-bae.

adjust in order to bring into agreement v.
milidiba.

admonish v.
sa'mjidiba.

adolescent n.
1. chature'.
2. *(bitch)* chauri.
3. *(cow)* kxurima.
4. *(buffalo)* thara.

adorn v.
siŋããrdiba'.

adult n.
ciba'.

advance on salary n.
peski'.

adverbialiser
-la, -le'.

advice n.
buj, sa'lla.

affected a.
nakali'.

affix v.
ṭããĩdiba'.

affix thumbprint v.
ṭhaudiba'.

afflict v.
syaa'ba.

affliction n.
ka'sṭa.

afraid (of plxa*)* v.
lõba', khyããba'.

after p.
liũdi'.

after that c.
jxaale'.

afternoon n.
txĩyãã.

again
1. c. phe'ri.
2. av. aarkai.

against p.
barkhela.

age n.
1. *(era)* juga.
2. *(of a person)* umer, aayu'.

agentive s.n.
-di, -ji, -le'.

agentive (emphatic) s.n.
-nna'.

agree v.
kxriba, ma'njur labaa'.

agreement n.
ma'njur, mi'laab.

agreement to use another's oxen, having none of own n.
paryaali'.

agreement between two persons n.
bandabasta.

agriculture n.
khedi' paadi'.

aim at v.
cxyaaba.

air n.
xaba.

aircraft n.
xaawa' jxaasa'.

airstrip n.
graaun.

alder-tree n.
gxyõsĩ'.

alertness n.
sajid, xegaa'r.

alight v.
1. *(from plane, boat)* khaa'rba.
2. *(of a bird; of a person from a vehicle)* udridiba'.
3. *(of bird, aircraft)* nxeba.

alike a.
pri'pri'.

all a.
khaa'gu, taan', to'ndori.

alone av.
ekaantaa', eklaasi, gxri'n.

also
1. s.n. -i.

2. s.n. *(agentive)* -jai.
3. pa. yaa[1].
4. av. dxari'.

alter v.
pherdiba'.

aluminium n.
silbaḍaa'.

always t.
khõĩ, khõyõĩ, sodaa'n, sodaa'.

amazed v.
cha'kka pardiba'.

amazement n.
cha'kka, aacamma.

ambassador n.
dud.

America n.p.
amrika'.

amidst p.
axdxari', mxããjuri, nxõnõna.

amuse v.
nilabaa'.

amused, be v.
nikhabaa'.

amusement n.
ni.

anaesthetised a.
sela tabaa'.

ancestors n.
jyujyu baaje, khe, xyõ.

and c.
1. *(sentence introducer)* daai, aba.
2. *(in numeral phrases only)* se'.
3. *(linking nouns)* ne, nego', nero'.

angel n.
so'rga dud.

angle n.
1. kunaa'.
2. *(of rice field)* ti.

angry v.
gaar mxããdiba, perdibaa', ṭxuba'.

anguish n.
pir.

animal n.
1. *(domestic)* bastu.
2. *(four-legged)* jantu, jibjantu.

ankle n.
gããṭho, pxali ka'blo.

anklet worn by small boys n.
kalli'.

another, the other person n.
aagu.

answer n.
juwaaba.

ant n.
na'bbru.

antlers n.
ru.

anus n.
mu'ji.

anxiety n.
phikkar, šok.

anyone pn.
khaba'e.

any time, at av.
belu ku'belu.

appear v.
mrõbaa'.

appearance n.
1. *(facial)* anuwaa'r.
2. *(physical form)* ru'b.

applicable v.
lxaidiba.

application of official nature (as for registration of land sale or for government employment) n.
dakhaasta.

apply v.
lxaidiba, thẽbaa'.

apply decorative spot to forehead v.
khyaabaa'.

apply medicine v.
phu'ba.

apply oil to head of effigy at post funeral ceremony v.

kra saa' labaa'.

appoint v.
khaḍidiba'.

approval n.
ma'njur, sadar, sai'.

approximately av.
de, karib.

apron-like garment (black, worn by married women) n.
ŋxyui'.

arbitrator n.
bxalaa'dmĩ.

area n.
eriyaa'.

areca n.
subaari'.

argue v.
pxõba, nxeba'.

argument n.
jxagaḍaa'.

arithmetic n.
xisaa'b.

arm n.
paakhru', yo.

armlet of gold or silver usually not a complete circle n.
rayãã.

armpit n.
ŋyãũlĩ'.

army n.
phoja.

aroma n.
thãã.

around p.
khaa'gu.

arrange v.
kxril labaa', kxrille thẽba'.

arrangement n.
bandabasta; bebasthaa.

arrangements n.
ṭhyãã'm ṭhĩ'm.

arrest v.
kxaaba, pagaḍdiba'.

arrive v.
phebaa', txõ khaba'.

arrogance n.
gxama'nḍi.

arrow n.
me.

arrow (especially associated with gods of Hindu mythology) n.
bããn.

artificial a.
nakali'.

ascetic (religious, normally a scholar with beard and yellow robes, often mendicant) n.
jogi.

as for s.n.
-la.

as for X..., Y on the other hand... p.
jadi... jadi.

ashes n.
khlyi, mebro'.

ask v.
ŋyu'iba.

ask for v.
xriba.

ask for more food v.
kxeba, kxegu labaa', khõba'.

asparagus-like vegetable n.
pattu'.

Assam n.p.
aasam.

assault (of dogs, quarreling people) v.
mxuba.

assemble v.
1. *(intransitive)* cxuba'.
2. *(machinery, etc.)* jordiba.
3. *(people)* khubaa'.

assembled a.
mru'.

assets n.
ryãã'ũ ṭhyãã'ũ.

assistance n.
saidaa'.

associate with
1. p. -ne baalu.
2. v. pxraba'.

associative s.num.
-na'.

asthma n.
dxamgi'.

astrologer n.
jaisi.

astrological birth sign (determined by the exact hour of birth) n.
nache'tra.

astrological calculation n.
laen.

astrological term for a particular occasion n.
khãã.

at p.
1. *(with place or time)* -ra, -ri.
2. *(with time expressions in days)* maa.

at first t.
paile'.

at last t.
balla.

attached to v.
pyaa'ba.

attack n.
ṭha'ḍa ṭhu'ḍu, aaṭek.

attain to a certain age v.
kxaaba.

attempt n.
košiš.

attend (house, grazing animals) v.
rũ'ba[1].

attention n.
1. *(care)* susaar.
2. *(concentration)* dxyããn, xegaa'r.

attentive v.
saẽ jxõba'.

aunt n. (see Appendix A)
1. *(FaErSi)* phaagaẽ', phubu'.
2. *(FaYrSi)* phojyõ.
3. *(Fa2dEtSi)* phaadẽ'.
4. *(FaYtBrWi)* amjyõ.
5. *(MoBrWi)* aŋŋi'.
6. *(MoErSi, FaEtBrWi)* anthebaa', aathe.
7. *(MoSi, FaBrWi - term of address)* aamaa.
8. *(MoYtSi - address and reference)* axjxyu', axccyõ'.

auspicious time for departing on journey n.
saaidu'.

auspiciousness n.
bxaru'ni, tithi'.

authoritative person s.n.
-dxiš'.

authority n.
1. adikaar.
2. *(delegated by a sovereign)* xa'k.

available v.
yõbaa'.

average av.
ṭhi'kkale.

avert the eyes in anger or disgust v.
mĩ'ṭxuba'.

awareness of surroundings n.
sajid.

awe n.
dagas.

awl for sewing rainshield together n.
nũ'[1].

axe n.
ta'.

axe head, back of n.
ta'kra.

axle of rice pounder n.
aulo'.

B

baboon n.
promĩ' yogaaraa.

baby (up to a few months) n.
o'lãã.

bachelor n.
khere.

back
1. v. *(pfx.)* e-.
2. av. waapas.

back n.
1. *(small of)* kre.
2. *(upper)* kxo.

back and forth av.
exor doxor.

back of hand or foot n.
pu.

back of knee n.
kunjyu'.

back of neck n.
ũsyu'.

backward loc.
pachaaḍi.

bad a.
axchyãã'ba, axgadilu'.

bad temper n.
murkha'.

bag n.
1. *(carpetbag)* xinbe'ga.
2. *(shoulder bag)* jxyolaa'.
3. *(for carrying grains up to 2 or 3 gallons in capacity)* nedo'.

baggage n.
maa'l.

balances n.
paa'raa.

balcony n.
kausi'.

ball n.
1. *(football, etc.)* bxugũ'nda.
2. *(lump)* ḍalla.
3. *(of wool)* kabae.

balls of ground yam, leaves, and lentils n.
ma'syããũru'.

bamboo n.
rĩ.

banana n.
mxajaa'.

bandage n.
paṭṭi'.

bandit n.
ḍããgu.

bangle n.
curaa.

bank of river n.
gxaaḍaa', ti'ra.

banquet n.
bxoj'.

bar of door n.
aulo'.

bargain v.
kõ' kasdiba'.

bark n.
phi.

bark (of a dog) v.
chu'ba.

barley n.
jxagu'.

barren a.
bed.

barter v.
ti'ba.

basic a.
mu'l.

basket n.
1. *(baby's crib)* jxogaa'.
2. *(closely woven, of varying size, for pounded rice)* ḍaalu.
3. *(large closely woven, for carrying)* korbyo'.
4. *(large, conical)* jxarãã'go.
5. *(open weave used for covering chickens to prevent them from wandering)* kurku', nũ'[2].
6. *(small, closely woven, for harvesting millet)* thublõ'.
7. *(triangular shaped scoop for collecting dung and dirt)* chu'ra.
8. *(large, closely woven, conical, for carrying loads on back, usually harvested grains)* swĩ'di.
9. *(large, conical, open-weaved, for carrying things on back, 45 to 90 cm. high)* pxi.

10. *(for storing carded yarn)* dxemyõ'.

bastard n.
progyaa.

bat n.
pho'bõ.

bathe v.
jyu khru'ba.

bathing n.
gxusul.

battery n.
1. beṭari.
2. *(dry cell)* gesa.

be v.
tabaa'.

beak n.
cucco'.

beam n.
1. sĩbi' buḍi.
2. *(central, supporting upper storey or verandah)* darlĩŋaa.
3. *(longitudinal, in gable roof)* ḍxaaḍe' balo.
4. *(sloping, of gable roof)* bxelsĩ'.
5. *(used in cattle shed)* saḍaa'.
6. *(of scales)* ḍanḍi.
7. *(of verandah)* karẽŋaa'.

beams and rafters - collective term n.
dar baar.

beans - french n.
simi.

bear
1. n. bxalu'.
2. v. *(endure)* khabdiba'.
3. v. *(carry)* no'ba.
4. v. *(give birth to)* phibaa'.

beard n.
daari.

beasts n.
janawaar.

beat v.
1. plããbaa', ṭĩba'.
2. *(a drum)* mxããda xraaba.
3. *(sheaves on ground for threshing)* pxruba'.
4. *(with a stick)* xoba'.

beautiful a.
chyããbaa'.

because
1. s.v. -badi.
2. p. sero'.
3. c. ta'lebiyãã.

become v.
pardiba', tabaa'.

become extinct v.
thũba'.

become loose v.
khumjidi'ba.

become numb v.
cxwiba.

become wet v.
usidibaa', sĩbaa'.

bed bug n.
nabli.

bed wetter n.
kũsyu.

bedstead (wooden) n.
khaa'ḍa.

bee n.
kxwe'.

beehive n.
gxaaraa', kxwe' ḍõḍaa, kxwe' la'.

beer n.
kxwipaa'.

beeswax n.
kyolõ'.

beetle (black, with a foul smell, around dung) n.
khlyi bebẽ.

before av.
1. *(in time)* talaa'.
2. *(in space)* ũĩ.
3. *(quickly, early)* yuna.
4. *(in time or space)* osõ', aasõ'.

beg v.
kxwiba, xriba.

begin v.
lxaudiba, šuru' laba', ṭhaaldiba'.

beginning n.
šuru'.

baguile v.
bxuldi'ba.

behind av.
lili, pachaaḍi, liũdi'.

behind one's back p.
plxari.

belch
1. n. axar, aaxr.
2. v. aaxr labaa'.

believe v.
kwẽ'ba.

bell n.
syõ.

belongings n.
saaman.

beloved a.
piyaaro'.

below loc.
pxriri.

bench n.
benca.

bend cane after heating v.
kurba.

bend in pipe n.
kudũ'.

benefactive (v.aux.)
-bxĩba'.

benefit n.
bxalo'.

benevolence n.
gun.

bent a.
kwaar.

bent over a.
kur, kurle', kuu.

bereft of spouse and children (a person) n.
bairaagi.

berry n.
1. *(a species in jungle)* timmru'.
2. *(small, dark blue)* cuduru'.
3. *(yellow, raspberry-like)* palãã'.

betel leaf eaten with areca nut n.
paa'n.

betel nut (hard brown and white flesh) n.
subaari'.

between p.
mxããjuri.

bewildered v.
bukka mxããdiba.

bewilderment n.
bukka.

beyond time of bearing children a.
bed.

Bhairawa (border town south of Pokhara) n.
bxairu'wa.

bicycle n.
saika'la.

bier n.
cxõ.

big a.
baḍi, khasro', thebrẽ', thebaa'.

bile n.
kãã'.

bill n.
1. *(beak)* cucco'.
2. *(account)* lesṭa'.

billy n.
1. baṭṭaa.
2. *(with lid)* syaa'mgo, ḍabba.

bind v.
1. *(a cummerbund)* khi'ba.
2. *(wrap round)* berdiba.
3. *(tie with rope)* phwi'ba.

binoculars n.
dirbin.

bird n.
1. *(general term)* nema.
2. *(species like a vulture, eagle)* ci'laa.
3. *(swallow)* cili'paaṭe'.
4. *(black drongo - long tailed, crow-like)* medgaa'.
5. *(myna)* mainãã'.

bird's food n.
swẽ'.

birth n.
janma.

birthday n.
janmaa din.

birthplace n.
janmaa tha'l.

bite v.
1. *(by dog or snake)* cxiba.
2. *(on chilli to improve bland meal)* kribaa'.

bits n.
cho'nõ.

bitter a.
kããbaa', kyũba'.

black a.
1. mlõgyaa.
2. *(of tea without milk)* phikkaa'.

black, very a.
mlõ ku'ji.

blacksmith caste n.
kamĩ'.

blade n.
1. *(of knife)* dxaara'.
2. *(of grass)* maudu'.

blame n.
1. chyaa'b, abgaal.
2. *(falsely laid)* doṣ.

blamed, be v.
kuubaa'.

blaze v.
lũ'ba.

bleed v.
ko' yu'ba.

blemish - physical n.
khoḍi'.

blemished a.
khurunḍa'.

blessing n.
aašik.

blind in one or both eyes a.
ka'naa.

blink v.
mĩ' cyũ' labaa'.

blister
1. n. phau.
2. v. phau raa'baa.

blood n.
ko'.

blouse worn by women n.
cola'.

blow
1. v. *(a fire into life)* phwibaa'.
2. v. *(one's nose)* naa' waabaa'.
3. v. *(upon sick person, usually done by a religious officiant)* ŋobaa'.
4. s.num. *(with knife)* -kkyo.

blow down v.
põbaa'.

blowfly n.
khlyi cyõmi'.

blue a.
ni'ra.

blunt-pointed a.
lxumḍe.

boastful v.
pxẽba.

boat n.
ḍuwãã, kyu' jxaasa'.

bobby pin n.
kiliba'.

body (of human) n.
jyu.

body gas n.
phi.

body hair n.
mwi'.

boil v.
plu'ba, xẽba.

boil jungle fibre with rice husks to facilitate combing v.
moloba'.

boiling n.
ṭhyaa'mmaa, khwaa'l khwaa'l.

boisterously av.
murkhaa' caalle.

bomb n.
bom.

bond n.
kaeda'.

bone n.
xriba².

book n.
1. *(exercise)* kaapi'.
2. *(printed)* pastugaa', kidaaba'.
3. *(of astrological information for a certain period giving auspicious days)* paadru'.
4. *(used by lama)* chwe, dam chwe.

boot, military n.
buḍ judaa.

border (of country or property) n.
sããdi'.

born v.
janmadiba, phibaa'.

born in the same year a.
dundrin.

Borneo n.p.
borne.

bosom n.
xri.

both
1. num. ŋxĩãḍo'.
2. pn. ŋxĩnaa' ŋxĩ'n.

both ... and ... pn.
nen ... nen ...

both sides (of paper) pn.
doxoran.

bottle n.
šiši.

bottom of container n.
asna'.

boundary n.
sããdi'.

boundary of a field n.
baara.

bouquet n.
ṭxa' naa.

bow down in respectful greeting v.
phyobaa'.

bow (for hunting, or carding wool) n.
txalĩ.

bowel motion n.
disaa, khlyi.

bowl n.
1. *(brass, 8 cm. high)* ḍugu.
2. *(brass, 10 cm. diam., for cooked vegetables, soup, or meat)* pxela.

box n.
1. *(general)* baagasa.
2. *(for food, lunchbox)* ḍabba.
3. *(on legs, for storing food)* mxudusa.

Brahmin n.p.
bomaẽ, pxrumaẽ.

braid n.
phula.

branch of tree n.
xããga'.

branches stripped of leaves by cattle n.
gxase'ḍa.

brand of burning sticks n.
miulũ'.

brass n.
pedaalaa'.

bravery n.
baadure.

bravo e.
syaabaas.

bread fried in oil n.
kxẽ.

breadth n.
cauḍaai, plxi.

break v.
chywi'ba, ciliba', cubaa', nxõba', ṭõbaa', tibaa'.

break branches of trees v.
praa'ba.

break open, apart v.
phordiba'.

break up v.
 ku'ba.

break up clods of dirt (in a wet field, with oxen) v.
 ma'eba.

break up clods of earth v.
 ṭhu'ba.

breaking up into small pieces a.
 pu'du pu'dule.

breast n.
 ŋxe.

breath n.
 so'.

breathe v.
 sẽ'ba.

brew beer v.
 kxwiba.

bribe n.
 gxus.

brick n.
 ĩ'ṭa.

*bride (*lit. *young woman)* n.
 phrẽsyo'.

bridegroom n.
 byaaulo.

bridge n.
 1. *(permanent)* pu'la.
 2. *(temporary, made of bamboo)* cãã.

briefly av.
 gxarchĩ'nna.

brigadier n.
 birgiḍiyar.

brigand n.
 ḍããgu.

bright a.
 su'kra.

bright lights of town life n.
 jxili ra mili.

brightly av.
 1. *(of lamp)* tejle.
 2. *(of sun shining)* sarla'kkale.

bring v.
 1. *(not from up or north)* bxaba'.
 2. *(down from higher altitude)* bxwi'ba'.

brinjal n.
 bxẽnḍa'.

Britain n.p.
 belaaid.

brittle a.
 cubaa'.

broad a.
 plxaaba.

broadcast publicly v.
 pracaar labaa'.

broom n.
 kuja.

brother n. (see Appendix A)
 1. *(address for older brothers and cousins, not eldest or youngest)* axwaa'.
 2. *(ErBr, not address)* aadaa, alaa.
 3. *(EtBr - address by younger siblings)* axgxĩ'.
 4. *(4thBr)* kaĩlaa'.
 5. *(full - used only in phrase* rĩ ne mxyõ *'brothers and sisters', not of two brothers)* mxyõ.
 6. *(2ndBr)* mxaĩlaa.
 7. *(3rdBr)* sãĩlaa'.
 8. *(YrBr - not used in address)* ali.
 9. *(YrBr - term of address)* bxaai'.
 10. *(YtBr - address and reference)* kanchaa', cyõ, cijyõ, bxaa'i cyõba.

brother-in-law n. (see Appendix A)
 1. *(HuYrBr)* dewar.
 2. *(ErSiHu)* aumo'.
 3. *(YrSiHu)* mxo.
 4. *(WiErBr)* aasyõ, jeṭhu.
 5. *(WiYrBr)* syõ'bu.
 6. *(WoSiHu)* saa'ḍu.

brothers n. (see Appendix A)
 daajyu bxaai', mũyũma'ẽ.

brothers - younger n.
 bxaaima'ẽ, alima'ẽ.

brown a.
 khaire'.

brush (thick, tangled undergrowth) n.

ȼxi.

bubbling n.
khwaa'l khwaa'l.

bucket with lid n.
gabu.

bud v.
paldiba'.

Buddhist chant ('O thou jewel in the flower of the lotus')
maa'ne paa'mẽ xum.

Buddhist priest n.
la'maa.

buffalo n.
1. *(bull)* rããgo'.
2. *(cow)* ma'gi.
3. *(adolescent cow)* thara.

bull n.
bxaaraa', khlxyaa' bxaara'.

bullet n.
goli.

bump into v.
thurbaa'.

bundle n.
1. *(of poles for carrying)* lũ'ḍi.
2. *(carried by porter)* txi'.
3. *(of wood, rattan poles carried as a load)* pxaẽ, -baẽ'.

burden n.
txi'.

burn v.
1. khrõbaa', lũ'riba'.
2. *(oil in a stove)* jalidiba.
3. *(flesh)* pi'rba[1].
4. *(cloth)* thi'ba.
5. *(as an offering, strictly incense but also butter or oil)* dxub' jxõba'.
6. *(wood as cooking, heating fuel)* phaabaa'.

burnt up v.
krobaa'.

burp n.
axar, aaxr.

burst v.
phadi xyaaba'.

bury a person v.
pxaaba'.

bus n.
basa.

bush n.
dxũ', jxyaaḍi'.

but c.
dile, dina, gi, tara.

butcher v.
saebaa'.

butt v.
1. thaabaa'.
2. *(of animals in fight)* thu'rba.

butter n.
1. *(unclarified)* maakhan, nuni'.
2. *(clarified)* chyugu'.

butterfly n.
txaamlo.

buttermilk n.
kolaa'.

buttocks n.
mae.

Butwal n.p.
baḍuli.

buy v.
kĩbaa'.

buy by measured volume v.
kxwẽba.

byway n.
po' gxyãã'.

C

cackle of a hen v.
kodobaa'.

cactus n.
syõ'ḍi.

cage-like trap n.
khora.

cake n.
ke'ga.

calamity, often invited by

ignoring advice of astrologers n.
ka'sṭa.

Calcutta n.p.
kalkada'.

calf of buffalo, up to one year old n.
kaḍawaa.

calf of leg n.
ligũ'.

call out to someone v.
xwiba'.

call the roll v.
mxildiba.

calling sound for dog n.
cywe' cywe', kudi' kudi.

calumny n.
culi.

camel n.
ũ'ḍa.

camp (of army) n.
ke'ma.

camphor n.
kaburaa'.

can n.
baṭṭaa.

cane n.
1. *(rattan plant)* mo'.
2. *(before splitting for weaving)* kapṭelu'.
3. *(dry, used as kindling or for torches)* medõ'.
4. *(offcuts)* lũṭhe.
5. *(piece carried by women in procession around effigy at puju's pae)* khwããlãã'.
6. *(strips used in weaving)* chae, chae khlyi, chae mĩ', gidra.

cap n.
kule'.

cape of wool worn by Thakalis n.
charkaali'.

caper v.
pyõ'ba.

captain (army rank) n.
subdaaraa'.

car n.
gaaḍi.

card
1. v. *(thread)* thutti'ba.
2. v. *(thread, not wool)* kha'eba.
3. v. *(wool, usually with bow)* pxuba.
4. n. *(playing cards)* taas.

care n.
1. *(charge, responsibility)* jimmaa.
2. *(anxiety)* phikkar.
3. *(attention, concern)* saer, susaar, yaa'd.
4. *(caution)* xos, xosyaa'r.

care for needs of another v.
ŋxyoba, se'k taak labaa', sayar susaar labaa'.

careful a.
ṭhyaa'kka.

carefully av.
aala'kkale.

carelessly av.
bijaar axlalle.

carpenter n.
sĩ' karmi'.

carpet n.
galẽja'.

carrier n.
bxaare'.

carrot n.
gaajar.

carry v.
kuubaa', no'ba.

carry away (of river) v.
bayaaba'.

carry child on one's back v.
pwibaa'.

carrying headstrap n.
1. *(for heavy bundles, made of thread)* choḍo'.
2. *(of rattan)* ṭxo' ṭobi'.

carrying net n.
phare.

carrying pole n.
no'la.

cart n.
gaaḍaa.

cartridge n.
ṭxodaẹ.

carve a figure v.
kobdibaa'.

caste n.
1. jaad.
2. *(within Gurung society)* jaade.
3. *(lower group of "sixteen" in Gurung society)* paẽma'ẽ.

castrate (goats and sheep) v.
khasi' labaa'.

castrated goat n.
khasi'.

cat n.
1. *(domestic)* nõwãã.
2. *(wild)* kxyonõwaaraa.

catch v.
1. *(grab, arrest)* kxaaba.
2. *(snag, get entangled)* kxoba.
3. *(catch up with - friend on road, thief, etc.)* syaa'ba.

cattle n.
khyodo.

cause n.
kaaran.

cause someone to do something v.
laba'r lxaidiba.

cause to alight v.
utaardiba'.

cause to enter v.
kxyuba.

cause to fly v.
u'ḍidiba.

cause to laugh v.
ni labaa'.

cause to separate - e.g. quarters of an orange v.
prebaa'.

caution n.
xoš', xošyaa'r.

cave n.
u.

cavity of earth due to subterranean caves n.
bxũn.

cell (prison) n.
ko'ḍ gxaaḍa'.

cemetery n.
cha'gõ.

censer n.
dxubaa'raa.

centipede n.
nxabre.

central a.
mu'l.

central gable of house under which lower caste people may not enter n.
dxuri'.

central shoot of plant grass or millet n.
kyugyũ'.

ceremonies which involve blood sacrifice n.
maa'r kaa'ṭ.

ceremony concluding pae, *the ritual chasing off of wife's brother* n.
aasyõ lxaaba.

certain a.
kxrosena', ni'scae, pakkaa', wochẽ.

chaff n.
1. *(from husking grains)* pwi'.
2. *(of rice)* pẽ'.

chain n.
sigri, sããũli'.

chair n.
kurji'.

chairman n.
saba'pati.

chalk for blackboard n.
pensal.

chamber pot n.
kobre'.

chance (opportunity) n.
maukaa'.

change
1. v. pherdiba'.
2. n. *(of money, strictly single rupee notes)* eusare', khusra.

change one's ways v.
phi'l labaa'.

channel for irrigation n.
kulu'.

charcoal n.
kroph̃u'.

charge n.
1. *(injunction not to repeat an offence)* kaeda'.
2. *(care, responsibility)* jimmaa.

charity n.
gun.

charming a.
sũ lachin.

chase v.
lxagaardiba.

chat v.
baad maardibaa', baad sebaa', gaph sa'b labaa'.

cheap a.
sastu'.

cheat v.
ṭhakdiba'; xyaarba.

check (verify) v.
mxildiba.

cheek n.
kxraamu.

cheep v.
ŋxeba.

cherished a.
piyaaro'.

chest n.
ku.

Chetri (a large Nepalese caste) n.p.
mxaẽ.

chevron n.
bilaa.

chew v.
ŋebaa'.

chicken n.
na'ga.

chicken pox n.
kujwir.

chief a.
sũ'ḍar.

child n.
kolo'.

childbirth v.
sudgyaari' tabaa'.

children n.
1. *(young people)* kolma'ẽ.
2. *(sons and daughters)* pxasxya pxasi.

chilli n.
khorsããni'.

chime (of clock, drum or gong) v.
ŋxeba.

chin n.
kãã'.

chips of wood n.
lũṭhe.

choke on food v.
mli'ba.

chores n.
ṭhyaa'm ṭhĩ'm, ma'dãã mu'dũ.

chorus (of song) n.
koras.

chrysanthemum-like plant, used as an antidote to nettle stings and in religious rites n.
cyõ'ḍi.

chunk (of meat or potato) n.
phũ.

church n.
manḍali.

churn butter into milk v.
lxubaa'.

chutney n.
1. *(of salt and chilis)* chu'.
2. *(rice accompaniment)* axjxaaraa'.

cigarette
1. n. curaaḍaa', kosa', sigreḍ.
2. s.num. -gyõ.

cigarette holder n.
khilli'.

cinder n.
krophũ'.

cinema n.
senimaa.

circumference n.
phero'.

city n.
šahaara.

city high life n.
jxili ne mi'li.

civil a.
ṡibil.

claim for oneself v.
pxwẽba.

clan
1. a. jaade.
2. n. *(the lower division of Gurung society - not actually sixteen clans)* so'raa jaad.
3. n. *(the upper division of Gurung society)* caa'r jaad - konma'ẽ, paĩgima'ẽ, plxonmaẽ, lemma'ẽ.

clarified butter n.
chyugu'.

clarify v.
ni'scae labaa'.

class n.
kilãäsa'.

classifier s.num.
1. *(for carpets, birds)* -ulõ'.
2. *(for clothes)* -jor.

claw n.
chĩ.

clay (white, used for whitewash) n.
phumaali'.

clean a.
saphphaa'.

clean jungle fibre prior to weaving v.
sabaa'.

clear a.
su'kra.

clear, sky is a.
mu thõŋŋyũ'.

clear throat v.
khona waabaa'.

clearing in jungle n.
khlxye.

cleave asunder v.
phordiba'.

clenched (of teeth) a.
bããdi.

clever a.
1. *(cunning, artful)* calaakh, baaṭṭho.
2. *(skilful)* si'baalu'.

cliff n.
pxro'[1].

cliff edge n.
ḍil.

climate n.
xaaba'.

climb (tree or mountain) v.
krebaa'.

cling to v.
xyõbaa'.

cloak n.
1. *(big, woven)* paspana'.
2. *(of goat's wool, water-resistant)* bakhu.
3. *(of homespun cloth)* bxulaa'.

clock n.
gxaḍi'.

clod of earth n.
ḍalla, ali'.

close v.
1. thundiba', tubaa'[3].
2. *(eyes)* cyũ' labaa'.
3. *(one eye, as in sighting rifle)* mĩ' saebaa'.

close succession, in av.
dxamaa' dxa'm.

close to p.
cẽdo', te'lẽ.

closed a.
bandaa.

closely av.
ti'nale.

closeness to death n.
ri'tta.

cloth n.
1. *(clothing)* kwẽ.
2. *(cotton, dyed or printed in various colours)* samphres.
3. *(printed with black squares on dark brown background)* chi're mi're.
4. *(raw, unprocessed)* koraa'.
5. *(white, worn as turban during mourning)* mre.
6. *(given at* pae *by maternal uncles)* aasyõ ṭaalu'.
7. *(white, carried by one man at head of funeral procession, before the* gxyãã'*, and later erected as a flag over the dead man's house during the* pae*)* ããlãã.
8. *(used in bathing - towel)* pachyoraa'.

cloud n.
nxããmjyo.

cloven hoof n.
khuraa.

club (stick) n.
phargu.

coagulated a.
cãã'ba.

coals (live) n.
mi phũ.

coarse a.
1. *(rough, big)* khasro'.
2. *(shameless, obscene)* nakaḍaa', phori'.

coarseness of speech n.
pidãã.

coast of sea n.
ti'ra.

coat (army greatcoat) n.
barenḍi.

cob of corn n.
gxyõ'.

cobbler caste n.
saargi'.

cockroach n.
khlyi bebẽ.

coconut n.
narwaala'.

coercion n.
ka'r.

coin worth half-rupee n.
mxoraa.

cold
1. n. *(ailment)* so'rmaẽ.
2. a. *(of fluids)* ŋyũ'ba.
3. a. *(of food)* sĩbaa'.
4. a. *(of day, and of person)* khũ'ba.

cold season (Nov. to Feb.) n.
pu'mãã, sarkha.

collaborate v.
thĩbaa'.

collapse v.
1. *(of landslide)* ṭwibaa'.
2. *(of house or building)* phubaa'.

collect v.
tũ'ba.

collide with v.
thurbaa'.

colonel n.
karnal.

colour n.
ra'ŋaa.

colour marker s.
-gya.

column n.
thãã'maa.

comb
1. n. *(of cock)* ṭii'.
2. v. *(hair)* swibaa'[1].

come v.
1. *(from other than uphill or north)* khabaa' (imp. kho).
2. *(down or from north)* ta'ba, yu'ba (imp. yu').

come loose v.
pyũbaa'.

come now! pa.
lu', lxau'.

come out v.
txõba.

comfort n.
kaa'ra, santok, sukha.

command v.
lxaidiba.

commoners as opposed to royalty n.
janta.

commotion n.
xaallaa'.

commotion of many talking n.
jyããũ jyããũ.

commotion of people n.
xul'.

community n.
samaaj.

community projects such as work on irrigation channels, roads, schools, animal pounds n.
jxaaraa'.

companion n.
thu.

company (group) n.
dapha.

compare v.
cxaẽba.

compared with p.
bxandaa'.

compassion n.
lxoyo.

compatible, be v.
krxiba, sa'idiba.

compel v.
lxaidiba.

competent, be v.
xraba.

complaint reported officially n.
jaer.

complete
1. v. *(to be ended)* nubaa'.
2. v. *(to finish a task, period of service or mourning, etc.)* umgadi'ba.
3. a. puraa'.

completely av.
kxyaanle, ŋithru'kkale, paṭakkan.

completely asleep, be v.
ṭobaa'.

completive aspect s.v.
-si, -waa, -xyaaba', -yaa.

comply with a suggestion v.
ma'njur labaa'.

compost n.
ma'la.

compress v.
khããdiba'.

compulsion n.
ka'r.

concern v.
yaa'd.

concerning
1. p. *(about)* baareri'.
2. s.n. *(as for)* -la.

conclusively av.
chyãã'n, chĩ'nle.

concrete n.
simenḍi'.

concrete construction n.
kralũ.

concurrent action s.v.
-ma.

condemnation n.
chyaa'b.

condiments n.
masalaa'.

conditional marker s.v.
-le, -syãã, -yãã.

conduct of one's affairs n.
caal calaan.

conference n.
sabxaa'.

confidence n.
bišwaas.

confined in space a.
sããŋgru', sããgru'.

confused, be v.
saẽ ŋxī' tabaa'.

confusion n.
gaḍabaḍ, golmol, kha'lbal, la'thaa lī'ŋ.

congenial, be v.
khrubaa'.

conscious of the consequences of one's actions, e.g. a child's awareness of danger v.
saẽ cxiba'.

consensus n.
mi'laab.

consent n.
ma'njur.

consent to a request v.
ma'njur labaa'.

consider v.
cxiba'.

consideration of matters n.
bijaara'.

conspiracy n.
ma'd.

constantly av.
dxama' dxam'.

consultation n.
buj, sa'llaa.

consultation with, in p.
-ne baalu.

consume v.
cwaabaa'.

container n.
1. *(tin can)* baṭṭaa.
2. *(drinking vessel for water)* bxaagu'na.
3. *(of cane matting for storing rice)* kaẽ koḍa.

contempt n.
1. *(neglect)* xe'l.
2. *(vocal ridicule)* billi.

content, be v.
majaa' tabaa', tī sī'ba.

contentment n.
1. majaa'.
2. *(with a meal)* sããũ'.

continuative s.v.
-ina, -ri, -sen.

continue v.
ṭibaa'.

continuous action s.v.
-na'...-n.

convenient, be v.
khrubaa'.

conversation n.
baad, tãã.

converse v.
exor doxor põ'ba, baad maardi'ba.

convince v.
kwẽ'l labaa'.

convulse (transitive) v.
lxaaba'.

cook
1. n. bxaancha're.
2. v. xyoba.
3. v. *(vegetables by browning initially in oil, then simmering in own juice or small amount of water)* txeba'.

cooked (very well) a.
phutru'kka.

cooking place n.
bxaancha'.

cooking pot n.
1. *(of copper or brass with ring handles)* kayaa'.
2. *(of white metal, various sizes, similar in shape to bxaagu'na)* baṭṭu'.
3. *(8" diam., 3" depth)* bxujuŋa.
4. *(for rice - large)* khargana'.

cool a.
sidaa'l.

coordinating c.
-ne.

copper n.
kyuraa'.

coral necklace n.

bxiru'.

corn n.
  1. makhaẽ'.
  2. *(roasted and popped)* pu'.
  3. *(flowers)* brubrũ.
  4. *(mash for cattle)* kũḍo', khole'.
  5. *(shoots, used ceremonially)* bru brũ.

corn stack frame n.
  suli'.

corner n.
  1. kunaa', ti.
  2. *(of cloth or mat)* ŋo.

corporal (military rank) n.
  naai'.

corpse n.
  sinu'.

correct
  1. a. ṭhi'k.
  2. v. sudaardiba.
  3. a. *(of speech)* khaa'sgari.

correct speaker n.
  phaṭkilo'.

correctly av.
  chenããle.

corrugated iron roofing n.
  jasta.

cost
  1. v. lxaudiba, phebaa'.
  2. n. sa'e.

cotton n.
  xruwaa.

cotton cloth (white) n.
  nainasu'd.

cough v.
  pxyũba.

council n.
  1. kajuri', sabxaa'.
  2. *(at village, district or national level)* pancaayat.

councillor (of village, district, or national government) n.
  sadaasi'.

counsellor n.
  bxaalaa'dmĩ.

count v.
  cxyoba'.

countenance n.
  mõḍaa'.

counting by days v.
  dinadi'.

country (nation) n.
  deša, muluk.

countryside (slopes surrounding villages) n.
  bana.

couplet sung by soloist n.
  ṭuka.

courageous, be v.
  saẽ bxõlle' ṭibaa'.

court
  1. v. *(flatter)* xwããba'.
  2. n. *(of law)* adlaasa', adaalat.
  3. n. *(yard of house)* xyu'.

courteous, be v.
  maa'n labaa'.

courteous person who keeps on good terms with all n.
  khojyãã.

courteous note added to request pa.
  xai.

courtesy n.
  maa'n.

courthouse n.
  gxaaḍa'.

cousin n. (see Appendix A)
  1. *(cross - term of address)* gyãã'.
  2. *(cross, female: FaSiDa, MaBrDa)* ŋõ'lõsyo.
  3. *(cross, male: FaSiSo, MoBrSo)* ŋõ'lõ.
  4. *(parallel, male: FaBrSo, MoSiSo)* bxaai'.

covenant as blood brothers v.
  cyaabaa'.

covenanted friend of a woman n.
  aagu, ŋxelsyo.

cover
  1. n. kaa'.
  2. v. *(something with something)*

kaa'ba.
3. v. *(oneself for sleeping)* pxoba'.
4. v. *(oneself from rain)* o'ttiba.
5. v. *(oneself with a blanket)* kuubaa'.
6. v. *(over)* xuba.

covetous, be v.
lobx labaa'.

covetousness n.
lobx.

cow n.
1. mxe'.
2. *(adolescent, not having borne young)* kurli'.

cowardly a.
kaaphaar.

crab n.
kwrẽ'.

crack v.
tibaa'.

crack open (of egg) v.
phadi xyaaba'.

craftsman n.
mistri'.

crane (bird) n.
jalgo kxure'.

cranny n.
khu'ndri.

crave for a specially tasty food (especially of a sick person) v.
mlãã'ba.

craw of bird for non-digested food n.
myu'.

crawl v.
gxesaa'rdiba.

crawl on all fours v.
karããba'.

crawling and toddling n.
ka'rãã ma'rãã.

crayfish n.
ku'ĩjiri tãã'ga.

crease in cloth n.
ɓoj.

create v.
banidiba.

creditor n.
saau'.

cremation platform on river bank n.
cha'.

cremation time n.
sa'la.

crevices above beam attached to external wall of house to support verandah roof n.
kre.

crier n.
kaṭwaale'.

crime n.
daaga.

crippled a.
ḍũḍaa.

crippled or deformed person n.
laŋgaḍa'.

critically ill a.
saar.

crocodile n.
gue.

crook of elbow n.
kunjyu'.

crooked a.
bããgo.

crop (harvest) n.
u'bjani.

cross v.
1. *(a bridge)* thaabaa'.
2. *(a lake or river)* tardiba'.

cross pieces in fence n.
saḍaa'².

cross-examine v.
kerdiba'.

crossroads n.
gxyãã' ti'ba.

crow
1. n. *(bird)* kagaa'.
2. v. *(of a cock)* u'rba.

crowd n.
1. thupro', xul', muluka'.

2. *(of people meeting at trail junction)* gxaaḍ.

crowd in v.
dxurdi'ba.

crown n.
1. *(of head)* kra pucu.
2. *(of king)* sripes.

crude (roughly made) a.
kacca'.

crumble v.
ku'ba, kujidiba'.

crumple (cloth or paper) v.
jxyũba'.

crush (jam finger in door) v.
pirbaa'.

cry
1. v. *(weep)* krobaa'.
2. v. *(of animals)* ŋxeba.
3. n. *(of cat)* ŋyããũ.

cubit n.
-gru, kru, naa'b.

cucumber n.
lakha'ẽ.

cud n.
kããchi.

cull v.
chiba'.

cultivate v.
khedi' lxaidiba.

cultivation n.
khedi' paadi'.

cummerband (about 12 feet long, wound round and round women's waists) n.
pha'gi.

cunning a.
calaakh, baaṭṭho.

cups of liquid s.num.
-khlyu.

cure v.
sxal' labaa', kho'j guwaar labaa'.

curious a.
caa'kh mxããdiba.

curried vegetable n.
ṭxaa.

curse
1. n. sa'rba.
2. n. *(of witch, causing loss of appetite leading to death)* bxed.
3. v. syaa'baa, kire kĩbaa'.
4. v. *(by splaying out the fingers of both hands in the direction of the person being cursed)* nããbri labaa', xĩ' labaa'.

curtain n.
parda.

custard-apple n.
ãã'ṭ.

custom n.
1. *(habit)* baani.
2. *(tradition)* calan.
3. *(ritual)* ri'ti, ri'ti thiti'.
4. *(obsolete word used of Rana period)* saasan.
5. *(at Tiwa festival, late October, of asking for gifts around the village in return for singing)* dausure.

cut
1. n. *(wound)* gxaa'.
2. v. *(meat, cloth, branch, general term)* kyãã'ba.
3. v. *(rice or grass at ground level)* kha'ẽba.
4. v. *(trees, canes)* tho'ba.
5. v. *(dry wood)* thubaa'.
6. v. *(meat)* tubaa'.
7. v. *(hair)* kribaa', waabaa'.

cut down (select, thin out) v.
chããḍibaa'.

cut out v.
tho'ba.

cut through v.
ṭõbaa'.

cuttings from hair n.
lũthe.

cylindrical container of bamboo for storing liquids (5" diam. by 18" long) n.
txu.

cymbals used by lama n.
chyolẽ.

D

dagger (Nepalese, with curved blade) n.
kxoja.

daily t.
dindinu.

damage n.
nausan, xi'na binaa', ḍyaamiḍa.

damp a.
ŋẽ'myãã ŋi'mi.

dance
1. n. naa'ja.
2. v. se'ba.

dance performed by puju' *at funeral* n.
labri'.

darkness n.
ane'ro.

dash against the ground v.
xoba'.

date n.
1. *(of the English month)* taarik.
2. *(of the Nepali month)* gate.

dative s.n.
1. *(for)* -la.
2. *(to)* -lai.

daughter n. (see Appendix A)
1. camĩ', cxamĩ'.
2. *(EtDa)* naa'ni.
3. *(2ndDa)* mxaĩli.
4. *(3rdDa)* saĩli'.
5. *(4thDa)* kaĩli'.
6. *(YtDa)* kããnchi, cxamĩ cyõ.

daughter-in-law (SoWi) n.
cõ, cxacõ.

dawn t.
sara.

day n.
din, txiyãã.

day after tomorrow t.
nũ'ĩmaa.

day before yesterday t.
ũĩ'mĩĩ'.

day, all ... long t.
txĩĩ tximĩ.

day, every t.
dindinu.

day of the week n.
baara.

days
1. s.num. *(with numerals up to 10)* -gaẽ'.
2. n. *(with numerals over 10)* din.
3. n. *(as opposed to nights)* txĩĩ.

daytime n.
txiyãã.

dazed a.
mxaliba.

deaf a.
nxausi, bairaa.

deal out cards v.
pããbaa'.

death n.
kaal.

debtor n.
asami.

decoit n.
lu'ki cu'ri, syura.

deceitfully av.
syutaa'le.

deceive v.
chaldiba', syur te'ba.

deception (lit. slippery matter) n.
cible tãã.

decide on a course of action v.
nirnae labaa'.

decision n.
nirnae.

decorate v.
siŋããrdiba'.

decorate effigy v.
pairidiba'.

decoration (Indian military) n.
joŋgi naa'm.

deed (recording division of land) n.
banḍa patra.

deem trustworthy v.
bišwaas mxããdiba.

deep (of water or hole) a.
gairo.

deer n.
pho.

defeat n.
kael.

defeated a.
xaardi'ba.

defecate v.
khlyi txõba.

defilement n.
1. *(sin)* paab.
2. *(ritual, 9-11 days after childbirth, 14 days after contact with corpse)* juḍa.

definite a.
ni'scae.

definitely av.
khai'lase.

delayed a.
kxaeba.

delirious a.
sajid axyõ'ba.

demand what has been given to another (especially of children) v.
prẽ'ba.

demon mask used at pae n.
taũri.

dent v.
kujidiba'.

deny an accusation v.
khyaabdiba'.

depart on a journey v.
txõba.

departure n.
bidaa.

deputy mayor n.
ubxaapradxaan.

deride v.
jxugu'diba.

derision n.
billi.

descend v.
khaa'rba, ta'ba, yu'ba.

descendants n.
santanaa'.

design n.
iskim.

desirable a.
saẽr ŋxããba'e.

desire n.
chutte', icchyaa', xraar.

despair n.
niraaš.

detested person n.
bairaagi.

detour v.
gxumdi'ba.

Devanagari alphabet (consonant symbols only) n.
kakha.

develop (of grains) v.
mrxiba'.

development n.
bikaaš.

devour v.
cwaabaa'.

devout a.
bxakti.

dew n.
si't.

diacritic - nasal (in Devanagari script, a superscribed dot) n.
nakhũ' sũ.

did you say? (seeking confirmation) pa.
ax.

die v.
1. sibaa'.
2. *(vulgar term)* gxyẽ'xyaabaa'.

different a.

na'ule, pha'raak, aargo'.

difficult a.
gaaro, muškil.

difficulties n.
sagas.

difficult breathing as a result of eating a certain plant v.
ilbaa'.

dig v.
txaaba'.

dig out things in the house v.
lxõba'.

direct a.
sojo'.

direction n.
disaa, paṭṭi.

directly av.
sa'raasa'r.

dirt n.
1. krxi.
2. *(rubbish)* kasĩ'.

dirty (of vessels, body, clothes) a.
mailaa'.

disagreement n.
la'tha lĩŋ.

disappointment n.
bukka.

disc n.
pada'.

discard v.
waabaa'.

discern v.
saẽr mxãẽba'.

discharge n.
1. *(pre-natal, from pregnant animal)* jxaja'e naa'.
2. *(of painful eye)* cywaa' cywaa' xyaaba'.

disciple n.
celaa'.

discovery aspect s.v.
-lãã', -mae, -na, -namu.

discussion n.
chalphal.

disease n.
bethaa.

disgruntlement n.
chorõ'.

disgust n.
bukka.

dish n.
bxããḍo', thali.

dish out v.
kywĩbaa'.

dishevelled (thrown all about) a.
saaḍãbuḍa.

dishonest (as of changing agreed land boundaries, or depriving wife of due property) a.
asa'tte.

dishonesty n.
bemaan.

disobedient a.
bibaa axŋẽ'ba, barkhela.

dispel evil influence v.
thaa kxaeba'.

disposition n.
bexora, su'baasa.

dissatisfaction n.
chorõ'.

dissension n.
phuṭ.

distant a.
xrẽgo.

distil spirits v.
paa' kwaalaaba'.

distinction (as of distinction between castes) n.
bxaba'.

distress (physical) n.
sagas.

distribute v.
cxũ'ba, cxuba', pããbaa'.

district (administrative, there being 76 in Nepal, each

district including about 50 village panchayats) n.
jillaa.

distrust n.
chyowaa.

ditch where buffalos wallow n.
ŋxyo.

diverted (as from grief) v.
saẽ bxuldi'ba.

divide v.
churiba', cxuba', cyãã'ba.

divine supernatural cause of illness n.
ŋxyoba, ŋxyob lxiba'.

diviner from lower caste n.
la'm kamĩ'.

divorce
1. n. paa'r.
2. v. paa'r labaa'.

divorcee - male n.
khere.

do v.
labaa'.

do good works and so gain merit for the after life v.
dxarma labaa'.

do work again which was done unsatisfactorily v.
kxegu labaa'.

document n.
1. *(recording division of land)* banḍa patra.
2. *(used to determine astrologically auspicious days)* mxuda.

dog n.
nagi.

domestic animal n.
khyodo.

donkey n.
gadaa.

door n.
mraa', ḍxogaa', duwaaraa, dailo.

doorway n.
gẽ, sãŋãã'raa.

dot n.
co', thablo.

doted on (of a child, with consequent spoiling) a.
piyaaro'.

double a.
ḍabal.

doubt n.
šãkaa'.

dove n.
ḍxugu'raa.

down loc.
1. *(direction)* oraa'lu, kyu'ru, ma.
2. *(place)* maa'i, prxiri, mari'.
3. *(emphatic of* ma*)* ma'ema.

drag v.
lxataardiba, gxisaa'rdiba.

drag oneself along v.
gxesa'rdiba.

dragon fly n.
kyu' aamaa.

drain out v.
taa'rdiba.

draw out v.
thutdiba'.

dream
1. n. mxõda.
2. v. mxõda mxõba'.

dress - form of n.
pošaka'.

dressed-up a.
ṭheṭaraa'.

driftingly av.
rĩ'li lili.

drink v.
thũ'ba.

drinking vessel n.
1. bxaagũ'na, loḍaa'.
2. *(without spout, about 15 cm. high, made of brass or silver)* ãkhoraa'.
3. *(with a spout but no handle, made of brass, copper or silver)* karwaa'.

drive a vehicle v.
calidi'ba.

drive away v.
lxaaba.

drive in stakes v.
kyo'ba.

drive out v.
lxaaba.

driver n.
ḍaaibara.

drizzle n.
bũbũ, nãã' bũbũ.

drop
1. v. khaa'rba.
2. n. *(of liquid)* thablo.
3. n. *(of water sprinkled for ritual cleansing)* chiḍ.

drum n.
1. *(large, double-sided, used in military)* ḍxola'.
2. *(tom tom, 8" diam., 20" long)* mxããda.
3. *(covered with cow leather)* dama.
4. *(used by lamas in religious rituals, made with goat's skin)* ŋxa.

drunk a.
ŋxeba.

drunkard n.
paa'ko.

dry
1. v. kaariba' kaarbaa'.
2. a. *(of wood, clothes)* kaar, sukkhaa'.
3. a. *(of ground)* o'bããnõ.
4. v. *(in the sun)* sõ'ba.
5. v. *(wool)* ṭẽbaa'.

dry up v.
ŋxaarba.

dubitative mood s.v.
-do', -e.

duck n.
xããsa'.

dumb person n.
1. *(female)* laadi'.
2. *(male)* laḍaa'.
3. *(idiot, mentally deficient)* axdxa kalsu'.

dung (of large cattle) n.
kobaa'ra.

dung-beetle n.
khlyi bebẽ.

duplicator (mimeograph machine) n.
chaabdiba'e sa'e.

durative aspect v.
-thẽbaa'.

dust n.
txula.

duty n.
ḍipṭi.

dwarf n.
baunebir.

dwell v.
ṭibaa'.

dye n.
raŋa'.

E

eagle n.
ci'laa, kxure'.

ear n.
nxa, nxemẽ.

ear edge, rim n.
nxa cxo.

ear lobe n.
nxa tẽ.

ear wax n.
nxa khlyi.

earlier av.
talaa'.

earring n.
1. *(with chain)* korlãã.
2. *(worn in centre of ear)* ḍxũḍi'.
3. *(small, round, worn on rim of ear)* si'lma'ndri.
4. *(small, in ear lobe)* cinjina, mãã'ḍuli.

earth n.
1. *(planet)* prithwi.
2. *(soil)* sa.

earthquake n.
sayo.

earthworm n.
kode'.

ease n.
kaa'ra, santok, sukha.

ease (of rain) v.
caebaa'.

easily offended a.
nxakhũ pra'ba.

east loc.
pu'rba.

easy a.
1. *(not difficult to do)* sa'jilo'.
2. *(not awkward)* khrubaa'.

eat v.
1. cabaa'.
2. *(roast grains, by tossing into mouth)* phe'ba.

echo
1. n. bxaarse'.
2. v. kobaa'.

economy n.
phar.

edge, at loc.
chyogari'.

edge of flat surface n.
cu'.

eel n.
bam tãã'ga.

effigy of dead person constructed at pae n.
plxo.

egg n.
phũ'.

eggplant-like fruit from jungle vine n.
malgaja.

eggs of head lice n.
ni'ri.

eight num.
pxre', aa'ṭh.

eighty num.
prxejyu'.

either... or c.
nãã'... nãã', yaa... yaa..., ki'... ki'...

elastic a.
tangadiba'.

elbow n.
kudũ'.

elder
1. a. *(of brothers)* thebaa'.
2. a. *(of siblings-sisters)* kxõba.
3. n. *(not eldest, brother, term of address)* txajyõ.

elders n.
cibnaab.

eldest daughter n.
thebsyo'.

eldest brother n.
ṭhaagu.

eldest sister n.
nãã'ni.

election n.
cunaab.

elephant n.
xaatti.

eleven num.
egxaaraa'.

eleventh day of Dasain n.
eka'dasi.

elk n.
1. *(Indian elk)* jaraayo.
2. *(a species of)* pe'daa.

elope v.
chyu'ḍi xyaaba', oḍaa'l xyaaba'.

elsewhere (at other times) av.
aaiba'ji.

embarrassed a.
pibaa'[1].

emblem of military rank n.
bilaa.

embrace v.
põ'sũ labaa'.

embroider v.
buṭṭa jxõbaa'.

embroidery n.
buṭṭa, phula.

emerge v.
txõba.

emphatic
1. *(on verbs)* -ai, -au, -sidi', -di, -m.
2. *(on past tense verbs)* -jon, -gon, -do'n.
3. *(on non past tense verbs)* -ma'n.
4. *(on verb roots)* -waa.
5. *(on nouns)* -di, -la, -mi, -i, -na', -m.
6. *(on agentive nouns)* -dai, -jyãã, -dãã.
7. *(on words ending in* -le'*)* -le'.
8. *(on words ending in* -l*)* -lãã'.
9. *(sentence final)* kuji'.
10. *(focus)* ga, ya.
11. *(on* taa'n*)* -madi'.
12. *(deictic)* axo-, aax-.

emphatically av.
kha'i lase.

employ agricultural labourers v.
nõ jxõba.

employ other's oxen, having none of own v.
gxẽba'.

employment n.
jaagir, no'kori.

empty
1. a. khaali', thedẽ'.
2. v. ũ'ba.
3. v. *(a vessel, or a room)* tebaa'[1].

enclose v.
1. *(with a fence)* thu'ba.
2. *(in a pen)* cyu'ba.

encourage v.
kwi'ba, manidiba'.

end n.
aakhi'ra, khatam.

endeavour n.
košiš.

endure v.
khabdiba', sa'idiba, thubaa'.

enemy n.
bairaagi, dušman, šaturaa'.

engage (occupy, render unavailable) v.
pxweba'.

English language; Englishman; English-speaking foreigner n.
ãŋgreji'.

enjoyable a.
raa'mid.

enjoyment of a loved one's company n.
mxayaa.

enlarge v.
syobaa', baḍiba.

enlarged a.
baḍi.

enlistment n.
bxardi'.

enmity n.
ṭha'ḍa ṭhu'ḍu.

enrolment n.
bxarna'.

entangled a.
bxuldi'ba, kxoba.

enter v.
khõ'ba.

entice v.
bxããḍi'diba.

entitlement n.
bxaau'.

envious of another's material comfort, good food, nice clothes a.
mro'ba.

envoy n.
dud.

envy n.
xraar.

epilepsy n.
carbane bethaa.

epoch n.
juga.

equally a.
baraabar, pri' pri'.

era in Hindu mythology n.
1. *(first of four)* satte' juga.
2. *(second)* dwaapar juga.
3. *(third)* treta' juga.
4. *(the present age)* kali juga.

erase v.
miḍiba'.

erect a.
ṭhaar.

erect (fence) v.
thu'ba.

errands, to go on v.
ki'l mi'l labaa'.

error n.
galdi.

escort v.
sa'dẽba.

estimate n.
aḍgal, andaaji'.

European n.
goraama'ẽ.

evaluation n.
bijaar.

evaporate v.
ŋxaarba.

even av.
dxari', pani.

even if, even though s.v.
-naa'bile, -se².

even now t.
axjxai.

evening n.
nesa', sãã'ja.

eventually av.
thaa' numa.

every a.
taan.

every day t.
dindinu, sodaa'n.

everywhere
1. loc. khanji' khanji, khantadan.
2. av. *(of child walking)* khe'rarale.

evidence n.
cakhilo'.

evil (loss, damage) n.
xaani'.

evil influence n.
thaasũ.

evil intent n.
daaga.

evil spirit able to appear as a headless form with eyes of lights in the shoulders n.
mxõ' ããlãã.

ewe (adolescent, before bearing) n.
kxyu' mxalwaa, kxyu' mxodõ'.

exact a.
ṭhyaa'kka.

exact likeness a.
dxuru'sta.

examination n.
jããj.

example n.
na'mũna.

exasperation n.
di'kka.

exceedingly pa.
maari'.

excellent a.
swaabaa'.

except a.
baaxek.

exchange v.
1. *(goods or money)* ti'ba.
2. *(labour)* nobaa'.

exchange of goods n.
sadaa'.

exclamation i.
1. *(really! indeed!)* xaid, xet.
2. *(of disgust)* axcya.
3. *(of frustration or evasiveness in response to an awkward request or question)* kho'i.
4. *(of pain when stung, burnt, scalded, pricked)* athu.
5. *(of pain when struck by hand,*

beam, rock, etc.) aya.
6. *(of puzzlement)* acya.
7. *(of surprise)* abwi'.
8. *(of wonder)* axmwĩ'.
9. *(look! most often used by shaman in trance)* xer.

exclamatory s.v.
-lãã'.

exclusively a.
sirib.

exert a bad influence on (as of adulterers, or youths spoilt by bad company) v.
bxããḍi'diba.

exhibition n.
melaa'.

exist v.
mubaa'.

expand v.
phuldiba'.

expect v.
xreba.

expend v.
mxaasdi'ba.

expended, be v.
ṭuḍi' xyaaba'.

expenditure n.
kha'rja, thaili.

expense n.
kha'rja.

expensive a.
mxããgu'.

explain v.
artha' kholdiba', maldab kholdiba', ni'scae laba', sa'mjidiba.

explain meaning of word, proverb v.
kholdiba'.

expletive - vulgar n.
mlxe.

explode v.
paḍgadiba'.

explosive charge (as used in killing fish) n.
bom.

expression i.
1. *(of disgust)* cya'.
2. *(of puzzlement)* xãã.

extend v.
thabdiba'.

extra a.
phalṭu'.

extract v.
thutti'ba.

extract confession, often by beating v.
kaeldiba'.

extremely av.
saaro'n.

extremity n.
bijed.

eye n.
mĩ'.

eye of needle n.
txa' mĩ'.

eyelid - lower n.
ŋããgora.

eyelids drooping in weariness a.
nxaru kxuba.

F

face n.
1. abbru', li', mõḍaa'.
2. *(honour)* ijed.

facing p.
sodaa'.

factory n.
kaarkhanaa'.

fade (of plants) v.
oilidi'ba.

faeces n.
khlyi.

faint
1. n. mursa'.
2. v. mursa' pardiba'.

fair
1. n. jaadra, melaa'.
2. a. *(acceptable, average)* ṭhi'kkan.

faith n.
bišwaas.

faithful a.
imaandaari, saẽ satte' tabaa'.

faithfulness (of wife to husband) n.
sa'da.

fall v.
1. pade' xyaaba', khaa'r xyaaba', tebaa', kxuri xyaaba'.
2. *(be obliged to)* txuba.
3. *(of large landslip)* ṭwibaa'.

fall asleep v.
nxaru cxwiba.

fall from tree (of fruit) v.
khaa'riba.

fallow ground n.
bããju.

falsehood n.
jxuṭṭaa', lu'ki cu'ri.

family n.
1. *(wife and children)* parwaa', jaan.
2. *(vertically extended)* khalag.

famine n.
ãngal.

fang n.
daare.

far away av.
xrẽgo.

fare n.
bxaaraa', gxyãã' kha'rja, kiraai.

fast
1. v. barta ṭibaa', upaas ṭibaa', sostani ṭibaa'.
2. n. upaas.
3. n. *(partial)* barjit.

fat
1. n. chi'.
2. a. chobaa', dxũba', kasdiba'.

father n.
aabaa.

father-in-law n.
kẽ.

fathom (distance between outstretched hands, approx. 180 cm) n.
bããũ.

fatty (nickname for obese people) n.
kabli.

fauna - crane n.
jalgo kxure'.

fauna - sambhar n.
ẽ.

fear n.
ḍar, ŋxĩji.

fearful a.
kaaphaar.

fearfully av.
tha'rarale.

fearless of strangers, to be v.
ŋo axcxyoba'.

feast n.
1. bxoj.
2. *(for wedding, hair cutting ceremony, post-funeral, etc.)* bxatyaa'ra.

feather n.
pxyaa.

fee n.
kiraai.

feed v.
1. *(solids to infant or invalid)* ko'ba.
2. *(liquid to a child or invalid)* tĩ'ba.

feed trough n.
ḍõḍaa.

feel pleased v.
chubaa'.

fellow villagers (lit. *relatives)* n.
isṭami'ttra.

female a.
1. *(of animal)* momãã.
2. *(of birds)* yõmãã'.

feminine suffix on nouns s.n.
-syo.

fence n.

baaraa.

fencing woven from cane (about 10 cm. mesh) n.
xraane.

fern n.
1. *(of which young shoots are eaten)* lauḍaa'.
2. *(like edible plant)* jalgo.

ferris wheel (made of rough timber, used only at Dasera) n.
xraa ku'di, ra ku'di.

fertile soil n.
nosa'.

fertilizer n.
1. *(chemical)* bikaaša ma'la, deši ma'la.
2. *(mixture of dead leaves and animal dung)* ma'la.

festival n.
1. caaḍa, jaadra.
2. *(major one in Hindu-Nepalese calendar, observed for ten days in Asoj, September to October, involving animal sacrifice)* dasaẽ.

fever n.
jar.

fever and weakness (loosely - illness generally) n.
na'b cha'ba.

few a.
kamdi'.

field n.
1. *(dry)* baari.
2. *(irrigated, usually for rice)* mrõ'.
3. *(close to one's house)* gxai mrõ'.
4. *(open and level common area)* mxaidan.

fields n.
khlxyo nxẽ.

field workers (assisting in the preparation of the flooded rice paddy for transplanting, paid by day) n.
baause.

fife n.
murli'.

fifty num.
ŋxajyu'.

fight v.
1. nxeba'.
2. *(with intent to kill)* saebaa' nxeba'.

file a lawsuit v.
mu'dda laba'.

file of documents n.
misil.

filigree n.
phula.

fill (mostly used with water) v.
khaabaa'.

films n.
senimaa.

final a.
akhkhiri, aakhi'ri, antim.

finally t.
balla, thaa' numaa.

find v.
1. *(obtain)* yõbaa'.
2. *(judge as, deem)* churiba'.

find something appeals to you v.
khobaa'.

finding (judgement) n.
nyaa'e.

fine
1. n. danḍa.
2. a. *(thin, small)* masinu', padlu'.
3. a. *(as of knitting needles)* pra'ba.

finely - very av.
masinkaa'le.

finger
1. v. koḍeba'.
2. n. ri, yori.

finger joint n.
yo cxi kxorbae.

finish
1. n. khatam.
2. v. khãã'ba, cxĩba, chõbaa', li'ba, nubaa', silidi'ba.

finish weaving edge or basket v.
ŋãã saebaa'.

fire
1. v. *(a rifle)* lxiba, prĩ'ba.
2. n. *(general)* mi.
3. n. *(of forest)* misaa'.

firefly n.
miwãã'.

fireplace n.
kodaa'.

firewood n.
sĩ'.

first av.
paile'.

first thing in the morning t.
nxããkharnaa'.

first fruits of rice harvest eaten at a special ceremony n.
nõwẽ'.

first-rate a.
pakkaa'.

fish n.
tãã'ga.

fish-hook n.
balchĩ.

fishing net n.
jaala.

fist - clenched n.
gxussa', muḍki'.

fistful n.
muṭhi.

fit into a given space v.
txeba.

fitting a.
tabaa'.

five num.
ŋxa'.

five hundred num.
ŋxabraa'.

flat a.
plenẽ, sa'mma.

flatus n.
phi.

flea n.
tomĩ'.

flesh n.
no.

flexible a.
ŋiliba'.

flicker (as of snake's tongue) v.
prũ prũ labaa'.

flinging back a.
xut'tale.

flock of sheep n.
bagal.

flood out (of faulty pen spilling ink) v.
okhaldiba'.

floor n.
1. *(earth, ground)* sa.
2. *(intermediate in a building)* aaḍi'.

flora n.
1. *(various species thus far unidentified)* bimraa dxũ', mxe' puju' dxũ', na'bbru sara' dxũ', naire' dxũ', na'upxyaa dxũ', nxaalgyõ, pxagi dxũ', sacyuli' dxũ', sagi' dxũ', aasuri' dxũ'.
2. *(a timber occurring in both red and white varieties)* olcae.
3. *(barley)* jxagu'.
4. *(coconut)* narwaala'.
5. *(fern)* jalgo.
6. *(orchid)* sail ṭxa'.
7. *(type of green vegetable)* ṭõnḍaa'.
8. *(type of shrub)* syo'wẽ.
9. *(wheat)* gaũ.
10. *(a type of tree)* puḍe.
11. *(dahlia)* saardile'.
12. *(rhododendron)* pu' ṭxa' dxũ'.
13. *(tubular plant 6'-12' high in forest at about 9000', used as a horn when dry)* mxaarbobõ.
14. *(root vegetable, calladium arumacise)* toyo'.

flour n.
1. *(general)* pxro'.
2. *(processed)* maidaa'.

flow v.
bagdiba.

flow of water n.
dxaara'.

flower
1. n. ṭxaa'.
2. v. *(of plants)* paa'riba.

fluent a.
phaṭkilo, le phiriba'.

fluffy av.
bũbũle.

fluttering (of a nestling learning to fly) n.
bxudududu.

fly
1. n. cyõmĩ'.
2. v. *(of bird, plane)* pxiriba.
3. v. *(kite)* u'ḍidiba.

fog n.
nxããmjyo.

folk songs n.
jxyaaure' kxwe'.

follow v.
1. *(physically)* lili khabaa'.
2. *(a religious system)* mxããdiba.
3. *(as a logical consequence)* di-.

following day t.
pxanxããgdũ'.

fontanel (membranous space in infant's head) n.
taalugaa'.

food contaminated by other's touch n.
juḍa.

food grains bought in market n.
besaa.

foot n.
1. *(of man or animal)* pxali.
2. *(of human)* paau.
3. *(measure of length)* phuṭ.

foot going to sleep v.
pxali nxar cxwiba.

footprint n.
mxae.

footrot (in cattle, treated with camphor) n.
khorẽ'.

for the benefit of p.
lxaagiri.

for the purpose of p.
lxaagiri, kaṛad, -male.

forbear v.
sa'idiba.

forbidden by astrology a.
ŋxaẽba.

forefathers n.
jyujyu baaje, khe, xyõ.

forehead n.
ŋo, ŋxo.

foreign (strange) a.
nau'le.

foreign country n.
bideš.

foreign woman of white skin n.
mi'm.

foreigner n.
bidesi.

foreleg n.
ũĩ pxali.

forest n.
bana.

forested area (high, 9000 feet) n.
khlyãã'.

foretell v.
liũba'e tãã bibaa.

forge n.
arẽ'.

forget v.
mli'ba.

forgetful a.
yaa'd axxreba'.

forgiveness n.
maa'ph.

form fruit after flowering v.
ru'ba.

formerly i.
uyãã'.

forsake v.
phi'l labaa', pi'ba.

forty num.
plxijyu', caalis.

forward loc.
ũĩ.

foundation n.
jaga.

fountain pen n.
phulḍinaa'.

four num.
plxi', caar.

fourteen num.
cauda'.

fowl (domestic) n.
na'ga.

fracture v.
cubaa'.

fragile (of glass) a.
kaaphaar, kacci.

fragments n.
1. *(of cloth)* kwẽ ṭaalaa' ṭuli'.
2. *(of long things)* lũṭhe.

fragrance n.
thãã.

fragrant a.
lĩ'bae thãã khabaa'.

frame for stacking corn cobs n.
suli'.

frames of cane bent over to form gable of cattle shed n.
dxaju'ra.

free fit (of parts) a.
kholẽba'.

free from disease a.
ni'ro'gi.

free of cost av.
chalen.

friend n.
1. *(companion)* thu.
2. *(covenanted relationship. usually of different caste)* ŋxela.
3. *(specially close)* dosti, mi'ttra.

fright n.
ŋxĩji.

frightened, be v.
ŋxĩba.

frog n.
1. kxau.
2. *(black in colour, lives in water)* ma'i wẽ'.

from p.
1. *(in space)* -ĩle', -ũle', ule'.
2. *(in time)* sero', wono'.

from the beginning of p.
laa'udo.

froth n.
pibi'.

frozen a.
ka'graa ku'gru.

fruit n.
1. *(general)* pha'l phu'la, ru'ḍu.
2. *(jack fruit)* kaṭara'.
3. *(tart flavour, size of apricot, rough brown skin, large brown stone)* kãlã.

fulfilled, be v.
behordiba.

full a.
ne'.

full moon n.
purne'.

full up, be v.
plẽbaa'.

full to the brim a.
ṭhyaa'mma.

funeral bier n.
mora'.

fungus n.
sĩ' nxẽmẽ.

fur n.
mwi'.

future n.
bxabi'sya.

future tense s.v.
1. *(normal non-past)* -m.
2. *(emphatic, 1st person sg.)* -syo.

G

gale n.
ããḍi'.

gall bladder n.
kãã.

gallon - one n.
pyõ'nõ.

gallons s.num.
-byõ.

gamble v.
juwaa khlyõba'.

gambler n.
juwaaḍe.

gambling n.
juwaa.

game n.
khe'l.

game of chance n.
baaji.

game with sixteen shells where players gamble on number falling right way up n.
kauḍi'.

gap between two things such as houses n.
anda'ra.

garden n.
bagaĩcaa, baari, gxai mrõ'.

gargle v.
khu'lu khu'lu labaa'.

garland n.
maa'laa.

garlic n.
nxu'.

garlic leaf preparation made by Tibetans n.
jimbu.

garment n.
1. *(worn by women)* ṭigisaa'.
2. *(worn by men in former times)* khaadi.

gate n.
ḍxogaa'.

gatepost for bar-gate (of stone) n.
tagara.

gather v.
tũ'ba.

gather into sheaves v.
txiba'.

gathered together (of people, flowers) a.
mru'.

generous a.
sae sxaba'.

genitals (male) n.
saa'l naa'l.

gentle a.
ŋiliba'.

genuine a.
khaa'sgari, pakkaa'.

geography n.
bxugol.

German, Germany n.p.
jarman.

gerund s.v.
-b, -ba, -baa, baa'.

gesture v.
xaastaa' labaa'.

get v.
1. kĩbaa', yõbaa'.
2. *(tickets)* tho'ba.

get rid, to v.
syo'ba.

get stuck v.
kxoba.

get thin (wear, of metal implements) v.
khiidiba'.

get up v.
ribaa'.

get wet v.
pãã'ba.

Ghachok (village NW of Pokhara) n.p.
kaju'.

ghee n.
chugu'.

ghost n.
mxõ', picaas, syaa'gi.

gift of the gab n.
lxe' põ'ba.

gift sent by mail or messenger, not handed in person n.
nasu'.

give v.
pĩbaa'.

give a dancer money in appreciation of good performance v.
krigi' labaa'.

give approval v.
ma'njur labaa'.

give back v.
ewaabaa'.

give birth v.
sudgyaari' tabaa'.

give it to me! pa.
khwe'.

give up v.
pi'ba.

glass n.
gilããsa.

glasses of liquid s.num.
-khlyu.

glasses (spectacles) n.
cašmaa'.

glean v.
tũ'ba.

gloriously av.
te'jle.

gluttonous a.
khõbaa'.

gnat n.
mo'so.

gnaw on (a bone, corn cob, etc.) v.
khri'ba.

go v.
xyaaba'.

go and... s.v.
-ne', -n.

go around v.
gxumdi'ba.

go clucky v.
nõ'ba.

go into trance for purpose of divination by communion with a spirit v.
nxebaa.

go shopping on various errands v.
kil mi'l labaa'.

go to sleep v.
cxwiba.

go to watch funeral or pae *of adult* v.
gxodaa' raa'ba.

goat n.
1. ra.
2. *(male, uncastrated)* bagya.
3. *(female, adolescent, before bearing young)* mxodõ'.

god n. (see Appendix B)
1. *(high god)* pramĩsara.
2. *(of senior class, including Ram, Vishnu, Krisna, Lakshman, to whom one offers flowers and grain offerings, but not blood sacrifice)* bxagawaa'n.
3. *(god of death, honoured during* dasaẽ *festival at* durga puja*)* durga.
4. *(local deities)* deudaa.
5. *(deity to whom a chicken is sacrificed in April and November, usually at edge of cliff)* bxayãã'r.

goddess n.
debi, devi.

go out v.
txõ-xyaabaa'.

goitre n.
gããḍa.

gold n.
mxaara'.

gold medallion in necklace n.
asurbi'.

goldsmith caste n.
sunaara'.

good a.
1. chyããbaa', swaabaa'.
2. *(astrological term)* amrita.
3. *(of character)* gadilu'.

good deeds n.

dxarmaa'.

good fortune n.
lachin.

good omen n.
saidu'.

goods n.
maa'l.

gore (of an animal) v.
thaabaa'.

gorge n.
gaŋgyu.

gossip v.
1. gaph sa'b labaa'.
2. *(reveal confidences)* nau' kisimle põ'ba.

gourd n.
tumbaa.

gourd (3' long fruit) n.
laugaa'.

grab v.
pxẽba, lxõba'.

grain n.
1. *(general)* andaa' paani'.
2. *(oats? barley? planted in November)* karu.
3. *(old)* krxo.
4. *(drying in sun)* sõ'gyaa.

granary (usually room above cattle shed) n.
dxancha'ra.

granddaughter (SoDa, DaDa) n.
kwẽmĩ'.

grandfather (FaFa, MoFa) n.
baajyu.

Grandmother (FaMo, MoMo) n.
bxujyu'.

grandson (SoSo, DaSo) n.
kwẽ.

grape n.
daakha.

grasp v.
cheba.

grasp to oneself v.
pxwẽba.

grass n.
1. *(fodder)* chi.
2. *(type used in making brooms)* baabyo.
3. *(a type of)* põ.

grassed area n.
bããju.

gratefully av.
gũnadi' gũnan.

grave n.
cho'gõ.

gravely ill, be v.
bijed tabaa'.

graze v.
rẽbaa'.

grazing ground (high above villages, sparse trees) n.
xe.

great-coat n.
barenḍi.

great-grandfather (FaFaFa, FaMoFa, MoFaFa, MoMoFa) n.
xyõ baajyu.

great-grandmother (FaFaMo, FaMoMo, MoFaMo, MoMoMo) n.
xyõ bxujyu'.

greatly av.
utille'.

greed n.
lobx.

greedy
1. a. khõbaa'.
2. v. *(show)* lobx labaa'.

green a.
pĩŋgyaa.

greens (of vegetables) n.
xa'riyo pariyo.

greeting word i.
bindi mu.

greeting word and action of holding hands in greeting i.
namaste.

grieve
1. v.i. saẽ na'ba.
2. v.t. saẽ na'l labaa'.

grind v.
1. *(grains with a handmill)* prxoba.
2. *(in mortar and pestle)* prxiba'.
3. *(through a machine)* mxaaba.

grit teeth v.
ka'ḍaḍa laba'.

groan v.
mxobaa'.

groom oneself v.
nakal te'ba.

ground n.
sa.

ground floor of house (lit. *inside house)* n.
dxĩ'nxõ.

group n.
1. dapha, paaṭi', ṭoli'.
2. *(co-operating for agricultural work)* nõgur.

grow v.
1. *(increase in size)* baḍiba.
2. *(hair, moustache, beard)* nxaba².

grow uncontrollably v.
chyu'ḍi xyaaba'.

growl (of dog) v.
ŋxururu labaa'.

grub (greenish-yellow, lives in khere dxũ', *corn, rice foliage in Srawan, irritates skin on contact)* n.
khere bicche.

guard (watch, attend) v.
rũ'ba¹.

guard duty n.
ḍipṭi.

guard house n.
ko'ḍ gxaara'.

guava n.
belaudi.

guest n.
pxrẽ.

guide
1. n. *(teacher)* guru.
2. v. *(as a shepherd guides flock)* ḍoridiba.

guilty a.
axpxraadi'.

gulley n.
piyããnaa'.

gum of teeth n.
sa ŋxe.

Gurkha Brigade (comprising Nepali troops in Indian and British armies) n.p.
gorkhaa.

Gurung n.p.
tamũ.

H

habit n.
1. su'baasaa.
2. *(particularly of negative tendency of character)* baani.

habituative s.v.
-brẽ.

Hades (the place or stage following death) n.p.
parlo'ga.

haggle v.
kõ' kasdiba'.

hail n.
tusyu'.

hair n.
1. *(body)* mwi'.
2. *(eyebrow or eyelash)* mĩjyãã.
3. *(head)* kra.

hair clip n.
kiliba'.

hair cuttings n.
kralũ.

half n.
axdxaa'.

half brothers n.
daajyu bxaai'.

half past the hour a.
saa'ḍe.

half-trained a.

mxakhanḍi.

halt v.
chyobaa', thaam dibaa'.

hammer v.
ṭĩbaa'.

hand n.
yo.

hand broom n.
kuja.

hand luggage n.
xinbe'ga.

hand over to someone else v.
sumdiba'.

hand-sized, round objects (cups, plates, cyapattis, bracelets, letters, coins, bras) s.num.
-bo.

handkerchief n.
xrumaala.

handle n.
1. *(on pot)* yu.
2. *(on plough)* anwaa'.

hang v.
cyobaa', xyõbaa', nẽjyoba'.

hang up v.
ṭããĩdiba'.

happen v.
tabaa'.

happiness n.
khuši', sa'nca.

happy a.
saẽ tõbaa', tĩ sĩ'ba.

hard a.
nisṭuri.

hard-hearted a.
ni'rmae, saẽ saaro'n tabaa'.

hard-working a.
imaandaari.

hare n.
kharaa'.

harm n.
xaani', xi'naa binaa.

harmonium n.
xarbin.

harmony n.
mi'laab.

harrow n.
ma'e.

harvest v.
1. *(millet)* tũ'ba.
2. *(of crops)* andaa' paani'.

haste n.
1. *(causing bungling)* lãã'ḍaa lũ'ḍe.
2. *(urgency)* axtxuri'.

hastily av.
axtxurle'.

hat n.
kule'.
(Ghandrung dialect: pulu'.)

haul v.
lxataardiba.

hate v.
xe'l labaa'.

have an appetite for v.
nibaa'.

have sexual intercourse v.
1. *(of humans)* mrĩ labaa'.
2. *(of animals)* prxcba.

have to (must) v.
pardiba', paardibaa', txuba.

hawk n.
baada.

hay n.
1. *(standing after millet harvest)* na'la.
2. *(rice)* praalaa.

haystack n.
kunnyo'.

he pn.
ca'.

he himself pn.
khi.

head
1. n. kra.
2. a. sũ'ḍar.

head man of village under pre-panchayat system in Nepal n.

muli', krxõ.

head of grain n.
nãã.

head of rice husking pounder n.
muslũ'.

head of river n.
si'r.

headgear n.
1. *(of white cloth)* krigi'.
2. *(worn ceremoniously by* pujyu', *made of wool with tassels hanging down back)* xraalbu.

headstone n.
deuraali.

heal
1. v.i. sxaba'.
2. v.t. sxa'l labaa'.

health n.
sa'nca.

healthy a.
ni'ro'gi.

heap n.
khaa'd, thupro'.

hear v.
theebaa'.

heart n.
1. *(physical organ)* tĩ.
2. *(mind)* ḍil, saẽ.

heat
1. n. garmi.
2. v. *(water, fluids)* kwaalaba', laabaa'.

heaven n.
swa'rga.

heavy a.
lxiba.

hedge n.
baara.

heed v.
dxyaan pĩbaa'.

heel v.
tĩjyu'.

height n.
kru.

hell n.
na'rga lok.

help n.
guwaar, madad, saidaa'.

help in starting a project v.
ããḍiba'.

hem of garment n.
ŋãã.

hen n.
1. yõmãã'.
2. *(before laying eggs)* lxããlõ.

henceforth t.
dxero'.

herdsman n.
prxõsaẽ.

here loc.
cu'r.

here and there loc.
khani' mxani.

hermit who remains alone n.
bairaagi.

hesitation stutter e.
axo-.

hesitation word, often initial to discourse in which delicate subject matter is to be discussed e.
txasi'.

hiccup v.
yugubaa'.

hide
1. v. lo'ba.
2. n. ṭxubi.

high a.
1. *(in stature or pitch)* nu'ba.
2. *(in altitude)* kxori.

highland n.
1. *(zone around 4000-6000 ft with small brush)* gxaari'.
2. *(beyond tree level but below summer snow line)* bugyaani.

hill n.
ḍããḍa.

hillside fields (unterraced) n.
khore'.

hind leg n.
  li pxali.

Hindi a.
  xindi'.

Hindu a.
  xindu'.

hire
  1. n. kiraai.
  2. v. *(oxen and plough paying with a portion of the crop)* pi'rba.

hiss n.
  ŋxeba.

history n.
  itihaas.

hit v.
  1. dxõba', plããbaa'.
  2. *(with a stick)* chyaabru'ba.

hither av.
  jxu'-.

hocus-pocus n.
  jyomẽ lyomẽ.

hoe
  1. v. txaaba'.
  2. n. *(short-handled)* kodaali'.

hold v.
  1. *(grasp)* cheba, kxaaba.
  2. *(closely, as of holding baby)* khwe'ba.

hold on! (wait!) v.
  thaaidu'.

hold out (a vessel to receive something) v.
  to'ba.

hold over oneself (covering) v.
  pxoba'.

hold tobacco in cheek v.
  pi'rba.

holder for oil lamp n.
  diyo.

hole n.
  1. khũ', xõ.
  2. *(small, in clothing, wall, rocks)* khu'ndri.
  3. *(in ground)* kholdõ.

holiday n.
  chuṭṭi'.

hollow a.
  1. *(especially of something which should have things in it, as peanut shell)* khogro'.
  2. *(of tree)* dxodro'.

hollow out a hole v.
  kundiba'.

hollowed log for beehive or feed trough n.
  kxwe' ḍõḍaa.

holy a.
  1. *(undefiled)* pawitra.
  2. *(ethically upright)* sojo', sudo'.

holy books n.
  silog.

holy man - Hindu n.
  jogi.

home n.
  1. dxĩ'.
  2. *(maternal)* maidaa'.

honest a.
  imaandaari, saẽ satte' tabaa', sajan, sojo'.

honesty n.
  imaansaa'th.

honey n.
  khudu'.

Hong Kong n.p.
  xaŋka'ŋ.

honour
  1. n. *(self respect)* abbru', ijed.
  2. n. *(respect to others)* maa'n.
  3. v. maa'n labaa'.

hood of sackcloth n.
  kuldu.

hoof n.
  khuraa.

hope v.
  xreba, aaša labaa'.

horizontally av.
  piru.

horns (of cow, deer) n.
ru.

horse n.
gxoḍaa'.

hortatory (1st plural) s.v.
-le'.

hospital n.
aspatala'.

hot a.
1. *(to touch)* cha'ba.
2. *(in taste)* sobaa'.
3. *(of fluids)* laa, la'la.

hot season n.
um.

hour n.
1. *(period)* gxanḍa'.
2. *(point of time)* ṭyãã'ma.

house n.
dxĩ'.

house and land n.
gxar khe'daa.

household members n.
paraa'.

households s.num.
-gĩ.

how av.
1. *(question word)* khaile.
2. *(emphatic, modifying adjective)* ka'tti.

how many, how much? av.
kadi'.

however c.
1. *(sentence initial)* dina.
2. *(sentence final)* gi.

howl v.
1. ŋxeba.
2. *(of witch at night)* cxuba.

hubbub n.
jyããũ jyããũ.

human being n.
mxi.

hunched up (from cold or fear) a.
kukru'ga.

hundred num.
prxa', sai.

hungry a.
pho' khrẽbaa'.

hunt v.
sigaar khlyõbaa', lxaaba.

hunter n.
sigaare'.

hurriedly av.
jxaab jxup', xa'ta pa'ta.

hurt v.
1. *(of an awkward load)* nxeba'.
2. na'ba.

husband n.
1. pyũ'.
2. *(less respectful term)* pha.

husband of a woman's covenanted friend n.
aagu.

husks of rice (very fine, obtained in second pounding) n.
ḍxuḍu'.

hymn of praise n.
bxajan.

hypocrisy n.
swããŋ.

hypocritical a.
nakali'.

hypocritical, be v.
swããŋ te'ba.

hypothetical result s.v.
-ma'la.

I

I pn.
ŋa.

identical a.
gxrinaa', khaal gxribaa'.

idiotic a.
ulḍu'.

idol n.
mu'rdi.

if s.v.
-syãã, -yãã, -du', -go', -du, -ju.

illegitimate child n.
progyaa.

illness n.
1. bethaa, na'ba.
2. *(caused by curse)* baan.

illumination n.
u'jyaalo.

illustration n.
na'munaa.

image n.
mu'rdi.

imitate v.
chyaattiba'.

immediately av.
dxamaa' dxam', ekkaasi', jxwaaṭṭan, xa't pata'.

immediately after p.
bittikan, todõn.

immigrant from another village (very derogatory term) n.
bxatwaa'.

impedimented speech n.
la'waaj.

imperative s.v.
1. -d.
2. *(if stem vowel is nasal)* -n.
3. *(polite)* -si.
4. *(nonfinal in sentence)* -du', -nu'.
5. *(on* bxau' 'bring'*)* -u'.
6. *(on* bxagu' 'bring'*)* -gu'.

implement n.
1. sããju'.
2. *(for carding wool)* kaa'.

important (of person) a.
thebaa'.

impression (likeness) n.
anman.

imprint n.
chaa'b.

imprison v.
thundiba'.

improve v.
sudaardiba'.

in s.n.
-maa, -nxõnõna, -ra, -ri.

in a few places loc.
khani' mxani, khani'.

in a little while t.
togo'.

in a massed manner av.
kha'ga khu'gule.

in agreement, be v.
thĩbaa'.

in company with p.
saada'r.

in front loc.
ũĩ, agxaaḍi.

in the case of s.n.
-la.

in the direction of p.
-ũdi'.

in turns av.
palo' palle'.

in-charge s.n.
-dxiš'.

inarticulate a.
la'waaj.

inauspicious, be v.
ŋxaẽba.

inauspicious time n.
garaa.

incantation n.
mantaraa'.

incarnation n.
autar.

incense n.
saa'ldxub, sigri, ṭu'lĩ, dxub.

increase v.
syobaa', thabdiba', xrĩn labaa'.

indeed
1. s.v. -gon.
2. pa. jxa'n, wochẽ.

index finger n.
yo ããmãã.

India n.p.
bxaara'da, deša, inḍiyaa', xindu'sthaa'n.

Indian a.
bxaarati.

indiscriminately av.

ma'n pari.

industrious a.
gadilu'.

inelastic a.
axta'ngadiba.

inexact a.
axsxuttu'.

inexpensive a.
sastu'.

infant n.
o'lãã, pxasi.

inferior in quality or rank a.
maamuli'.

influence (evil, causes disharmony in home) n.
thaa.

information n.
thaahaa, pattaa.

infrequently av.
khaa'gae.

ingrate n.
baigune.

inheritance n.
ãŋšaa.

injection n.
swi.

injure v.
ne' myõ'ba.

injure joint (usually as a result of a fall) v.
khribaa'.

ink n.
masi'.

inn n.
xoṭe'l, bxaaṭi'.

inoffensively av.
aala'kkale.

insect n.
1. *(general term including maggots, caterpillars, and grubs)* pxulũ, pxalãã pxulũ.
2. *(which flies, bites, and is smaller than a fly)* mo'so.

insert v.
chwi'ba.

inside
1. p. nxõ.
2. loc. nxõũba'.

inspection n.
jããj.

instantly av.
gxarchi'n, xa'ta pata'.

instead c.
baru.

instead of p.
saṭṭaa'.

instruments for cutting n.
lxoji.

intelligence n.
buddi, dimaag.

interest on loan n.
byaaja.

interjection of puzzlement i.
xũ.

interpretation n.
artha'.

interpret v.
artha' kholdiba', maldab kholdiba'.

interrogate v.
kerdiba'.

interrogative particle pa.
ki, u.

intestines n.
nxaanũ.

into p.
nxõ.

invert a vessel (chiefly used of emptying manure out of basket) v.
khlyuba'.

inverted a.
padkhu'.

investigation n.
jããj buj.

invisible a.
axmro'ba.

invitation n.
nimdu'.

invite a person v.
nimdu' labaa'.

IOU n.
tamsug.

Iran n.p.
iraan.

Iraq n.p.
iraag.

iron n.
pwe'.

iron sheets (galvanized, for roofing) n.
ṭi'na.

irrigate (a field) v.
kyu' jxõba'.

irritation caused by bites of small insects or secretion of plants n.
so.

is v.
1. *(existential)* mubaa'.
2. *(equative)* xo, ya, ga, ba, ŋxĩba'.

isn't it? c.
gi, xwaa'.

it pn.
ca'.

Italy n.p.
idli.

itch
1. v. kebaa'.
2. n. *(scabies)* ludu'.

itchy because of caked mud and insects in planting season a.
kyogyõ'.

J

jackal n.
selaa'.

jail n.
jxyaalkha'na.

jam v.
kxoba.

Japan n.p.
jaapan.

Japanese a.
jaapani.

jar (usually earthenware) n.
sure.

jaw n.
bãgra.

jealousy n.
ikh.

jeep n.
jib.

jewellery n.
gxaanãã'.

jock strap n.
phaasu'.

join v.
1. gaĩdiba, jordiba.
2. *(of rivers)* kõba'.

joint
1. n. cxi.
2. n. *(of knee, ankle, elbow, knuckle)* ka'blo.
3. s.num. *(of cane)* -jãã.

joke
1. n. ṭhaṭṭaa'.
2. v. ṭhaṭṭaa' maardiba.

Jomosom (town on road to Mustang) n.p.
jxumsaa'.

joy n.
khuši'.

judge
1. n. nyaa'edxiš.
2. v. *(a case)* nyaa'e labaa'.
3. v. *(deem)* churiba'.

judgement n.
ni'yaa, nyaa'e.

juice n.
1. *(of fruits)* ra'sa.
2. *(produced in cooking food)* caulaani'.

juicy a.
ra'silo'.

jump v.
pyõ'ba.

jump over v.
ŋwe'ba.

jump up v.
uphaardiba, uphridibaa'.

jumper n.
swiṭara'.

jungle n.
bana, jãgal.

jungle clearing used for shearing n.
khlxye.

just (deictic used ostensively) av.
o', xo.

just because av.
chalen, phaa'karnaa'.

just like av.
dxõle'.

just now t.
bxakhaa'r.

just so i.
chaba'na.

justice n.
ni'yaa.

K

Kathmandu (capital city of Nepal) n.p.
kaaṭhmanḍu.

Kathmandu Valley n.p.
nxebaal.

keep v.
1. *(animals)* nxaba.
2. *(possessions)* pxwẽba.

kernels (of corn, etc.) n.
phũ.

kettle n.
killi'.

key n.
kuji', sããju'.

kick n.
laatta'.

kidney n.
kha'i.

kill v.
saebaa'.

killing two birds with one stone av.
ek kaam dui banda.

kilt of white cloth worn by men n.
kaa'sa.

kind n.
jaad, khaal, kisim, tha'ri.

kindling n.
sĩ' jxĩjyãã'.

kindness n.
lxoyo.

king n.
mrũ, raa'jaa.

kingdom n.
raa'je.

kinship relationship n.
sainũ'.

kiss v.
mwẽ' labaa'.

kitchen cupboards (upon which are placed undefiled dishes) n.
phaesũ, phwisũ.

knead thoroughly v.
cẽ'ba.

knead with feet v.
nxeba'.

knee n.
cxi.

kneel v.
cxi dxũba'.

knife (penknife) n.
cakku'.

knit v.
ro'ba.

knock v.
ṭhaudiba'.

knock down v.
1. *(thing)* khaa'rwaaba.
2. *(opponent)* pachaardiba'.

knot n.
1. *(in rope)* gããṭho.

2. *(in wood)* ka'blo.

know v.
1. *(recognise)* ŋo se'ba.
2. *(a skill)* xraba.

knowledge n.
gyaan, thaa.

knuckle n.
cxi, yo cxi pxrirbae.

L

labourers for agricultural work (work party) n.
nõ.

lace (of boot) n.
tani.

Ladakh (region in north-west India) n.p.
lataga'.

ladder n.
1. *(with rungs)* bxryaŋaa'.
2. *(stepped pole)* li.
3. *(for collecting honey from cliff ledge hives)* prẽ.

ladle n.
1. *(flat, round, about 12" long, for serving out rice)* panyo'.
2. *(for soups)* ḍaḍu.

Lahachok (village just west of Ghachok) n.p.
labji'.

lake n.
samundra, taa'laa.

lama n.
la'maa.

Lamjung (a major village of the eastern dialect of Gurung) n.p.
la'mjũ.

lamp n.
1. *(small kerosene lamp, and small butter lamps used in Buddhist religious rites)* badi.
2. *(pressure)* mainṭolaa'.

lamp-stand for oil wick lamp n.
paanasaa'.

land
1. v. *(aircraft, bird)* utaardibaa', nxeba'.
2. n. *(as opposed to sea)* jamin.
3. n. *(agricultural)* khlxyo nxẽ.

land reform n.
bxumi' su'darar.

landslide n.
ṭwibaa'.

language n.
kxyui', -gi.

lap
1. n. kwẽ'.
2. v. lxẽba.

large a.
dxũbaa'.

last
1. a. akhkhiri.
2. v. khabdibaa', thubaa'.

lasting one night (of pae*)* a.
ekaraa'de.

late
1. av. axbelle.
2. v. *(be late)* kxaeba.

later t.
1. *(on the same day)* komãã'.
2. *(beyond the immediate future)* pxanã liũd.
3. *(in a few days' time)* pxanxãlii.

later born a.
nxõũba'.

laugh v.
nisyubaa'.

laugh at v.
jxugu'diba.

laughter n.
ni, ŋri.

law (edict) n.
aen, kaanun, saasan, xuku'm.

law case n.
mu'dda.

law court (district) n.
gosar.

lawlessness n.
khaici'ji.

lawn n.
bããju.

lawsuit n.
jxagaḍaa', mu'dda.

lay down v.
nebaa'.

lazy a.
alchi'.

lead
1. v. sa'dẽba.
2. n. *(metal)* sisaa'.

leaders n.
cib naab.

leaf n.
pxo, la.

leak v.
yu'ba.

lean (of man, animal, meat) a.
ḍyããŋgraa, kadrãã.

lean back, lean on v.
gxẽba'.

lean hand on another's shoulder v.
dxẽbaa'.

learn v.
lubaa'.

learn by rote v.
saẽr mxaẽ' thẽbaa'.

leather n.
ṭxubi.

leather yoke in ox harness n.
nxaraa.

leave n.
1. chuṭṭi'.
2. *(military)* ḍib.

leaves surrounding corn cob n.
khoyaa'.

leavings of a meal n.
juḍaa, puraa'.

ledge of cliff n.
tẽ'.

leech n.
1. *(in grass, leaves)* tibe'.
2. *(lives in water and enters nostrils of animals drinking, then living as parasite on animal's blood)* nããbli'.

left (opposite of right) a.
txebbre, txargyo.

left-handed person n.
txebbre paale'.

left over, be v.
ca'eba, ŋa'eba.

left-overs n.
ṭhãḍaa ṭhũḍe, ṭhũḍe.

leg n.
pxali.

leisure n.
phursada', ṭyaam.

lemon n.
mxĩba.

lend v.
1. *(a durable article, esp. clothing or jewellery)* ŋẽbaa'.
2. *(food or small amount of money, not at interest)* khi'ba.

length n.
kru, lambaai.

lengthen v.
xrin labaa'.

lenthened (of footprints on slick surface; of vowel sounds) a.
lasgadiba.

lentil n.
1. *(green)* caana.
2. *(species of)* tããŋgra.
3. *(black grain)* maa'sa.
4. *(red gram)* masuri'.
5. *(general term)* daala.

leopard n.
cituwaa'.

leprosy n.
kore'.

less a.
gxaḍi, kamdi'.

let v.
1. *(a house)* baalar pĩbaa'.

2. *(land to share farmers)*
axdxe' pi'ba.

letter n.
citthi'.

letter of alphabet n.
acher.

level a.
sa'mma.

level ground n.
mxaidan, sa'mma khlxyo.

lever out of the way v.
uwaabaa'.

lever up v.
ple'ba.

liar n.
syurgu'.

lick v.
lxẽba.

lid n.
kaa'.

lie
1. n. jxuttaa', syura.
2. v. syur te'ba.

lie down v.
ro'ba.

lieutenant (military rank) n.
lepten.

life n.
1. *(lifetime)* cha, aayu'.
2. *(lot)* juni, jyuni.
3. *(breath)* so'.

lift v.
kwi'ba, no'ba, sywi'ba.

light
1. a. *(of rain)* bũbũle.
2. v. salgadiba'.
3. n. u'jyaalo.
4. v. *(a lamp)* mrobaa', kho'mro bxĩba'.
5. a. *(in colour)* phikka'.
6. a. *(in weight)* yõbaa'.

light red a.
gulaaphi.

lightning n.
tipli kaamli'.

lightning strike v.
murbaa' yu'ba, nããbri yu'ba.

likable a.
mxayaalu.

like
1. p. -dõ'.
2. v. khobaa', ma'n pardiba'.

like that
1. av. chaaba'na, cxagana.
2. a. chaabaa'.

liking n.
xraar.

lime n.
1. *(white colouring)* phumaali'.
2. *(small chartreuse citrus fruit)* kaagadi'.

limp v.
khu'jũ khu'jũ xyaaba'.

limply (hanging loosely) av.
brĩ brĩ.

line n.
1. *(on paper or cloth)* dxarge'.
2. *(of arrangement on parade)* laen, lxaasyaarle tibaa.

lineage n.
khalag.

lion n.
sĩgaa.

lip n.
madi'.

liquid (of thin or weak liquids) a.
kyu'gyu.

listen v.
theebaa'.

little (amount) a.
cyugu' cyugu', kamdi'.

little finger n.
yo kanchi.

live v.
so'ba.

live again (rise from dead) v.
bauridiba, so'xyaaba.

live harmoniously v.
saẽ krxiba.

live humbly v.
cyẽnle ṭibaa'.

liver n.
u'iḍaa.

living a.
so'gõ.

living things n.
so' muba'e sa'e.

lizard n.
chi'baarge'.

load n.
txi'.

loan at interest n.
che'.

lobe of ear n.
tẽ.

locality (surrounding area) n.
khol ṭolaa'.

location n.
khlxyo.

lock n.
1. *(on house, etc.)* sããju' pããũru.
2. *(of hair on crown of head)* tamũ'.

locust n.
tiri'.

lodging place for one or two nights n.
baas.

loin cloth n.
phaasu'.

long (in distance or pronunciation) a.
xrĩgyo.

long ago t.
syõmãã syõmãã.

long live! i.
jay.

longing for absent friends or relatives n.
sãã.

look after v.
nxaba, ŋxyoba.

look at v.
ŋxyoba.

loom n.
kwẽḍo' saa'daa.

loop to secure carrying strap on basket n.
nxaji.

loose a.
kholẽba'.

loosely av.
brĩbrĩ.

loot v.
luḍiba'.

lose v.
1. *(in contest)* xaardi'ba.
2. *(especially of concrete objects)* mxaba, mxoba.
3. *(one's bearings)* mxaliba.
4. *(one's way)* phlebaa'.

loss n.
nausan.

lot in life n.
jyuni, juni.

lottery n.
ci'ṭṭha.

loudly (of voice) av.
dururule, carkole.

louse (head and body) n.
se'.

lovable a.
mxayaalu.

love n.
mxayaa.

low a.
1. *(in height or pitch)* mo'ba.
2. *(pitch or volume of voice)* ma'duro.

lower a.
pxriũba'.

lower back n.
kre.

lower caste people n.
puni'maẽ.

lower in altitude a.
maaba', ma.

lucky a.
lacchin.

luggage n.
saaman.

lullaby word n.
nũ'.

Lumle (a village west of Pokhara) n.p.
lxũli.

lump n.
ḍalla.

lung n.
khlxyoba.

M

machine n.
misina, ka'l.

mad a.
dimaag ṭhig axxreba', xaawaa' nxõxyaaba', sobaal taba'.

madness (as of religious sadhus, or mentally unbalanced people who don't live in a socially acceptable manner) n.
sobaala.

Magar (large ethnic group of West Nepal) n.p.
mxagaa'ra.

maimed a.
ḍũḍaa.

maimed person (usually congenital) n.
lãŋgaḍaa', lulaa'.

main a.
mu'l.

main road n.
mu'l gxyãã'.

maintain v.
nxaba.

maize n.
makha'ẽ.

major (military rank) n.
mẽ'jar.

make v.
banidiba.

make certain v.
ni'scae labaa'.

make thread from fibre v.
perbaa'.

make tired v.
naarwaaba'.

make up (dress up) v.
nakal te'ba.

malaria n.
aulo', kwĩne'.

Malaya n.p.
malaai.

male a.
1. *(of humans)* mxarda.
2. *(of animals)* txoba.

male relatives of second ascending generation n.
baajyu.

males - human n.
aamuĩma'ẽ.

malice n.
ikh.

mallet n.
1. *(for breaking up clods)* gxanmase.
2. *(flat, heavy, for breaking previously unused ground)* tu'.

man n.
1. *(human being regardless of sex)* mxi.
2. *(male human)* aamuyũ'.

mandarin (fruit) n.
sundalaa.

mange
1. n. *(in animals)* ludu'.
2. v. mwi' tixyaaba.

manger n.
khlxyaa' ḍõḍaa.

mango n.
ããbaa'.

manner n.
calan, kaaidaa'.

mantle n.
1. *(fabric on pressure lamp)* jaali.

2. *(woven of jungle thread or cotton, worn by men)* xrẽgaa'.

many a.
lxe'.

mark n.
cakhilo'.

market n.
bajaar.

marriage n.
byaa.

marrow of bone n.
ṭõ.

marsh n.
simãã.

mash n.
1. *(thin, of flour and water, fed to animals)* prokhu', khole', kũḍo'.
2. *(of corn or millet flour, eaten as thick porridge)* paigũ'.

mask of demon, worn at pae n.
taũri.

master n.
saabaa'.

master of slave n.
krxõ.

mat n.
1. *(small, round, of maize husks, for sitting on)* cauḍi'.
2. *(thick, woven of rice straw, used as floor covering)* sukul.
3. *(cane, finely woven, large, 5 feet by 8 feet, used mostly for sun drying grains)* pxyo.
4. *(about 6 feet by 3 feet, woven of rice straw)* gundri.
5. *(of cane, 4' by 13'6", finer than* cidra*, often used as roofing on shepherds' huts and cattle sheds)* bxagaa'ri.
6. *(cane, thickly woven)* cidra.

match
1. v. krxiba, kxyããba.
2. n. *(for lighting fire)* sale'.

matching rim or edge n.
cxyaarba.

matter n.
tãã.

mattock (small) n.
kuḍi.

mature (of wine, tree, animal, human) a.
cigõ'.

meal
1. n. chaage'.
2. s.num. -cho.

meaning n.
artha', maldab, maa'ne.

measure v.
1. naabdiba'.
2. *(volume)* kxwẽba.
3. *(length in cubits)* krubaa'.

measure of volume n.
1. *(approx. 20 gallons = 90 litres)* mxuri.
2. *(approx. one gallon = 4.5 litres)* padi, pyõ'nõ -byõ.
3. *(approx. one pint = 570 ml.)* mxana.
4. *(approx. 2 oz. = 57 ml.)* muṭhi.

measure of weight n.
1. *(approx. 2.4 kg, comprising 8 ser in Pokhara or 3 ser = 12 pau in Kathmandu)* dxaarne.
2. *(approx. 300 g in Pokhara)* ser.

measurement n.
naa'b.

measuring unit for stored grain (if mat is used as an upright bottomless cylinder) n.
bxagaa'ri.

meat n.
1. se.
2. *(lean)* no.

mechanic n.
mistri'.

meddle v.
chwibaa'.

medicine n.
maẽ.

medium av.

ṭhikkale.

medium-sized a.
andare'.

meek a.
ŋiliba'.

meet v.
txoba.

meeting n.
1. kajuri', miṭing.
2. *(to plan community projects)* aŋ sabaa'.

melon (about 6" diameter, with hairy green skin and white flesh, used in Dasain sacrifices) n.
kubinḍaa'.

melt v.
bilidiba.

member (of council) n.
sadasi'.

memorial n.
1. *(general)* cinu'.
2. *(monument on a grave)* deuraali.

memorize v.
saẽr mxaẽ thẽbaa'.

memory n.
yaa'd.

mend v.
gaĩdiba, kywẽ'ba, tundiba', ṭaaldiba.

menstruate v.
ko' yu'ba, kra khru'b tabaa'.

meow v.
ŋxeba.

mercy n.
lxoyo.

merit acquired by doing good deeds n.
dxarmaa'.

message n.
khabar, samjaa'r.

method n.
tarigaa'.

midday n.
txiyãã axdxaa'.

middle
1. p. mxããjuri.
2. a. *(in phrase 'middle school')* miḍil.

middle, in the p.
axdxari'.

middle finger n.
yo naa'ni.

middle-aged a.
axdxa' barse.

mild a.
ŋiliba'.

military n.
milḍeri'.

military cross n.
em si.

military medal n.
em em.

military service abroad n.
laa'khure.

milk
1. n. ŋxe.
2. v. *(a cow or buffalo)* ŋxeba.

milk pail (wooden, for storing milk and buttermilk) n.
paru'.

mill (water-driven) n.
gxaṭṭe'.

mill stone for home grinding n.
xrẽdo.

millipede n.
tuĩ' pxuri.

mimic v.
chyatiba'.

mind n.
ḍil, saẽ.

mingled av.
ma'li.

Minister of government n.
mandri.

minor road n.
po' gxyãã'.

mirror n.
aina'.

mischievous (of child or baby animal) a.
biṭhẽ.

mislead v.
xyaarba.

misled, be v.
bxuldi'ba.

misled, cheated a.
chagadiba.

mist n.
nxããmjyo.

mistake n.
galdi.

mix v.
1. kõba'.
2. *(husks of grain with jungle fibre for strengthening)* chibaa'.
3. *(lemon with spices)* sããdiba'.

mixed up av.
ma'li, che'laa ma'li.

moan with pain v.
mxoba'.

mock v.
jxugu'diba.

moderate a.
andare'.

moment (one) n.
chi'ndri, chi'n gxri', ti'syaa.

momentarily av.
gxarchi'nna.

money n.
mxwi', paisaa'.

mongoose n.
nyauri muso.

monkey n.
1. yogaara.
2. *(white-faced)* sobaa'rgi.

monosyllables n.
-ji.

monsoon n.
barkha.

month n.
1. mxaina, -la.
2. *(1st of Nepali calendar, mid-April to mid-May)* baišaka.
3. *(2nd of Nepali calendar, mid-May to mid-June)* jeṭh.
4. *(3rd of Nepali calendar, mid-June to mid-July)* asaar.
5. *(4th of Nepali calendar, mid-July to mid-August)* sãã'wẽ.
6. *(5th of Nepali calendar, mid-Aug. to mid-Sep.)* bxadu'.
7. *(6th of Nepali calendar, mid-Sep. to mid-Oct.)* asoda'.
8. *(7th of Nepali calendar, mid-Oct. to mid-Nov.)* kaartika.
9. *(8th of Nepali calendar, mid-Nov. to mid-Dec.)* mxaĩsir.
10. *(9th of Nepali calendar, mid-Dec. to mid-Jan.)* pu's.
11. *(10th of Nepali calendar, mid-Jan. to mid-Feb.)* mxaaga.
12. *(11th of Nepali calendar, mid-Feb. to mid-March)* phaawẽ'.

moon n.
la'yãã.

moon, full n.
purne'.

moon, new n.
aũsi'.

more av.
bardaa.

morning n.
nxããga.

morsel n.
tya'te'.

mortgage (the money lender pays the land owner a sum, less than the purchase price of the land, and has use of the land until the owner refunds the money and redeems the land) n.
bandaki.

mosquito n.
lxa'mkhuṭṭe'.

mosquito net n.
jxulaa'.

moss n.
lede'.

mother n.
ããmaa.

mother-in-law n.
syumi.

mother's husband (used in oath) n.
ampha.

motor vehicle n.
moṭora'.

mount v.
kreba'.

mountain peak n.
1. kadaa'sũ.
2. *(abode of the gods - mountain top)* kailaas.

mourning (distress) n.
bedan.

mourning rites performed up to the thirteenth day after death n.
kire'.

moustache n.
muraa.

mouth n.
sũ.

mouthful n.
gaasa.

move
1. v. yogõba'.
2. v.t. *(a cowshed)* ku'ba.
3. v.t. *(something to a different place to make room)* syo'ba, sardiba', kuubaa'.
4. v.t. *(hands)* xaastaa' labaa'.
5. v. *(unrestrainedly, recklessly, in dancing)* nalgadiba'.

much a.
jyaadaa, utille', bele.

mucus n.
naa'.

mud n.
xilaa'.

mug n.
ma'ga.

multiple av.
dobara tebara.

multiply v.
syobaa'.

murderer n.
jyaanmaaraa'.

mushroom n.
cxyããbu.

musical instrument (generic) n.
baajaa.

must v.
txuba.

mustard n.
turi.

mute n.
laḍaa'.

mutilated a.
ḍũḍaa.

muzzle (for ox, woven from cane) n.
mxũũlu.

N

nag v.
kaj kaj labaa', bururu laba'.

nail n.
1. *(metal)* kããḍi'.
2. *(of toe or finger)* chĩ, sĩ'.

naked (of person) a.
khlyunaa'.

name n.
mĩ.

nape of neck n.
kujyõ.

nard n.
jatamanse.

narrow a.
1. cyugu' plxaaba, sããgru'.
2. *(of badly woven mat)* rubaa'.

nasal pronunciation n.
nakhũ' sũ.

native of s.n.
-thẽ.

nature n.

behora, su'baasaa.

naughty a.
badmaša.

Nautanwa n.p.
na'utuna.

navel n.
padi'.

near p.
badẽ, cẽdo', chyogari', dana, jare.

near side p.
cõjãã'.

nearness n.
ri'tta.

nearly equal in size a.
gxoyõ mayõ.

neatly finished (of rope) a.
khiridiba'.

neck n.
kha'ri.

neck of jar n.
kha'ri.

necklace n.
1. xaaraa'.
2. *(of beads worn by women other than widows. In Brahmin custom, only by married women with living husbands)* kããji'.
3. *(of coral)* bxiru'.

need (of goods, money, facilities) n.
khããj.

needed, be v.
caidiba'.

needle n.
txa'.

negative prefix (on verb)
ax-.

neglect n.
xe'l.

neigh v.
ŋxeba.

neighbour n.
ŋxeb ṭxub.

Nepal n.p.
nxebaal.

Nepali (a citizen of Nepal) n.p.
nxebaali, gorkhaali.

Nepali language n.
prxu kxywi'.

nephew n. (see Appendix A)
1. *(MaSiSo, WoHuSiSo)* bxaani'ja.
2. *(WoBrSo)* kwẽ.

nervous a.
aadidiba', kaaphaar.

nest n.
cxõ.

net for fish n.
jaala.

nettle n.
pulu.

nevertheless c.
dile.

new a.
chaa'ra, na'ule, na'yãã.

Newar (a large ethnic group in Nepal, particularly in Kathmandu Valley) n.
nxewaar.

newcomer n.
syãã.

news n.
baen, khabar, na'yãã tãã, samjaa'r.

next a.
aargo'.

next day t.
pxanxãgdu'.

next year t.
kxurima.

nickname (not given by astrologer) n.
ce.

niece n. (see Appendix A)
1. *(MaSiDa, WoHuSiDa)* bxaanji'.
2. *(WoBrDa)* kwẽmĩ'.

night n.
1. mxwĩsa, -ro.
2. *(used mainly in conjunction*

with Nepali ordinals)
raa'daa.

night of death (many animals die on night of kaalraa'di. *Many people stay awake on this night, viz. eighth day of Dasain called* asṭami', *to "cut the death")* n.
kaalraa'di.

nine num.
1. ku'.
2. *(in Nepali loan phrases)* nau.

nineteen num.
unes.

ninth day of Dasera festival n.
naumĩ'.

nip off v.
chywi'ba.

nipple (of breast) n.
ŋxe kra.

noise n.
aawaj.

nonpersonal (suffix on loan numeral) s.num.
-oḍa.

nonserviceman n.
ḍxaagre'.

noon n.
txiyãã axdxaa'.

north loc.
ka'ẽḍu, taai', uttar.

nose n.
na.

nostril n.
nakhũ'.

note (currency) n.
no'ḍa.

note book n.
kaabi'.

notice n.
su'cana.

now t.
aba, coro', dxero', togo'.

nowadays t.
coro', tĩĩ' joro', ti'nxããga.

nudge v.
koḍeba'.

numb a.
1. ṭobaa'.
2. *(with cold)* gaŋgridiba, kaaṭhidiba', kõ'ba, ṭhiridiba'.

number n.
nxambar.

nurse n.
1. *(medical)* susaare'.
2. *(for child)* dxaraa'le.

O

O i.
o'.

O.K. pa.
jei, tam, õ.

o'clock (used in conjunction with Nepali numerals) n.
baje.

oath n.
1. *(vow)* baacchaa, kasam.
2. *(curse)* kire kĩbaa'.

obey v.
ŋẽbaa'.

oblique a.
bããŋgo-ṭeḍo'.

obscene a.
gairo, phori'.

obscenity n.
pidãã.

observe v.
mxããdiba.

obstruction (as interrupting light or of child standing between two people talking) n.
che'l.

occasion n.
1. *(opportunity)* maukaa'.
2. txi, belaa.
3. *(astrological)* joga, belaa.

occasion of importance (marriage, pae, house building - which necessitates astrological guidance) n.
kaarjya.

occupation n.
ilaam.

occupy v.
pxweba'.

ocean n.
samudra.

odour n.
baasan, thãã.

of (possessive) s.n.
-la, -e.

of the present time a.
dxowo'.

of two minds a.
saẽ ŋxĩ' tabaa'.

off-centre loc.
chyogari'.

offence n.
gaar.

offend v.
saẽ na'l labaa'.

offended, be v.
gaar mxããdiba.

offer v.
1. *(an animal sacrifice, especially to consecrate various parts of new house)* khro pĩbaa'.
2. *(sacrifice)* pujdiba'.
3. *(to ancestors)* chywebaa'.

offering n.
1. *(of rice given priests for use in ceremonies, the bulk being kept as part of his payment)* acheda'.
2. *(to gods or priests, usually money)* bxeṭi'.

office n.
1. *(government)* aḍḍaa', adlaasa'.
2. *(of district administration* gosar.
3. *(clerical)* aphis.

official n.
aphisar.

official responsible s.n.
-dxi'š.

offspring of animal n.
jxaja'.

oh i.
xo, oho, au.

oh, I see (signifying that one has now understood) i.
xe, ŋxe.

oil n.
1. te'la.
2. *(cooking)* chyugu'.

old (of cloth) a.
thaũni.

old man n.
khiba'.

omit v.
biridiba.

on loc.
phiri'.

on behalf of p.
lxaagiri.

on heat (of animals, lit. *husband seeking), be* v.
pha mxaeba.

on the upper side of loc.
kxowãã pxadẽ.

once av.
ekaali'.

once upon a time t.
paile', syomãã, syomãã syomãã.

one num.
1. e'k, gxri', kri'.
2. *(with suffixes)* ti-.

one after another av.
dxamaa' dxa'm.

one and a half num.
ḍer.

one by one av.
palo' palle'.

one ... the other pn.
khaen ... khaen.

oneself pn.
khi.

onion n.
pyaa'ja.

only a.
khaali', ma'ttre', sirib.

open
1. v. *(as of road's completion, switching on a radio, opening a box for customs inspection, commencing an army career)* kholdiba'.
2. a. *(of ground, road, box)* khullaa'.
3. v. *(door)* thõbaa'.
4. v. *(eyes - of human)* churbaa'.

open out
1. v.t. phaebaa'.
2. v.i. *(of flowers)* pxaariba.

opinion n.
bijaara', saẽ bicaara'.

opportunity n.
maukaa'.

opposed to p.
barkhela.

or c.
athaba', u, yaa, ki'.

orange n.
sundalaa.

order (governmental) n.
xuku'm.

order goods from a distant place (esp. from someone coming from overseas) v.
thobaa'.

orders n.
xa'k.

ordinary a.
maamuli', sadxaran, saadaa'.

organisation n.
caal calaan, samaaj, bebasthaa.

originally t.
syomãã.

other a.
aargo', aaru, phaalṭu'.

other side of p.
kyõjãã'.

ought
txuba.

our pn.
ŋi'e.

outlay n.
thaili'.

outside loc.
baairu.

over p.
phiri'.

over and over av.
gxari'.

over there loc.
ca'ri, jxaa-.

over-indulge (in food, drink) v.
chyaalbaa'.

overcast - of sky, be v.
kxũba.

overflow v.
lxuba.

overflowing n.
jal tha'l.

overhead a.
phibi.

overturn v.
palṭidi'ba.

own (reflexive pronoun)
xrõsa, khemaẽ.

owner n.
khlxye.

ox n.
khlxyaa'.

P

paddle of wood about 18" long used for beating jungle fibres n.
mxũru.

page n.
pe'na.

pain n.
naane.

pair n.
joḍaa.

palace n.
darbaara.

pale a.
phikkaa', saadaa'.

palm of hand n.
plo.

pan n.
1. *(handleless, metal)* ḍibji.
2. *(long-handled, for frying food)* taabge'.
3. *(for scales)* nau'li.
4. *(of brass)* tasala'.

panic v.
aadidiba'.

panther n.
cyõ'ḍi cituwaa'.

paper n.
kaagaadaa'.

parade (military) n.
pareḍaa'.

parade ground n.
ṭũḍikhe'la.

parallel av.
piru.

parallel male cousins n.
daajyu bxaai'.

paralysed a.
kõjura xyaaba', kagraa ku'gru.

pardon n.
maa'ph.

parents-in-law of one's own child n.
samdi'.

parrot n.
sugaa'.

part n.
-bãã, xissa'.

part in hair n.
o'gyãã.

partition (wooden, in house) n.
kaḍbaa'ra.

partner n.
1. sajai.
2. *(as of two friends)* joḍaa.

party n.
dapha, paaṭi', ṭoli'.

pass through v.
kyulbaa'.

pass
1. v. *(urine, bowel motion)* txõba.
2. v. *(wind rectally)* syubaa'.
3. n. *(graduation)* paa's.

past repetitive tense s.
-ma'la.

past tense s.
-i, -di, -ji -lu -la.

pasture for cattle (uncultivated) n.
paḍa, gaucaran.

patch
1. v. khẽbaa'.
2. n. ṭaalu'.

path n.
gxyãã'.

pattern n.
dxããja'.

pawpaw n.
mewaa.

pay (salary) n.
tanakha'.

pay attention v.
dxyaan pĩba'.

pea n.
tããŋgra'.

peace n.
šantok.

peace-maker n.
sũ lachin.

peacock n.
mũ'juraa, na'utõ.

peak (of tree, mountain, stick or beam, top of statuette) n.
cxo.

peanut n.
badama.

peel
1. n. bogro, phi.
2. v. chaa'ba.

peg in verandah floor to hold loom n.
thuri.

pen (cage) n.
cyõ.

penalty n.
danḍa.

penis of adult man n.
mlxe.

penknife n.
cakku'.

people of a kingdom or country n.
janta.

pepper n.
ma'rija.

peppery a.
sobaa'.

percent av.
saikaṭa.

perfect a.
1. satte'.
2. *(in physical excellence, of humans)* mxaarba.

perfect aspect s.v.
-ŋŋyũ.

perforate v.
cwibaa'.

perforated a.
sũ tabaa'.

perform v.
labaa'.

perhaps pa.
saed.

perhaps... perhaps c.
na'... na'.

permanently av.
igurle'.

permission n.
xuku'm.

permission to leave n.
bidaa.

permissive a.
-bxĩba'.

permit (as for cutting timber) n.
phurji'.

perpendicular a.
ṭhaaḍo'.

perplexed a.
almallaa'.

persimmon fruit n.
xalwaa'.

person n.
mxi.

person whose nose is continually runny n.
naa'ble.

perspiration n.
chaeba.

persuade v.
1. *(of truth of something)* kwẽ'l labaa'.
2. *(to do something)* xwããba'.

pertain to v.
pyaa'ba.

petticoat worn under sari n.
peṭṭi'ko'ḍa.

pewter n.
kããsu'.

pheasant n.
parwaa', ti'ntiri.

phlegm n.
khona.

photo n.
na'kasa, tasbir, photo'.

physical blemish (of man or animal, such as scar, birthmark, crossed eyes, twisted limb, any malproportion) n.
khoḍi'.

piano accordion n.
xarbin.

pice (one hundredth part of rupee) n.
paisaa'.

pick at (as a dumb person pokes at people to draw attention) v.
khoḍeba'.

pick up v.
tubaa'.

pickle made from radish leaves (pounded in a bamboo cylinder then allowed to stand for a week till fermented. They are then sun dried and stored for later

use) n.
gundru.

picture n.
na'kasa, phoṭo, tasbir.

piece of old canework (as used in thaa sũ waabaa' *ceremony)* n.
cxaablẽ.

pieces n.
cho'nõ.

pierce v.
cwibaa'.

pig n.
1. *(domestic)* tili'.
2. *(wild)* tõ.

pigeon (domestic) n.
parwaa'.

pile n.
khaa'd.

pill n.
goli, phũ.

pillar n.
1. thaa'maa, txo.
2. *(central, set first in building a house)* mu'l txo.

pillow n.
kregũ.

pimple n.
ci.

pin (safety) n.
pĩ'na.

pineapple n.
bxaĩ'kaṭar.

pink a.
gulaaphi.

pints s.num.
-mna.

pious person n.
bxakti.

pipe n.
nalgi'.

pipe band n.
paai bẽ'n.

pipe for hookah n.
paaeba cilĩ.

pipe of bamboo for smoking n.
kulbi.

pipe of clay about 2" inches long, for smoking tobacco n.
cilĩ.

pitch (of song) n.
bxaagaa'.

pity n.
lxayo.

place
1. n. khlxyo.
2. v. thẽbaa'.

place for dancing n.
khaal.

place in forest where dead trees are available n.
gxaaraa'.

place where one lays head for sleeping - towards fireplace n.
kregũ.

place where woman sits in cooking n.
kxorbae khlxyo.

plague affecting cattle n.
xri.

plain (ordinary) a.
saadaa', saadxaran.

plains dwellers from Terai and north India n.
mxadise.

plait v.
1. *(rope)* khrĩbaa'.
2. *(hair)* pebaa'.

plait of black cotton (plaited in with woman's own hair) n.
kramĩ'.

plan n.
1. *(design)* iskim.
2. *(purpose)* bijaar.

plane (aircraft) n.
jxaasaa'.

plant
1. n. *(generic)* dxũ'.
2. n. *(with red berry in Nov.-Dec.)* e'ra.
3. v. *(crops)* ruĩbaa'.

plants shooting close together n.
jaũle.

plastic n.
ra'bara.

plate (for rice, about 10" diam.) n.
thaali.

platform n.
1. *(upper floor of house)* aaḍi'.
2. *(resting place under shady tree)* caudara.

play v.
1. *(games)* khlyõbaa'.
2. *(musical instruments, radio)* xraaba.
3. *(on swing or ferris wheel)* mxaeba'.

playful baby animal n.
biṭhẽ.

pleasant a.
kxyaalaba, ra'mid, swaabaa'.

please (courteous, polite particle, sentence final on requests) pa.
o.

pleased a.
tĩ sĩ'ba.

pledge not to repeat offence, the signing of which is a condition for release from prison n.
kael.

pliable (of cloth, skin) a.
ra'bara, na'ram.

plough
1. n. kxora, xa'la.
2. v. kxyoba'.
3. v. *(after spreading manure, repeatedly)* ugaasdibaa'.

plough share (metal) n.
phali.

ploughman n.
khlxyaasa'ẽ.

pluck v.
thubaa'.

pluck ripe grains only v.
prubaa'.

plunder v.
luḍiba'.

plural marker s.n.
1. jaga, jau.
2. *(for humans and animals)* -ma'ẽ.
3. *(for things and perhaps cattle)* budũ.

pocket n.
guji.

point n.
1. mlxu, mrxu.
2. *(of compass)* disaa.

poison n.
bikh, megãẽ.

pole n.
ḍããḍa, daara, saḍaa'.

police n.
pulisaa'.

polish v.
1. mijiba'.
2. *(by rubbing with a cloth)* moldiba'.

pollen n.
saa'raa.

pond n.
xraa'.

pony n.
ṭaṭṭu.

pool n.
kuwaa.

poor a.
garib.

poor person n.
khlyããnu'.

pop (grains) v.
ŋxoba.

porch n.
1. *(downstairs)* pĩḍĩ.
2. *(usually upstairs on end of house, usually enclosed, to which lower caste people are given entrance)* baartali'.

porcupine n.
dxũsĩ'.

portents used by shaman in divination n.
txẽ-chyaa.

porter (contemptuous term) n.
ḍxaagre'.

possessions n.
1. dxan sampati', dxĩ'naa, sampati'.
2. *(goods and money brought back from service abroad)* saa'di.

post n.
1. txo.
2. *(to which threshing oxen are tethered)* mxẽ.
3. *(some inches in diameter, used particularly for tethering cattle, bigger than* phargu *or* prxe*)* kyulu'.

post-funeral ceremony (to conduct a departed spirit to the resting place of the dead) n.
pae.

pot with handle (of aluminium, for ghee, milk, etc.) n.
syaa'mgo.

potato n.
aalu'.

pots and pans n.
bxããḍũ' kũḍũ'.

pounce upon v.
xwẽba, mxuba.

pound
1. v. *(rice)* dxõba'.
2. n. *(for animals)* kãje xaaus.

pour v.
jxõba'.

powdered a.
pauḍara'.

power (spiritual of gods or religious officiants) n.
šakti.

praise (sung to a god) n.
aaraa'ti.

prawn n.
kwĩ'jiri tãã'ga.

prayer n.
praarthana'.

prayer flag (erected on bamboo poles before Buddhist monasteries and homes) n.
luŋta.

preach v.
pracaar labaa'.

precise a.
ṭhyaa'kka.

precisely
1. av. *(exactly)* chenããle.
2. i. *(affirmative response)* xo.

predict v.
liũba'e tãã bibaa.

pregnant woman n.
kxone muba'e camĩ'ri.

prejudiced a.
gxama'nḍi.

prepare v.
1. *(meal, ceremony)* cxuba'.
2. *(vegetables for cooking, cutting out waste)* swibaa'.

prepared a.
kasdiba', tayaar.

present
1. n. *(gift)* nasu'.
2. a. *(on duty)* xããji'r.
3. n. *(of food taken by a woman visiting her relatives)* kosyaali'.

presently t.
togo'.

press
1. v. khããdiba', mxaaba.
2. v. *(with foot)* nõ'ba, ããṭhidiba'.
3. n. *(for extracting oil or sugar juice)* kulaa.
4. v. *(mud on paddy wall)* al dxẽba'.

prestige n.
ijed, abbru'.

prestigious man (usually foreign) n.
saabaa'.

pretence n.
ni'ũ, swããŋ.

pretend to do something (as a

pretext to cover one's real intent) v.
ni'ũ labaa'.

pretext n.
ni'ũ.

pretty a.
chyããbaa'.

previously t.
asõ', osõ', syõmãã, uyãã'.

price n.
kõ', sa'e.

prick n.
cwibaa', kobdiba', mlxubaa'.

pride n.
sikki'.

priest n.
1. *(Buddhist)* la'maa.
2. *(Hindu)* pujaare'.

prime (physically, usually of men, but also of animals) a.
phrẽ.

print v.
chaabdiba'.

printed (of paadru' *'astrological calendar')* a.
chaapwaa', kããsi' waale'.

prise up v.
ku'ba.

privately av.
ekaantaa'.

proclaim (news, announcement) v.
gxaudi'ba.

proclamation n.
su'cana.

prodigal n.
mxaaswaa'.

produce n.
ubjani.

profession n.
ilaam.

profit (especially from corrupt practices) n.
naphaa'.

progress n.
bikaaš.

prohibition n.
baan.

promise
1. n. baacchaa.
2. v. kabol labaa'.

prone a.
padkhu'.

property n.
1. *(house, land)* gxa'r khe'daa.
2. *(baggage)* maa'l.
3. *(possessions)* nxur.

proportionate to p.
xisaab.

prosperity n.
cha.

prosperous a.
1. *(wealthy)* plxoba'.
2. *(successful)* xyõ lachin.

prostitute n.
raṇḍi baaji.

protect v.
jugudiba, racche labaa'.

protection n.
saer.

proud, be v.
pxẽba.

proverb n.
ukhaan.

provide v.
khulidiba'.

prune v.
chããḍiba', khasi' labaa'.

pull v.
caẽbaa'.

pull apart v.
ṭõbaa'.

pull out v.
thutti'ba.

pulse (lentils) n.
daala.

pumpkin n.

ũsya.

Pun (an ethnic group of Nepal, often regarded as a subgroup of Magars) n.p.
prõmaẽ.

punch v.
1. *(with fist)* bachaardiba.
2. *(hole in paper)* thõbaa'.

pundit (religious scholar) n.
panḍidma'ẽ.

punishment designed to reform offender n.
sajaẽ'.

pure a.
1. *(ritually)* cokho', suddo'.
2. *(clean)* saphphaa', pawitra.
3. *(morally)* su'do, satte'.

purpose n.
kaḍa, maldab.

purposelessly av.
khero.

purr (of cat) v.
ŋxruba'.

purse (cloth, women's, for money) n.
jxilge'.

pursed lips (for blowing up fire) n.
phu'.

pursue v.
lxagaardiba.

pus n.
nxo.

push v.
kxaeba'.

push through a hole v.
chwi'ba.

put (place something) v.
thẽbaa'.

put in (bolt in place, seeds in ground, sugar in tea, chickens under basket, feed in manger) v.
jxõba'.

put to bed v.
nebaa'.

put up with v.
khabdiba'.

Q

qualified people (either referring to arbitration of quarrels, or to divination, or technical skills) n.
xrab se'bmaẽ.

quarrel
1. n. jxagaḍaa'.
2. v. pxõba.

quarter n.
1. *(one fourth)* caũthẽ'.
2. *(area of town)* ṭola.

quarters n.
ḍeraa.

queen n.
mrũsyo.

question n.
prašna.

question particle (seeking confirmation of statement) pa.
aa, xwaa'.

quickly av.
gxari'nna, gxar chi'nna, jxaab jxup, yumanaa.

quill of porcupine n.
mlxu.

quoted speech marker pa.
ro.

R

rabbit n.
kharaa'.

rabies (of dogs) n.
sobaala.

races (sports) n.
khel.

rack n.
1. *(over fireplace)* ṭxõwãã.
2. *(for stacking rice straw)* ṭowaa.

radish n.
1. labu'.

2. *(sliced and dried)* cana'.
3. *(pickle of leaves)* gundru.
4. *(preserved)* kyũḍa.

raffle n.
ci'ṭṭhaa.

rafter n.
balo, masi'.

ragged a.
thauni.

rags n.
kwẽ ṭaalaa' ṭuli'.

rain
1. n. nãã'.
2. v. nãã' yu'ba.

rainbow n.
xyaago.

rain hat n.
chadri kule'.

rainy season n.
barkha.

raised portion (verandah, bank of gully, etc.) n.
ḍil.

ram n.
1. sãã'ḍe.
2. *(full grown)* kxyu' sãã'ḍe.
3. *(young, one to two years)* kxyu' khaarbu.

rat n.
nimũ.

rat hole n.
ro.

rate of goods or services n.
kõ'.

rather c.
baru, jxan'.

rattan cane n.
mo'.

rattle v.
gxaji'diba.

ray (of sun or star) n.
sa'ra.

razor blade n.
ispaadaa'.

reach v.
syaa'ba.

read v.
khe'ba.

ready a.
tayaar, so'j, kasdiba'.

real a.
krxosena.

really! (in amazement) i.
xet'teri, xo.

reap v.
1. *(full stalks)* kha'ẽba.
2. *(heads of grain)* thubaa'.

reason n.
kaaran.

rebuke v.
gaal ke'ba, xaudiba'.

receipt n.
lesṭa'.

receive v.
kĩba'.

recently t.
1. bxakha'r.
2. *(a few days ago)* axyãã ũĩ'.
3. *(before yesterday)* ũĩ' mĩĩ'.

recess in wall (to hold lamp so that work can be done at night) n.
khoba'.

recital (given during Tiwa festival late Oct. for which offerings are expected) n.
bxailo'.

recitation (memorized) n.
mu'waar.

recite from memory v.
mu'waar caḍiba'.

reckoning n.
xisaab.

recognise v.
ŋõ se'ba, se'ba.

recollect v.
saẽr mxaẽba'.

record (on tape, film) v.
khitti'ba.

recorder (musical instrument) n.
murli'.

recover (from illness) v.
na'b sxaba'.

recovered slightly a.
khajij.

red a.
olgyaa'.

red powder used for tika n.
sĩdur.

redeem mortgaged property v.
khaa'ba.

reduce v.
1. *(pay, army)* tho'ba.
2. *(in size)* gxaḍi'ba.

regard as v.
churiba'.

regiment n.
palḍan.

regret n.
pachit.

regulations n.
riti thiti.

reign v.
raaj labaa'.

related by kin, be v.
phebaa'.

relative n.
naathu', sainũ'.

relative who performs son-in-law's responsibilities at a pae n.
mxo.

relatives n.
isṭaa' mi'ttra.

relax v.
kũ'ba.

release v.
1. pi'ba, te'ba.
2. *(from curse of witch or evil spirit)* txẽba.

reliability n.
bxar.

religion (traditional, animistic, sacrificial) n.
santan dxarma'.

religious officiant (indigenous Gurung, of shamanistic Tibetan Bon tradition) n.
khlxebri, pucu.

religious rules n.
riti thiti'.

religious teacher n.
dxarma' guru, guru.

reluctance n.
kaes.

remain v.
1. *(left over)* ca'eba, ŋa'eba.
2. *(stand still)* chyobaa.
3. *(abide)* ṭibaa'.

remainder n.
1. bããgi.
2. *(of uncompleted work)* ekwaa', tõ.

remember v.
cxiba', mxaẽba'.

remembrance n.
cinu'.

remnant of cloth n.
ṭaalu'.

remorse n.
pachit.

remorsefully av.
dxaradxara.

remove a paddy wall in order to enlarge rice paddy v.
piridiba.

render unavailable v.
pxweba'.

rent n.
1. bxaaraa', kiraai.
2. *(on house)* baala.

repair v.
banidiba, gaĩdiba, kywẽ'ba.

repeat words after someone v.
lili lili bibaa.

repeated a.
ḍabal.

repeatedly av.
gxari'.

replacement n.
bxarna'.

reply n.
juwaaba.

report
1. n. *(reputation)* baen.
2. n. *(gossip spoken behind one's back)* phram tãã.
3. v. *(for duty)* xããji'r tabaa'.

repose n.
aaram.

reprimand v.
gaal ke'ba.

reputation n.
ijed, baen.

request n.
bindi.

required, be v.
lxaidiba, lxaudiba.

resemble v.
byõba, xri khabaa'.

resembling a.
dxuru'staa.

residue n.
ekwaa'.

resolve (a dispute) v.
ṭobaa'.

respect v.
1. maa'n labaa'.
2. *(as a person)* mxi labaa', mxi cxiba.

respectful address for any older man n.
txajyõ.

response to greeting (respectful) i.
xajur.

response to call i.
xwe'.

responsibilities associated with funeral or post-funeral ceremonies n.
ma'dãã mu' dũ.

rest
1. n. aaram.
2. v. bxõ' nxaba.

rest day (work or travel forbidden) n.
ko'sa prim.

rest house (built for travellers as a meritorious work) n.
ṭhããḍi.

rest one's foot on v.
nxeba.

rest upon v.
dxũba'.

restaurant n.
xoṭe'l.

resting platform on roadside n.
nxẽ.

restore v.
sẽ'ba.

restrain (in pen or trap) v.
thundiba'.

restraint (moral or social) n.
chyaar.

resurrected, be v.
bauridiba.

retail v.
lõbaa'.

retaliate v.
badalaa labaa'.

retracted (of lamp wick), be v.
gaaḍiba.

return
1. v.i. eba'.
2. v.t. ewaaba'.
3. n. saḍaa'.
4. v.t. *(goods)* sẽ'ba.
5. v.i. *(on the same day from a journey)* khwi'ba.

revenge v.
saḍaa' pĩbaa'.

reward v.
saḍaa' mxaeba.

rice n.
1. *(as opposed to less preferred staple foods)* mlxogõ.

2. *(cooked)* kaẽ.
3. *(freshly harvested)* siraaũlu'.
4. *(husked, uncooked)* mlxasi'.
5. *(insufficiently cooked or not ripe)* si.
6. *(variety)* ciniyãã'.
7. *(paddy from seed to husking)* mlxa.
8. *(roasted, thrown by women relatives at corpse and at* plxo *at a* pae, *also offered in* puja*)* lxawaa.
9. *(type of better quality than* ciniyaa', *planted early* asar, *ripens late* ḳaartik*)* mxaarsi.

rice straws (prepared by extruding boiled mashed rice, drying in sun, and frying in deep fat for eating) n.
khyuni', jxilge'.

rice flakes n.
cyura'.

rice fragments broken during husking n.
kãgaa'.

rice gruel (sticky) n.
kxole.

rice pounder n.
kuni.

rich a.
plxoba'.

riches n.
nxor.

ride v.
1. *(on a swing or ferris wheel)* ku'di mxaeba'.
2. *(car or animal)* krebaa'.

ridge n.
ḍil.

ridge pattern (imprinted on palm by leaning on gundri, *or in seed plot)* n.
ḍyaamaa.

right
1. n. *(authority)* adikhaar, xa'k.
2. a. *(correct)* ṭhi'k.
3. a. *(body parts)* kyolo.
4. av. *(direction)* kyolo paṭṭi'.

right size a.
plxi kru krxiba.

right to speak n.
põ'bae gxyãã'.

right way up (as of woven mat) a.
sulḍu'.

righteous a.
gadilu'.

rim (of basket) n.
ŋãã.

ring
1. v. xraaba.
2. n. *(finger)* cyaa', aũṭhi'.
3. n. *(iron surrounding bamboo container)* kããju'.
4. n. *(worn in nose)* phuli'.

rip off v.
chywi'ba.

ripen (of fruit and grains) v.
mĩ'ba.

rise v.
1. *(of people)* ribaa'.
2. *(of dough)* rõ'ba, phuldiba'.
3. *(of sun)* mlxoba'.

rise and fall (of voice pitch) v.
gxumdi'ba.

rite n.
1. *(initial used to neutralize witch's curse)* paaldu' waabaa'.
2. *(second used to negate curse of witch)* dobaaḍe waabaa'.
3. *(third to neutralize witch's curse)* ŋxaẽ sẽ'ba.
4. *(conducted in post-funeral ceremony)* cxemphar labaa'.

rites n.
riti thiti'.

ritual fast (for special days, perhaps eating only one meal, or fruit only, or only what one has cooked oneself, or eating in silence) n.
barjit.

ritually clean a.
cokho'.

river n.
1. syõ.

2. *(in place names)* kholaa'.
3. *(joining Seti east of Ghachok)* syaatti syõ.

rivulet n.
pxalẽ.

road n.
gxyãã'.

roast v.
1. *(in pan)* ŋxoba.
2. *(in coals)* khrõbaa'.

robber n.
ḍããgu.

rock
1. n. ŋyu'mãã, yu'maa.
2. v. *(a baby)* lxaaba'.

rocky area (hard to make way through) n.
gxõ'.

roll call parade n.
xããji'r.

roll over v.
oleba'.

roll over and over v.
rali rali labaa'.

roll up (mat, paper) v.
berdiba.

roof
1. v.t. sywibaa'.
2. n. *(covering verandah or sleep-out)* paali'.

roof garden with balustrade n.
kausi'.

roof of mouth n.
sããso.

room (in house) n.
koṭhaa'.

rooster n.
bxaale'.

root n.
jara.

rope n.
chu, xrasi.

rose n.
gulaaph.

rot (of vegetation) v.
krãã'ba.

rotate
1. v.t. gxumdi'waaba.
2. v.i. *(of millstone, propeller, wheel)* mxyaarba'.

rotten (of eggs) a.
kxwiba.

rotund a.
chobaa'.

rough a.
khasro'.

round about p.
jare, kaa'rgyu, khaa'gu.

rows of stitching s.num.
-syaar.

rub hard v.t.
1. *(as hands together, for warmth; or a cloth, to get dirt out)* mijiba'.
2. *(tobacco into flakes)* moldiba'.

rude a.
axlachin sũ, axkho'jyãã sũ.

rug n.
1. *(type for sitting on)* pãŋgale'.
2. *(for floor, used for sitting and sleeping on)* xraḍi.
3. *(woven of sheep or goat's wool)* kaamlo'.

rule sternly, authoritatively v.
ro-ro pi-pi labaa'.

ruled a.
xrekha.

rum n.
paa'.

rumour (generally false) n.
phram tãã.

run v.
kxyoba.

run away v.
bxaudi'ba, chyu'ḍi xyaaba'.

rupees n.
mxwi'.

rye-like grain (eleusine corasana) n.
naare'.

S

sack n.
1. *(small)* nẽdo'.
2. *(for holding grains or flour, 10* padi *or more)* kuldu.

sacred thread of Hindu (worn on neck or wrist) n.
jane.

sacrificial rites (generally intended to appease spirits) n.
pujaa'.

sad a.
khuši' axxreba', pir mubaa', saẽ na'ba.

sadness n.
aaphsos, so'ga.

salaried position n.
jaagir.

salary n.
talaba'.

sale n.
bikri.

salt n.
caja.

salute n.
solọd.

salvation n.
mu'kti, ra'cche.

sambhar n.
jaraayo, e.

same a.
gxrinaa'.

sample (food) v.t.
mxyõba.

sanction n.
sadar.

sand n.
balwaa.

sandal n.
cabli.

sane a.
satte'.

sapling n.
txura.

sari n.
phariya'.

satisfactory a.
ṭhi'kan.

satisfied a.
1. *(usually of food)* mrẽ 'ba.
2. *(with a meal)* sããũ' tabaa'.

saucepan n.
tasala'.

sauerkraut n.
1. *(made from radish)* kyũḍaa'.
2. *(made of garlic leaves)* jimbu.

save v.
jugudiba.

save up v.
sãã'diba.

saving of money n.
thi.

savour n.
swaad.

say v.
bibaa.

scabies (in man) n.
ludu'.

scale (of fish) n.
katle'.

scales n.
1. *(balances - with lead weight on one end)* paa'raa.
2. *(with trays both ends for measuring gold)* kããḍa.

scar n.
ṭaḍe'.

scarce a.
mxããgu'.

scarcity n.
ãgal.

scare v.
plxa lõwaaba'.

scarf n.
  1. *(long, woollen, worn by men)* galbandi.
  2. *(worn on woman's head)* kramũ'.

scatter v.t.
  1. *(paper)* paẽbaa'.
  2. *(seed on field)* plxuba'.

school n.
  skula'.

scissors n.
  kaĩji'.

scold v.
  pxõba, xaudiba'.

scolding n.
  bururu.

scorch
  1. v.t. thi'ba.
  2. v.i. krobaa'.

score v.
  kordiba'.

scorpion n.
  tximmru bicche.

scour v.
  myaa'ba.

scourer (straw, husks, corn cob, etc.) n.
  lxũḍi.

scrap n.
  ṭaalu'.

scrape
  1. v.t. *(bark)* khurkudiba'.
  2. v.t. *(dishes clean)* myaa'ba.
  3. v.i. *(of door, etc.)* ŋxeba.

scraps (of cloth) n.
  kwẽ ṭaalaa' ṭuli'.

scratch
  1. v.t. ru'iba.
  2. v.i. *(as of a pen)* kordiba'.
  3. v.t. *(by a thorn)* roebaa'.

screen (on windows to keep out insects) n.
  jaali.

screw top n.
  kaa'.

screw up v.
  cxyurba.

scriptures of a religion n.
  dxarma šastra', šaastara.

scrubby area (with cyõ'ḍi, dhurse'*)* n.
  padyaani'.

scrubland (about 6000 feet to 8000 feet) n.
  dxusaa'.

scrupulous about religious regulations (such as washings, diet, etc.) a.
  bxakti'.

sea n.
  samudra.

seal n.
  chaa'p.

search for v.
  mxaeba.

season (food, with spices) v.
  masala' jxõba'.

second a.
  dosro.

second-born daughter n.
  mxaĩli.

second-born son n.
  mxaĩla.

second day after a given date t.
  nũ'ĩmdũ.

second day after dasmi n.
  duwaadasi.

second line of couplet n.
  kaa'.

second-rate a.
  kacca'.

secretary n.
  sajib.

section
  1. n. *(part)* xissa'.
  2. s.num. -jãã.

sediment in pan after boiling milk n.
  kuraani', kaũri.

see v.

mrõbaa'.

seed n.
plxu'.

seeds (of pumpkin, etc.) n.
mrxe.

seek v.
mxaeba.

seek an auspicious day v.
ŋxyoba.

segments (of fruit - orange, etc.) n.
phũ.

segregate v.
chããḍiba'.

seize v.
kxaaba, pagḍidiba', pxẽba.

select v.
1. chããḍiba'.
2. *(after carefully comparing various choices)* txããba.

self pn.
xrõsa.

self-control n.
gyaan.

self-respect n.
abbru', ijed.

selfish person n.
kugaaḍaa', khõ'ḍa.

sell v.
cũ'ba, lõbaa'.

selvage (of cloth) n.
ŋãã.

semblance (poor copy, in derogatory sense) n.
anman.

send v.
1. *(a thing, letter)* pibxĩba'.
2. *(a person on an errand)* kulbaa', kul bxĩba'.

send back v.
sẽ'ba.

senior person n.
cibaa'.

sense (wisdom) n.
buddi, dimaag.

senses n.
plxa.

sentence (penalty) n.
sajaẽ'.

separate
1. v.t. phribaa'.
2. v.t. *(wool, fluffing it with bow after washing process)* prẽbaa'.
3. v.i. churiba'.

sergeant (in Indian or Nepalese Army) n.
xaawoldaar.

serpent form of a god n.
lu.

serrated (as of elephant's trunk, rat-eaten pages of book, saw teeth) a.
ŋri'ba ŋri'ba.

serve out (rice from pot) v.
kywĩbaa'.

service n.
1. *(employment)* no'kori.
2. *(attending to needs)* susaar.

set
1. v.i. *(of sun, moon)* li'ba.
2. v.t. *(aside for later use)* so'j labaa'.

set fire to v.
salgadiba'.

set in order v.
krxil labaa', krxille thẽbaa', mxildiba.

set out on a journey v.
saidu' labaa', gxyãã' kxaaba.

set up (prepare) v.
cxuba'.

Seti river gorge n.
gaŋgyu.

settle (of earth, wall) v.i.
bxaasi'diba.

settlement (of a dispute) n.
chi'na phaa'naa.

seven num.
1. ŋi'.
2. *(in loan phrases)* saa't.

seven hundred num.
ŋi'braa.

seventy num.
ŋi'jyu.

several a.
aanek.

severe a.
1. *(of person)* nisṭuri.
2. *(of famine)* carko'.

severely av.
dururule.

sew v.
ṭxuba'.

sexually aroused (of male animals) a.
caldiba'.

shade n.
sidaa'la.

shade of meaning n.
bxaaba'.

shadow n.
chyaa.

shake
1. v.t. lxaaba'.
2. v.i. yogõba'.
3. v.t. *(a door)* gxaji'diba.
4. v.i. *(in chill, fright, shaman's trance)* txaarba.

shake head in negation v.
kra lxaaba', kra saliba'.

shake loose (as of dust off one's feet) v.
samet khaar thẽbaa'.

shake oneself (of animal shaking water off after rain) v.
khaa'rba.

shake to and fro (of cat with a mouse) v.
mxuba.

shaking (of fruit falling from trees being shaken) n.
bxudududu.

shaman (who divines supernatural causes of illness, etc.) n.
pujyu'.

shameless a.
nakaḍaa'.

share n.
ã'šaa.

share
1. s.num. -bãã.
2. n. bxaau', xlssaa'.

share farming n.
axdxe'.

share out (food) v.
pããbaa'.

sharp a.
chyaa'rba.

sharp edge (as of axe) n.
dxaara'.

sharpen (a point) v.
myũbaa'.

shave (wood) v.
khurkudiba'.

shawl n.
1. *(worn sash-like by mature women)* pro'.
2. *(worn as head covering)* pachyuraa'.

she pn.
ca'.

she herself pn.
khi.

sheaf
1. n. lũ'daa.
2. s.num. *(grass or fibres)* -jyaa.
3. n. *(of grain)* muṭhaa'.

sheath of Nepali dagger n.
syu.

shed n.
1. *(near house, thatched roof)* sinĩ'.
2. *(temporary shelter for cattle)* prxõ.

sheep n.
kxyu'.

sheet n.
1. *(of white cloth carried ahead of corpse)* gxyãã'.
2. *(used on bed)* cyaadar.

shelf n.
1. *(above fireplace to hold wood, meat for drying)* ṭxõwãã.
2. *(for big pots and water jars)* takhada'.

shell
1. v. *(husks off corn)* pi'ba.
2. n. *(of snail)* gxãã'.

shelter
1. v.i. *(from rain)* o'ttiba, kru'ba.
2. n. *(temporary, built in fields distant from home where workers stay over-night)* ṭhããḍi.
3. n. *(above rice housing place)* syõ'rããni.

shelves n.
a'lmuḍi.

shepherd
1. v. chabaa'.
2. n. chaẽ.

shift
1. v.t. sardiba'.
2. v.i. yogõba'.

shin n.
khlxyõ, nali', pxali ḍããḍa.

shine v.
1. *(of sun)* pre'ba.
2. *(with brightness)* ṭalgadiba'.

ship n.
kyu' jxaasa'.

shirt n.
1. kamẽja'.
2. *(Nepali style)* bxoḍo'.

shiver v.
1. txaarba.
2. *(with fever)* kwĩbaa'.

shoe n.
juda.

shoot n.
1. maudu'.
2. *(new, of edible lily)* gaba.
3. *(of barley grown indoors for ceremonial purposes - at Dasain)* jamra.

shop n.
dukhaan.

short a.
1. *(in length)* ranṭhi'.
2. *(of man)* mo'ba.

short person n.
puḍke.

short-tempered a.
nxakhũ pra'ba.

short-tempered person n.
jxaḍĩ'yãã, jxaḍĩge.

shortage n.
khããj.

shortly t.
dxowo', togo'.

shorts n.
jxããge.

shot-gun n.
bandxu'.

shot-put n.
chyolo.

shoulder n.
1. *(especially towards neck)* kããdaa'.
2. *(especially away from neck)* pxaẽdo.

shout v.
gxaudi'ba, kae te'ba.

shouting in confusion av.
cyããũ cyãã'ũle.

show v.
tẽbaa', u'ĩba.

shriek v.
cijidiba'.

shrimp n.
kwĩ'jiri tãã'ga.

shrine n.
1. *(small, for offering religious rites to* deudaa*)* deuraali.
2. *(to a god, smaller than* ma'ndir*)* thaa'na.

shrink (of cloth or of hole) v.
gxaḍi'ba, rubaa'.

shrouded completely (of wearing cape) av.
gxublukkale.

shuffle through (in looking for something lost) v.
lxiba'.

shut v.
1. *(a door)* tubaa'.
2. *(eyes)* mĩ' cyũ' labaa'.

shut up (imprison) v.t.
thundiba'.

shy, be v.
pibaa'.

siblings (blood brothers and sisters) n.
ti'maẽ, saget.

sick, be v.
na'ba.

sickle n.
ããsi'.

side with v.
lxaidiba.

sieve n.
1. *(cane, for winnowing grains)* pwiga'ẽ.
2. *(winnowing tray for small grains)* ce'na.

sigh
1. v. xui labaa'.
2. n. xa'ger xa'ger.

sights n.
jxill ra mi'li.

sign in Devanagari script indicating that no vowel sound follows a consonant (lit. *'foot cutting'*) n.
pxal tho'ba.

signature n.
sai'.

significance n.
bxaabaa', pattaa.

silver n.
cããdi'.

similar p.
-dõ'.

similar, be v.
krxiba.

simmer v.
plu'ba.

simultaneously av.
ticyaarnaa'.

sin (ritual defilement) n.
paab.

since p.
sero', wono'.

sinew n.
nasa.

sing v.
1. *(a song)* prĩ'ba.
2. *(first line of a solo couplet)* ubaa'.

singe (an animal after killing) v.
khrõbaa'.

singly av.
ekaali'.

sink v.
1. *(of earth)* bxaasi'diba.
2. *(of boat)* ḍubdiba.

sir n.
saabaa'.

sister n. (see Appendix A)
1. *(EtSi, address by younger siblings, relatively rare)* axgxẽ'.
2. *(ErSi)* anãã.
3. *(YtSi)* kanchi.
4. *(YrSi)* ãŋãã'.
5. *(2nd)* mxaĩli.
6. *(3rd)* saĩli'.
7. *(4th)* kaĩli'.

sister-in-law n. (see Appendix A)
1. *(HuYrBrWi)* deurããni.
2. *(WiYrSi)* sali'.
3. *(ErBrWi)* cõ.
4. *(YrBrWi)* buwaari.

sisters (MaSi, WoHuSi) n.
rĩ', rĩ'maẽ.

sit v.
1. kũ'ba.
2. *(of hen on eggs)* nõ'ba.

Siva (Hindu deity) n.
siba.

six num.
ṭxu'.

sixty num.
ṭxujyu'.

skein of thread n.
cyaa'.

skid v.
plebaa'.

skilful a.
si'baalu'.

skin n.
1. ṭxubi.
2. *(of goat used at* pae *ceremony)* khaal.

skirt n.
1. lũgi', syããmãã'.
2. *(worn by young girls)* jããmaa.
3. ṭigisaa'.
4. *(of dark checked cloth worn by Gurung women)* musre' ŋxywi'.

skull n.
khoplẽ.

sky n.
mu.

sky gods (sun and moon, regarded as remote, not requiring animal sacrifice or other offerings) n.
parameš̌wara.

sky is clear v.
mu thõŋŋyũ'.

slander n.
culi.

slanting a.
bããgo-ṭeḍo.

slap with open hand v.
chẽraaba'.

slaughter (animal) v.
tho'ba.

slave n.
keb.

sleepout (enclosed side verandah often occupied by widowed, adolescent, or divorced members of family) n.
khubi'.

sleepiness n.
nxaru.

sleeping place n.
khlxyo.

slender a.
padlu'.

slip v.
plebaa'.

slip of the tongue n.
sũ phlebaa'.

slither on stomach (of infant unable yet to crawl) v.
khlyããbaa'.

slothful a.
alchi'.

slow a.
ḍxile'.

slowly av.
nũ'jile.

slug n.
1. ka'bu.
2. *(large, usually 2"-3" long)* maina' ka'bu.

small a.
1. cyõbaa', jxaja'.
2. *(in size)* cyugu' thiri'.

small as that a.
cxi siri', cxi thiri'.

small portion eaten by convalescent n.
tya'te.

small quantity of rice n.
gaasa.

smaller a.
gxaḍi'.

smallpox n.
biphar.

smart a.
calaakh.

smash v.
phordiba'.

smell
1. v.i. nãã'ba, thãã nãã'ba.
2. n. thãã.

smile (in friendliness or mockery) v.
ni xe'rara labaa'.

smoke
1. n. migu'.
2. v. *(cigarettes, etc.)* thũ'ba.

smooth a.
1. *(of flour, cloth, skin, surfaces)* masinu'.
2. *(of surface)* ci'llo.

smooth mud and cowdung on walls and floor v.
syaa'laba.

snag v.
kxoba.

snail n.
ka'bu gxãã'.

snake n.
1. *(in religious texts)* lu.
2. *(small)* pxuri.
3. *(large)* khlxõbae.
4. *(python)* sãã'be.
5. *(green, with poor eyesight and painful bite)* ããdi', ããdi' pxuri.
6. *(with poor eyesight and painful bite)* pi'bi pxuri.

snarl of tiger (onom.) n.
xãã.

snatch away v.
pxẽba.

sneeze v.
chĩbaa'.

snobbish a.
maattiba'.

snore v.
ŋxruba'.

snot n.
naa'.

snow n.
khlyĩ'.

snow peak n.
kadaa'sũ, kailaas.

so
1. c. cxamare', dabae, diyãã, diyããre'.
2. av. *(... big, fat, etc.)* cxaa.

soak v.
kyobaa'.

soaked a.
pãã'ba.

soap n.
saabaanaa'.

society n.
samaaj.

sock n.
juraabaa.

soda (a rising agent) n.
soḍaa'.

soft a.
galdiba, kamalo', masinu', na'ram, ŋiliba'.

soil n.
sa.

soldier n.
laa'khure.

soldier guards n.
paale'.

sole of foot n.
paidala', plo.

solid (not hollow, of jewellery) a.
khanwaa'.

some days ago t.
ũĩ'mi'.

some people pn.
ku'i.

some people's pn.
ku'ilaa.

someone, something a.
phalanaa.

something pn.
to' budũ tãã.

sometimes t.
khaa'gae, khõyõ khõyõ, ku'ila.

sometimes... other times t.
khõyõ... khõyõ.

son n. (see Appendix A)
1. cxa.
2. *(adopted)* dxarma' pu'tra.
3. *(first)* ṭhaagu.
4. *(second)* mxaĩlaa.
5. *(third)* saĩlaa'.
6. *(fourth)* kaĩlaa'.
7. *(youngest)* kanchaa', cyõ.

son-in-law (DaHu) n. (see Appendix A)
mxo.

son-in-law of household (who lives in wife's house and, in absence of son, inherits through wife) n.
gxa'r jawẽ.

song n.
1. kxwe'.
2. *(of praise)* bxaja'n.
3. *(folk)* jxyaaure' kxwe'.
4. *(ballad sung in responsive parts)* dokhore kxwe'.

soot above fireplace n.
krxiji.

sore n.
gxaa', pura.

sores on face n.
khorẽ'.

sorrow
1. n. aaphsos.
2. v. saẽ na'ba.

sort (variety) n.
jaad.

soul n.
plxa, saẽ.

soup n.
khu'.

sour a.
axmĩ'ba, kyũbaa'.

south loc.
dakhin, kyu'ru maai.

sow by scattering v.
plxuba'.

space between poles in a rack for stacking corn cobs n.
khaal.

spade n.
belca.

span of hand n.
bittaa.

spare a.
phalṭu'.

spare time n.
phursada'.

sparrow n.
ko'rmẽ.

speak v.
põ'ba.

speak truthfully v.
saccaa' põ'ba.

speak indiscriminately v.
nau' kisim bibaa.

special a.
ṭheṭaraa'.

species n.
jaad, thari.

speckled (of animals or cloth) a.
jxyaale' maale'.

speech n.
baagyaa.

speechless (with fury, or joy, or any strong emotion) a.
baagyaa axkho'ldiba.

speed
1. n. spiṭ.
2. v. *(in motor vehicle)* kuttiba'.

spend (money, resources) v.
mxaaidi'ba, mxaasdi'ba.

spendthrift n.
mxaaswaa'.

spew out of the mouth (rinse water, spittle) v.
swaalbaa'.

spices n.
masala'.

spicy a.
sobaa'.

spider n.
tximmru.

spike n.
thuri.

spill v.
ŋxeba', okhaldiba'.

spilling av.
pakha'r.

spin
1. v.t. gxumdi'waabaa'.
2. v.i. yurbaa'.

spinning wheel n.
xaaḍa'.

spirit n.
1. *(ghost)* picaas.
2. *(wine)* paa'.
3. *(not flesh)* aadmaa'.
4. *(evil, inhabitant of* na'rga*)* mxũgi'.
5. *(evil)* bxut, ligyãã'.
6. *(evil, of a person or animal who has died as a result of falling from a cliff)* syo'.
7. *(evil, of a person who has suffered a violent death, can be aroused by witch to hurt people)* syaa'gi.
8. *(evil, of dead person who has been unable to reach the village of the dead, dwells around cemeteries)* masana'.
9. *(evil, of fire)* sarwẽ'.
10. *(which dwells in forest areas)* xesaẽ.
11. *(of waterfall)* muhãã.

spit v.
tu' waabaa'.

spit at (usually contemptuously) v.
tu'd praa'baa.

spite n.
ikh.

spitting pan n.
kobre'.

spittle n.
tu'.

splash v.
praa'ba.

splashing n.
1. jal tha'l.
2. *(of liquid out of a receptacle)* pakha'r.

split v.
1. tibaa'.
2. *(cane)* ku'ba.
3. *(cane or wood lengthwise)* khlyi'ba.

split cane or wood (used as fork) n.
kaa'bro.

sponge n.
ispan.

spoon (big) n.
camja'.

spot of religious significance on forehead, usually red n.
cxae'.

spotted a.
jxyaale' maale' phulaa.

spout of water from vessel n.
dxaaraa'.

sprain v.
khribaa'.

spread v.
1. *(news)* phailidiba'.
2. *(infection)* ku'ba, sardiba'.

spread out v.
1. *(paper)* paẽbaa'.
2. *(blanket, mat)* tibaa'.

sprig of bush n.
nãã.

spring n.
kyu'waadxũ', mu'laa.

spring up v.
mlxoba'.

sprinkle (as in ritual cleansing) v.
praa'ba.

sprout
1. n. maudu'.
2. v. paldiba', mlxoba'.

sprout profusely - of leaves v.
mxããba.

spun yarn n.
sarbu'.

squash v.
kujidiba'.

squeak v.
ŋxeba.

squeeze v.
cxyurba.

squint v.
mĩ' ṭa'k saebaa'.

stab v.
cwibaa', mlxuba'.

stable for oxen n.
se'rãã dxĩ'.

stack n.
1. *(wood)* rẽ.
2. *(hay)* ṭowaa.
3. *(sheaves)* kunnyo'.

staff (stick) n.
prxe.

stake n.
1. kilo', phargu, thuri.
2. *(forked, which supports eaves of the cattle shed)* pẽdo'.
3. *(in gambling)* baaji.

stale a.
sĩ.

stalk n.
1. *(of plant such as maize)* ḍããḍa.
2. *(of millet)* na'la.

stall (usually for cows) n.
sinĩ'.

stamp n.
1. *(seal)* chaa'p.
2. *(postage)* ṭigaḍ.

stand
1. v. *(rest one's weight on)* dxũba'.
2. v. *(take erect position)* raa'ba.
3. n. *(for earthen water pot, ring woven of rice straw)* bẽḍa.
4. n. *(of copper, for ritual offerings)* chaabri'.

stand on v.
mxaeba.

stand up v.
ribaa', raa'ba.

stand upright v.
ṭhaardiba'.

star n.
musaa'ra.

startled, be v.
plxa lõbaa'.

starve (of men and animals) v.
ruḍiba'.

statement n.
bxaannãã'.

station (railway) n.
isṭesan.

statue n.
mu'rdi.

statuette (of rice flour used in religious ceremonies, especially funeral and post funeral) n.
ka'ẽḍu.

statutory labour n.
jxaaraa'.

stay v.
ṭibaa'.

steal v.
xyoba'.

steam
1. v.i. lom khabaa'.
2. n. lomãã.
3. v.t. plu'ba.

stem n.
ḍããḍa.

step v.
kwãã'ba.

step on v.
nxeba', mxaeba.

step over v.
ŋwe'ba.

stepfather n.
kaga' aaba.

stepmother n.
amjyõ aamaa.

stepped pole n.
li.

steps (portable, wooden) n.
bxryããŋãã'.

stepson n.
1. *(of a woman)* jxaṭke'lu cxa,
2. *(of a man)* progyaa.

stern a.
nisṭuri.

stew v.
plu'ba.

stick
1. n. prxe.
2. v. xrẽba.

stiff a.
1. *(of limbs, due to cold)* ka'graa ku'gru.
2. *(of cloth, stone, timber)* rũ'du.

stiffness in joints (due to vitamin deficiency probably) n.
naane.

stile n.
gũḍaa.

still t.
axjxai.

sting of nettles n.
khrõbaa'.

stink (always with thãã*)* v.
nãã'ba.

stir
1. v.t. *(liquids)* ruduba'.
2. v.t.,v.i. oleba'.

stirrer - wooden n.
ke'ba.

stomach n.
bxũḍi, pho'.

stone
1. n. ŋyu'mãã, yu'maa.
2. v. *(something or someone)* phai'rĩba.

stony ground or soil n.
bagra.

stool n.
1. *(bowel motion)* disaa.
2. *(circular, made of bamboo)* mõḍaa'.

stoop v.i.
kurbaa'.

stooped a.
kwaar.

stooping a.
kur.

stop v.i.
1. chyobaa', thaamdiba.
2. *(doing something)* pi'ba.

stopped a.
bandaa.

store (as opposed to spending or using money or clothes) v.
sããdiba'.

store-room for foodstuffs (near cooking area) n.
cxyogõ.

storey (of house) n.
tale'.

story n.
1. bxaannãã'.
2. *(fable or history)* kathaa'.

straight
1. av. *(directly)* sa'raasa'r.
2. a. sidaa', sojo'.
3. a. *(of character)* saẽ satte' tabaa'.

strands twisted together (in rope or plaits) s.num.
-brẽ.

strange a.
nau'le.

stranger n.
syãã.

strap for carrying load on back n.
ṭobi', ṭxo'.

straw n.
praalaa.

stream (seasonal) n.
bxolaa'.

strength n.
bxõ'.

stretch v.i.
tãngadiba'.

stretch out arm v.
syõbaa'.

stretched, be v.i.
lasgadi'ba.

stretcher-like construction on which corpse is placed n.
mora'.

stride v.
lamgadi'ba, te' kwãã'ba.

strike
1. v.t. dxõba', ṭhaudiba', ṭĩba'.
2. v.t. *(bell, instrument)* xraaba.
3. v.i. *(of projectile, curse)* ṭaba'.
4. v.i. *(of clock)* battiba.
5. v.t. *(corn cobs against each other to get grains off)* ṭhi'ba.

strike against v.
thurbaa'.

strip of land - narrow and long, between adjoining fields n.
dxarge'.

strip off v.
pi'ba.

stripe (as on ruled paper, shirt) n.
dxarge'.

striped a.
xrekha.

strive v.
xwẽba.

stroll v.
ḍuldiba, gxumdi'ba.

strong a.
1. *(of cloth, paper)* baaklo.
2. bxõba', pakkaa'.

stub (toe) v.
thurbaa'.

stubble of crops n.
phugaa'ra, ṭhuḍu'.

stubborn a.
gxama'nḍi.

stubs of cigarettes n.
lũṭhe.

study v.
khe'ba.

stumps n.
lũṭhe.

stupid a.
murkhaa'.

stutter v.
kawiba'.

stye in the eye n.
nimur.

submitting a.
kael.

substitute n.
saaṭṭo'.

suckle v.
mwẽ' mwẽ' labaa'.

sudden change from sunshine to threatening rain n.
xa'ra xu'ri.

suddenly av.
ekkaasi'.

suddenly and completely av.
ḍxyaa'ppa.

suffice v.
tabaa', yu'ba, thubaa'.

sugar n.
1. *(refined)* cini'.
2. *(raw)* guraa.

sugar-cane n.
ũsyu.

suit well (usually of clothes) v.
ŋxẽba.

suitable, be (congenial) v.
khrubaa'.

sulky a.
nxakhũ pra'ba.

summer n.
um.

sun n.
txiyãã.

Sunday n.
aaitabaara'.

sunlight n.
txiyããe' jyoti.

sunrise t.
sa'ra.

supervision arising from knowledge of bad tendencies (ensuring sentries do not sleep at post, cattle graze at crops, husbands philander) n.
cyowaa, yaa'd.

support v.t.
1. *(maintain)* nxaba.
2. *(encourage)* kwi'ba.
3. *(orally)* manidiba'.

supremely av.
taan bxandaa'.

surprise n.
bukka, cha'kka.

surrounding p.
kaa'rgyu.

surrounding area n.
khol ṭolaa', eriyaa'.

survey (as of damage in accident) n.
naa'b-jaab.

survive (from disaster or disease) v.
so'ba.

suspend
1. v.t. ṭããĩdiba'.
2. v.i. cyobaa', mẽ'jyoba'.

suspicion n.
chyowaa, šãkaa.

swaddling clothes n.
thaũni.

swallow
1. n. cili' paaḍe'.
2. v. khlxyõba.

swamp n.
simãã.

swear an oath v.
1. phwi'ba.
2. *(invoking curse on oneself if oath is broken)* kasam kĩbaa', kasam cabaa'.

sweater n.
swiṭara'.

sweep rice back into hole during pounding v.
kywĩbaa'.

sweep up v.
phyo'ba.

sweet a.
ki'giba'.

swell v.
1. mrxiba', phuldiba'.
2. *(of flesh)* rõ'ba.
3. *(of popped corn)* pxəariba.

swim v.
kywaaliba'.

swing with bamboo uprights n.
la'ĩku'di.

sword n.
1. *(weapon)* tarwaali'.
2. *(part of weaving apparatus)* krõmãã'.

syllabary of Devanagari script n.
baarkhari'.

T

tablet n.
goli, phũ.

tadpole n.
cyoblaa'.

tahr of Himalayas n.
pe'da.

tail of animal n.
mi.

tailor caste n.
txuli.

take v.
kĩba', bobaa.

take away v.
bayaaba.

take it! v.
1. nãã'.
2. *(somewhat disrespectful)* lu'.

take off (clothes) v.
plibaa'.

take photos v.
khitti'ba.

take root v.
cyõbaa'.

talk v.
põ'ba.

talkative v.
khaebaa'.

tall a.
nu'ba.

Tamang n.p.
la'mmaẽ.

tantrum of child n.
raar.

tap, piped water n.
ka'l, dxaru'.

tape-recorder n.
ṭebrikoḍ.

taste
1. v. mxyõba.
2. n. swaad.

tasty a.
1. lĩ'ba.
2. *(of goat meat)* kasdiba'.

tax n.
1. *(on land)* baali.
2. ṭeksaa'.

taxi n.
ṭyaaksi'.

tea n.
1. cxaa'.
2. *(drunk on first arising,* lit. *'bed tea')* beṭicxyaa'.

teach (usually with causative particle, but not always) v.
lubaa'.

teacher n.
1. *(especially religious)* guru.
2. *(school)* maasṭara'.

tear v.
1. *(clothes, paper)* ṭo'ba.
2. *(into pieces)* lũbaa'.

tears n.
mili.

telescope n.
dirbin.

tell v.
1. *(a lie)* syur te'ba.
2. *(the truth)* saccaa' põ'ba.
3. *(a story, narrative)* sebaa'.

temple n.
1. *(of head)* ŋẽŋẽ'.
2. *(dedicated to Hindu rites)* ma'ndir.

tempt v.
bxããḍi'diba.

ten num.
cyu', das.

tender a.
kamalo', kaaphaar.

tenth day (after a given date, esp. of dasaẽ *festival)* n.
dašmi.

terrace n.
1. bĩḍi.
2. *(of paddy fields)* nõ, nxõ'.
3. *(field - dry)* pakh mrõ'.

test n.
bijaar, jããj.

testicle n.
kxalphũ.

tether v.
cywĩbaa'.

tethering peg n.
kilo'.

thank you! p.
1. *(to equal or superior, but rarely used)* dxanyaa'baad.
2. *(to child or servant)* syaabaas.

Thak (Gurung village east of Pokhara) n.p.
thosõ.

Thakali (ethnic group inhabiting the Thak Khola) n.p.
pxaemaẽ.

than p.
bxandaa'.

that pn.
ca'.

that way a.
cxa.

that's the way it is av.
chalen, cxagana.

thatch n.
kxi'.

the more pa.
jxa'n.

the most av.
taan bxandaa'.

the place of p.
ŋaar.

themselves pn.
khemaẽ.

then c.
cxarare', dabae, daai, diyãã, jxaale', phe'ri.

there loc.
1. ca'ri, kya.
2. *(way over there)* ke' kyari'.

therefore c.
cxa tamaa', daaiga, diyãã, diyããre', jxaasero'.

thick a.
1. dxũba', rũ'du.
2. *(of cloth, paper)* baaklo.

thief n.
xyo'.

thigh n.
pxãã.

thin a.
1. ḍyããgra, kadrãã, pra'ba, ṭãã'gu.
2. *(of cloth, paper)* padlu', pobaa'.

thing n.
sa'e.

thinness a.
sibi' cheba.

third a.
tesro'.

third finger n.
yo mxaĩli.

third of four eras of Hindu mythology n.
dwaapaar.

thirsty a.
kyu' pii, pibaa'.

thirteen num.
te'roḍa.

thirty num.
sõ'jyu.

this pn.
cu'.

this much a.
1. cxaa, cxo, ja.
2. *(usually a small amount)* cxaga.

this side
1. p. cõjãã'.
2. av. jxu-.

this small a.
cxi thiri'.

this (correlative with cha *'thus')* c.
chu.

thither av.
jxaa-.

thong n.
cabli.

thorn n.
puju'.

thought n.
1. *(reflection)* bijaaraa', saẽ bicaara'.
2. *(concern)* yaa'd.

thousand num.
xa'jar.

thrash v.
prxuba'.

thread
1. n. ru'.
2. v. syu'ba.
3. n. *(spun)* sarbu'.
4. v. *(a needle)* kyulbaa'.
5. n. *(extracted from bush plant)* naĩ'.
6. n. *(worn around neck for supernatural protection)* ru'ba.

three num.
sõ'.

thresh v.
nxeba'.

threshing floor (area cleared in the rice field for threshing at harvest time) n.
khalaa'.

threshing of grain with oxen n.
daẽ.

threshold n.
gẽ, sũ, sãgaa'raa.

thrice av.
tintiyaali.

thrive (of plants) v.
sobaardiba'.

throat n.
1. *(internal)* mlõ'gu.
2. *(internal, rarer than* mlõ'gu*)* orgõ.
3. *(external)* kha'ri.

throb (of wound) v.
balag balag labaa'.

throne n.
raa'j gatti.

throughout p.
bxori', ti'laa.

throw (a brick) v.
prĩ'ba.

throw away
bxyõba', waabaa', bxyããba'.

thrust in v.
kxyuba.

thumb n.
yo aabaa.

thumbprint n.
sai'.

thunder (lit. *'sky roaring')* n.
mu ŋxeba.

thus
1. av. cxa.
2. c. cxamare'.

Tibet n.p.
bxoḍ, ṭibaaḍe.

Tibetan n.p.
bxoḍe', cyobraa'lmaẽ.

ticket n.
ṭigaḍ.

tiger n.
cẽ.

tight a.
1. *(narrow)* sããŋgru'.
2. *(of rope, belt, binding)* kasdiba'.

timber (sweet-smelling) n.
gxyõsĩ'.

time n.
1. *(occasion)* belaa, txi, ṭyãã'maa, yaa'm.
2. *(occasion, astrological)* joga.
3. *(turn)* laa, palu'.

time of very heavy rain n.
gxaanaa' gxoḍ'.

time to die n.
kaal.

times s.num.
-ble.

tin (can) n.
baṭṭa.

tire v.
naariba'.

toad n.
pxadgu.

tobacco n.
1. kãgaḍaa'.
2. *(chewing)* sordi'.
3. *(smoking)* tamaakhu'.

today t.
tiyãã'.

toddling unsurely n.
kaa'rãã ma'rãã.

together
1. a. khaa'gu.
2. av. khaa'gule, baalu.

together with p.
saathaa'ri, -ne baalu.

tomato n.
golbxẽḍaa'.

tomcat n.
nowãã ḍxaaḍe'.

tomorrow t.
pxanxããga.

tomorrow morning t.
pxanxããri'.

tongs for fire n.
cimḍaa'.

tongue n.
le'.

tonight (future) t.
kom nesaa'.

tooth n.
1. sa.
2. *(protruding)* daare.

top n.
cxo.

topknot n.
tamũ'.

topsy-turvy a.
ulṭaa' paalṭaa'.

total
1. n. jamma.
2. a. puraa'.
3. n. *(of pay entitlement)* ṭoḍol.

touch v.
chwibaa'.

towards p.
1. *(of time)* badẽ.
2. *(of place)* paṭṭi', -ũdi'.

towel n.
pachyoraa', tauliyaa.

town n.
1. *(market)* bajaar.
2. *(village)* nãã'sa.
3. *(city)* šahaara.

town crier n.
kaṭwaale'.

trace n.
cakhilo', cinu', sagẽ', ṭhyaa'ppa.

track (minor road) n.
po' gxyãã'.

trade n.
bepaari, chõ.

train (railway) n.
rel gaaḍi.

trance with shaking (of religious officiant) n.
gur.

transfer of land title permanently n.
raa'jinaa'm.

transparent a.
saũlo'.

transplant seedlings v.
ruĩbaa'.

trap n.
1. khoraa, ŋo'.
2. *(cage-like)* cyõ.

travel cost n.
gxyãã' kha'rja.

tray (wicker, about 30" in diameter used for winnowing) n.
na'ũli.

tread upon v.
plibaa'.

treat v.
1. *(an illness)* kho'j guwaar labaa'.
2. *(medically)* maẽ labaa'.

tree n.
1. *(generic)* dxũ'.
2. *(like the ginger tree which produces a sweet smelling white or yellow flower in September)* keuraali.
3. *(species, when branch of which is crushed and soaked in river fish are poisoned and easy to catch)* khere.
4. *(kind of)* prumũ'.

tree without leaves n.
chadrãã.

tremble v.
txaarba.

trick n.
cible tãã.

trip (cause to fall) v.t.
kxurwaaba.

triply av.
tintiyaali.

tripod over fire (for cooking pots) n.
jxõgu'.

trouble n.
du, ka'ṣṭa.

trousers (long) n.
paldũ.

truck n.
gaaḍi.

true a.
krxõsena', satte'.

trunk n.
1. *(box)* baagasa.
2. *(of tree)* mu'l xããga'.

trust
1. n. bišwaas.
2. v. bišwaas mxããdiba.

trustworthiness n.
bxar.

trustworthy, be v.
bišwaas mxããdiba.

truth n.
saccaa'.

truthful a.
sajan.

truthfulness n.
imaansaa'th.

try n.
košiš.

tube n.
nalgi'.

Tuesday n.
mxanglaa baaraa'.

tuft n.
jxyaaḍi'.

tumpline n.
choḍo', ṭxõ'.

tune n.
bxaagaa'.

turban n.
krigi'.

turmeric n.
besaara.

turn
1. v.t. gxumdi'waaba'.
2. v.i. yurbaa'.
3. n. *(one in a number)* palu'.

turn inside out v.t.
su'ba.

turn over v.t.
palṭidi'ba.

turn round v.t.
sẽ'ba.

turquoise n.
tudu'.

turtle n.
kachuwaa'.

tusk n.
daare.

twelfth day of dasaẽ n.
duwaadasi.

twelve num.
baara.

twenty num.
bis, ŋxisyu.

twenty-one num.
ekaais.

twenty-four num.
caubis.

twenty-nine num.
unantis, untis.

twice av.
duwaali, ŋxible.

twine v.
1. *(rope)* khrĩba'.
2. *(two strands of thread together for strength in weaving)* dunidiba.

twined tightly, be v.
khirididiba'.

twins (of offspring of normally monogenetic animal) n.
jaũle.

twist (rope, cane) v.
cyaa'riba.

two num.
1. dui, ŋxĩ'.

2. *(emphatic)* ŋxĩããḍõ'.

two hundred num.
ŋxibraa.

two together pn.
ŋxĩnaa' ŋxĩ'n.

type v.
chyaabdiba'.

typewriter n.
chaabdiba'e sa'e.

U

udder of a cow n.
mlõ.

umbilical cord n.
1. *(animal)* simããlaa'.
2. *(human)* koloe' thu.

umbrage n.
gaar.

umbrella n.
1. chada'.
2. *(head cover made of woven cane interlined with leaves)* kxũ.

unbending a.
ni'rmae.

uncle n. (see Appendix A)
1. *(FaBr, MoSiHu)* aabaa.
2. *(FaEtBr, MoEtSiHu)* aathebaa'.
3. *(FaYtBr)* aabjyõ.
4. *(Fa2ndBr)* axma'ĩlaa.
5. *(MoYrBr, MoErBr)* maa'maa.
6. *(paternal, oldest in own family)* kaagĩ'.
7. *(Fa3rdBr)* aabsaĩlaa'.

uncles (paternal) n.
aappa'e.

uncompassionate a.
saẽ saaro'n tabaa'.

uncontaminated a.
pabitra.

uncontrollably av.
murkhaa' caalle.

uncontrolled a.
murkhaa'.

uncooked (of meat, vegetables, not rice) a.
syu.

uncover (remove blanket or veil) v.
syuiba'.

uncultivated hillside n.
pakhaa'.

undefiled a.
1. pabitra, šuddha.
2. *(especially of food but also of people)* cokho'.

undergrowth n.
cxi.

underneath a.
nxõũba'.

underpants n.
jããge, mae kwẽ, xab jããge.

understand v.
kxoba.

unfriendly a.
maattiba'.

ungenerous person n.
khõ'ḍa, ku'gaaḍaa'.

ungrateful man n.
baigune'.

uniform, be v.
kxyããba.

unirrigated (field) a.
o'bããnõ.

unit (in army) n.
palṭan.

unjust a.
asa'tte.

unkind a.
ni'rmaẽ.

unladen (of porter) a.
thedẽ'.

unleavened bread n.
plaagẽ'.

unmotivated a.
phaa'karna'.

unprovoked av.
phaa'karna', ani'yaa.

unrestrainedly (of women fighting) av.
ḍũrũne mũ'rule.

unripe (of berries, fruit) a.
axmxĩba', kaji ka'duraa.

unruled (of paper) a.
saadaa'.

unselfish, be v.
saẽ sxaba'.

unskilled a.
mxakhanḍi.

unteachable a.
gxama'nḍi.

untie v.
pla'ba.

until p.
sa'mmaa.

unveil v.
syuibaa'.

unwillingness n.
kaes.

up loc.
ta, taai.

up to p.
sa'mma.

upend v.
khlyubaa'.

uphill
1. loc. tae'taadi'.
2. av. ukhaalu'.

upon loc.
phiri'.

upper back n.
kxo.

upright a.
1. *(ethically)* gatilo', su'dho, sojo'.
2. *(vertical)* ṭhaaḍo'.
3. *(standing upright)* thaar.

uprights (central forked poles of a cattle shed) n.
kũdo'.

uproar n.
gaḍbaḍ, kha'l bal, xallaa'.

uproot v.
syu'iba.

upside down a.
ulḍu'.

upturned (of a vessel holding liquid to tip out the last bit) a.
kyu'ru prõ'.

upwards av.
ka'ẽḍu.

urinate v.
kũ txõba.

urine n.
kũ.

use up (usually recklessly) v.t.
mxaasdi'ba.

used up, be v.
ṭuḍi' xyaaba'.

usefulness n.
keraa'.

utter v.
te'ba.

uvula n.
o'lmẽ.

V

vaccinate v.
kobdiba'.

vain, be v.
pxaẽba.

variegated in colour a.
jxyaale' maale'.

variety n.
khaal, kisim.

various a.
aanek.

various kinds of a.
na'u ul.

vegetable n.
1. *(generic)* ṭxaa.
2. *(green, generic)* ṭxaa ṭxu.
3. *(fern)* cible'.
4. *(spinach)* paasagi'.
5. *(arum colocasia)* lxauna.

6. *(like bamboo shoots)* karmaudu'.
7. *(of forest - bracken-like)* kudruge'.

vehemently av.
cargo'le.

vehicle n.
1. *(road)* gaaḍi.
2. *(air or sea)* jxaasa'.

vein n.
ca, na'sa.

vengeance, take v.
badalaa labaa'.

verandah onto which lower caste people are given entrance n.
pĩḍi.

vertical a.
ṭhaaḍo'.

vertical stroke in Devanagari script for aa *vowel* n.
kanda'ni.

very av.
bele, beseri, bxudu'kan, khu'b, lxe'.

vessel n.
1. *(cooking)* bxããḍo'.
2. *(metal water pot about 10 litres)* gauri.
3. *(large pot, for cooking rice)* khargana'.
4. *(for collecting wine in still)* pu.
5. *(for carrying fire when making offerings)* dxubaa'raa.
6. *(earthen water pot)* gxaĩḍi'.
7. *(for eating or cooking)* tõ'.

vestibule of house n.
thõ.

vexation n.
di'kka.

victory to... i.
jay.

view n.
tããn' chenle mrõl yõbaa'.

viewmaster n.
dirbin.

village n.
nãã'saa.

villagers n.
nãã'sthẽmaẽ.

vine n.
nxorĩ'.

violent
1. n. *(of man or animal)* jxaḍi'yãã.
2. a. *("hit first, speak afterwards" reaction)* murkhaa'.

violently av.
ḍũrũne' mũ'rule.

virgin (of male or female) n.
kanne'.

visible, be v.
mrõbaa'.

vision n.
daršan.

vomit v.
ogaaldiba', ru'iba.

vomitus n.
ru'i.

vow revenge v.
daagaa thẽba'.

vulture n.
kxure'.

W

wages paid to ploughmen in kind, generally rice n.
mu'juri.

waist n.
kaṭṭi'.

wait
1. v. bxaẽba'.
2. (imperf.) thaidu'.

wakefulness (in contrast with sleep) n.
saẽmaa.

walk v.
prxaba'.

walking stick n.
prxe.

wall n.
1. *(standing alone, usually of stone)* baanu.

2. *(of house, mud plastered)* bxedaa'.
3. *(of stone)* gaara.
4. *(of terrace field)* kallãã'.

walnut tree n.
kadu'.

wander v.
gxumdi'ba.

wander off (neglecting one's responsibilities, as of a rolling stone) v.
badaardi xyaaba'.

want to (with reduplication of monosyllabic verb stem) v.
ŋxããba.

want to follow (of child after parent) v.
ṭwibaa'.

war n.
laḍẽ'.

ward of village or town n.
1. *(geographical area)* ṭolaa'.
2. *(political - about 140 adults)* o'ḍaa.

warm (of clothes) a.
ṭxoba'.

warm oneself at a fire v.
txiba.

warmth (of weather) n.
garmi.

warning n.
su'cana.

wart n.
chi'bula.

wash v.
khru'ba.

wasp n.
na'bbru kuji'.

waste n.
khlyi.

watch
1. n. gxaḍi'.
2. v. rũ'ba.

water n.
kyu'.

water frog, reddish in colour n.
penḍo'.

water hole (small) n.
kuwaa.

water pot n.
1. *(earthen)* gaĩdi'.
2. *(metal)* gauri.

water source n.
dxaru', kyu'waa dxũ', mu'laa.

water vessel n.
1. *(copper, 3" high, storage)* xroja.
2. *(small round)* kasũḍi'.

water-pipe n.
nalgi'.

waterfall n.
chaare'.

watermill n.
chyodo.

wave around v.
syurbaa'.

waves n.
bxelga'.

wax n.
1. *(for sealing)* lxaa.
2. *(of bees)* kyõlõ'.

way n.
1. *(custom)* calan.
2. *(method)* tarigaa'.
3. *(of pronunciation)* kaaidaa'.

we pn.
1. *(exclusive)* ŋi.
2. *(inclusive)* ŋxyo'.
3. *(plural exclusive)* ŋija'ga.
4. *(plural inclusive)* ŋxyo'jaga.

weak a.
1. axbxõba', kacca', kaaphaar.
2. *(thin - of cloth)* padulu', pobaa'.

weakness n.
kamjo'ri.

wealth n.
dxan sampati', dxĩ'naa, gacche, nxora, pũji', sampati'.

wear v.
1. *(head covering)* kuubaa'.

2. *(a knife in the belt or feathers in headband)* khyaabaa'.
3. *(clothes or jewellery)* khibaa'.

wear away v.
khiidiba'.

weariness n.
1. nxaru.
2. *(with a certain food)* nar.

weary
1. v.i. naariba'.
2. v.t. naarwaaba'.

weary, be v.
nxaru yu'ba.

weave v.
ro'ba.

wedding n.
byaa.

Wednesday n.
budabaar.

weed v.
no syu'iba.

weed out v.
chããḍiba'.

weeds n.
no.

week n.
sada', xaptaa'.

weep v.
krobaa'.

weigh v.
1. kwi'ba.
2. *(in balances)* tauldiba'.

weight for balance-scales n.
ḍxaag'.

welcome hospitably v.
chen kxyuin labaa'.

welfare n.
bxalo'.

well
1. av. chenããle, chenle, sarla'kkale.
2. n. *(large)* inaar.
3. a. *(of health, of person)* sxaba'n.

well-being i.
sa'nca.

well done a.
syaabaas.

well-proportioned a.
plxi kru kxriba.

wet
1. v.t. kyobaa'.
2. a. sĩbaa'.
3. a. *(of firewood or clothes)* syu.

what pn.
to'.

what kind of a.
khai, to'laa.

what manner av.
khaile.

wheat n.
gaũ.

wheel n.
1. *(of machine)* ca'kka.
2. *(of vehicle)* pããuru, xwil.

when t.
khõyõ.

whenever av.
khõyõ bile, khõyõm.

whenever desired av.
belu ku'belu.

where loc.
1. khani'.
2. *(of movable objects or people)* kho'i.

wherever pn.
khani'.

whet (a blade) v.
myaa'ba.

which a.
khab.

while s.v.
-ŋere', -male'.

whip
1. v. kurra'd prĩ'ba.
2. n. kurraa'.

whiskers n.
daari.

whisky n.
xuski'.

white a.
taargyaa.

white ants n.
dxami'ro.

white foreigner n.
goraama'ẽ.

white metal n.
kããsu'.

white of egg n.
cããdi'.

white woman n.
mi'm.

whiten (of hair) v.
saa'riba.

whittle v.
khurkudiba'.

who pn.
khab.

whoever pn.
khab.

whole a.
puraa', satte'.

whose a.
khaba'la.

why av.
ta'le.

wick of lamp n.
daraa.

wicked a.
badmaaša.

wicked person n.
badmaaš, badmaaši.

wide a.
plxaaba.

widow n.
xraaḍi, bidhuwaa.

widower (insulting term) n.
khere.

width n.
cauḍaai, plxi.

wife n.
mrĩ, phrẽsyo.

wife of a man's covenanted friend n.
ŋxelsyo.

wild animals n.
janawaar, banarba'e jantu.

win v.
ṭxoba.

wind
1. n. kha'ẽ.
2. v. *(bandage around wound)* berdiba.

window n.
jxyaalaa'.

wine bibber (disrespectful term) n.
paa'ko.

wing n.
1. pxyaa.
2. *(less common than* pxyaa*)* pxyaagõ.

winnow v.
1. *(shaking tray up and down)* ṭaa'ba, cyaa'ba.
2. *(from side to side)* cxiba'.
3. *(rice from above the head, in the wind)* phyurbaa'.

winter n.
sarkha.

wire n.
taa'raa.

wisdom n.
gyaan.

wise men n.
xrab se'bmaẽ.

wish n.
chutte', icchyaa', xraar.

wisps n.
1. *(of barley, rice, wheat)* kho.
2. *(of corn ear)* bxudlaa'.
3. *(of hair growing out of corn cob)* makha'ẽ muraa.

witch (a living person who works malice against fellow villagers, either personally or by raising up certain evil forces to do

her bidding) n.
pumsyo.

witch's male relative n.
bausa.

witch-doctor n.
jxããkri'.

with p.
1. baalu, -ne baalu, saada'r.
2. *(in consulation)* ma'ne.

wither v.
oilidi'ba.

withered ear n.
pẽ'.

within p.
anda'rari'.

without a.
binaa.

without cause av.
phaa'karna'.

without considering others av.
ma'n pari.

without delay av.
gxari'nna.

without restraint (often sentence initial and often with beseri*)* pa.
mããri'.

without special cause av.
chalen.

witness (of an act) n.
saaji'.

woman n.
1. cami'ri, cxamiri, mrĩsyo'.
2. *(young, 16 to 30 years)* chamĩ'.
3. *(old)* mããba'.
4. *(in childbirth or period of confinement following)* sudgyaari'.
5. *(young)* rĩ'maẽ.
6. *(middle-aged)* axdxa'barse.

wonder n.
aacammaa', chakka.

wood n.
sĩ'.

woodpecker n.
xugaa' xraabae nemãã, sĩ' nemãã.

woods n.
bana.

wool n.
1. pae.
2. *(fine)* bxuwaa'.

word n.
1. tãã, šabda.
2. *(simulating lama's reading of Tibetan chants)* jyomẽ lyomaẽ.

work
1. n. kxe'.
2. v. *(for hire in fields)* ta'ba.
3. n. *(incomplete, to be resumed)* tõ.

workable (of earth) a.
galdiba.

workman n.
mistri'.

world n.
duniyaa, prithwi'.

worm n.
1. *(earth)* kode'.
2. *(water)* nããbli'.
3. *(intestinal, round worm)* pxebe.
4. *(in rectum, thread worm)* curnaa'.

worry n.
di'kka, du, phikkar, šo'k.

worship n.
ara'ti.

worship shrine near holy man's house for his own use n.
guphaa.

worthless a.
1. badmaaš.
2. *(of person, or of animal which breeds poorly)* axgadilu'.

worthless person n.
badmaaši.

wound n.
gxaa'.

wounded, be v.
ne' myõ'ba.

wrap around v.t.
berdiba.

wrap oneself with blanket v.
pxoba'.

wrap up v.
berdiba, mxuriba.

wriggle v.
khlyããbaa', oleba'.

wriggling av.
1. swaa swaalle'.
2. *(as of a snake)* garlaane gudlile.

wring out v.
cxyurba.

wrinkle
1. n. *(in skin)* boj.
2. v. *(skin)* mxyũba'.

wrinkled, be v.
khumjidi'ba, ŋri'ba ŋri'ba.

wrist n.
naari'.

write v.
prxiba.

writing paper n.
kaabi'.

X

X-ray examination n.
eksre'.

Y

yam n.
ti'mĩ.

yard n.
1. *(measure of length)* gaj.
2. *(of a house)* xyu'.

yawn v.
kãã'ba, xa'i labaa'.

year n.
1. *(as unit of time)* barṣa.
2. *(as unit of time, or in reference to a particular year)* saa'l.

year, last t.
tugyũmaa.

year, next t.
kurimbaa.

year, this t.
tidĩmaa.

year after next t.
na'udimaa.

year before last t.
naidi'maa.

year of birth in Tibetan 12 year cycle (changes each year about Dec. 31) n.
lxo.

year of the bird (1945,57,69, 81) n.
nemaa lxo, cxe lxo.

year of the cat (1951,63,75,87) n.
xi lxo, nõwãã lxo.

year of the cow (1949,61,73,85) n.
lõlo.

year of the deer (1947,59,71, 83) n.
pho lxo.

year of the dog (1946,58,70,82) n.
nagi lxo, khi lxo.

year of the horse (1942,54,66, 78) n.
gxoḍaa' lxo, ta lxo.

year of the monkey (1944,56,68, 80) n.
pra lxo, yogaara lxo.

year of the rat (1948,60,72,84) n.
cyuilo', nimũ lxo.

year of the sheep (1943,55,67, 79) n.
lxu lxo, kxyu' lxo.

year of the snake (1941,53,65,77, 89) n.
sabri' lxo, pxuri lxo.

year of the tiger (1950,62,74, 86) n.
cẽ lxo, to lxo.

year of the vulture (1940, 52, 64, 76) n.
mubru' lxo, kxure' lxo.

years s.num.
-dĩ.

years past t.
tugyũ'm naidi'maa.

yell v.
cijidiba', kae te'ba.

yellow a.
urgyaa.

yes (acknowledging statement or expressing approval) pa.
õ.

yesterday t.
telaa'.

yet t.
axjxai.

yoke of oxen
1. s.num. guraa.
2. n. kha'rgũ, xa'la.

yolk of egg n.
mxaara'.

you pn.
1. *(singular)* kxi.
2. *(plural)* kxemaẽ.

you know? i.
to'.

young (tender, of plants and men) a.
kalilo'.

young but full-grown a.
phrẽ.

young man - 16-30 years old n.
phrẽsĩ'.

youngest (of child or animal) a.
cyõbaa'.

youngest born male n.
1. *(affectionate diminutive)* cxijyõ.
2. *(calling name)* cyõ.

Z

zigzag a.
bããgo-ṭiŋgo', ṭeḍo'.

zinc n.
jasta.

zone (one of 14 into which Nepal is divided for administrative purposes) n.
ãcalaa'.

NEPALI-GURUNG INDEX

नेपाली – गुरुङ्ग

शब्द कोश

The purpose of this glossary is to allow the reader access to Gurung vocabulary entries by way of Nepali glosses. The first portion of each entry is Nepali and the glossary is arranged in Devanagari alphabetical order. This glossary will form an index in Devanagari script to the Gurung-Nepali-English dictionary.

अ

अं -- ओं ।

अंक -- न्हम्बर ।

अंगार -- क्रोफुं ।

अंग्रेजी -- अंग्रेजी ।

अंचल -- अंचला ।

अंध्यारो -- अनेरो ।

अंवा -- बेलौदो ।

अंश -- अंशा, औशा ।

अवे र -- अवे र ।

अगतिलो -- अह्गदीलु ।

अगाडि -- अघाडि, उंह्रं, सोदा ।

अगुत्टो -- मीउलुं, मेदों ।

अगेनु -- कोदा ।

अग्लो -- नुब ।

अघाउनु -- म्रैंब ।

अधि -- तलु, आसों, ओसों, तला ।

अचार -- अह्फारा ।

अफै -- अफै ।

अटाउनु -- त्हेब ।

अडकल -- अडगल ।

अडिनु -- क्ष्योबा ।

अड्कनु -- क्होब ।

अड्डा -- अड्डा ।

अथवा -- अथबा ।

अथा -- अथु, अत्थु ।

अदालत -- अद्लास ।

अढकल्चो -- अह्ध कल्सु ।

अधिकार -- अदिकार ।

अधिकारी -- अफीसर, अदिकारी ।

अधियां -- अह्धे ।

अधीन -- ग्यान ।

अनि -- अनि, दाई।

अनिकाल -- अंगल ।

अनुमान -- अन्मान ।

अनुसार -- अनुसार, हीसाबले ।

अनुहार -- अनुवार ।

अन्डरप्यान्ट -- हाब जांगे ।

अन्तर -- अन्दर ।

अन्दाज -- अन्दाजी ।

अन्न (आंखामा) -- नीमुर ।

अन्न (बाली) -- अन्दा,

अन्दापानी । तीफुंदे ।

अन्याय -- अनीया ।

अफसोस -- आफसोस, शोक ।

अब -- अब, धेरो ।

अबेर -- अ्हबेल्ले ।

अमीलो -- क्युंबा, क्युं ।

अम्खोरा -- अंखोरा ।

अम्बा -- बेलाउदी ।

अम्वि -- अ्हम्ह्वीं ।

अरीङ्०गाठे -- तुईप्हुरी ।

अरू -- आरू ।

अरू बेला -- आईबजी ।

अर्को -- आगु, आर्गो ।

अर्थ -- अर्थ ।

अर्थ खोल्नु -- अर्थ खोल्दीब,
मल्दब खोल्दीब ।

अर्थात -- अथबा ।

अलमल्ल -- अल्मल्ला ।

अलि -- दे, सरी, ते, तेर्ले ।

अलि अलि -- च्युगु च्युगु, खागए ।

अलि बिसेक -- खजीज़ ।

अल्किति -- तीब्रंदे, तीनदे,

अल्छी -- अल्छी ।

अल्जिनु -- कृहोब ।

अल्जो गर्नु -- प्ह्बेब ।

अल्पिनु -- म्हलीब ।

अवतार -- औतार ।

अशी -- प्ह्रेज्यु ।

अष्टमी -- अष्टमीं ।

असन -- आस्ना ।

असफर्ी -- असुर्बी ।

असल -- स्वाबा ।

आसामी -- असमी ।

असार -- असार ।

असिना -- तुस्यु ।

असुराको बोट -- आसुरी धुं ।

असोज -- असोद ।

अस्ति -- उंई मींई ।

अस्ति भर्खरै -- अहयां उंई ।

अस्पताल -- अस्पताल

अह्लिे -- धोवो, तोगो ।

आ

आंखा -- मीं ।

आंखा चिम्लनु -- मीं च्युं लबा ।

आंखा झिम्काउनु -- मीं सस्बा, मीं ट्हुब ।

आंखा बन्द गर्नु -- च्युं लबा ।

आंखाको पटल -- ङ०गोर ।

आंखे रौं -- मींज्यां ।

आंट्नु -- आंडीब ।

आंधी -- आंदी ।

आंप -- आंबा ।

आंसु -- मीली ।

आइज -- खो ।

आइतवार -- आइतबारा ।

आउ -- ल्हउ, यु ।

आउनु -- खबा, युब ।

आउने साल -- व्हुरीम ।

आकाश -- मु ।

आकाशमा बादल लाग्नु -- मु क्हुंब ।

आखिर -- आखिर ।

आखिरी -- आखिरी ।

आगन -- ह्यु ।

आगो -- मी ।

आग्लो (दैलो वा ढीकीमा राख्ने) -- औलो ।

आज गएर आजै आउनु -- ख्वीब ।

आज बेलुका -- कोम् नेसा ।

आजकल -- तींई जोरो, तीन्हांग ।

आठ -- आठ, प्ह्रे ।

आडलाउनु -- वैंब ।

आतिनु -- आदीदीब ।

आत्तुरी -- अहत्हुरी ।

आत्मा -- प्ल्ह, सएं, आद्मा ।

आदर गर्नु -- क्वैंब डे०ब, म्हादींब ।

आधा -- अहधा ।

आनन्द (सुबिस्ता) -- कर योंब, सजीलो ।

आन्द्रो -- न्हानुं ।

आफु -- खी, ह्रोंस ।

आफुहरू -- खेमए जग ।

आबै -- अबृवी ।

आमा -- आमा ।

आमाको कान्छी बहिनी -- अहच्च्यौं, अहम्फ्युु ।

आमाको दिदीहरू -- आथे ।

आमाको सौता -- अम्ज्यौं आमा ।

आयु -- आयु, छ ।

आरति -- आराती ।

आरन -- आरौं ।

आराधन -- आराती, सेवा ।

आराम -- आरम ।

आराम गर्नु -- पौं न्हब ।

आर्को किसिमको -- स्योब ।

आली (हालु) -- अली ।

आली लाउनु -- अल धैंब ।

आलू -- आलू ।

आवाज -- आवाज़, कए ।

आशा गर्नु -- ब्रेब ।

आशिक -- आशिक ।

आश्विन -- असौज ।

आहाल -- इoह्यो ।

इ

इक्का -- क्युत्तं, इक्क्या ।

इज्जत -- अव्बु, इजेद ।

इतिहास -- इतिहास ।

इन्द्रेनी -- ह्यागौं ।

इलाका -- एरीया ।

इशारा गर्नु -- हास्ता ल्ब ।

इष्टमित्र -- इस्टमित्त्र ।

इस्टेसन -- इस्टेसन ।

इस्पात -- इस्पदा ।

ई

ईटं -- ईटं ।

ईख -- ईख ।

ईमान साथ -- इमान्साथ ।

ईमान्दार -- इमान्दारी, सएं सात्ते तब ।

उ

-उं -- ले ।

उंट -- उंड ।

उंधो मुन्टो -- क्युरू प्रों ।

उंधोको -- माब ।

उंभो -- तादी, कस्ंडु ।

उकालो -- उखालु ।

उकास्नु -- उगास्दीबा ।

उक्कीनु -- कुब ।

उखान -- उखान ।

उखु -- उंस्यु ।

उखेलु -- स्युईब ।

उग्राउनु -- कांछी डे०ब ।

उचाल्नु -- क्वीब ।

उजिन्नो -- न्हजी ।

उज्यालो -- उज्यालो ।

उठाउनु (धान) -- त्हीब ।

उठ्नु -- रीबा ।

उडाउनु -- उडीदीब ।

उड्डुस -- नल्ली ।

उड्नु -- प्हीरीब ।

उता -- क्यादी ।

उता पट्टि -- फ्रापट्टि,
क्यापट्टि ।

उतार्नु -- उर्तादीब, ताबा ।

उत्तर -- कस्ंडु, तई, उत्तर ।

उत्तिसको (वोट) -- घ्र्योंसीं ।

उत्रनु -- उद्रीदीब ।

उद्याउनु -- म्याब ।

उनन्तीस -- उनन्तीस, उन्तीस् ।

उन्नु -- स्युब ।

उन्नैस -- उनेस् ।

उपकिनु -- कुब ।

उपचार गर्नु -- खोज गुवार ल्ब ।

उपद्र्याह -- उपत्द्रे ।

उप प्रधान पंच -- उभाप्रधान ।

उपल्लो -- त, क्होर्ब ।

उपवास -- बर्जीत, उपास् ।

उपवास बस्नु -- उपास टीबत् ।

उपाय -- ईस्कीम ।

उपियां -- तोंमी ।

उप्काउनु -- प्लेब ।

उफ्रनु -- उफ्रीदीबा ।

उब्जनी -- उब्जनी ।

उब्जाउनु -- खेदी ल्हीदीब, उब्ज लब ।

उभिनु -- राब ।

उमाल्नु -- ख्वाल ख्वाल ।

उमेर -- उमेर ।

उम्कनु -- उम्गदीब ।

उम्रनु -- म्ल्होब ।

उल्टा-पुल्टा -- उल्टा पुल्टा ।

उल्टो -- उल्डु ।

उल्टो गर्नु -- सुब ।

उवा -- करू ।

उसिन्नु -- प्लुब, हैंब ।

ऊ

ऊन -- पए ।

ऋ

ऋण -- क्षे ।

ए

ए -- हे, इ०हे ।

-ए पनि -- -ना बीले ।

एक -- एक, घ्री ।

एक कप -- तीरुल्यु ।

एक पन्थ दुई काम -- एक काम-दुई बन्द ।

एक छिन्मै -- घरीन्न ।

एक दर संग मिल्नु -- व्ह्यांब ।

एक पाथी -- प्योनो ।

एक फेर -- एकाली, तीव्ले ।

एक रातको -- एकरादे ।

एक रुपियांको नोट -- सउसरे, खुस्त्र ।

एक्ले -- घ्रीन, एक्ले बीर ।

एकादशी -- एकदशी ।

एकान्त -- एकलासी, एकान्ता ।

एकासी -- एकासी ।

एकै -- घ्रीन ।

एकै चोटि -- तीच्यारन् ।

एकै नासको -- खाल् ग्रीब ।

-एको -- -ब्, -ब, -ईमु, -इ०इ०युं ।

-एको थियो -- -मल ।

एकोहरो-दोहरो -- एहोर दोहोर ।

एक्काईस -- एक्काईस ।

एक्सरे (खिच्नु) -- एक्सरे ।

एघार -- एघारा ।

-एछ -- -न, -नमु ।

-एर -- -बीरी, -सैरे, -सी ।

ए

ऐसेलु -- पलां ।

ऐन -- अस्न्, सास्न् ।

ऐना -- ऐन ।

ऐया -- अया ।

ओ

ओइलनु -- ओईलीदीब ।

ओकल्नु -- ओगल्दीब ।

ओखर -- कदु ।

ओटा -- ओडा ।

ओठ -- मदी ।

ओथारो बस्नु -- नौंब ।

ओडार -- उ ।

ओदनु -- ओत्तीब, प्होब, कूबा ।

ओत बस्नु -- कूब ।

ओदान -- फ्रौंगु ।

ओबानो -- ओबानो ।

ओम माने पादमे हुं -- माने पामैं हुम् ।

ओरालो -- ओरालु ।

ओर्लनु (जहाज, तरा) -- न्हैब ।

ओर्लिनु -- तब ।

ओल्टयाङ० पल्टयाङ० गर्नु -- ल्हीब ।

ओहो -- अह्म्ह्वीं ।

ओहोर दोहोर -- एहोरदोहोर ।

औ

औठीं -- औठी, च्या ।

औलो -- री, योरी ।

औलोको जोर्नी -- यो च्ही ।

औतार -- ओतार ।

औले जरो -- अउलो क्वीने ।

औषधि -- मएं ।

औषधि गर्नु -- मएं ल्बा ।

क

कक्रक्क -- क्ग्राकुड़, कोंब ।

कखहरा -- क ख ।

कच्चा (काम) -- कच्च ।

कछाड -- कास ।

कछुवा -- कछुवा ।

कटहर -- कटर ।

कटेरो -- सेरांधीं, सीनीं,
स्योंरानी ।

कट्टु -- जांगे ।

कठवार -- कडबार ।

कडा -- सएं, सारो तबा ।

कति -- कदी ।

कति -- काचि ।

कत्ला -- कत्ले ।

कथा -- कथा ।

कनिका -- कंगा ।

कन्चट -- डेँ० डेँ० ।

कन्दनी -- कन्दनी ।

कन्ना पछाडि -- प्ल्हरी ।

कन्या -- कन्ने ।

कन्याउनु -- रुईब ।

कपाल -- क्र ।

कपाल काट्नु -- पेबा ।

कपास -- हुवा ।

कपूर -- क्बुरा ।

कबुल गर्नु -- कबोल ल्बा ।

कम -- घडी ।

कमलो -- कमलो, ड०लीब ।

कमाउनु -- तब ।

कमारो -- केबु ।

कमिलो -- नब्बु ।

कमीज -- कमेंज ।

कमेरो -- फुमाली ।

कम्जोरी -- कम्जोरी ।

कम्ती -- कम्दी ।

कम्मर -- कट्टी ।

कर काप गर्नु -- कऱ् लब ।

कराउनु -- कए तेब, ङ०हैब ।

कराउनु (बिरालोले) -- ङ०हुब ।

करिब -- करिब ।

करूवा -- कऱ्वा ।

कर्कलो -- ल्हउन ।

कर्नेल -- कर्नेल ।

कल -- कल, मिसीन ।

कलमी काट्नु -- खसी लबा ।

कलह गर्नु -- प्ह्रोंब ।

कलि युग -- कलि जुग ।

कलिलो -- कलिलो ।

कलेजो -- उईडा ।

कल्चौडो -- म्लों ।

कल्ली -- कल्ली ।

कष्ट -- कष्ट, नब् छ्ब ।

कसम -- कसम् ।

कसम खानु -- कसम् चाबा, कसम किंब ।

कसरी -- खैले ।

कसिङ०गर -- कसीं ।

कसिनु -- कस्दीब ।

कसेको -- कस्दीब ।

कसैगरि -- खैलसे ।

कसौंडी -- कसूंडी ।

कस्को -- खबल ।

कस्तो ? -- खैब ?

कहां (को घरमा) -- (ङ०) ङ०ांर ।

कहां ? -- खनी ?

कहां छ ? -- खनीमु ?

कहिले ? -- खोंयों ?

कहिले कहिले -- खोंयो खोंयो ।

कहिले काहीं -- खोंयों (खोंयो-म्हयो) ।

कांक्रो -- लखएं ।

कांचो -- स्यु, कदुर, कजी, अहम्हींब ।

कांटी -- कांडी ।

कांड -- मे (त्हलीं) ।

कांढो -- खो ।

कांढो -- पुजु ।

कांस -- कांसु ।

काईली -- कैंली ।

काइंलो -- कैला ।

काइदा (तरिका) -- काइदा ।

काका -- आब फेबृमएं जग ।

काका बा -- क्गा आबा ।

काख -- क्वैं ।

काखी -- ङ्०यौली ।

काग -- क्गा ।

कागत -- कागादा ।

कागती -- कागदी ।

काट्नु -- क्यांब, थोब ।

काट्नु (डल्ला) -- ठुब ।

काट्नु (धान) -- खास्ंब ।

काट्नु (मासु) -- तुबा ।

काठिनु -- काठिदीब, कौंब ।

कातर -- काफार ।

कान -- न्ह, न्हेमैं ।

कान नसुन्ने -- न्हउसी ।

कानमा लाउने गहना -- कौंलां ।

कानुन -- कानुन ।

काने गुजी -- न्ह ल्त्यी ।

कानो -- क्ना ।

कान्छा बाबा -- आञ्ज्यौं ।

कान्छा बाबुको श्रीमती -- अम्ज्यौं ।

कान्छा भाइ -- च्यौं ।

कान्छा भाइ (पियारो बोलि) -- च्हीज्यौं ।

कान्छी -- कान्छी ।

कान्छी फुपू -- फोज्यूं ।

कान्छो -- कन्छा ।

काप -- काब्रो ।

कापी -- काबी ।

काफार -- काफार, कच्चा ।

काम -- क्हे ।

काम लाग्नु -- केर त्हुब ।

कामी -- कर्मी ।

काम्नु -- क्वींबा, त्हार्ब ।

काम्लो -- द्रुडी, काम्लो ।

कायल -- कएल ।

कायल गर्नु -- कएल्दीब ।

कारण -- कारन् ।

कारखाना -- कारखना ।

कार्तिक -- कार्तिक ।

कार्यक्रम -- कांज्य ।

काल -- काल ।

काल रात्री -- कालरादी ।

कालिज -- पर्वा ।

कालो -- म्लोंग्या ।

कालो (बेसरी) -- म्लों कुजी ।

कालो निहुरो -- कुद्गे ।

कासी वाले -- कांसी वाले ।

कि -- -ए, गी, कि, उ ।

कि कि -- न न ।

कि त कि -- कि -कि,
या -या ।

किचकिच गर्नु -- कज् कज् लब ।

किच्नु -- पीबाँ, आंठीदीब ।

किताब -- किदाब ।

किद्लो -- किल्ली ।

किन -- तले ।

किनभने -- तलेबीयां ।

किरण -- सर, हवी व्ही ।

किराया -- किराई ।

किरिया -- किरे ।

किरिया खानु -- किरे कींबा ।

किलो -- थुरी, फर्गु, किलो,
क्युलु ।

किलो (दांई हाल्ने) -- म्हें ।

किल्किले -- ओल्में ।

किसम् -- किसीम् ।

कीरो -- प्हुलुं ।

कीरोहरू -- प्हलं प्हुलुं ।

कुंडो -- कुंडो ।

कुंद्नु -- कुन्दीब ।

कुइनो -- कुदुं ।

कुइरो -- न्हाम्ज्यो ।

कुकुर -- नगी ।

कुकुरको बर्ष -- नगी ल्हो,
खी ल्हो ।

कुकुक -- कुक्रा ।

कुखुरो -- नग ।

कुखुरो थुन्ने कोक्रो -- नुं ।

कुखुरोको फुल बिक्रिनु -- क्हुइब ।

कुखुरी (भर्खर हुर्केको) -- ल्हांलों ।

कुचो -- कुज ।

कुच्याउंनु -- कुजीदीब, चीलीब ।

कुटो -- कुडी ।

कुट्नु -- धोंब ।

कुदाउनु -- कुत्तीब ।

कुन- खब् ।

कुना -- ती, कुनुं, ड०ी ।

कुनियो -- कुन्यो ।

कुनियो लगाउनु -- कुन्यो फ्रोंब ।

कुन्जिएको -- कुंजुर ह्याम ।

कुप्रो -- क्वार, कुप्रे ।

कुबिन्डो -- कुबिन्ड ।

कुम -- कांदा, प्हसंदो ।

कुमारी -- कुमारी ।

कुरा -- तां ।

कुरिलो -- पत्तु ।

कुरौनी -- कुरानी ।

कुर्कच्चा -- तींज्यो ।

कुर्सी -- कुंजी ।

कुलो -- कुलु ।

कुल्चनु -- प्लीबा ।

कुल्ला गर्नु -- खुलु खुलु लबा ।

कुवा -- कुवा ।

कुहुनु (घांस) -- क्रांब ।

कुहुनु (हातको) -- कुइनुं, कुदुं, कुंन्जयु ।

के ? -- तो ?

के को ? -- तोला ?

केउराली -- केउराली ।

केटाकेटी -- क्षतुरे, कोल्मसं ।

केरा -- म्हाज ।

केराउ -- तांग्र ।

केर्नु (प्रश्न सोध्नु) -- केर्दीब, ख्याव्दीब ।

केलाउनु -- च्हीब, प्रेंबा, सुर्इब ।

केहि कुरा -- तो बुदुं तां ।

केहि छैन -- तोई अहद्रे ।

केहि पनि न- -- तोई अद्र- ।

केही.. केही -- खस्र.. खस्र

कैंची -- कैंजी ।

कैलास -- कैलास ।

को ? खब् ?

-को -- -बए, -ए, -ल, -मसं ।

कोक्रो -- फ्रांगो ।

कोक्रो (कुखुरा छोप्ने) -- कुर्गु ।

कोक्रो (बालख सुत्ने) -- फ्रोग ।

कोट -- क्वी ।

कोट्टयाउनु -- कोडेब ।

कोठा -- कोठा ।

कोठा (ठानामा) -- कोड घार ।

कोण परेको -- कुदुं ।

कोत्रनु -- रोस्ब ।

कोदाली -- कोदाली ।

कोदो -- नारे ।

कोपरा -- को०रे ।

कोर -- कोरे ।

कोरा -- कोरा ।

कोरालो (बाच्छी) -- कुर्ली, क्हुरीम ।

कोर्नु (कपाल) -- स्वीबा

कोर्नु (कागत) -- केर्दोब ।

कोर्रा -- कुर्रा ।

कोर्रा लाउनु -- कुर्रा प्रींब ।

कोल -- कुला ।

कोशिश -- कोशिश ।

कोसेली -- कुस्याली ।

कोहि -- खबए, कुई ।

कोहिको -- कुईला ।

कौडी -- कौडी ।

कौसी -- कौसी ।

क्याम्प -- केम ।

कृष्ण -- कृष्ना ।

क्लास -- कीलास ।

क्वार क्वार गर्नु (कुखुरीले) -- कोदोब ।

ख

खंदिलो -- खन्वा ।

खकार्नु -- खोंन वाबा ।

खजुरो -- न्हा०रे ।

खटाउनु -- खडीदीब ।

खट्कौलो -- क्या, (खगर्न) ।

खतम -- खतम् ।

खन्नु -- त्हाब ।

खप्नु -- खव्दीब ।

खप्पर -- खोप्लें ।

खबर -- खबर, नयां तां, फ्रम् तां ।

खर -- क्ही ।

खरानी -- मेंरो ।

खरायो -- खरा ।

खर्क (बन्मा) -- ख्ल्ह्ये ।

खर्च -- खर्ज, थैली ।

खल्क -- खलाग ।

खल्ती -- गुजी ।

खलो -- खला ।

खलबल -- खल्बल ।

खसी -- खसी ।

खसी पार्नु -- खसी ल्वा ।

खस्नु -- खह्र्याबि, खारीब, तेबा ।

खप्रे भ्यागुतो -- प्ह्यादगु ।

खप्रो -- खस्रो ।

खांचो -- खांज् ।

खांद्नु -- खांदीब ।

खाइदिनु -- च्वाबा ।

खाट -- खाड ।

खादी (लोग्ने मानिसको पुरानो पोशाक) -- खादी ।

खानमा दु:ख पाउनु -- रूडीब ।

खानु -- चाबा ।

खानु (चुरोट) -- थुंब ।

खानु (मकै) -- फेब ।

खाने कुरा -- च्वबए सए ।

खाने समान राख्ने कोठा -- च्ह्योगों ।

खान्दान -- ईजेंद ।

खाम -- चिट्ठी खोल ।

खाल -- खाल ।

खाल (जुवा) -- खाल ।

खाल (थरि) -- खाले ।

खालि (मात्रै) -- खालि ।

खाली (रित्तो) -- थेर्दे, खाली ।

खाली गर्नु -- तेब ।

खाल्टो -- हों ।

खास -- खासगरि ।

खास्टो -- मुला ।

खिइनु -- खिदीब ।

खिच्नु -- तित्तीब ।

खिराको रूख -- खेरे ।

खुकुरी -- क्होज ।

खुकुलो -- खोलेंब ।

खुट्किलो -- गुंडा ।

खुट्टा -- प्हली ।

खुत्रु खुत्रु -- खद्र खुद्ध ।

खुदो -- खुदु ।

खुद्रा -- खुद्रा ।

खुब -- खुब ।

खुम्चिनु -- खुम्जीदीब, फ्युंब ।

खुर -- खुरा ।

खुर्कनु -- खुर्कुदीब ।

खुर्सानी टोक्नु -- क्रीबा ।

खुला -- खुल्ला ।

खुवाउनु -- कोब ।

खुशी -- खुसी ।

खुशी लाग्नु -- -तीं सींब,
सएं तींबा ।

खेत -- म्रों ।

खेती पाती -- खेदी पादी ।

खेद्नु -- ल्हाब ।

खेर -- बर्दै ।

-खेरि -- डे०रे ।

खेल -- खेल ।

खेल्नु -- ख्ल्योंबा ।

खेल्नु (पीड०) -- म्हस्ब ।

खैरो -- खैरे ।

खोइ ? (कहां) -- खोई ?

खोइ (जवाफ दिने शब्द) -- खोई ।

खोक्नु -- प्ह्युंब ।

खोक्ने खकार -- खोन ।

खोच्याउनु -- खुजुं खुजुं ह्याब ।

खोज्नु -- म्हस्ब ।

खोट -- खोडी ।

खोतल्नु (घरको कुरा) -- ल्होंब ।

खोपा -- खोब ।

खोपी (कोठा) -- खुबी ।

खोपी (प्वाल) -- खोल्दों ।

खोप्नु -- कोव्दीब, खोब् फोंब ।

खोर -- खोरा, च्यों ।

खोरण्डो -- खुरूण्ड ।

खोरिया -- खोरे ।

खोर्सानी -- खोर्सानो ।

खोले -- खोले, कुंडो खोले ।

खोलो -- खोल, स्यों ।

खोल्नु -- खोल्दीब, खुलीदीब ।

खोल्सा खोल्सी -- घों ।

खोस्नु -- प्हेँब ।

ख्वाउनु (खाने कुरा) -- कोब ।

ख्वाउनु (पिउने कुरा) -- तींब ।

ग

गंगटो -- क्र्वें ।

गंगारिनु -- गंग्रदीब ।

गड्यौंलो -- कोदे ।

गई जानु -- क्युडी ह्याब ।

गएको सालमा -- तुग्युम ।

गच्छे -- गच्छे ।

गज -- गज ।

गजबको -- म्हार्ब ।

गड्बड -- गड्बड ।

गडाड० गुडुड० गर्नु -- ड०हेब ।

गतिलो -- गदिलु ।

गते -- गते ।

गधा -- गदा ।

गनाउनु -- थांनाब ।

गन्ध -- थां ।

गन्नु -- ल्ह्योब ।

गफ गर्नु -- बाद मार्दीब, गफ सब् लबा, तां सेब ।

गवुवा -- गबु, स्याम्गो ।

गरीब -- गरीब, ख्ल्यानु

गरो -- नों, न्हों ।

गर्दन -- उंस्यु, गर्दन ।

गर्न लाग्नु -- लबर ल्होदीब ।

गर्नु -- लबा ।

गर्मी मौसम -- उमा ।

गर्व -- सीक्की ।

गला लाग्नु -- म्लीब ।

गलेबन्द -- गल्बन्दी, पस्पन ।

गलैंचा -- गलैंज ।

गल्नु -- गल्दीब ।

गहना -- घाना ।

गहीरो -- गैरो ।

गहूं -- गउं ।

गह्रौ -- ल्हीब ।

गांठो -- गांठो ।

गांड -- गांड ।

गांस -- गास ।

गांस्नु -- गैंदीब ।

गाई -- म्हे ।

गाई बर्ष -- लौं लो, म्हे
ल्हो ।

गाउं -- नांस ।

गाउंलेहरू -- नांस्थेंमएं ।

गाउनु -- प्रींब ।

गाग्री -- गौरी ।

गाजर -- गाजर ।

गाडा -- गाड ।

गाडी -- गाडी ।

गाड्नु -- प्हाब, क्योब,
गाडीब ।

गारा (नराम्रो दिन) -- गरा ।

गारो -- गार, बांनुं ।

गाल -- क्ल्हांमुं ।

गाली गर्नु -- गाल केब ।

गाह्रो -- गार ।

गाह्रो मान्नु -- गार म्हांदीब ।

गाह्रो लाग्नु -- कयास,
म्हांदीब ।

गिजो -- सङ०हे ।

गिज्याउने शब्द (लामालाई) --
ज्योमैं ल्योमैं ।

गिद्ध क्हुरे ।

गिद्ध बर्ष -- क्हुरे ल्हो,
मुब्रु ल्हो ।

गिद्रो -- गिद्र ।

गीत -- क्ह्वे ।

गिलास -- गिलांस ।

गीलो भात -- क्होले ।

गुंड -- च्हौं ।

गु (दिसा) -- ख्ल्यी ।

गुएंली -- तीम्रु ।

गुण -- गुन ।

गुन्युं -- ङ०ह्यवी ।

गुन्द्री -- गुन्द्री ।

गुभो -- क्युग्युं ।

गुये कीरा -- ख्ल्यी बेबें ।

गुरांसको बोट -- पुदह धुं ।

गुरू -- गुरू ।

गुला -- क्हल्फुं ।

गुलाफ -- गुलाफ ।

गुलाफी -- गुलाफी ।

गुल्यिो -- कीगीब ।

गुहार -- गुवार ।

गेडा -- रुड्ड, फुं ।

गोठ -- प्ह्रौं ।

गोठालो -- प्ह्रौंसएं, क्रएं ।

गोबर -- कोबार ।

गोराहरू -- गोरामएं ।

गोरू -- एल्ह्या ।

गोर्खाली -- गोर्खाली ।

गोलभिंडा -- गोल्भेंडा ।

गोल्माल -- गोल्मोल ।

गोली -- गोली, फुं ।

गोली गांठो -- प्ह्ली कव्लो, गांठो ।

गोल्फ (बनको फलफूल) -- मलाज ।

गोस्वारा -- गोसर ।

गोही -- गुए ।

गौंथली -- चीलीपाटे ।

गौचरन -- गौचरन ।

ज्ञान -- ग्यान ।

ग्राउन -- ग्राउन ।

घ

घचेट्नु -- क्हस्ब ।

घच्चयाउनु -- घजीदीब ।

घट्ट -- क्ष्योदो, घट्टे ।

घट्नु -- घडीब ।

घडी -- घडी ।

घण्टा (टाइम) -- घन्ड ।

घण्टा (बज्ने) -- स्यो ।

घमण्ड -- सीक्की ।

घमण्डी -- घमन्डी ।

घर -- धीं, -गीं ।

घरखेत -- घर खेदा ।

घर-ज्वांइ -- घर जवें ।

घर मित्र -- धीं न्हों ।

घरि घरि -- घरी ।

घस्रनु -- घेसरदीब ।

घांटी -- खरी, म्लोंगु, ओर्गु ।

घांस -- क्ष्री ।

घाउ -- घा, पुर ।

घाद -- घाडा ।

घाम -- त्हीयां ।

घाम लाग्नु -- प्रेब ।

घाम नलाग्नु -- क्हुंब ।

घिउ -- छ्युगु ।

घिच्नु -- च्ह्याल्बा ।

घिसार्नु -- घिसार्दीब,
ल्हतार्दीब ।

घुंडा -- च्ही ।

घुच्चुक -- कुज्यों ।

घुमाउनु -- घुम्दीवाब ।

घुम्निु -- म्ह्यार्ब ।

घुम्नु -- घुम्दीब ।

घुर्नु -- ङ०हुब ।

घुस -- घुस ।

घुसार्नु -- छ्वीब, क्ह्युब ।

घुस्सा -- घुस्सा ।

घूम -- क्हुं ।

घैटो -- घैडी ।

घैया बारी -- घै म्रों ।

घोगो -- घ्र्यों ।

घोचो -- फर्बु ।

घोच्नु -- च्वीबा, म्ल्हुब ।

घोड़ा -- घोड़ ।

घोड़ा बर्ष -- त ल्हो ।

घोताने -- कोन्मरं ।

घोप्टो -- पद्बु ।

घोप्ट्याउनु -- ए्ल्युबा, उंब ।

घोषणा गर्नु -- घउदीब ।

घोषण गर्ने मानिस -- दट्वाले ।

ङ

ङ०यार ङ०यार गर्नु (कुकुरले) --
ङ०हुरूरू ल्बा ।

च

चकटी -- चौडी ।

चक्का -- चक्क ।

चक्कु -- चक्कु ।

चड्कने -- नांब्री ।

चड्कने पर्नु -- मुर्ब ।

चद्नु -- क्र्वेबा ।

चतुर -- चन्डाल ।

चन्दन् -- ओल्वए ।

चन्द्रमा -- चन्द्रमा ।

चपल -- चव्ली ।

चपाउनु -- डे०बा ।

चम्चा -- चम्ज ।

चरो -- नेम ।

चरा बर्ष -- नेम ल्हो, च्हे ल्हो ।

चराउनु -- छ्बा ।

चराको गांड -- म्यु ।

चर्खो -- ह्राडा ।

चर्नु -- रेंबा ।

चलन -- चलन ।

चलाउनु -- चलीदीब, क्युह्बा, ओलेब, रूदुब, चल्दीब ।

चलाक -- चलाख ।

चलन त्याग्नु -- फील ल्बा ।

चल्नु (रुपियां) -- चल्दीब ।

चल्मलाउनु -- ओलेब ।

चांडै -- युन ।

चांदी -- चांदी ।

चाक -- मए ।

चाख्नु -- म्ह्योंब ।

चाक्लो -- प्ल्हाब ।

चाड० -- रैं ।

चाट्नु -- ल्हेंब ।

चाड -- चाड ।

चाना (मूलाको) -- चन ।

चामल -- म्ल्हसी ।

चार -- चार, प्ल्ही ।

चारा -- स्वें ।

चालचलन -- चाल चलान ।

चालीस -- चालीस, प्ल्हीज्यु ।

चाल्नु -- प्वीगएं, चेन ।

चाहिनु -- चैदीब ।

चिउंडो -- कां ।

चिक्नु -- म्रीं ल्बा ।

चिच्याउनु -- चीजीदीब ।

चिज -- सए ।

चिट्ठा -- चिट्ठा ।

चिट्ठी -- चिठी ।

चितुवा -- च्योंडी चितुवा, चितुवा ।

चित्रा -- चिद्र ।

चिन्नु -- सेब ।

चिप्ले कीरो -- क्बु, क्बु घां, मैना क्बु ।

चिप्लो -- प्लेबा ।

चिया -- च्हा ।

चिर्नु -- रुल्यीब, कुब ।

चिलाउनु -- केबा ।

चिलाउने चिज -- सो ।

चिल्लो -- चिल्लो ।

चिसो हुनु -- सींबा, ङ०युब, उसीदीबा ।

चिहान -- छ्गों, छोगों ।

चीनी -- चीनी ।

चीनु -- चीनु ।

चीबे -- मेद्गा ।

चील -- चीला ।

चीलीम -- चीलीं ।

चुईं चुईं आवाज गर्नु -- ङ०ह्लेब ।

चुक्लि -- चुली ।

चुच्चो -- चुच्चो ।

चुट्नु -- प्रहुब, होब ।

चुत्रो -- चुदुरू ।

चुनाउ -- नुनाब ।

चुरा -- चुरा ।

चुरोट -- चुराड ।

चुरोटको कोसा -- खिल्ली -ग्यों ।

चुरोटको पाइप -- कुल्बी ।

चुलेत्र (बोट) -- पुडे ।

चुल्लो -- फरसुं ।

चेप्नु -- पीर्ब ।

चोक्टा -- फुं, तीफुंदे ।

चोखो -- चोखो ।

चोट लाग्नु -- म्यांब, ने म्यांब ।

चोयो -- छ्र ।

चोरी -- ह्यो ।

चोर्नु -- ह्योब ।

चोलो -- चोल ।

चौडाइ -- प्ल्ही, चौडाइ ।

चौतारी -- चौदर ।

चौथाइ -- चौथैं ।

चौध -- चौद ।

चौबीस -- चौबीस ।

च्याउ -- च्ह्यांबु ।

च्यात्नु -- टोब ।

छ

-छ -- -म्, -मौ, -मुं, -मु ।

६ (अंक) -- ट्हु ।

-छ कि -- -मा ।

छकाउनु -- छल्दीब ।

छकिनु -- -छगदीब ।

छक्का -- छक्का ।

छल -- चीव्ले तां ।

छलफल -- छल्फल ।

छहरो -- छारे ।

छांउनु -- स्युईब ।

छांट्नु -- छांडीब ।

छाउरी -- छौरी ।

छाक -- छागे ।

छाता -- छ्द ।

छाती -- कु ।

छाद्नु -- रूइब, ओखल्दीब ।

छाप -- छाप, छाब ।

छापिस्को -- छप्वा ।

छाप्नु -- छाब्दीब ।

छाप्रो -- ठांडी ।

छायां -- सीदाल ।

छारे रोग -- चर्बने बेथा ।

छाला -- ट्हुबी ।

छिंक्नु -- छिंबा ।

छिट् गर्न्युं -- मुप्रे ङ०ह्युङ ।

छिटो (चांडो) -- युमना ।

छिटो (थोपो) -- छीड ।

छिटो रिसाउनु -- न्हखुं प्रब ।

छिन -- छिन ।

छिन (एक) -- तीस्या ।

छिन भरि -- घर्छीन्न ।

छिनाफाना गर्नु -- छिन फांना ।

छिनाल्नु -- थुबा, टोंवाबा ।

छिन्नु -- टोंब ।

छिपिस्को -- चीगों ।

छिमेकी -- ङ०हेब ट्हुब ।

छिर्नु -- क्युल्बा ।

छुटाउनु -- फ्रीवाब ।

छुट्टिट -- छुट्टी ।

छुनु -- छ्वीबा ।

छेउ -- छ्योगरी, सांदी ।

छेकाइ -- छेल ।

छेपारो -- छोबार्गे ।

छेलो (हान्नु) -- छ्योलो ।

छोटो -- रन्ठी ।

छोडाउनु (मकै) -- प्रीब, पीब ।

छोडनु (वस्तु) -- पीब ।

छोप -- छु ।

छोप्नु -- काब ।

छोरा बुहारी -- च्ह चों ।

छोरी -- चमीं, च्हमीं ।

छोरी जुवाइं -- म्हो ।

छोरो -- च्ह ।

छ्या -- अच्या, अहच्या, च्या ।

छ्याप्नु -- प्राब ।

छ्युं गर्नु -- छिंबा ।

ज

जंगल -- जंगल ।

जंड्याहा -- पा को ।

जग -- जग ।

जग्गा जमीन -- ल्ह्यो न्हें ।

जतातते छरिनु -- सडांबुड, टांह्याब ।

जतासुकै -- सन्जी सन्जी, सन्तदन ।

जति -- जदी... जदी ।

जनता -- जनता ।

जनावर -- जनवार ।

जनै -- जने ।

जन्म -- जन्म ।

जन्म थल -- जन्म थल ।

जन्म दिन -- जन्म दिन ।

जन्मनु -- जन्मदीब, फीब ।

जमरा -- जम्र ।

जमीन -- जमीन ।

जम्नु -- चांब ।

जम्मा -- जम्म, खागु, मु ।

जम्मा गर्नु -- खुबा ।

जम्मा गर्नु (पैसा) -- थी लब ।

जम्मा हिसाब -- टोडोल ।

जम्मा हुनु -- च्हुब, तुंब ।

जम्ल्याहा -- जौले ।

जय -- जय ।

जरायो -- जरायो ।

जरीवाना -- डण्ड ।

जरो -- जर ।

जलाउनु -- जलीदीब ।

जलेसी -- जलो ।

जल्नु -- छुंरीब ।

जवाफ -- जुवाब ।

जसरी -- धौंले ।

जस्ता -- जस्त

जस्तो -- -दौं ।

जस्तो देखिनु -- दौं व्यौंब ।

जहां -- खनी ।

जहां तहीं पुग्नु (बालक) -- खेरले ।

जहाज -- जहास ।

जहान -- जान, परा, पंवा ।

जहिले -- खौंयौं ।

जहिले पनि -- खौंयौं बीले ।

जांच -- जांज ।

जांचबुझ -- जांजबुज ।

जांड -- क्ह्वीपा ।

जांड बनाउनु -- क्हुब ।

जांतो -- ह्रंदो ।

जांठा -- ज्यांठा, ढ्वां ।

जाउं -- क्ष्यो ।

जागीर -- जागीर ।

जाडो -- खुंब ।

जाडो मौसम -- सर्ब, पुम ।

जात -- जाद ।

जानु -- ह्याब ।

जान्नु -- सएं च्हीब, ह्रब ।

जान्ने सुन्नेहरू -- ह्रब सेबमएं ।

जामा -- जाम ।

जाल -- जाल ।

जाली -- जाली ।

जिजु -- ह्यौं बाज्यु ।

जिजु बाजे -- ज्युज्यु बाजे, खे, ह्यौं ।

जित्नु -- ट्होब ।

जिप -- जिब ।

जिभ्रो -- ले ।

जिम्बु -- जिम्बु ।

जिल्ला -- जिल्ला ।

जीउ -- ज्यु ।

जीजु आमा -- ह्यों भुज्यु ।

जीवजन्तु -- जीबजन्तु ।

जीविका -- सोगों ।

जीवित (प्राणी) -- सो मुबए सए ।

जुंगा -- मुरा ।

जुक्ति -- ईस्कीम ।

जुग -- जुग ।

जुत्नु (भैंडा) -- थुर्ब ।

जुता -- बुड जुदा, जुद ।

जुन -- ल्यां ।

जुनकीरी -- मीवां ।

जुनी -- जुनी ।

जुम्रो -- से ।

जुम्रोको लिखो -- नीरी ।

जुवाई -- जवैं, म्हो ।

जुवा (खेल्नु) -- जुवा ।

जुवा (हाल्नु) -- खर्गु ।

जुवा खेल्नु -- जुवा एल्योंबा ।

जुवारे -- जुवाडे ।

जूका (नाकको) -- नांव्ली ।

जूका (पेटको) -- प्हेबे ।

जूका (बनको) -- तीबे ।

जूठो -- जुड ।

जेठा बाबा -- कार्गी, आथेबा ।

जेठान -- आस्यों, जेठु ।

जेठी -- नानी, थेब्स्यो ।

जेठी आमा -- अन्थेबा ।

जेठी दिदी -- अह्घएं ।

जेठी फुपू -- फागएं ।

जेठो -- ठागु, थेब ।

जेठो दाइ -- अह्घीं ।

जेलखाना -- फ्यालखन ।

जोग -- जोग ।

जोगाउनु -- जुगुदीब ।

जोगी -- जोगी ।

जोडा -- जोडा ।

जोत्नु -- क्ह्योब ।

जोर्नी -- कव्लो ।

जोर्नु -- जोडदीब, जोदीर्ब ।

जौ -- फ्गु ।

ज्यादा -- सारोन ।

ज्यादा रीस उठ्नु -- झडियां ।

ज्यादा सिंघाने -- नाल्चे ।

ज्यानमारा -- ज्यान्मारा ।

ज्यामी -- बौसे, जेला कींब्रमरं ।

ज्यास्ता -- ज्यादा ।

ज्योतिषी -- जैसी ।

झ

झक्कड -- रार ।

झगडा -- झगडा ।

झट्ट -- झ्वाट्टन ।

झड्केलो छोरो -- झट्केलु च्ह ।

झन -- झन ।

झम्टनु -- म्हुब, हवेंब ।

झरी पर्नु -- नां युब, झर तब ।

झर्नु -- खार्ब, खारीब ।

झांक्री -- झांक्रीं, ङल्ह्येब्री, पुज्यु, लम्कामी ।

झांट्नु (अन्न) -- प्ह्लब ।

झाड (बनको) -- च्ही, झ्याडी ।

झापक्कुप्प -- झ्याब झुप ।

झार उखेल्नु -- नो स्युर्ब ।

झारल -- पेद ।

झारा -- झारा ।

झार्नु -- खावर्ब ।

झिंजो (दाउराको) -- झिंज्यां ।

झिकिदिनु -- स्युब, टहुइवाब ।

झिल्ङ्गे -- ख्युनी, झीले ।

झिलिमिली -- झिलि र मीली ।

झिसमिसे -- पसा पुसु ।

झींगे -- क्वींजीरी तांग ।

झुक्किनु -- छगादीब ।

झुक्क्याउनु -- ङ्यार्ब ।

झुण्डिनु -- च्योबा, ङ्योंबा ।

झुण्ड्याउनु -- मैंज्योब ।

झुल्कनु -- म्ल्होब (त्हीयां) ।

झूट -- झूट्टा ।

झूटो बोल्ने मान्छे -- स्युर्गु ।

झूल -- झूल ।

झोल -- खु ।

झोला (सर्कारी) -- झ्योला, रूपसई, नाम्ज्यो ।

झ्याउं झ्याउं -- ज्याउं ज्याउं ।

झ्याउ -- ईस्पन, लेंदे ।

झ्याउरे गीत -- झ्यौरे क्ह्वे ।

झ्याल -- झ्याला ।

झ्याली -- क्ष्योलें ।

ट

टट्टु -- टट्टु ।

टल्कनु -- टलादीब ।

टांका -- म्लु ।

टांगो (लामो लट्ठी) -- टागुं ।

टांग्नु -- टांईदीब ।

टांसिनु -- ह्रेंब ।

टाटो -- टडे ।

टालो -- टालु ।

टाल्नु -- खेंबा ।

टिप्नु -- तुबा, थुबा ।

टिप्नु (पाकेको कोदो मात्रै) -- प्ुब ।

टिमुर -- प्रुमु ।

टीका लगाउनु -- ख्याबा ।

टुक्का (गीतको खण्ड) -- टुक ।

टुक्रा -- क्ह्राब्लें ।

टुट्नु -- टोंह्याब, चीलीवाब ।

टुपी -- तमुं ।

टुसा -- मौदु ।

टुंडीखेल -- टुंडीखेल ।

टेक्नु -- धुंब, म्हस्ब, न्हेब ।

टेढो आंखा भएको हुनु -- मीं (सस्बा) ।

टेढो-मेढो -- टेडो ।

टेवा -- पानसा ।

टोक्नु -- क्ह्रीब ।

टोपी -- कुले, पुलु, मख्खु ।

टोल -- टोल ।

टोली -- टोली ।

टोलको वरिपरि -- खोल टोला ।

ट्याक्क -- ठ्याक्क ।

ट्याक्सी -- ट्याक्सी ।

ठ

ठक्कर लाग्नु -- थुर्बा ।

ठग्नु -- ठक्दीब ।

ठटाउनु -- टींबा ।

ठट्टा -- ठट्टा ।

ठट्टा मार्नु -- ठट्टा मार्दीब ।

ठस्कनु -- म्होब ।

ठांटिनु -- ठांई ठुई ।

ठाउं -- एल्ह्यो ।

ठाडो -- ठाडो, ठार ।

ठिटो -- फ्रें, फ्रेंसीं ।

ठिहिरिनु -- ठिरिदीब, कोंब ।

ठीक -- ठीक ।

ठीकै -- ठीकन, ठीक्कले ।

ठीकैको -- अन्दरे ।

ठुटो -- लुंठे, ठुइ ।

ठुस्सिनु -- न्हबु प्रब ह्रीसखब ।

ठूलो -- थेब, थेब्रें ।

ठूलो उन्यू -- लोंडा ।

ठूलो चिप्ले कीरा -- माईंना क्बु ।

ठूलो ठालो -- चीबृनांब ।

ठूलो पानी पर्ने बेला -- घानाघोड ।

ठूलो मानिस -- चीबा ।

ठूलो मानिसहरू -- चीब नाब ।

ठेउला -- कुज्वीर ।

ठेकी -- परू ।

ठेगाना -- ठेगन ।

ठेटर (आजकलको नाच) -- ठेटरा ।

ठोकिनु -- थुर्बा ।

ठोक्नु -- ठौदीब ।

ड

डंडी फोर -- ची ।

ड -- चो ।

डकार -- अहर ।

डकार्नु -- आहर ल्बा ।

डढेलो -- मीसा ।

डदनु -- क्रोबा ।

डदनु (लुगा) -- थीब ।

डण्डी -- डण्डी ।

डफा -- दफ ।

डबल -- डबल ।

डब्बा -- डब्ब ।

डर -- डर, ड़ाहींजी ।

डराउनु -- ड़ाहींब ।

डल्लैंठो -- घन्मसे ।

डल्लो -- डल्ल ।

डल्लो फर्नु -- ठडा ठुड्ड ।

डाकू -- डांगु ।

डांठ -- डांड ।

डांडो -- डांड ।

डाम्भर -- डाम्बर ।

डाडू -- डडु ।

डालो -- डालु ।

डालो (सानो, पुवा काटेर राख्ने) -- धेम्यौं ।

डाहा लाग्नु -- म्रोब ।

डील -- डील, चु ।

डुंगा -- डुंवां ।

डुंड -- डोंडा ।

डुंडे -- डुंडा ।

डुब्नु -- डुक्दीब ।

डुल्नु -- डुल्दीब ।

डेढ -- डेर ।

डेग्ची -- डीबृजी ।

डेरा -- डेरा ।

डोको -- प्ही ।

डोरी -- ह्रसी ।

डोऱ्याउनु -- डोरीदीब ।

ड्याङ० -- ड्यांमा ।

ड्याप्पा (आवाज) -- दयाप्प ।

ढ

ढक -- ढग ।

ढाक्नु -- हुब ।

ढांट्नु -- स्युर तेब ।

ढाक्नु -- हुब ।

ढाक्रे -- ढाग्रे ।

ढाड -- क्रे ।

ढाड़े -- नोवां ढाड़े ।

ढिस्को -- तैं ।

ढींडो -- पैगुं ।

ढीकी -- कुनी ।

ढीकीको दांत -- मुस्लुं ।

ढीलो -- ढीले ।

ढुकुर -- ढुकुर ।

ढुङ०गो -- युम, ङ०युमां ।

ढुङ०गो उप्काउनु -- उवाबा ।

ढुङ०गोले हान्नु -- फैरीब ।

ढुड०ग्री (कानमा) -- ढुंडी ।

ढुङ०ग्रो (दूध हाल्ने) -- त्हु ।

ढुङ०ग्रो (फुक्ने -- फदी ।

ढुटो -- ढुडु ।

ढुसी -- सीं न्हेमैं ।

ढोका -- ढोगा, दैलो, म्रा ।

ढोका खोलु -- थोंब ।

ढोक्नु -- फ्रयोबा ।

ढौंतरी -- दुन्द्रीन् ।

दयांग्रो -- ड०ह ।

त

तं -- क्ही ।

त -- -ऐ, -दी, -ग, -मृ, -मी, -न, -द् ।

त नि -- कुजी, -सीदी ।

तखता -- तखद ।

तगारो -- तगर ।

तताउनु -- क्वाल्ब, लाबा ।

तनखा -- तनख ।

तन्काउनु -- तंगदीब ।

तपाइं -- क्ही ।

तपाइंहरू -- क्हैंमएं ।

तब -- तब ।

तमसुक -- तम्सुग ।

तमाखु -- तमाखु, कंगडा ।

तमाड०ग -- लम्मएं ।

तयार -- अन्, तयार ।

तयार हुनु -- कस्दीब ।

तर -- गी, तर ।

तरवार -- तर्वाली ।

तरीका -- तरीगा ।

तरूनी -- छमीं ।

तरूनीहरू -- रींमएं ।

तरूल -- तीमीं ।

तर्नु -- तर्दीब, थाबा ।

तर्नु (आंखा) -- ट्हुब ।

तर्सनु -- ख्यांबा, लौंबा ।

तर्साउनु -- प्ल्ह लौंवाब ।

तल -- म ।

तलको -- प्हीउंब ।

तलतिर -- प्हीरी ।

तलब -- तलब ।

तला -- तले, आडी ।

तल्लो -- प्हीर्ब ।

तल्लो तिर -- क्युरू, मार्ई ।

तसला -- तसल ।

तस्वीर -- तस्बीर ।

ताक्नु -- व्ह्याब ।

ताती -- छ्ब, लल, ला ।

तान (बुन्ने) कल -- क्वेंडो सादा ।

तान्नु -- तंगदीब, चसंबा ।

ताप्के -- ताबुगे, ताण्णे ।

ताप्नु (आगो) -- त्हीब ।

तामो -- क्युरा ।

तार -- तारा ।

तारा -- मुसार ।

तारीख -- तारीक ।

ताल -- ताला ।

तालु -- पुचु (क्र) ।

ताल्वा -- सांजु पंउरूं ।

तास -- तास ।

तास्नु -- छाब ।

तिखानु -- म्युंबा, म्ल्हुलबा ।

तिखो -- म्ह्रु ।

तिग्रो -- प्हां ।

तिते टुसा -- क्मोंदु ।

तितो -- कांबा ।

तिथी -- तिथी ।

तिथीहरूको नाम -- असुनी ।

तिमी -- क्ही ।

तिमीहरू -- क्हेमएं ।

तिर -- जरे, तिर, -उंदी ।

तिरो बाली -- बाली ।

तिखाउनु -- पीबा ।

तिर्सना गर्नु -- तीर्सना लब ।

तिहुन -- टह, टहा टहु ।

तीन -- सौं ।

तीनफेर -- तीन्तीयाली ।

तीस -- सौंज्यु ।

तुरून्त -- तोदोन् ।

तुहाउनु (गर्भ) -- प्हसी वाबा, प्युल्ह वाबा ।

तेजिलो -- तेज्ले ।

तेति हो -- च्हगन ।

तेरा -- तेरोड ।

तेर्सो -- पीरू ।

तेल -- तेल ।

तेम्रो -- तेम्रो ।

तै पनि -- दीले, दीन ।

तोरी -- तुरी ।

तौलनु -- तौल्दीब ।

तौलिया -- पछ्योरा, तौलीया ।

त्यस -- च ।

त्यसकारण -- छ्तमा, च कारण ।

त्यसै -- छ्लेन ।

त्यसो भएर पो -- दाङ्गा ।

त्यसोभने -- दीयांरे, दीयां ।

त्यस्तै -- छ्ाबन ।

त्यहां -- के क्यारी, चरी ।

त्यहांदेखि -- फ्ासेरो ।

त्यहांबाट -- फाले ।

त्यो -- च ।

थ

थप दिनु -- क्लेगु पींब ।

थप माग्नु -- क्लेब ।

थप्नु -- थब्दीब ।

थम्बा -- मुल हांग ।

थरि -- थरि, जादे ।

थकाली -- प्हस्मएं ।

थाकलको बोट -- म्हे पुजु धुं ।

थाक्नु -- नारीब ।

थाङ्नो -- थौनी ।

थान (देउताको) -- थाना ।

थाप्नु -- तोब ।

थाप्लो -- ताल्हु ।

थाम -- त्हो, थामा ।

थाम्नु -- थाम्दीब ।

थार -- ए ।

थारो -- थरा ।

थाल (एक किसिम, सानो) --
  डुगु ।

थाली -- थली ।

थाल्नु -- ठाल्दीब ।

थाहा -- थाह ।

थिच्नु -- नोंब ।

थुक -- तु ।

थुक फाल्नु -- तु वाबा ।

थुक्नु -- तुद प्राबा, स्वाल्बा ।

थुत्नु -- थुदीब, थुत्तीब ।

थुन्नु -- थुन्दीब, च्युब ।

थुन्से -- कोंव्यों, स्वींदी ।

थुन्से (कोदो टिप्ने) -- थुल्लों ।

थुप्रो -- साद, थुप्रो ।

थुबुक्क -- आलक्कले ।

थैली -- फीलो ।

थैलो -- कुल्दु, नैंदो ।

थोप्लो -- थल्लो ।

द

दगुर्नु -- क्ह्योब ।

दमा (बजाउने) -- दम ।

दमाइ -- त्हुली ।

दया -- ल्होयो ।

दराज -- अल्मुडी ।

दर्बार -- दरबार ।

दर्शन -- दर्शन ।

दर्खास्त -- दर्खास्त ।

दलिन (ठूलो) -- दलींडoT ।

दल्दल -- सीमां ।

दश -- च्यु, दश ।

दशमी -- दशमी ।

दशैं -- दसएं ।

दांज्नु -- च्हसंब, त्हांब ।

दांत -- स ।

दांतले मकै कोर्पनु -- ख्रीब ।

-दा -- -म ।

-दा.. दा -- -म.. -म,
  -न.. -न ।

-दा खेरि -- -मले, -म डे०रे ।

दांइ -- दएं ।

दाइ -- आदा ।

दाइ र बहिनी -- म्ह्यों ।

दाउरा -- सीं ।

दाउराको गांठो -- कव्लो ।

दाख -- दाख ।

दाग -- दाग ।

दाजु -- त्हज्यों ।

दाजु भाइ -- मुयुंमएं, दाज्यू भाइ, ती, तीमएं, भाइमएं ।

दानी -- सएं स्हब ।

दानी नहुने मान्छे -- खोंड, कुगाड ।

दाप -- स्यु ।

दाबिलो -- केब ।

दाम्लो -- कु ।

दाल -- दाल ।

दाहिने -- क्योलो ।

दाहिने पट्टि -- क्योलो पट्टि ।

दाह्रा किट्नु -- कडड लबा ।

दाह्री -- दारी ।

दाह्रो -- दारे ।

दिउंसो -- त्हीयां, त्हीयांरी ।

दिक -- दिक्क ।

दिदी -- आना, रीं ।

दिन -- दिन, -गएं, त्हीं‌ईं ।

दिनकादिन -- दीन्दीनु ।

दिन भरि -- त्हीं‌ईं त्हीमीं ।

दिनले -- दीनदी ।

दिनु -- पींबा, भोंब ।

दिमाग -- दिमाग ।

दिल -- डील ।

दिशा -- दिशा ।

दिसा -- दिसा, ए्ल्यी ।

दीयो -- दीयो ।

दुई -- दुई, ड०हीं ।

दुई पल्ट -- दुवाली ।

दुई सय -- ड०हीब्रा ।

दुईटा -- ड०हींअंडों ।

दु:ख -- दु:ख ।

दु:ख दिनु -- सएं नए लब ।

दुःख लाग्नु -- सएं नब ।

दुःखी हुनु -- खुसी अह्ह्रेब, सजीद अह्र्योंब, सएं नब ।

दुख्नु -- नब ।

दुख्नु धेरै -- बल्ग् बल्ग् ल्बा ।

दुनिया -- दुनिया ।

दुब्लो -- ङ्यांग्र, क्द्रां, सीबी सेब ।

दुम्सी -- धुंसीं ।

दुम्सीको काढ़ो -- म्ल्हु ।

दुरूस्त -- धुरूस्ता ।

दलहा -- ब्याउलो ।

दुबै -- ङ०हींना ड०हींन् ।

दुशमन -- दुशमन ।

दुहुनु -- ढ०हेब (मगी) ।

दूत -- दूत् ।

दूध -- ङ०हे ।

दूध (ङ्ढेको) -- कौंरी ।

दूध ख्वाउनु -- तींब ।

दूधको मुन्टो -- ङ०हे ढ्ढ ।

दूर्बीन -- दीर्बीन ।

देउता -- देउदा ।

देउरानी -- देउरानी ।

देउसुरे -- दउसुरे, दौसुरे ।

देखाउनु -- तैंबा, उंर्इब ।

देखि -- -ईले, सेरो, वोनो ।

देखिनु -- म्रौंबा ।

देख्नु -- म्रौंबा ।

देखरेख -- च्योवा ।

देब्रे हात चले -- त्हेव्ब्रे पाले ।

देश -- देश ।

देशीमल -- देशीमल ।

देवर -- देवर ।

देवी -- देवी ।

-दै गर्नु -- -ब्रैं ल्बा ।

-दैछ -- -ईनमु ।

दैलो -- दैलो, दुवारा, -गैं ।

दोकान -- दुकान ।

दोबर -- डबल ।

दोष -- दोस, क्ष्याब ।

दोष लाग्नु -- क्ष्याब कुब ।

दौस्त -- दोस्ती ।

दोप्रो -- दोप्रो ।

द्वादशी -- दुवादशी ।

द्वापर -- द्वापर ।

ध

धणु -- त्हलीं ।

धतुरो -- धजुरा ।

धन -- न्होर ।

धनी (मालिक) -- एल्ह्ये ।

धनी (सेठ) -- प्ल्होब ।

धनसम्पत्ति -- धन सम्पती,
पुंजी ।

धनसार -- धन्छार ।

धपाउनु -- ल्हाब ।

धमाधम -- धमा धम् ।

धमीरो -- धमीरो ।

धम्की -- धम्गी ।

धुरू धुरू रूनु -- धाधर ।

धर्को -- धर्गे, ड्रेख ।

धर्म -- धर्मा ।

धर्म पुत्र -- धर्म पुत्र ।

धर्म शास्त्र -- सास्तर ।

धाई -- धराले ।

धाक लगाउनु -- प्हस्ंब ।

धागो -- रू ।

धागो (कपालमा) लगाउने) --
क्र्मीं ।

धान -- म्ल्ह ।

धान (मार्सी) -- म्हांसी ।

धान राख्ने भकारी -- कएं कोड ।

धानको वालो -- नां ।

धानको भूस -- पैं ।

धामी -- लम्कर्मी ।

धामी काम्नु -- गुर न्हेब ।

धार -- धारा ।

धारा -- धरू, धार ।

धारिलो लाग्ने -- क्र्यार्ब ।

धार्नी -- धार्नें ।

धिश -- धिस ।

धुइरो -- धुर्दीब ।

धुनु -- खुब ।

धुपौरो -- धुबारा ।

धुरी -- धुरी ।

धुरी खम्वा -- कुंदो ।

धुलो -- पोडर, त्हुल ।

धूप -- धूब, साल धूब ।

धूप हाल्नु -- धूब म्हर्नोंब ।

धूंवा -- मीगु ।

धूवांसो -- क्हीजी ।

धेरै -- बेले, ल्हे ।

धेरै कुरा बोल्ने -- सस्बा ।

धेरै मुक्नु -- चैंब ।

ध्यान -- ध्यान, याद ।

ध्यान दिनु -- ध्यान पींबा, सएं म्हर्नोंब ।

न

-न -- -बर ।

नकटो(लाज नमान्नु) -- नकडा ।

नक्कल गर्नु -- क्ष्यतीब ।

नकली -- नकली ।

नक्कल पार्नु -- नकल तेब ।

नक्सा -- नक्स, फोटो ।

नङ०ग्रो -- क्हीं ।

नजिक -- रीत, चैंदो, तेलैं, तीनले ।

नपाकेको -- अह्मींब, कजी ।

नभएको -- अहह्रेब ।

नमस्ते -- बीन्दी मु, नमस्ते ।

नमान्ने -- बीबा अहर्डें०ब ।

नमुना -- नमुना ।

नम्र निबेदन गर्नु -- क्हवीब ।

नयां -- नयां, छार ।

नरक -- नर्गें ।

नरम -- नरम ।

नराम्रो -- अहक्ष्यांब ।

नरिवल -- नर्वाल ।

नल -- तल ।

नली -- नगी ।

नलीहाड -- र्ल्ह्यों, नली ।

नसो -- च, नस ।

नाइक (पल्टनमा) -- नाईं ।

नाइटो -- पदी ।

नाइरो (गोरूको जुवामा) -- न्हरा ।

नाक -- न ।

नाक्को प्वाल -- नखुं ।

नाक्को स्वर -- नखुं सुं ।

नाग -- लु ।

नाग्नु -- ङ०वेब ।

नाङ०गो -- एल्युना ।

नाङ०लो -- नौली ।

नाच -- नाज ।

नाच्नु -- सेब ।

नाता -- नाथु ।

नाति -- क्वैं, नाती ।

नातिनी -- क्वैंमीं ।

नाना किसिम -- नौ उल ।

नाप -- नाब ।

नाप (६ फुटको) -- बांउं ।

नाप-जांच -- नाब-जांब ।

नाप्नु -- कूबा, नाव्दीब ।

नाम -- मीं ।

नाम्लो -- छोडो, टोबी, टहो ।

नारी -- नारी ।

नाल -- सीमांला ।

नालिश -- जएर ।

नासो -- नासु ।

-नि -- -दोन, -गोन् ।

नि -- हे ।

निउंरो -- चीबूले ।

निकाल्नु -- तेब ।

निको पार्नु -- स्हल ल्बा ।

निको हुनु -- स्हब ।

निखन्नु -- खाब ।

निगालो -- मो ।

निगालोको कप्टेरो -- कप्टेलु ।

निचोंनु -- च्ह्युर्ब ।

निदाउनु -- न्हरू च्ह्वीब ।

निदाउनु (भुसुक्कै) -- टोबा ।

निदाउरो -- अन्यारो, लुक्हो तब ।

निद्रा -- न्हरु ।

निफन्नु -- च्याब, टाब ।

निबुवा -- म्हींब ।

निम्तो -- नीम्दु ।

निम्त्याउनु -- नीम्दु ल्बा ।

नियुक्त काम -- डीप्टी ।

निर -- बर्दैं, दन ।

निराश -- निराश ।

निरोगी -- निरोगी ।

निर्णय -- निर्नए ।

निर्णय गर्नु -- निर्नए ल्बा ।

निर्बलियो -- काफार, अह्मोंब ।

निर्दयी -- निर्मए ।

निलो -- नीर ।

निलु -- एल्ह्योंब ।

निश्चय -- निस्चए ।

निश्चय गर्नु -- टोंबा ।

निस्कनु -- त्होंब ।

निहुं -- निउं ।

निहुं पार्नु -- निउं ल्बा ।

निहुरिनु -- कुर् तब, क्वार तब ।

निहुराउनु -- कुर्बा ।

-नी (स्त्रीलिङ्ग) -- -स्यो ।

-नु -- ल ।

नुन -- चज ।

नुनु गर (सुताउने शब्द) -- नुं ल्द् ।

नुहाउनु -- ज्यु खुब ।

नुहाउने चलन -- घुसुल ।

-नै -- -ब्, -ब, -बए ।

नेपाल -- न्हेबाल ।

नेपाली -- न्हेबाली ।

नेपाली भाषा -- प्ह्रु क्ह्यूवी ।

नेवाल -- न्हेवार ।

नैन सूत -- नैनसुद ।

नोकरी -- लाखुरी, नोकोरी ।

नोक्सान -- नौसान, नोक्सन्, डीपेट पर्दोंब ।

-नोस -- -सी ।

नौ -- कु, नौ ।

नौनी -- नुनी ।

नौलो -- नौले, स्यां ।

न्याउरी मूसा -- न्यौरी मुसो ।

न्यानो -- ट्ह्रोब ।

न्याय -- नीया, न्याए ।

न्याय गर्नु -- न्याए ल्बा ।

न्यायधिस -- न्याएधिस ।

न्याम्रो -- सां ।

प

पकाउनु -- त्हेब, ह्योब ।

पक्का (अवश्य) -- पक्का ।

पक्का (राम्रो) -- पक्का ।

पक्नु -- क्हाब, पग्डीदीब ।

पखेटो -- प्ह्यागुं ।

पग्लनु -- बीलीदीब ।

पचास -- ङ०हज्यु ।

पछाडि -- लीउंदी, पछाडि ।

पछाडिको खुट्टा -- ली प्हली ।

पछार्नु -- पछार्दीब ।

पछि -- बाद, लीली, लीउंदी ।

पछि पछि आउनु -- लीली खबा ।

पछि लाग्नु (आमाको) -- ट्वीबा ।

पछिको -- न्हौंउंब ।

पछुताउ -- पछीद ।

पछेउरा -- पोछ्योर ।

पटुका -- फगी ।

पट्टिट -- पट्टिट ।

पट्टी -- पट्टी ।

पठाउनु (मानिस) -- कुल्बा ।

पठाउनु (समान) -- पीभींब ।

पडकनु -- पड्गदीब ।

पढनु -- खेब ।

पत्याउनु -- क्वेंब ।

पत्यार पर्नु -- क्वेंल ल्बा ।

पत्लुन -- पत्लुं ।

पनि -- -धरी, -जै, पनि, या, -ई, -दै ।

पन्छाउनु -- स्योंब ।

पन्यालो (रस, झोल) -- क्युग्यु ।

पन्यु -- पन्यो ।

परलोग -- परलोग ।

परसर्नु -- क्र खुब तबा, को युब ।

परागुं -- नोंदीम ।

परार -- नैंदीमा ।

पराल -- प्राला ।

परालको टुवा (कुनियो) -- टोव ।

परेवा -- पर्वा ।

पर्खनु -- भस्ंब ।

पर्नु -- पदींब, त्हुब ।

पर्म गर्नु -- नोंबा ।

पर्‌याली (गोरूको भाडा) -- पीर्ब ।

पर्सी -- नुंर्ह्म ।

पर्सी पल्टो -- नों ईम्दुं ।

पलाउनु -- पलीदीब, प्हुब ।

पल्ट (चोटि) -- ल्वे ।

पल्ट (पछिल्लो दिन) -- -दुं ।

पल्टन -- पल्टन्‌ ।

पल्टाउनु -- पल्टीदीब ।

पशुहरूलाई थुन्ने खोर -- कंजे हाउस ।

पश्चाताप -- बेदन ।

पसार्नु -- स्योंबा ।

पसाल्नु -- क्ह्युब ।

पसीना -- क्ळ्ब ।

पस्कनु -- क्युंर्ब ।

पस्नु -- खोंब ।

पहरा दिनु -- रुंब ।

पहिलो -- पैले ।

पहिलेनै -- स्योमां ।

पहेँलो (फुल्को) -- म्हार ।

पांच -- ङ०ह ।

पांच सय -- ङ०हब्रा ।

पाइलो -- म्हए ।

पाइलो सार्नु -- क्वांब ।

पाउ (बुट्टा) -- पाउ, प्लो ।

पाउनु -- योंबा ।

पाक्नु -- मींबा ।

पाकेको (बेसरी) -- फुत्रुक्क ।

पाखामा -- पखर ।

पाखी -- क्कर्ालि ।

पाखुरो -- पाखु ।

पाखो -- धारी, पखा ।

पाचुके -- पार ।

पाटा -- पड ।

पाटी (टोली) -- पाटी, दफा ।

पाटी (बस्ने ठाउं) -- ठांडी ।

पाठशाला -- स्कूल ।

पात -- प्हो, ल ।

पातो -- प्हसंदो पद ।

पात नभएको रूख -- छद्रं ।

पाती (एक किसिमको वोट) -- च्योंडी ।

पात्रो -- पाद्ग ।

पात्लो -- पद्लु, पोबा ।

पाथी -- पदी, -व्यों ।

पाद -- फी ।

पादल (बनको एक भाग) -- ग्ल्यां ।

पाद्नु -- स्युबा ।

पान -- पान ।

पाना -- पेन ।

पानी -- क्यु ।

पानी (बर्षा हुने) -- नां ।

पानी जहाज -- क्यु म्हास ।

पानी तिर्खा लाग्यो -- क्यु पीब ।

पानी पनेरो -- क्युवाधुं ।

पानी पर्नु -- नां युब ।

पानी बिदो हुनु -- चस्बा ।

पानी राख्ने घ्याम्पो -- ढ्रोज ।

पानी लाउनु -- क्यु म्हाँब ।

पानी हाल्नु -- क्यु म्हाँब ।

पानीको निकास -- पीयाना ।

पाप -- पाप ।

पारी -- क्योंजां ।

पार्नु -- पादोंब, ठीब ।

पाली (चोटी) -- -क्यो ।

पाली (छानु) -- पाली ।

पालीको भाटो -- कोंड० ।

पाले पालो -- पलो पल्ले ।

पालो -- पलु ।

पाल्नु -- न्हब ।

पासो -- ड०ो ।

पासो थाप्नु -- ड०ो च्हुब ।

पाहा (खोलामा) -- पैं, टुटीं ।

पाहा (बनमा) -- क्हो, हेपा ।

पाहुनु -- प्ह्रें ।

पिंडालु -- तोयो ।

पिंडालुको गाभा -- गब ।

पिंडोला -- लीगुं ।

पिंढी -- पींडीं ।

पिंध्नु (जांतोले) -- प्ह्रोब ।

पिउन -- सिपाई, प्युंन् ।

पिउनु -- थुंब ।

पिउरी -- कबए ।

पिचास -- पिचास, स्यागी ।

पिट्नु -- धोंब, प्लांबा ।

पिठो -- प्ह्रो ।

पिठ्यू -- क्हो ।

पित -- कां ।

पितल -- पेदाला ।

पितृलाई चढाउनु -- क्ष्योस्ब ।

पिप -- न्हो, पीबी ।

पिरो -- सोबा ।

पिर्नु -- पर्दीब ।

पिलो -- रूं ।

पिसाब -- कुं ।

पिसाब गर्नु -- कुं त्होंब ।

पीड० -- कुदी ।

पीड० (चर्खे) -- व्रा कुदी ।

पीड० खेल्नु -- कुदी म्हस्ब ।

पीड़ा -- नब् छब ।

पीर -- पीर ।

पीर हुनु -- पीर मुबा ।

पुगिनु -- थुबा, युब ।

पुग्नु (ठाउंमा) -- फेबा ।

पुच्छर -- मी ।

पुड्को -- पुड्के ।

पुतली -- त्हाम्लो ।

पुन (जात) -- प्रोंमएं ।

पुरा -- पुरा ।

पुरानो अन्न -- क्र्हो ।

पुरूष -- आमुयुं ।

पुरूष हरू -- आमुईमएं ।

पुर्याउनु -- सदेंब ।

पुल -- पुल ।

पुलिस -- पुलिसा, सिपाई ।

पुवा -- नई ।

पुवा काट्नु -- खस्ब ।

पुवाको भूसलाई फाल्ने चिम्टो
-- का ।

पुष्टिनु -- म्ह्रीब ।

पुस्तक -- पुस्तगा ।

पूजा -- पूजा ।

पूजा गर्नु -- पूज्दीब, पूजा लब ।

पूजारी -- पूजारे ।

पूरा -- पुरा ।

पूर्खा -- ह्र्यों, खे ।

पूर्खा बाजे -- क्हों बाज्यु ।

पूर्खा बजै -- ह्र्यों भुज्यु ।

पूर्नी -- पुर्नै ।

पूर्ब -- पुर्ब ।

पृथिवी -- पृथिवी ।

पेट -- फो ।

पेटको जुगा -- प्हेबे ।

पेटिकोट -- पेट्टीकोड ।

पेलु -- म्हाब ।

पेशा -- ईलाम ।

पेश्की -- पेश्की ।

पैचो गर्नु -- खीब, ङ०स्बा ।

पैताला -- पैदल, म्हली प्लो ।

पैलो -- म्हए ।

पैसा -- पैसा ।

पोइल जानु -- ओडाल ह्याबा, फर ह्याब ।

पोखरा -- पुखु ।

पोखिनु -- ङ०हैब ।

पोते -- कांजी ।

पोथी -- योमां ।

पोलु -- ब्रोंबा ।

पोशाक -- पोशाक ।

पोइनु -- क्यूवालीब ।

पौडी खेलु -- क्यूवालीब ।

पौष -- पुष ।

प्याज -- प्याज ।

प्यारो -- पीयारो ।

प्रकाश (सूर्यको) -- त्हीयांए ज्योति ।

प्रचार -- प्रचार लबा ।

प्रार्थना -- प्रार्थन ।

प्वांख -- प्ह्या ।

प्वाल -- खुं, खुन्द्रो ।

प्वाल पार्नु -- थोंब ।

फ

फकाउनु -- ह्र्वांब, मनीदीब ।

फट्काउनु (ऊन) -- प्हुब ।

फट्याइ०ग्रो -- नम्ज्यो, फट्यांउरू ।

फरक -- फरक ।

फर्काउनु -- सैंब ।

फर्किनु -- एब ।

फर्सी -- उंस्य ।

फल मासु -- नो ।

फलानो -- फलाना ।

फलाम -- प्वे ।

फल्नु -- ल्ब ।

फलफूल -- फलफूल ।

फसाउनु -- भांडीदीब, फसीदीब, भुल्दीवाब ।

फाड्नु -- प्योंब ।

फारो -- फर ।

फाली -- फली ।

फाल्टु -- फाल्टु ।

फाल्नु -- भ्यांब, वाबा ।

फिजाउनु -- पसंबा ।

फिक्का -- फिक्का ।

फिक्री -- फिक्कर ।

फित्ता -- तनी ।

फिर्ता आवाज -- भार्से ।

फिर्ता गर्नु -- एवाब ।

फिर्ता नआउने -- झुर्ले ।

फुकाउनु -- फस्बा ।

फुक्नु (आगो) -- फुवीबा ।

फुक्नु (गांठो) -- प्युंबा ।

फुक्नु (विरामिलाई) -- ङोब ।

फुट्नु -- तीबा ।

फुत्कनु -- स्युर्बा ।

फुपू -- फुबु ।

फुल -- फुं ।

फुली -- फुली ।

फुल्नु -- फुल्दीब, प्वारीबा ।

फुल्नु (कपाल) -- सारीबा ।

फूट (रूल) -- फूट ।

फूर्सत -- फूर्सद ।

फूल (लाउने) -- ट्ह ।

फेटा -- क्रोगी, म्रे ।

फेद (जमिन माथीको) -- मुल दांग ।

फेरि -- दबए, फेरि ।

फेरि गर्नु -- क्लेगु ल्बा ।

फेरो -- फेरो ।

फेर्नु -- फेर्दीब ।

फेल गर्नु -- फील ख्बा ।

फैलनु -- फैलीदीब ।

फोक्सो -- एल्ह्योब ।

फोड्नु -- फोर्दीब ।

फोहोर (चिलाउनु) -- क्योग्यों खबा ।

फोहोरी -- फोहरी ।

फोहोरी शब्द -- पीदां ।

फौजी -- मील्डेरी, फौजी ।

ब

बकस -- बकस ।

बक्खु -- बक्खु ।

बगाल -- बगल ।

बगैंचा -- बगैंचा ।

बङ्गारो -- बंग्र ।

बच्चो -- फ्रज ।

बच्चो (२,४दिन भएको) -- ओलां ।

बजाउनु -- ह्राब ।

बजार -- बजार ।

बज्नु -- बत्तीब, ङहेब ।

बज्यै -- भुज्यु ।

बटार्नु -- छींब, छीरीदीब, ख्रींब, दुनीदीब ।

बट्लु -- तुंब ।

बढाउनु -- स्योबा ।

बढार्नु (कसेर) -- फ्रयोब ।

बढी -- बडी ।

बद्ता -- बर्दा ।

बदनु -- बडीब ।

बताउनु -- फ्रयुर्बा ।

बत्ति -- बदी ।

बत्तिको फित्ता -- दारा ।

बदमाश -- बद्माश ।

बदमाशी -- बद्माशी ।

बदाम (जमिन भित्र फल्ने) -- बदम ।

बन -- बन ।

बन (सानो सानो रूख भएको) -- धुसा ।

बनको जन्तु -- बनर्बए जन्तु ।

बनको बिरालो -- क्ह्योनोंवारा।

बनको भूत -- ह्रेसएं ।

बनमा हुने एक किसिमको बजाउने चिज -- म्हाबोंबों ।

बनाउनु -- बनीदीब ।

बनेल (बनमा बस्ने) -- तो ।

बन्चरो -- त ।

बन्चरोको पासो -- त क्र ।

बन्डा पत्र -- बन्डा बत्र, अंश ल्ब ।

बन्द -- बन्दा, बन् ।

बन्द गर्नु (ढोका) -- तुबा ।

बन्दूक -- बन्धू ।

बन्दोबस्त -- बन्दबस्त, ठ्याम् ठीम् ।

बन्धकी -- बन्दकी ।

बन्धन -- फुवी क्ठु ।

बम -- बोम ।

बमोजिम -- बमोजीम ।

बयान -- बएन् ।

बराबर -- बराबर, प्रीप्री ।

बरु -- बरु ।

बर्त बस्नु -- बर्त टीबा ।

बल -- भों ।

बलीयो -- भोंब ।

बलेंसी थाम -- पेंदो ।

बलो -- बलो, भेल्सीं, ढाडे बलो ।

बल्छी -- बल्छीं ।

बल्नु -- लुंब ।

बल्ल -- बल्ल ।

बस -- बस ।

बस्नु -- कुंब, टीबा ।

बहर -- भारा ।

बहर (सांढे) -- एल्या भार ।

बहादुर -- सएं भोंल्ले टीब ।

बहादुरी -- बादुरे ।

बहिनी -- अंड०ा, रीं ।

बहिनी ज्वाई -- म्हो ।

बहिनी दिदीहरू -- रींमएं ।

बहिरो -- बैरा ।

बांकी -- बांगी, चस्ब, ङ०स्ब ।

बांच्नु -- सोब ।

बांझो -- बांजु ।

बांड्नु -- च्हुब, पांबा ।

बांदर -- योगार ।

बांदर बर्ष -- प्रा ल्हो, योगार ल्हो ।

बांध्नु -- फ्वीब ।

बांस -- रीं ।

बाउन्ने -- बौनैबीर ।

बाउसो -- तु ।

बाकस -- बागस ।

बाक्लो -- बाक्लो, रूंदु ।

बाख्रा -- र ।

बाघ -- चैं ।

बाघ बर्ष -- चैं ल्हो ।

बाइ०गो -- बांगो, कुईदुं ।

बाचा -- बाच्का ।

बाज -- बाद ।

बाजा -- बाजा ।

बाजी -- बाजी ।

बाजे -- बाज्यु ।

बाज्नु -- फ्लोंब ।

बाज्ये -- बाजे ।

बाटा -- -ईले, -उंले ।

बाटो -- घ्यां ।

बाट्नु -- च्यारीब, ख्रोंबा, पेर्बा ।

बाठो -- बाट्ठो ।

बाण -- बान ।

बात मार्नु -- मार्दीब ।

बातचीत -- बादचीत ।

बादल -- न्हांम्ज्यो ।

बानी -- बानी, सुबासा ।

बान्नु -- च्युइंब ।

बान्नु (पट्का) -- सीब ।

बाफ -- लोमां ।

बाफिनु -- लोम् खबा ।

बाबियो -- बाव्यो ।

बाबु (बा) -- आबा ।

बाबुहरू -- आप्पए ।

बाम माक्रो -- बम तांगा ।

बायां -- त्हेव्क्रे, त्हग्यों ।

बार (गारो) -- बार ।

बार (घरको, एक किसिम) -- लुइ०त ।

बार (दिन) -- बार ।

बार बार्नु -- थुब ।

बारी -- बारी ।

बारुलो -- नव्बु च्युवी ।

बारखरी -- बार्खरी ।

बारदली -- बार्तली ।

बार्नु (कुनै दिशा) -- ङ०हस्बं ।

बाल काट्नु -- क्रीब ।

बालक -- प्हासी, कोळो ।

बालकहरू -- कोल्मएं ।

बालक बोक्नु -- प्वीबा ।

बालुवा -- बल्वा ।

बाल्टीन -- गबु, बाल्टीन ।

बाल्नु -- सोम्रो भींब, म्रोबा, फाबा ।

बास -- बास ।

बासी -- सीं ।

बास्ना -- बासन्, थां ।

बास्नु -- उरीब, उर्ब ।

बाहिर -- बाईरू ।

बाहुनहरू -- बोमएं, प्ह्रुमएं ।

बाहेक -- बाहेक ।

बाह्र -- बार ।

बिउंझिनु -- छुर्ब ।

बिक्री -- बिक्री ।

बिक्री गर्नु -- लौंबा, सुक्री बिक्री लबा ।

बिग्रनु -- न्होंब ।

बिचरो -- ओछें ।

बिचेत -- बिजेद ।

बिचेत हुनु -- बिजेद तबा ।

बिच्छी -- त्हीम्ह्रु बीच्छे ।

बिछ्याउनु -- तीबा ।

बिफाउनु -- न्हेब ।

बिट -- ङ०ां ।

बिटो -- ठुंडा, -ब्रएं ।

बित्ता -- बित्ता ।

बित्तिकै -- बित्तिक् ।

बिदा -- बिद ।

बिना -- बिना ।

बिन्ती -- बिन्दी ।

बिफार -- बिफार ।

बिमिराको बोट -- बीम्रा धुं ।

बियां -- म्ह्रे ।

बिराउनु -- बिरीदीब ।

बिरालो -- नौंवा ।

बिरामी -- नब् छ्ब ।

बिरालो बर्ष -- नाँवा ल्हो, ही ल्हो ।

बिर्को -- का ।

बिर्सनु -- म्लीब ।

बिर्सनु (बाटो) -- फ्लेबा ।

बिल्ला -- बील्ला ।

बिसाउनु -- न्हब ।

बिसाउने ठाउं -- न्हें ।

बिसेक हुनु -- सजीज तब ।

बिस्कुन -- साँग्या ।

बिस्तारै -- नुंजीले ।

बिहान -- न्हांग ।

बिहानै -- न्हक्कर्ना ।

बींड -- यु ।

बीउ -- प्लु ।

बीच्मा -- अह्धरी, म्हांजुरी ।

बीस -- बीस, इ०हीस्यु ।

बुझ्नु -- क्होब ।

बुट्टा -- बुट्टा, फूल ।

बुट्टा हाल्नु -- बुट्ट झर्बँ ।

बुधवार -- बुदबार ।

बुद्धि -- बुद्दी ।

बुन्नु -- रोब ।

बुहारी -- बुवारी ।

बूढी -- मांब ।

बूढी औंलो -- यो आबा ।

बूढो -- खीब ।

बेईमानी -- बेमान् ।

बेग्लै बेग्लै -- आनेक ।

बेच्नु -- चुंब ।

बेत -- बेद् ।

बेन्च -- बेन्च ।

बेपार -- छौं ।

बेपारी -- बेपारी ।

बेबस्था -- बेबस्था ।

बेर हुनु -- क्हरब ।

बेर्नु -- बेर्दीब, म्हुरीब ।

बेला -- बेला, ला, ट्याम, त्ही ।

बेलायत -- बेलाईद ।

बेलुका -- नेस ।

बेलौती -- बेलौदी ।

बेसरी -- बेसेरी, भुदुकन, उतील्ले ।

बेसार -- बेसार ।

बेसाहा -- बेसा ।

बैना -- बैना ।

बोको -- बग्या ।

बोक्नु -- कुबा, नोब ।

बोक्रो -- बोग्रो, फी ।

बोक्सी -- पुम्स्यो ।

बोक्सी कराउनु -- च्हुब ।

बोक्सीको छोरा कि छोरी -- बोस ।

बोक्सीलाई दिने पहिलो भोग -- पाल्दु ।

बोक्सीलाई दिने दोस्रो भोग -- दोबाडे ।

बोक्सीलाई दिन (आर्को भोग) -- पुतीबर ल्हैं डु०हरं सैंब ।

बोट -- धुं ।

बोधो -- ल्हुम्डे ।

बोलाउंदा बोलिने शब्द -- ह्वे ।

बोलाउनु -- ह्वीब ।

बोल्नु -- पोंब ।

बोलचाल -- पोंसुं ।

बोसो -- छी ।

बौलाहा -- हावा न्होंह्याब, सोबाला ।

व्याउलो -- व्याउलो ।

व्याज -- व्याज ।

व्याट्री -- बेटरी, गेस ।

भ

भंगेरो -- कोमैंएं ।

भए पनि -- -न बीले य ।

भएको -- तबा ।

भकुण्डो -- भुगुंड ।

भक्त -- भक्ती ।

भक्भके -- क्वीब ।

भगवान -- भगवान ।

भजन -- भजन ।

भटमास -- कोया ।

भट्टी -- भाडी ।

भड्कनु -- (लोंब) छ्युडीह्याब ।

भतिजी -- क्वेंमीं ।

भतिजो -- क्वें ।

भतुवा -- भत्वा ।

भत्कनु -- फुबा ।

भत्यार -- भत्यार ।

भनाइ -- भनाई ।

-भने -- -ले, स्यां, -यां ।

भन्दा -- भन्दा ।

भन्नु -- बीबा ।

भन्सार -- टेक्सा, भन्सार ।

भरखर -- भक्खर ।

भरपर्नु -- भर ।

भरपाइ -- लेस्ट, भरपाई ।

भरी -- तील, भरी ।

भरीएको -- नै ।

भरीएर पोख्नु -- ल्हु ह्याब ।

भरीया -- भारे ।

भरे -- कोमां ।

भर्ती -- भर्दी ।

भर्ना -- भर्न ।

भर्नु -- क्होसेंब, प्लैंबा ।

भर्याङ -- प्रें, भर्याङ ।

भलादमी -- भलाद्मीं ।

भल -- भोला, प्हलें ।

भलो -- भलो ।

भविष्य -- भविस्य ।

भविष्य बताउनु -- लीउंबस्तां बीबा ।

भांग्रो -- ड्रैंग ।

भांच्नु -- चुबा, प्राब ।

भांडा -- भांडो ।

भांडाहरू -- तों, भांडुं कुंडो ।

भाइ -- अली, भाइ ।

भाउ -- कों ।

भाखा -- भागा ।

भाग -- बां, भाउ ।

भाग्नु -- भउदीब ।

भाड़ा -- भारा, ध्यां खर्ज, -बाल ।

भाड़ा दिनु -- बालर पींबा ।

भात -- कएं, म्ल्होगों ।

भात (नपाकेको) -- सी ।

भानिज -- भानिज ।

भान्जी -- भान्जी ।

भान्सा -- भान्छा ।

भान्से -- भान्छे ।

भारत -- इंण्डीया, भारद,

हीन्दुस्थान
भारती -- भारती ।
भारी -- त्ही ।
भालु -- भलु ।
भाले (कुखुरो) -- भाले ।
भाले (सबलाई) -- त्होब ।
भाव -- भाब ।
भाषा -- क्ह्युई ।
भासिनु -- भासीदीब ।
भिजेको -- पांब ।
भिडाउनु (दांज्नु) -- त्हांब ।
मित्र -- न्हों, न्होंउंब ।
मित्रै -- न्होंनोंन ।
मिनाज्यू -- ओमो ।
मिर्नु -- ख्याबा ।
भीर -- फ्रो ।
भुंडी -- भुंडी ।
भुइंकटहर -- भेंकटर ।
भुइंको प्वाल -- भुन ।
भुइंचालो -- सयो ।
भुक्नु -- क्छुब ।
भुजुड्०गो -- भुजुड० ।
भुटनु -- इ०होब ।
भुतुक्क -- भुदुकन ।
भुते -- ल्हुम्डे, भुत्ते ।
भुत्लो -- भुद्ला ।
भुल्नु -- म्लीब, भुल्दीब ।
भुवा -- भुवा ।
भूगोल -- भूगोल ।
भूत -- भूत ।
भूत (अनेक किसिमको) -- म्हों, म्हों आंलां ।
भूमी सुधार -- भूमी सुदर ।
भूस -- प्वी ।
भेटी -- भेटी ।
भेदनु -- त्होब, स्याब ।
भेड़ो -- क्ह्यु ।
भेड़ो बर्ष -- क्ह्यु ल्हो, ल्हु ल्हो ।
भैंसी -- मगी ।
भैंसीको पाठो -- कडवा ।
भोक लाग्नु -- फो ब्रेंबा ।
भोग दिनु -- ब्रो पीबा ।
भोज -- भन्यार, भोज ।

भोट -- भोड ।

भोटे -- भोडे, च्योब्राल्मएं ।

भोटो -- भोडो ।

भोलि -- प्ह्न्हांग ।

भोलिपर्सि -- प्ह्न्हां लिउंद, प्ह्न्हांलीई ।

भोलि पल्ट -- प्ह्न्हाग्दुं ।

भोलि बिहान -- प्ह्न्हांरी ।

भ्याउन खोज्नु -- ह्वैब ।

म

मंगलवार -- म्हङ्०लाबारा ।

मंसिर -- म्हैंसिर ।

म -- ङ० ।

म धनी हुं भन्ने -- प्ह्सेंब ।

मकै (भुटेको) -- पु ।

मकैको खोस्टा (भुत्लो) -- खोया ।

मकैको जमरा -- बुबुं ।

मक्खन -- मखन ।

मखन्डी (सीप नभएको) -- म्हखन्डी ।

मग -- मग ।

मगर -- मगर ।

मगाउनु -- थोबा ।

मजेत्रो -- क्रमुं ।

मज्जा -- मजा ।

मज्जा लिनु -- मजा तबा ।

मतलब -- मल्दब, माने ।

मद्दत -- मदद, सास्दा ।

मधिसे -- म्हदीसे ।

मधुरो -- मदुरो ।

मध्याह्न -- त्हीयांअह्धा ।

मन -- सएं ।

मन पराउनु -- मन पर्दीब ।

मन पर्नु -- खोबा ।

मन भुलाउनु -- सएं भुल्दीब ।

मन रमाइलो हुनु -- छुबा ।

मनाउनु -- मनीदीब ।

मन्जूर -- मन्जूर ।

मन्जूर गर्नु -- मन्जूर लबा ।

मन्त्र -- मन्त्रा, मन्तरा ।

मन्त्री -- मन्ड्री ।

मन्दिर -- मन्दिर ।

मनपरी -- मन्परी ।

मनलाग्नु -- ङ्०हांब ।

मरमत गर्नु -- क्योएंब ।

मरिच -- मरिज ।

मर्कनु -- ख्रीब ।

मर्काउनु -- नलदीब ।

मर्दना -- म्हर्दा ।

मर्नु -- सीबा, घेंल्याब ।

मल्नु -- मोल्दीब ।

मल्ल (एक किसिमको फल) -- एर ।

मसला -- मसल ।

मसला हाल्नु -- मसल फ्नोब ।

मसान (भूत प्रेत) -- मसन ।

मसान (लाश गाड्ने) -- क्र्याँ ।

मसिनो -- मसिनु, प्रब ।

मसी -- मसी ।

मसुर -- मसुर, अहङ्०हींबए म्ही ।

मसुरको दाल -- मसुरी

महंगो -- म्हांगु ।

मह -- खुदु ।

महि -- कोला ।

महीना -- -ल, म्हैन ।

-मा -- -र, -री, -मा ।

माङ्त -- मैद ।

माईज्यू -- अङ्०डॉं ।

माउ -- मोमां ।

माउरी -- क्ह्वे, क्वे ।

माउरीको घर -- क्होए डोंडा ।

माकुरो -- त्हीम्ब्रु ।

माखो -- च्योमीं ।

माग्नु -- ह्रीब ।

माघ -- म्हाग ।

माछा -- तांग ।

माफ्नु -- म्याब ।

माटो -- स ।

माटो दिनु -- प्हाब ।

माड्नु (पराल) -- न्हेब ।

मात्नु -- मात्तिब ।

मात्रै -- मत्त्रे ।

माथि -- क्होरी, क्होउं, फोरी, ताईं ।

माथि निर -- क्होवां प्ह्रदें ।

माथिबाट आउनु -- युब ।

मादल -- म्हांद ।

मादल बजाउनु -- म्हांदद्राब ।

मान -- मान ।

मान गर्नु -- मान ल्बा ।

मानिस -- मुनुखे, म्ही ।

मानु -- म्हंन ।

माने -- माने ।

मान्नु -- डे०स्बा, म्हांदीब ।

माफ -- माफ ।

मामा -- मामा ।

मामुली -- मामुली ।

माया -- म्हाया ।

मायालु -- म्हयालु ।

मारकाट -- मारकाट ।

मार्नु -- सस्बा ।

मार्नु (भैंसीले) -- थाबा ।

मार्नु लइनु -- सस्बा न्हेब ।

माल -- माल ।

माला -- माला ।

मास -- मास ।

मासी (हाडमित्रको) -- टों ।

मासिनु (प्राणी) -- थुंबा ।

मासु -- से ।

मास्नु -- म्हास्दीब, म्हाईंदीब ।

मास्टर -- मास्टर ।

माहिली -- म्हैली ।

माहिली फुपू -- फादें ।

माहिलो -- म्हैल ।

माहिलो बाबा -- अहम्हैल ।

मिच्नु -- मीजीब ।

मिजासीलो -- धुं लच्छीन्, मीज्यासी ।

मिठो -- लींब ।

मिडील -- मिडील ।

मित -- इ०हेल ।

मित (मितिनीको लोग्ने) -- आगु ।

मित लाउनु -- च्याबा ।

मितिनी -- इ०हेलस्यो, आगु ।

मित्र -- मित्त्र ।

मिगौंलो -- खई ।

मिल्जुल -- थोंब ।

मिलाउनु -- क्ह्रील् ल्बा, क्हील्ले थेंबा, म्हीलीदीब, म्हील्दीब ।

मिलाप -- मिलाब ।

मिल्ने -- तीप्ली काम्ली ।

मिलु -- क्ह्रीब ।

मिसाउनु -- कोंब ।

मिसाउनु (पुवा र धानको भूस) -- मोलोबा ।

मिसिल -- मिसिल ।

मिसिन -- मिसिन ।

मिस्त्री -- मिस्त्री ।

मुख (अनुहार) -- ली, मोंडा ।

मुख (बोल्ने) -- सुं ।

मुखले बिराउनु -- सुं फ्लेबा ।

मुखिया -- मुली, क्ह्रों, नेता ।

मुख्य थाम -- मुल त्हो ।

मुगा -- भीरू ।

मुगामा राख्ने चिज -- तुदु ।

मुङ्ग्रो -- म्हुउंरू ।

मुङ्लो (गोरूको मुखमा लाउने) -- म्हुउंलु ।

मुजी -- मुजी ।

मुजुरी (ज्यालाको लागि दिने अन्न) मुजुरी, म्हुंजुरी ।

मुजूर -- मुंजुरा, तौतो ।

मुट्ठ -- तीं ।

मुट्ठो -- मुट्ठा ।

मुठ्ठी -- मुठी ।

मुड्की -- मुड्की ।

मुड्कीले हान्नु -- बक्कादींब, प्रींब ।

मुत्वा -- कुंस्यु ।

मुद्दा -- मुद्द ।

मुद्दा गर्नु -- मुद्द ल्बा ।

मुनि -- न्होंबं, फ्रोरी ।

मुन्डे घर -- क्रुलुं धीं ।

मुन्द्रा -- चीन्जीन ।

मुन्द्रा (कानमा लाउने) -- मडुली ।

मुरली -- मुर्ली ।

मुरी -- म्हुरी ।

मुर्कट्टा -- मुल कट्ट ।

मुर्छा -- मुर्स ।

मुर्छा पर्नु -- मुर्स पर्दीब ।

मुर्दाको अगाडि लाने झण्डा -- आंलां ।

मुलुक -- मुल्क ।

मुश्किल -- मुश्किल ।

मुसी -- मसी ।

मुस्कुराउनु -- नी खबा ।

मुहार -- मुवार ।

मूर्ख -- मूर्खा ।

मूर्ख चाल्ले -- मूर्खा चाल्ले ।

मूर्ति -- मूर्ति ।

मूर्ति (भातको) -- कएंदु ।

मूल (पानीको) -- मूला ।

मूल (मुख्य) -- मूल ।

मूल रुख -- मूल हांग ।

मूला -- ल्बु ।

मूल बाटो -- मूल घ्यां ।

मूसो -- क्षीबुल, नीमुंर ।

मूसो बर्ष -- नीमुं ल्हो ।

मूसाको घर -- रो ।

मृग -- फो ।

मृत्यु -- काल, सीब ।

मेटाउनु -- मीडीब ।

मेन्टोल -- मैन्टोला ।

मेम साब -- मीम साबा ।

मेरो -- ङ०ला ।

मेल मिलाप -- थींबा, क्ह्यांब ।

मेला -- मेला ।

मेलो -- ताँ, एक्वा ।

मेवा -- मेवा ।

मेसो -- ताँ ।

मैदा -- मैदा ।

मैदान -- म्हैदन ।

मैन -- क्योलों ।

मैना -- मैनां ।

मैलो पन -- क्ह्री, मैल ।

मोइ -- मए ।

मोजा -- जुराबा ।

मोटर -- जीप, मोटर ।

मोटे -- कल्ली ।

मोटो -- धुंब, क्षोबा ।

मथ्नु -- ल्हुब ।

मोल -- सए ।

मोल पर्नु -- फेबा ।

मोहोर -- म्होरा ।

मौरी -- क्होए, क्वे ।

म्वाइ खानु -- म्वैं ल्बा ।

य

यता पट्टि -- फुदी ।

यति -- च्हग ।

यति सानो -- च्ही सीरी,
च्ही थीरी ।

यति -- च्हौ ।

यसो -- छा, छु ।

यस्तो -- छाबा ।

यहां -- चुरी ।

या -- या ।

यात्रा -- ह्रेगौं - फ्ह्रब ।

याद -- याद ।

युग -- जुग ।

यो -- चु ।

-यो -- -दी, -दु, -ई, -जी,
-ल, -छ ।

-यो त -- ठो ।

-यो नि -- जोन् ।

यो सालमा -- तीदींम ।

योग -- जोग ।

योगी -- जोगी

र

र -- नैगो, नैरो ।

रवा गर्नु -- रच्छे ल्बा ।

रक्सी -- पा ।

रक्सी थाप्ने भाडो -- पु ।

रक्सी बनाउनु -- पा क्वालब ।

रक्सी लागेको -- न्हेब ।

रगत -- को ।

रगत आउनु -- को युब ।

रगत बार्नु (काम गर्न हुन्न) --
कोस प्रीम् ।

रड० -- रड० ।

रण्डी -- रन्डी ।

रमाइलो -- रामीद ।

रमाइलो हुनु -- क्ह्यालब ।

रस -- रस ।

रसिलो -- रसिलो ।

रह -- ह्रा ।

-रहनु -- -डी ।

रहनु -- टीबा ।

रहर (लाग्नु) -- ह्रार ।

-रहेछ -- -मना ।

रांगो -- रांगु ।

रांड़ो -- खेरेंगु ।

राखि छोड्नु (पानीमा) -- क्योबा ।

राख्नु -- थेंबा ।

राख्नु (कांधमा हात) -- थेंब ।

रागन (जोर्नी दुख्नु) -- नाने ।

राज गद्दी -- राज गत्ती ।

राज गर्नु -- राज ल्बा ।

राजा -- मुं, राजा ।

राजीनामा (मुक्त हुनु) -- राजीनाम् ।

राज्य -- राजे ।

राती -- म्हुईस, रादा, -रो ।

रातो -- ओल्ग्या ।

रानी -- मुंस्यो ।

राम्रो (मासु) -- कस्दीब ।

राम्रो वास्ना आउने -- लींबए थां खबा ।

राम्रो संग -- छेन्ले ।

रिङ्ग -- माड्ली ।

रीति -- रीति थीती ।

रिबन -- ह्रमीं ।

रिसाउनु -- ह्रीस खब ।

रुघा -- सोर्मएं ।

रुचाउनु -- नीबा, खोब ।

रुनु -- क्रोबा ।

रुमाल -- ह्रुमाल ।

रूप -- रूप ।

रूल -- फूट ।

रे -- रो ।

रेल गाडी -- रेल गाडी ।

रोग -- बेथा ।

रोटी -- क्हें, प्लागें ।

रोडा -- रोडा, मसीनु युकां फुं ।

रोप्नु -- रूईंबा ।

रौं -- म्वी ।

ल

लंगडो -- लंगडा ।

ल -- लु, न ।

लक्षण -- लछीन ।

लखेट्नु -- ल्हादींब ।

लगाउनु (औषधि) -- फुब ।

लगाउनु (काम गर्न) -- ल्हैदीब ।

लगाउनु (दोष) -- ल्हगैदीब ।

लगाउनु (लुगा) -- खीबा ।

लगौटी -- फासु ।

लट्ठी -- फर्गु, फ्रे ।

लट्ठीले हान्नु -- क्ष्याबुब ।

लडाइ -- लडैं ।

लडाउनु -- क्हुर्वांब ।

लडि बडी खेल्नु -- ओलेब ।

लड्नु (खस्नु) -- क्हुरीह्याबा ।

लड्नु (लडाइ गर्नु) -- न्हेब ।

लत्ता कपडा -- क्वैं टालाद्गुली ।

लथालिङ० -- लथलीङ० ।

लबटाले हान्नु -- क्षैंराब ।

लस्सी -- कंलं ।

लमाइ -- लम्बाइ ।

लम्कनु -- लम्गदीब, तेक्वांब ।

लाम्छाने (गुरुंगको जात) -- लेम्मएं ।

लम्जुङ० -- लम्जुं ।

लसुन -- न्हु ।

लहरो -- न्होरीं ।

-लाई -- -लाई ।

लाग्नु (खर्च) -- ल्हौदीब ।

लाग्नु (समय) -- ल्हैदीब ।

लाग्नु (सराप, गोली) -- टबा ।

लाग्नु (हिलो) -- ङ०होस्ब ।

लाटी -- लाडी ।

लाटो -- लडा ।

लात्ती -- लात्ता ।

लामखुट्टे -- ल्हम्खुट्टे ।

लामा -- लमा ।

लामाहरू -- लम्मएं ।

लामो -- द्रीङ०ग्यो ।

लामो कोट -- बौंडी ।

लामो बनाउनु -- लस्गदीब ।

लास -- मोर ।

लाहांचे -- सीं नेमां, हुगा ह्राबए नेमां ।

लाहा (चिट्ठीको) -- ल्हा ।

लिलि -- ओल्मएं ।

लिनु -- ख्वेब, कींब ।

लिप्नु -- स्यालब ।

लिस्नु (एक किसिमको भऱ्याङ०) -- ली ।

लुकाउनु -- लोब ।

लुकीचोरी -- लुकी-चुरी ।

लुक्नु -- लोब ।

लुगा -- क्वैं ।

लुगा फुकाउनु -- प्लीबा ।

लुच्चा-फटाहा -- लुच्चा ।

लुछ्नु -- छ्युर्ब्ब, रोस्ब, टोंब ।

लुट्नु -- लुडीब ।

लुलो -- ठुला ।

लूतो -- लुदु ।

ले -- -दं, -दी, -जी, -ज्या, -ल, -ले ।

लेक -- बुग्यानी, हे ।

लेप्नु -- फ्रीब ।

लैजानु -- बयाब, बोबा ।

लोग्ने -- फ ।

लोग्ने खोज्नु -- फ म्हस्ब ।

लोटा -- भागुन, लोडा ।

लोट्नु -- क्हुरीह्याब ।

लोती -- न्ह तैं ।

लोभ -- लोभ ।

लोभ गर्नु -- लोभ ल्बा ।

लोभ गर्नु (खाने बेलामा) -- खोंबा ।

लौ (लिनुस) -- नं ।

लौका -- लौगा ।

ल्याउनु -- भब ।

ल्याउनु (माथीबाट) -- म्वीब ।

ल्वाङ०ग -- ल्होगौं ।

व

वमन गर्नु -- रूईब ।

वरिपरि -- खागु, कार्ग्यु ।

वर्ष -- बर्ष, -दीं ।

वर्षा -- बर्षा ।

वस्तु -- बस्तु ।

बस्तु (गाई, गोरू, भैंसी) -- ख्योंदो ।

वस्तु मर्ने रोग -- ह्रीं ।

वा... वा -- या... या ।

वाक्य -- बाग्य ।

वाक्य नउठाउनु -- बाग्या अहखोल्दीब ।

वापस -- वाफस, ए- ।

वान्त -- रुई ।

वायु -- स्यागी, स्यो ।

वारी -- चौंजं ।

वास्ता नगर्नु -- हेल ल्बा ।

वाह्या जननेन्द्रियहरू (लोग्ने मानिसको) -- सालनाल ।

विकास -- बिकास ।

विकास मल -- बिकास मल ।

विचार -- बिचार, सएं बिचार ।

विचार गर्नु -- म्हसंब (सएंर) ।

विदेश -- बिदेश ।

विदेशी -- बिदेशी ।

विधवा -- म्री ह्रांडी ।

विपना -- सएंम ।

विरोधी -- बर्बैल ।

विवाह -- व्या ।

विवाह विच्छेद गर्नु -- पार ल्बा ।

विश्वास -- बिश्वास ।

विश्वास मान्नु -- विश्वास म्हांदीब ।

विष -- बिख, मेंगएं ।

वेदना -- बेदन् ।

वैगुनी -- बैगुने ।

वैलनु -- ओईलीदीब ।

श

शक्ति -- सक्ती ।

शङ्का -- शंका ।

शत्रु -- सतुरा ।

शर्माउनु -- पीबा ।

शहर -- शहार ।

शाखी -- शाजी ।

शाली -- शाली ।

शिकारी -- शिगारे ।

शिकार खेल्नु -- शिगार एल्योंबा ।

शित -- शित ।

शितल -- शिदाल ।

शिर मुन्द्री -- शिलमन्द्री ।

शिर बिन्दु -- नखुं सुं ।

शिशी -- शिशी ।

शीशा (मेन्टलको) -- शीशा ।

शुरु गर्नु -- शुरु लबा ।

शोक -- शोक ।

शेफ्टी पिन -- पिन ।

श्रावण -- सावें ।

श्रीपेच -- श्री पेच ।

श्रीमती -- म्रीं ।

श्रीमान -- प्युं ।

श्लोक -- शीलोग ।

ष

षड्यन्त्र -- मद् ।

स

संघार -- संगार ।

सकस -- सगस ।

सकिनु -- च्हीँब ।

सक्नु -- खांब ।

सखर -- गुरा ।

संग -- -नै बालु, -नै प्री ।

सङ्गै -- खागुले, बालु ।

सङ्लो -- सौलो ।

सचिब -- सजीब ।

सच्चा -- सजन ।

सजाय -- सजएं ।

सजिलो -- सजिलो ।

सट्टा -- सट्टा, सट्टो ।

सतीत्व -- सद ।

सतरी -- ङोज्यु ।

सत्य -- सत्ते ।

सत्य युग -- सत्ते जुग ।

सदर -- सदर ।

सदस्य -- सदसी ।

सधैं -- सोंई, सोदा ।

सन्चो -- सन्च, स्हबन् ।

सन्तान -- सन्तना ।

सन्तोष -- सन्तोक ।

सपना -- म्होंड ।

सप्रनु -- सोबादींब ।

सफा -- सफ्फा ।

सब -- तोन्दोरी ।

सबभन्दा -- तानभन्दा ।

सबै -- तान् ।

सभा -- कजुरी, सभा, अंसभा,
मीटीङ० ।

सभपति -- सबपती ।

समाचार --सम्जार ।

समाज -- समाज ।

समात्नु -- क्वेब, क्वाब, स्याब ।

समुद्र -- समुद्र ।

सम्झनु -- च्हीब, म्हसंब ।

सम्झाउनु -- सम्जीदीब ।

सम्धि -- सम्दी ।

सम्म (पुग्नु) -- सम्म ।

सम्म (मैदान) -- सम्म ।

सम्म जग्गा -- सम्म ख्ल्ह्यो ।

सम्पत्ति -- न्हुर, धींना, सम्पती ।

सय -- प्ख्र, सै ।

सयकडा -- सैकड ।

सरंग -- ट्होंवां ।

सराप -- सराब ।

सराप्नु -- स्याब, सराप् फ्रोंब ।

सरासर -- सरासर ।

सर्नु -- कुब, सर्दीब ।

सर्प -- प्हुरी, ख्ल्ह्योंबए ।

सलक्क -- सर्लक ।

सलह -- तीरी ।

सलाई -- सले ।

सलाम -- सोलुङ ।

सल्काउनु -- सलादीब ।

सल्लाह -- बुज, सल्ल ।

ससुरो (स्वास्नी वा लोग्नेको बा)
-- -कैं ।

ससुरो (दिदी सासूको लोग्ने)
-- साङु ।

सस्तो -- सस्तु ।

सहनु -- सईदीब ।

सही -- सै ।

सांघुरिनु -- रुबा ।

सांघुरो -- सांगु ।

सांघू -- चां ।

सांचो (ताल्चा) -- सांजु, कुजी ।

सांचो (सत्य) -- सच्चा ।

सांचो भन्नु -- साच्चा पोंब ।

सांच्चे -- क्रोसेन ।

सांच्नु -- सांदीब ।

सांझ -- सांज ।

सांढ -- क्ह्यु सांडे, सांढे ।

सांप -- प्हुरी, रल्ह्योंबए ।

सांप बर्ष -- प्हुरी ल्हो, सब्री ल्हो ।

सांहिली -- सैली ।

सांहिलो -- सैला ।

सांहिलो बाबु -- आबसैला ।

साइत -- सैदु ।

साक्खै -- सगेत ।

साग -- पासागी ।

साइ०लो -- सांउंली, सीग्री ।

साटो (गर्नु) -- सडा ।

साटो (बांसको) -- सडा ।

सादनु -- तीब ।

साठी -- दहज्यु ।

साढे -- साडे ।

सात -- ड०ी ।

सात सय -- ड०ीब्रा ।

साता -- सद ।

सातो -- प्लह ।

साथमा -- सादर ।

साथसाथ -- साथारी ।

साथी -- थु ।

साधा -- सादा ।

साधारण -- साधारन ।

सानो -- च्योंबा, च्युगु थीरी ।

सानो जात -- पुनी ।

साबुन -- साबाना ।

सामान -- सामन ।

सायद -- सएद ।

सारस -- जलो क्हुरे ।

सारी -- फरीया ।

सार्की -- सार्गी ।

सार्नु -- कुब ।

साल -- साल ।

साली ज्वाइं -- साडु ।

सालो -- स्याँबु ।

सावेल -- बेल्च ।

सास -- सो ।

सास थुन्नु -- ईल्बा ।

सास फेर्नु -- सैंबा ।

सासू -- स्युमी ।

साहिनु -- सैनुं ।

साहिनु पर्नु -- फेबा ।

साहू -- साउ ।

साहेब -- साबा ।

साहै -- सारोन ।

सिंगार्नु -- सिड०दीबि ।

सिंघान -- ना ।

सिंघान फाल्नु -- ना वाबा ।

सिंदूर -- सिंदूर ।

सिंह -- सिंगा ।

सिउंदो -- ओग्यां ।

सिकर्मी -- सिंकर्मी ।

सिकाउनु -- लुबा ।

सिकिस्त -- सार ।

सिक्नु -- लुब ।

सिक्री -- सिग्री ।

सित -- मने ।

सिद्धिनु -- खांब ।

सिद्याउनु -- लीब, नुबा ।

सिनु -- सिनु ।

सिनु पोल्ने बेला -- सल ।

सिन्की -- क्युंडा, गुन्द्रु ।

सिपालु -- सिबालु ।

सिपाही -- लाखुरे, सिपाई, पाले ।

सिमसिमे पानी -- नां बुंबुं ।

सिमी -- सिमी ।

सियो -- त्हा ।

सियोको नाथ्री -- त्हा मीं ।

सिरानी -- क्रेगुं ।

सिरौला -- सिरांउंलु ।

सिलाउनु -- ट्हब ।

सिलौटो -- सिल्बडा ।

सिस्नु -- पुलु ।

सिहुंडी -- स्योंडी ।

सीङ० -- रू ।

सीधा -- सीद ।

सीम -- सीमां ।

सीसा (बन्दूकमा हाल्ने) -- सीसा ।

सुइ -- स्वी ।

सुकाउनु -- सौंब ।

सुकाउनु (ऊन) -- टैंबा ।

सुकुल -- सुकुल ।

सुकेको -- कार, कारीब ।

सुक्नु -- कार्बा ।

सुक्नु (पोखरीमा पानी) -- ङ०हार्बा ।

सुक्र -- सुद्र ।

सुख -- सुख ।

सुखा -- सुखा ।

सुगा -- सुगा ।

सुताउनु -- नेबा ।

सुत्केरी -- सुदग्यारी ।

सुत्केरी हुनु -- सुदग्यारी तबा ।

सुत्नु -- रोब ।

सुन -- म्हारा ।

सुनाउनु -- सुनीदीब ।

सुनार -- सुनार ।

सुनिनु -- रौंब ।

सुन्तला -- सुन्दला ।

सुन्नु -- थेस्बा ।

सुपारी -- सुबारी ।

सुम्पनु -- सुम्दीब ।

सुल्टो -- सुल्डो ।

सुसार -- सुसार ।

सुसारे -- सुसारे ।

सुहाउनु -- ङ०हैंब ।

सूचना -- सूचन ।

सूत -- नैनसूद ।

सूर्य -- त्हीयां ।

सेती खोला -- गङ०ग्यु ।

सेतो -- ताग्र्या ।

सेर -- सेर ।

सोच गर्नु (पैसा जम्मा गर्नु) -- थी लबा ।

सोफ्नो -- सोजो ।

सोध्नु -- ङ०युङ्ब ।

सोल्टि (बाबुको दिदी बहिनीको छोरा, आमाको दाजु भाइको छोरा) -- ङ०लोंलों ।

सोल्टिनी (बाबुको दिदी बहिनीको छोरी, आमाको दाजु भाइको छोरी) -- ङ०लोलोंस्यो ।

सोह्र जात -- पसंमएं ।

स्याखु (घूम) -- क्हुं ।

स्याखु सिलाउने सियो -- नुं ।

स्यावास -- स्याबास ।

स्यामा (तामाङ०नीहरूको आफ्नो लुगा) -- स्यामां ।

स्याल -- सैला ।

स्याहार -- सएर, सुसार ।

स्वर्ग -- स्वर्ग ।

स्वर्गको दूत -- परमेश्वरए सिपाई ।

स्वाङ० गर्नु -- स्वांङ० तेब ।

स्वाद -- स्वाद ।

स्वास्नी मान्छे -- च्मीरी, चमीरी ।

स्वास्नी मान्छे (मान नभएको) -- म्रीस्यो ।

स्वीटर -- स्वीटर ।

ह

हं (नबुझेर सोध्ने शब्द) -- हां ।

हसिंया -- आंस्यी ।

हक -- हक ।

हगि -- ह्वा, आ, तो ।

हजार -- हजर ।

हजुर -- हजुर ।

हतार हतार गरी -- अहत्हुलें ।

हतियार (काट्ने) -- ल्होजी ।

हत्केलो -- यो प्लो ।

हतपत -- हतपत ।

हवेरी -- हैद, हैत ।

हप्काउनु -- होदीब ।

हप्ता -- हप्ता ।

हमला -- आटेक ।

हराउनु -- म्हब, म्होब ।

हरियो -- पींग्या, हरियो ।

हरियो परियो -- हरियो परियो ।

हरियो माखो -- एल्यी
च्यौंमीं ।

-हरू -- बुदुं, जग, -जौं, -मएं ।

हल -- -गुरा, हल ।

हलन्ट -- प्हल थोब ।

हली -- एल्ह्यासएं ।

हल्को -- यौंबा ।

हलुवाबेद -- हल्वा ।

हलो -- क्होर ।

हल्लनु -- ल्हाब ।

हल्ला -- हल्ला ।

हल्लाउनु -- ल्हाबा ।

हल्लिनु -- योगौंब ।

हवल्दार -- हावल्दार ।

हवाइ जहाज -- हवा फ्रास ।

हां (बाधको शव्द) -- हां ।

हांगो -- हांग ।

हांगो (पात नभएको) -- घसेड ।

हांगो (सुकेको) -- धारा ।

हांस -- हांस ।

हांसो -- नी ।

हांस्नु -- नी स्युबा ।

हाइ आउनु -- है ल्बा, कांब ।

हाजिर -- हांजिर ।

हाजिरी -- हांजिरी ।

हाड -- क्रीब ।

हात -- यो ।

हात (नाप्नु) -- गु, -कु ।

हात गोडा टेकेर हिंड्नु --
कारां मांरां ।

हात वा बुट्टाको भाग -- -पु ।

हाती -- हाती ।

हानि -- हानि ।

हान्नु -- ल्हीब, प्रींब ।

हामी (तपाइं बाहेक) -- ङ०ी ।

हामी (तपाइं हामी) -- ङ०ह्यो ।

हामीहरू -- ङ०ीजग, ङ०ह्योजग ।

हाम्रो -- ङ०ीए, ङ०ीला,
ङ०ह्योए, ङ०ह्योला ।

हार (लडाइमा) -- हारा ।

हार्नु -- हादींब ।

हाल्नु -- फ्रौंब ।

हावा -- खएं, हब ।

हावा कुरो -- फ्रम तां ।

हिउं -- ल्यीं ।

हिउंद -- सर्ब, पुम ।

हिक्क लाग्नु -- युगुब ।

हिजो -- तेला ।

हिनामिना -- हीनबीन ।

हिन्दी -- हिन्दी ।

हिन्दु -- हिन्दु ।

हिन्दुस्थान -- हिन्दुस्थान ।

हिमाल -- कदासुं ।

हिलो -- हिला ।

हिसाब -- हिसाब् ।

हिस्सा -- हिस्सा ।

हुकुम -- हुकुम ।

हुत्याउनु -- हुतले ।

हुनाले -- -बदी ।

हुनु -- मुबा, तबा ।

हूल -- हूल ।

हूल (बाटोको) -- घाड ।

हेर्नु -- ङ०ह्योब ।

है -- औ (अउ) ।

हो (प्रश्नमा) -- ज ।

हो -- ग, ङ०हींब, हो, य ।

हो कि ? -- अह, गे, ह्वा, आ, तो ?

होचो -- मोब ।

होटेल -- होटेल ।

होला -- -लै, लसे ।

होश (नभएको) -- होश सजीद् ।

होशियार -- होस्यार ।

होशियारी -- होस्यारी ।

-होस -- -द्, -गु, -न्, -नु ।

हौसला दिनु -- क्वीब ।

APPENDIXES

APPENDIX A

GURUNG KINSHIP TERMS

The Gurung kinship system is basically an Iroquois system in that sibling terms are extended to parallel cousins; but separate terms are used for cross cousins from both patrilineal and matrilineal descent.

Descent and inheritance are patrilineal. Residence is patrilocal with daughters going to live at the residence of their husbands after marriage. Cross cousin marriages are preferred and, in Ghachok area at least, there is no expressed preference as to whether the mate is chosen through the maternal or the paternal link. Although Doherty (1974) reports sister-exchange marriage as favoured in West Gurung, sister exchange between lineages (khalag) is prohibited in Ghachok area.

The Gurung population is endogamous as also are the two moieties within the Gurung society. These two major moieties are called the *'four clans'* (caa'r jaat) and the *'sixteen clans'* (so'raa jaat). In actual fact neither name is correctly representative of the exact number of clans in each group.

GENERAL COMMENTS ON KIN TERMS

1. Members of the vertically extended clan are called one's txamaẽ while members of one's own generation within one's clan are called ti'maẽ. Members of other clans within the moiety are called ŋẽmaẽ and the people of these clans provide potential marriage mates for members of the clan. rī'maẽ are the female siblings of a male ego or the female siblings of a female ego's husband. muyũma'ẽ are the male siblings of a female ego.

2. In most kin terms there is a distinction made if the person referred to is older or younger than ego. It has been suggested that the prefix a- is diagnostic of the terms for those older than ego. While

this is true in many cases, it is not consistently so, as in ali *'younger brother'* and angaa' *'younger sister'*.

3. People junior to ego are addressed according to their order of birth, using terms borrowed from Nepali except for the first born and last born children of each sex:

1st born son			ṭhaagu	*1st born daughter*			naa'ni
2nd	"	"	mxaĩla	*2nd*	"	"	mxaĩli
3rd	"	"	saĩlaa'	*3rd*	"	"	saĩli'
4th	"	"	kaĩlaa'	*4th*	"	"	kaĩli'
last	"	"	cyõ	*last*	"	"	cxamĩ cyõ, kaaji

The terms (of reference and address) for *FaBr* (23, 27 on chart) and *MoYrSiHu* (36) are, according to the man's order of birth in his own family:

			FaBr	*MoYrSiHu*
1st born son			aathebaa'	kaagĩ'
2nd	"	"	axmxaĩ'la	axmxaĩ'la
3rd	"	"	aabsaĩlaa'	aabsaĩlaa'
4th	"	"	aabkaĩlaa'	aabkaĩlaa'
last	"	"	aabjyõ	aabjyõ

Terms of address for other affinal relations senior to ego are generally based on consanguine links, typically maa'maa, baajyu, or aumo for men. (The terms for women show more variety, because affinally related women, such as mother-in-law, frequently belong to the same clan as a male ego.) So the terms of address for these relations are marked only by three dots in the key to the kin chart.

4. If a male ego's youngest female sibling is older than himself he calls her anjyõ, that is aana + cyõ. (The Gurung phonemic system requires stops to be voiced when they occur medially in a word. Hence cyõ becomes -jyõ when word medial.)

If a female ego's youngest male sibling is older than herself she calls him txajyõ. In fact all one's elder male siblings except the eldest, can be addressed as txajyõ or axwaa'.

If the first born male sibling is younger than a female ego she calls him ṭhaagu. If the first born female sibling is younger than a male ego he calls her naa'ni. Father's female siblings who are not the eldest or youngest are called phaadẽ'.

KEY TO KINSHIP CHART

Number	*Generation*	*Term of address*	*Term of reference*
1.	G+O	axgxĩ'	aadaa
2.		cõ	cõ
3.		axgxaẽ'	aanaa
4.		aumo	aumo
5.		..-ma'e aamaa	..-ma'e aamaa, mrĩ
6.		cyõ	ali
7.		...	buwaari
8.		kaaji	aŋaa'
9.		ṭhaagu, etc.	mxo
10.		...	saa'ḍu daai
11.		...	aasyõ
12.		...	jeṭh šali'
13.		...	šali'
14.		...	syõ'bu
15.		ṭhaagu, etc.	saa'ḍu bxaai'
16.		ŋõlõ'syo	ŋõlõ'syo
17.		ŋõlõ'	ŋõlõ'
18.		ṭhaagu, etc.	bxaai'
19.		naa'ni, etc.	rĩ'
20.		naa'ni, etc.	(no term in use)
21.	G+1	aabaa	aabaa
22.		aamaa	aamaa
23.		aathebaa'	aathebaa'
24.		aathe, anthebaa'	anthebaa'
25.		phaaga'ẽ	phaaga'ẽ
26.		phojyõ	phojyõ
27.		aabjyõ	aabjyõ
28.		amjyõ	amjyõ
29.		...	kẽ
30.		...	syumi
31.		maa'maa	maa'maa
32.		aŋŋi'	aŋŋi'
33.		aathe, anthebaa'	aathe, anthebaa'
34.		aathebaa'	aathebaa'
35.		axjxyu'/axccyõ	axjxyu'/axccyõ
36.		kaagĩ', etc.	kaagĩ', etc.

continued overleaf

Key to Kinship Chart - *continued*

Number	*Generation*	*Term of address*	*Term of reference*
41.	G+2	baajyu	baajyu
42.		bxujyu'	bxujyu'
45.	G-1	ṭhaagu, etc.	cxa
46.		naa'ni, etc.	cxamĩ
47.		cyõ	cxa
48.		kaaji	cxamĩ cyõ
50.		naa'ni, etc.	cxa cõ
51.		ṭhaagu, etc.	cxami mxo
52.		ṭhaagu, etc.	bxaanja', bxaani'ja
53.		naa'ni, etc.	bxaanji'
55.	G-2	ṭhaagu, etc.	kwẽ
56.		naa'ni, etc.	kwẽmĩ'
60.	G-3	ṭhaagu, etc.	naati, panaati
61.		naa'ni, etc.	naatini, panaatini

APPENDIX B

RELIGIOUS TERMS

1. SUPERNATURAL BEINGS

In his daily activities the Gurung villager is vitally concerned with the world of the supernatural because he believes that all of life's misfortunes are at least potentially, and most probably, caused by supernatural beings. These beings fall into three main categories: gods, evil spirits, and witches.

1.1. *GODS.* There are two levels of deity expressed by the villager in his discussion about gods. The high god is referred to as paramešwara or bxagawaan. The high god has appeared in the world in several incarnations (autara), namely sitaa, kri+ṣṇaa, bišnu and lakšmaṇ. Somewhat lower than the high god are the godlings (deutaa), whom the villager fears more than the high god because of their apparent power to curse him. mahaadew, durga, saarašwati, guje suri, jaŋge suri, pašupati, salle' naraayaaṇ, šitala dewi, bxayãã'r, deuraali, salbi, kabo, side, bauddxa, simbu, dev ghar, and siva have all been named as deutaa.

1.2. *EVIL SPIRITS* are also feared by the villager and come in many manifestations.

ligyãã manifests itself to children and dogs only in the form of a hairy man with his feet back to front.

mu'l kaṭṭa or mxõ' ããlaa takes a headless form with eyes seated in the shoulders.

syo' is the ghost of a person or animal who has suffered a violent death.

sawa mana is the ghost of a person who has been killed when digging out clay from the mountain sides.

masana is the ghost of a person who has not been able to reach the village of departed men's souls and usually dwells around cemeteries.

syaa'gi is the ghost of a person who through suffering a violent death has not been able to reach the village of departed men's souls. Unlike the syo' these spirits are able to leave the scene of the death and roam around the village to attack the villagers.

mxõ' or bxuṭ is the ghost of any person who has died and not yet reached the village of departed men's souls.

sarwẽ' is a spirit which manifests itself as fire which consumes anything new.

xesaẽ is a spirit which lives in the forested areas and manifests itself as a horse carrying a deity.

thaa is a spirit which manifests itself by causing disharmony in the home.

1.3. The *WITCH* pumsyo is a living person who works malice against the villagers either personally or by causing certain evil spirits, the mxo', syaa'gi and masana, to do her bidding.

2. RELIGIOUS OFFICIANTS

2.1. *SEERS* are people who can divine the supernatural origins of a misfortune and are called ŋxyoba mxi' *'a looking person'*. la'm kami, of the blacksmith caste, is considered by many to be the most competent type of seer.

jaisi are skilled in the art of reading astrological calendars and horoscopes and are often called for by the villager to use this science to divine the causes of illness or calamity.

bomaẽ *'Brahmin'* is of the Hindu tradition. Because of his skill in reading astrological calendars and horoscopes he is also sometimes consulted by the Gurungs.

2.2. *SHAMANS* are religious officiants who can not only divine the supernatural causes of misfortunes, but also prescribe and perform the curative rituals.

pujyu' (P) is of the indigenous Gurung tradition, of the soraa jaad (*sixteen clans*) moiety. He frequently officiates in association with the khlxyebri.

khlxyebri (K) is also of the indigenous Gurung tradition and a member of the soraa jaad.

la'maa (L) is a Gurung who has taken special training in the Buddhist monastery and officiates using the Buddhist scriptures.

la'm kami (LK) - see under *Seers*.

3. RITUALS

3.1. Many *RELIGIOUS RITUALS* can be carried out by the untrained householder without need of calling a shaman or a seer.

sxywaa labaa' is a rite which involves placing both hands on the head or shoulders of one who has had a bad fright or been exposed to evil influences thus endangering the security of his own souls, plxa. (Men are thought to possess nine plxa and women seven plxa.) The placing of the hands on the head is intended to hold in these potentially escaping plxa.

ru'ba jxõba *'putting on the thread'*. When a person has been sick or exposed to evil spirits through death rituals or other calamity, then friends, neighbours and relatives come and place a cord around his neck knotted with seven or nine knots according to the sex of the sufferer. This also is expressive of the desire to preserve intact within the body all of the plxa as is necessary for one's well-being.

3.2. *CURATIVE RITUALS* which require the services of a trained officiant are listed below in chart form for clarity of display.

CURATIVE RITUALS

Name	*Calamity*	*Sacrifice*	*Officiant*
probrõ' labaa'	being cursed by mxõ'	baby goat	L,K
plxa xui' labaa'	having lost one or more of one's plxa resulting in sickness		L,P
thaasũ waabaa'	disharmony in home as a result of presence of evil influences		P,K
mxõ' puja	to dispel ghost of dead person from home	chicken	P
gaara tho'ba	protection from attack of evil spirits causing sickness	chicken	P,L
xyõ khubaa'	one's wealth and property have diminished		L,K
chẽ txẽ	sickness due to attack by ligyã̃	eggs, sheep and goat's wool, and grains, rooster	P

continued overleaf

Curative Rituals - *continued*

Name	*Calamity*	*Sacrifice*	*Officiant*
dxĩ' baar labaa'	sickness in household	rooster, river water and sand	P,L
pae labaa'	the ghosts of dead are still wandering in the village potentially causing harm to relatives	sheep (if K officiates)	L (P & K)
paaldu' waabaa'	curse by witch	fermented millet and rice	L,P,K
dobaaḍe waabaa'	" " "	chicken	L,P,K
ŋxaẽ sẽba or	" " "	kid	P
nxo ŋxaẽ or	" " "		
phi ŋxaẽ or	" " "		
txẽ laba	" " "		L,LK
cho'p chebaa'	curse by witch upon hunting dog	rooster	

3.3. *REGULAR VILLAGE AND HOUSEHOLD RITUALS* are also performed throughout the year. These also are displayed in the chart below.

Ritual	*Month*	*Purpose*	*Sacrifice*	*Officiant*
panca bxoli'	jethaa *(May-June)*	to dispel illness and plagues from village	5 creatures: pidgeon, kid, fowl, sheep, calf	ritually prepared villager
kul' pujaa'	aasa'ra *(June-July)*	to ensure good rainfall for planting season	kid	B
saa'wẽ sakrãanti pujaa'	saa'wẽ *(July-Aug)*	to dispel illness from village	fowl	householder
txode labaa'	"	to dispel evil spirits from village	millet and fowl	young boys
bxayãã'r pujaa'	bxadu' *(Aug-Sep)*	to ensure evil spirits leave house	fowl	P,L

continued next page

Regular Rituals - *continued*

Ritual	*Month*	*Purpose*	*Sacrifice*	*Officiant*
dasaẽ	asauj *(Sep-Oct)*			
debi pujaa'	"	to placate goddesses	hen	house-holder
durga pujaa'	"	to placate god Durga	rooster	"
dxĩ baar labaa'	kaartika *(Oct-Nov)*	to dispel sickness from house-hold	rooster	P,L
tihaara	"	to honour dogs, oxen, cows, and brothers	-	house-holder
si'ldo pujaa'	pu'ṣ *(Dec-Jan)*	to beg for sunshine or rain	fish	villager
satte' narayaaṇ pujaa'	mxaaga *(Jan-Feb)*	to gain aus-picious favour of gods - to gain ritual purity for household	grain and food	B
mxaaga sakraanti	"	no expressed purpose	-	house-holder
ṭxoḍẽ labaa'	caida *(Mar-Apr)*	to dispel evil spirits from village	millet and fowl	youths
gaara tho'ba	"	to gain pro-tection from evil spirits, sickness	fowl	P,L
dxĩ baar labaa'	"	*see above*	*see above*	*see above*

REFERENCES

BENEDICT, Paul K.

1972 *Sino-Tibetan: a Conspectus. Princeton-Cambridge Studies in Chinese Linguistics*, vol.2. Cambridge: Cambridge University Press.

CHANG, Kun, and Betty Shefts

1964 *A Manual of Spoken Tibetan (Lhasa Dialect)*. Seattle: University of Washington Press.

DOHERTY, Victor

1974 'The Organizing Principles of Gurung Kinship'. *Kailash* 2:273-301. Kathmandu: Ratna Pustak Bhandar.

GLOVER, Warren W.

1969 *Gurung Phonemic Summary*. Kathmandu: Summer Institute of Linguistics.

1974 *Sememic and Grammatical Structures in Gurung (Nepal). SIL Publications in Linguistics and Related Fields*, vol.49. Kathmandu: SIL.

GLOVER, Warren W. and John K. Landon

n.d. 'Gurung Dialects'. To appear in *Pacific Linguistics*, A.53.

LANG, Adrianne, Katherine E.W. Mather, and Mary L. Rose

1973 *Information Storage and Retrieval: a Dictionary Project. Pacific Linguistics, D.8*. Canberra: Australian National University.

MEERENDONK, M.

1960 *Basic Gurkhali Dictionary (Roman Script)*. Nepal agents: Ratna Pustak Bhandar, Kathmandu.

PATHAK, R.C., comp. and ed.

1966 *Bhargava's Standard Illustrated Dictionary of the Hindi Language (Hindi-English Edition).* Varanasi: Bhargava Book Depot.

PITTMAN, Richard S., and Jessie R. Glover

1970 'Proto-Tamang-Gurung-Thakali'. In: *Tone Systems of Tibeto-Burman Languages of Nepal. Part II: Lexical Lists and Comparative Studies.* Edited by Austin Hale and Kenneth L. Pike, pp.9-22. (*Occasional Papers of the Wolfenden Society*, edited by F.K. Lehman, vol.3) Urbana: Department of Linguistics, University of Illinois.

REGMI, M.P.

n.d. *Anglo-Nepali Dictionary.* Varanasi: M.P. Sharma.

SINGH, Chandra Lall

1971 *Nepali to English Dictionary.* Kathmandu: Educational Enterprise.

PACIFIC LINGUISTICS

Series A, Nos. 1-9, Series B, Nos. 1-6, Series C, Nos. 1 and 3, and Bulletins 1 and 2 were called **LINGUISTIC CIRCLE OF CANBERRA PUBLICATIONS.**

All publications (including reprints of earlier items) subsequent to July 1967 bear the new name **PACIFIC LINGUISTICS.**

After each entry, ISBN numbers have been added. Where there are two ISBN numbers given, the first one refers to the complete set of volumes, and the second to the individual volume or part.

Prices are subject to alteration without prior notification.

SERIES A - OCCASIONAL PAPERS

No. 1 **WURM, S.A.** *Some Remarks on the Role of Language in the Assimilation of Australian Aborigines.* 1963; 12 pp. Reprinted 1966. ISBN 0 85883 006 X — $1.00

No. 2 **HEALEY, Alan** *Handling Unsophisticated Linguistic Informants.* 1964; iii + 30 pp. Reprinted 1967, 1972, 1973, 1975. ISBN 0 85883 007 8 — $1.50

No. 3 **PENCE, Alan, Ellis Deibler Jr, Phyllis M. Healey, and Bruce A. Hooley** *Papers in New Guinea Linguistics* No.1. 1964; iv + 42 pp. Reprinted 1971. ISBN 0 85883 008 6 — $1.50

No. 4 **WURM, S.A.** *Papers in New Guinea Linguistics* No.2. 1964; iv + 41 pp.; 1 map. Reprinted 1971. ISBN 0 85883 009 4 — $1.50

No. 5 **HEALEY, Phyllis M.** *Papers in New Guinea Linguistics* No.3. 1965; iv + 53 pp. Reprinted 1972. ISBN 0 85883 010 8 — $2.00

No. 6 **BEE, Darlene** *Papers in New Guinea Linguistics* No.4. 1965; iv + 68 pp. Reprinted 1971. ISBN 0 85883 011 6 — $2.50

No. 7 **FRANTZ, C.I. and M.E., D. and J. Oatridge, R. Loving, J. Swick, A. Pence, P. Staalsen, and H. and M. Boxwell** *Papers in New Guinea Linguistics* No.5. 1966; viii + 93 pp. Reprinted 1971. ISBN 0 85883 012 4 — $3.00

No. 8 **SHETLER, J., R. Pittman, V. Forsberg, and J. Hussey** *Papers in Philippine Linguistics* No.1. 1966; iv + 38 pp. Reprinted 1971. ISBN 0 85883 013 2 — $1.50

No. 9 **NGUYEN DANG LIEM, A. Tran Huong Mai, and David W. Dellinger** *Papers in South East Asian Linguistics* No.1. 1967; iv + 43 pp. + 30 tables + 3 chart tables + 27 charts. Reprinted 1970. ISBN 0 85883 014 0 — $3.50

PACIFIC LINGUISTICS

Occasional Papers - *continued*

No.10 **GLASGOW, D. and K., Jean F. Kirton, W.J. Oates, and B.A. and E.G. Sommer** *Papers in Australian Linguistics* No.1. 1967; v + 59 pp. Reprinted 1972. ISBN 0 85883 015 9 — $2.00

No.11 **VON BRANDENSTEIN, C.G., A. Capell, and K. Hale** *Papers in Australian Linguistics* No.2. 1967; iii + 73 pp. + 7 maps. Reprinted 1971. ISBN 0 85883 016 7 — $3.00

No.12 **McELHANON, K.A. and G. Renck** *Papers in New Guinea Linguistics* No.6. 1967; iv + 48 pp. Reprinted 1971. ISBN 0 85883 017 5 — $2.00

No.13 **GODDARD, J. and K.J. Franklin** *Papers in New Guinea Linguistics* No.7. 1967; iv + 59 pp. Reprinted 1971. ISBN 0 85883 018 3 — $2.50

No.14 **AGUAS, E.F. and D.T. Tryon** *Papers in Australian Linguistics* No.3. 1968; iii + 46 pp. + 1 map. Reprinted 1971. ISBN 0 85883 019 1 — $2.00

No.15 **CAPELL, A., G.J. Parker, and A.J. Schütz** *Papers in Linguistics of Melanesia* No.1. 1968; iii + 52 pp. + 1 map. Reprinted 1971. ISBN 0 85883 020 5 — $2.00

No.16 **VOORHOEVE, C.L., K.J. Franklin, and G. Scott** *Papers in New Guinea Linguistics* No.8. 1968; iv + 62 pp.; 2 maps. Reprinted 1971. ISBN 0 85883 021 3 — $2.50

No.17 **KINSLOW HARRIS, J., S.A. Wurm, and D.C. Laycock** *Papers in Australian Linguistics* No.4. 1969; vi + 97 pp.; 3 maps. Reprinted 1971. ISBN 0 85883 022 1 — $3.50

No.18 **CAPELL, A.; A. Healey, A. Isoroembo, and M. Chittleborough; and D.B. Wilson** *Papers in New Guinea Linguistics* No.9. 1969; vi + 110 pp.; 1 map. Reprinted 1971. ISBN 0 85883 023 X — $3.50

No.19 **MILLER, J. and H.W. Miller** *Papers in Philippine Linguistics* No.2. 1969; iii + 32 pp. Reprinted 1971. ISBN 0 85883 024 8 — $1.50

No.20 **PRENTICE, D.J.** *Papers in Borneo Linguistics* No.1. 1969; iv + 41 pp. Reprinted 1971. ISBN 0 85883 025 6 — $2.00

No.21 **CAPELL, A., A. Chowning, and S.A. Wurm** *Papers in Linguistics of Melanesia* No.2. 1970; v + 105 pp.; 5 maps. ISBN 0 85883 002 7 — $3.50

PACIFIC LINGUISTICS

Occasional Papers - *continued*

No.22 **LAYCOCK, D.C., Richard G. Lloyd, and Philip Staalsen** *Papers in New Guinea Linguistics* No.10. 1969; v + 84 pp. ISBN 0 85883 026 4 — $3.00

No.23 **BUNN, G. and R.; Alan Pence, Elaine Geary, and Doris Bjorkman; H. and N. Weimer; and O.R. Claassen and K.A. McElhanon** *Papers in New Guinea Linguistics* No.11. 1970; v + 78 pp.; 1 map. ISBN 0 85883 001 9 — $3.00

No.24 **ABRAMS, N., J. Forster, and R. Brichoux** *Papers in Philippine Linguistics* No.3. 1970; vi + 77 pp. ISBN 0 85883 000 0 — $3.00

No.25 **VOORHOEVE, C.L., K.A. McElhanon, and Bruce L. and Ruth Blowers** *Papers in New Guinea Linguistics* No.12. 1970; iv + 60 pp. + 1 map. ISBN 0 85883 027 2 — $2.50

No.26 **BLOWERS, B.L., Margie Griffin, and K.A. McElhanon** *Papers in New Guinea Linguistics* No.13. 1970; iv + 48 pp. ISBN 0 85883 028 0 — $2.00

No.27 **KIRTON, Jean F.** *Papers in Australian Linguistics* No.5. 1971; iv + 70 pp. ISBN 0 85883 029 9 — $2.50

No.28 **DUTTON, T., C.L. Voorhoeve, and S.A. Wurm** *Papers in New Guinea Linguistics* No.14. 1971; vi + 172 pp.; 8 maps. ISBN 0 85883 030 2 — $5.50

No.29 **GLOVER, Warren W., Maria Hari, and E.R. Hope** *Papers in South East Asian Linguistics* No.2. 1971; iv + 78 pp.; 1 map. ISBN 0 85883 031 0 — $3.00

No.30 **DELLINGER, D.W., E.R. Hope, Makio Katsura, and Tatsuo Nishida** *Papers in South East Asian Linguistics* No.3. 1973; iv + 82 pp. ISBN 0 85883 091 4 — $3.00

No.31 **LEWIS, R.K., Sandra C. Lewis, Shirley Litteral, and P. Staalsen** *Papers in New Guinea Linguistics* No.15. 1972; v + 69 pp. ISBN 0 85883 032 9 — $2.50

No.32 **HOHULIN, R.M. and Lou Hohulin** *Papers in Philippine Linguistics* No.4. 1971; iv + 32 pp. ISBN 0 85883 033 7 — $1.50

No.33 **COURT, C. and R.A. Blust, and F.S. Watuseke** *Papers in Borneo and Western Austronesian Linguistics* No.2. 1977; vi + 132 pp.; 1 map. ISBN 0 85883 164 3 — $5.00

PACIFIC LINGUISTICS

Occasional Papers - *continued*

No.34 **ALLEN, Janice and M. Lawrence** *Papers in New Guinea Linguistics* No.16. 1972; iii + 46 pp. ISBN 0 85883 081 7 $2.00

No.35 **BEAUMONT, C., D.T. Tryon, and S.A. Wurm** *Papers in Linguistics of Melanesia* No.3. 1972; vii + 113 pp. + 6 maps. ISBN 0 85883 083 3 $4.00

No.36 **SCHEBECK, B.; and L.A. Hercus and I.M. White** *Papers in Australian Linguistics* No.6. 1973; iv + 72 pp. + 4 pages of photographs + 2 maps. ISBN 0 85883 095 7 $3.00

No.37 **FURBY, Christine E., Luise A. Hercus, and Christine Kilham** *Papers in Australian Linguistics* No.7. 1974; iv + 73 pp. + 1 map + 3 photographs. ISBN 0 85883 116 3 $3.00

No.38 **HOLZKNECHT, K.G. and D.J. Phillips** *Papers in New Guinea Linguistics* No.17. 1973; iii + 78 pp. ISBN 0 85883 097 3 $3.00

No.39 **SHARPE, M.C., L. Jagst, and D.B.W. Birk** *Papers in Australian Linguistics* No.8. 1975; v + 78 pp. ISBN 0 85883 126 0 $3.50

No.40 **CONRAD, R. and W. Dye; N.P. Thomson; and L.P. Bruce Jr** *Papers in New Guinea Linguistics* No.18. 1975; iv + 102 pp. + 5 maps. ISBN 0 85883 118 X $4.00

No.41 **CHANDLER, Donna Hettick, E. Ruch, and Jeannette Witucki** *Papers in Philippine Linguistics* No.5. 1974; iv + 74 pp. ISBN 0 85883 114 7 $3.00

No.42 **HUDSON, Joyce and Barbara J. Sayers** *Papers in Australian Linguistics* No.9. 1976; iv + 79 pp. ISBN 0 85883 140 6 $3.50

No.43 **HEADLAND, T.N. and A. Healey; and Jeannette Witucki** *Papers in Philippine Linguistics* No.6. 1974; iii + 74 pp.; 1 map. ISBN 0 85883 108 2 $3.00

No.44 **HOOKER, B., D. Behrens, and P.M. Hartung** *Papers in Philippine Linguistics* No.7. 1975; iv + 60 pp. ISBN 0 85883 135 X $3.00

No.45 **REESINK, G.P., L. Fleischmann, S. Turpeinen, and P.C. Lincoln** *Papers in New Guinea Linguistics* No.19. 1976; v + 105 pp.; 2 maps. ISBN 0 85883 156 2 $4.50

No.46 **WITUCKI, Jeannette, M.R. Walrod, and Jean Shand** *Papers in Philippine Linguistics* No.8. 1976; iv + 89 pp. ISBN 0 85883 146 5 $4.00

PACIFIC LINGUISTICS

Occasional Papers - *continued*

No.47 **KIRTON, Jean; B. Sommer; S.A. Wurm and Luise Hercus; and P. Austin, R. Ellis and Luise Hercus** *Papers in Australian Linguistics* No.10. 1976; iv + 78 pp.; 3 maps; 11 photographs. ISBN 0 85883 153 8 — $3.50

No.48 **THOMAS, D.D., E.W. Lee and Nguyen Dang Liem, eds** *Papers in South East Asian Linguistics* No.4: *Chamic Studies*. 1977; x + 124 pp. ISBN 0 85883 163 5 — $5.00

No.49 **BRADLEY, D.** *Papers in South East Asian Linguistics* No.5. 1977; iv + 98 pp. ISBN 0 85883 158 9 — $4.00

In preparation:

No.50 **JOHNSTON, E.C., H. Weins, Jo Ann Gault, P. Green and B. Grayden** *Papers in Philippine Linguistics* No.9

No.51 **KIRTON, Jean F., R.K. Wood and Luise Hercus** *Papers in Australian Linguistics* No.11

No.52 **GETHING, T.W. and Nguyen Dang Liem, eds** *Papers in South East Asian Linguistics* No.6; *Tai Studies in Honour of William J. Gedney*

No.53 **TRAIL, R.L., H.T. Rathod, G. Chand, C. Roy, I. Shrestha and N.M. Tuladhar; P.J. Grainger; W.W. Glover and J.K. Landon; A. Hale and T. Manandhar; and B. Schöttelndreyer** *Papers in South East Asian Linguistics* No. 7

SERIES B - MONOGRAPHS

No. 1 **WURM, S.A. and J.B. Harris** *POLICE MOTU, an introduction to the Trade Language of Papua (New Guinea) for anthropologists and other fieldworkers*. 1963; vi + 81 pp. Reprinted 1964, 1965, 1966, 1967, 1969, 1970, 1971, 1973. ISBN 0 85883 034 5 — $3.00

No. 2 **WURM, S.A.** *Phonological Diversification in Australian New Guinea Highlands Languages*. 1964; iii + 87 pp.; 1 map. Reprinted 1971. ISBN 0 85883 035 3 — $3.00

No. 3 **HEALEY, Alan** *Telefol Phonology*. 1964; iii + 1 figure + 53 pp. + 5 tables. Reprinted 1972. ISBN 0 85883 036 1 — $2.50

No. 4 **HEALEY, Phyllis M.** *Telefol Noun Phrases*. 1965; iii + 51 pp. Reprinted 1972. ISBN 0 85883 037 X — $2.00

PACIFIC LINGUISTICS

Monographs - *continued*

No. 5	**HEALEY, Phyllis M.** *Levels and Chaining in Telefol Sentences.* 1966; iv + 64 pp. Reprinted 1971. ISBN 0 85883 038 8	$2.50
No. 6	**TRYON, Darrell T.** *Nengone Grammar.* 1967; x + 91 pp. Reprinted 1971. ISBN 0 85883 039 6	$3.50
No. 7	**TRYON, Darrell T.** *Dehu Grammar.* 1968; ix + 111 pp. Reprinted 1971. ISBN 0 85883 040 X	$4.00
No. 8	**TRYON, Darrell T.** *Iai Grammar.* 1968; xii + 125 pp. Reprinted 1971. ISBN 0 85883 041 8	$4.50
No. 9	**DUTTON, T.E.** *The Peopling of Central Papua: some Preliminary Observations.* 1969; viii + 182 pp. Reprinted 1970, 1971. ISBN 0 85883 042 6	$5.50
No.10	**FRANKLIN, K.J.** *The Dialects of Kewa.* 1968; iv + 72 pp.; 20 maps. Reprinted 1971. ISBN 0 85883 043 4	$3.50
No.11	**SOMMER, B.A.** *Kunjen Phonology: Synchronic and Diachronic.* 1969; iv + 72 pp.; 3 maps. ISBN 0 85883 044 2	$3.00
No.12	**KLOKEID, T.J.** *Thargari Phonology and Morphology.* 1969; viii + 56 pp.; 1 map. ISBN 0 85883 045 0	$2.50
No.13	**TREFRY, D.** *A Comparative Study of Kuman and Pawaian.* 1969; iv + 94 pp.; 1 map. ISBN 0 85883 046 9	$3.50
No.14	**McELHANON, K.A.** *Selepet Phonology.* 1970; v + 47 pp.; 1 map. ISBN 0 85883 003 5	$2.00
No.15	**TRYON, D.T.** *An Introduction to Maranungku (Northern Australia).* 1970; vi + 111 pp.; 1 map. ISBN 0 85883 047 7	$4.00
No.16	**McELHANON, K.A. and C.L. Voorhoeve** *The Trans-New-Guinea Phylum: Explorations in Deep-level Genetic Relationships.* 1970; v + 107 pp.; 4 maps. Reprinted 1978. ISBN 0 85883 048 5	$4.00
No.17	**KUKI, Hiroshi** *Tuamotuan Phonology.* 1970; ix + 119 pp.; 2 maps. ISBN 0 85883 049 3	$4.00
No.18	**YOUNG, R.A.** *The Verb in Bena-Bena: its Form and Function.* 1971; v + 68 pp. ISBN 0 85883 050 7	$2.50
No.19	**PATON, W.F.** *Ambrym (Lonwolwol) Grammar.* 1971; xi + 128 pp.; 1 map. ISBN 0 85883 051 5	$4.50

PACIFIC LINGUISTICS

Monographs - *continued*

No.20 **CAPELL, A.** *Arosi Grammar.* 1971; iv + 90 pp.; 1 map. $3.50
ISBN 0 85883 052 3

No.21 **McELHANON, K.A.** *Selepet Grammar. Part I: From Root to Phrase.* $4.00
1972; vi + 116 pp. ISBN 0 85883 085 X and ISBN 0 85883 086 8

No.22 **McELHANON, K.A.** *Towards a Typology of the Finisterre-Huon Languages, New Guinea.* 1973; vii + 73 pp.; 1 map. $3.00
ISBN 0 85883 094 9

No.23 **SCOTT, Graham** *Higher Levels of Fore Grammar.* Edited by Robert E. Longacre. 1973; x + 88 pp. $3.50
ISBN 0 85883 088 4

No.24 **DUTTON, T.E.** *A Checklist of Languages and Present-day Villages of Central and South-East Mainland Papua.* 1973; iv + 80 pp.; 1 map. $3.00
ISBN 0 85883 090 6

No.25 **LAYCOCK, D.C.** *Sepik Languages - Checklist and Preliminary Classification.* 1973; iv + 130 pp.; 1 map. $4.50
ISBN 0 85883 084 1

No.26 **MÜHLHÄUSLER, P.** *Pidginization and Simplification of Language.* $5.00
1974; v + 161 pp. Reprinted 1978. ISBN 0 85883 113 9

No.27 **RAMOS, Teresita V.** *The Case System of Tagalog Verbs.* 1974; $5.50
viii + 168 pp. ISBN 0 85883 115 5

No.28 **WEST, Dorothy** *Wojokeso Sentence, Paragraph, and Discourse Analysis.* Edited by Robert E. Longacre. 1973; x + 181 pp. $6.00
ISBN 0 85883 089 2

No.29 **ELBERT, Samuel H.** *Puluwat Grammar.* 1974; v + 137 pp. $4.50
ISBN 0 85883 103 1

No.30 **METCALFE, C.D.** *Bardi Verb Morphology (Northwestern Australia).* $6.50
1975; x + 215 pp.; 1 map. ISBN 0 85883 121 X

No.31 **VOORHOEVE, C.L.** *Languages of Irian Jaya: Checklist. Preliminary Classification, Language Maps, Wordlists.* 1975; iv + 129 pp.; 17 maps. $5.00
ISBN 0 85883 128 7

No.32 **WALTON, Janice** *Binongan Itneg Sentences.* 1975; vi + 70 pp. $3.00
ISBN 0 85883 117 1

No.33 **GUY, J.B.M.** *A Grammar of the Northern Dialect of Sakao.* 1974; $3.50
ix + 99 pp.; 2 maps. ISBN 0 85883 104 X

PACIFIC LINGUISTICS

Monographs - *continued*

No.34 HOPE, E.R. *The Deep Syntax of Lisu Sentences. A Transformational Case Grammar.* 1974; viii + 184 pp. + 1 map. ISBN 0 85883 110 4 — $6.00

No.35 IRWIN, Barry *Salt-Yui Grammar.* 1974; iv + 151 pp. ISBN 0 85883 111 2 — $5.00

No.36 PHILLIPS, D.J. *Wahgi Phonology and Morphology.* 1976; x + 165 pp. ISBN 0 85883 141 4 — $5.50

No.37 NGUYEN DANG LIEM *Cases, Clauses and Sentences in Vietnamese.* 1975; v + 89 pp. ISBN 0 85883 133 3 — $3.50

No.38 SNEDDON, J.N. *Tondano Phonology and Grammar.* 1975; viii + 264 pp. ISBN 0 85883 125 2 — $8.00

No.39 LANG, Adrianne *The Semantics of Classificatory Verbs in Enga (and other Papua New Guinea Languages).* 1975; xii + 234 pp.; 2 maps. ISBN 0 85883 123 6 — $7.00

No.40 RENCK, G.L. *A Grammar of Yagaria.* 1975; xiii + 235 pp.; 1 map. ISBN 0 85883 130 9 — $7.00

No.41 Z'GRAGGEN, J.A. *The Languages of the Madang District, Papua New Guinea.* 1975; vi + 154 pp.; 1 map. ISBN 0 85883 134 1 — $5.00

No.42 FURBY, E.S. and C.E. *A Preliminary Analysis of Garawa Phrases and Clauses.* 1977; viii + 101 pp. ISBN 0 85883 151 1 — $3.50

No.43 STOKHOF, W.A.L. *Preliminary Notes on the Alor and Pantar Languages (East Indonesia).* 1975; vi + 73 pp. + 2 maps. ISBN 0 85883 124 4 — $3.00

No.44 SAYERS, Barbara *The Sentence in Wik-Munkan: a Description of Propositional Relationships.* 1976; xvii + 185 pp. ISBN 0 85883 138 4 — $6.00

No.45 BIRK, D.B.W. *The Malakmalak Language, Daly River (Western Arnhem Land).* 1976; xii + 179 pp.; 1 map. ISBN 0 85883 150 3 — $6.00

No.46 GLISSMEYER, Gloria *A Tagmemic Analysis of Hawaii English Clauses.* 1976; viii + 149 pp. ISBN 0 85883 142 2 — $5.00

No.55 LYNCH, John *A Grammar of Lenakel.* 1977; vii + 135 pp.; 1 map. ISBN 0 85883 166 X — $4.50

PACIFIC LINGUISTICS

Monographs in preparation:

No.47 BEAUMONT, C.H. *The Tigak Language of New Ireland*

No.48 CLARK, Marybeth *Coverbs and Case in Vietnamese*

No.49 FILBECK, David *T'in: a Historical Study*

No.50 SMITH, Kenneth D. *Sedang Grammar: Phonological and Syntactic Structure*

No.51 LEE, Jennifer R. *Notes on Li Hawu (Eastern Indonesia)*

No.52 KILHAM, Christine A. *Thematic Organization of Wik-Munkan Discourse*

No.53 VESALAINEN, Olavi and Marja *Clause Patterns in Lhomi*

No.54 SNEDDON, J. *Proto-Minahasan: Phonology, Morphology and Word List*

No.56 ROSS, M. and John Natu Paol *Waskia Grammar Sketch and Vocabulary*

No.57 CHAN-YAP, Gloria *Hokkien Chinese Borrowings in Tagalog*

No.58 GONZALEZ, Andrew *Pampangan: Outline of a Generative Semantic Description*

No.59 LUZARES, Casilda E. *The Morphology of Selected Cebuano Verbs: a Case Analysis*

No.60 SOBERANO, Rosa *The Dialects of Marinduque Tagalog*

SERIES C - BOOKS

No. 1 LAYCOCK, D.C. *The Ndu Language Family (Sepik District, New Guinea)*. 1965; xi + 224 pp.; 1 map. ISBN 0 85883 053 1 — $7.00

No. 2 GRACE, George W. *Canala Dictionary (New Caledonia)*. 1975; x + 128 pp. ISBN 0 85883 122 8 — $4.50

No. 3 NGUYEN DANG LIEM *English Grammar (A Contrastive Analysis of English and Vietnamese* vol.1). 1966; xliv + 177 pp. Reprinted 1970. ISBN 0 85883 054 X and ISBN 0 85883 055 8 — $6.50

No. 4 NGUYEN DANG LIEM *Vietnamese Grammar (A Contrastive Analysis of English and Vietnamese* vol.2). 1969; xlvi + 209 pp. Reprinted 1975. ISBN 0 85883 054 X and ISBN 0 85883 056 6 — $7.50

No. 5 NGUYEN DANG LIEM *A Contrastive Grammatical Analysis of English and Vietnamese (A Contrastive Analysis of English and Vietnamese* vol.3). 1967; xv + 151 pp. Reprinted 1971. ISBN 0 85883 054 X and ISBN 0 85883 057 4 — $5.00

PACIFIC LINGUISTICS

Books - *continued*

No. 6 **TRYON, Darrell T.** *Dehu-English Dictionary.* 1967; v + 137 pp. Reprinted 1971. ISBN 0 85883 058 2 — $4.50

No. 7 **TRYON, Darrell T.** *English-Dehu Dictionary.* 1967; iii + 162 pp. Reprinted 1971. ISBN 0 85883 059 0 — $5.00

No. 8 **NGUYEN DANG LIEM** *A Contrastive Phonological Analysis of English and Vietnamese (A Contrastive Analysis of English and Vietnamese* vol.4). 1970; xv + 206 pp. ISBN 0 85883 054 X and ISBN 0 85883 004 3 — $6.50

No. 9 **TRYON, D.T. and M.-J. Dubois** *Nengone Dictionary. Part I: Nengone-English.* 1969; vii + 445 pp. ISBN 0 85883 060 4 and ISBN 0 85883 061 2 — $12.50

No.10 **OATES, W. and L. Oates** *Kapau Pedagogical Grammar.* 1968; v + 178 pp. Reprinted 1971. ISBN 0 85883 062 0 — $5.50

No.11 **FOX, C.E.** *Arosi-English Dictionary.* 1970; iv + 406 pp.; 1 map. ISBN 0 85883 063 9 — $11.00

No.12 **GRACE, George W.** *Grand Couli Dictionary (New Caledonia).* 1976; vii + 113 pp. ISBN 0 85883 154 6 — $6.00

No.13 **WURM, S.A. and D.C. Laycock, eds** *Pacific Linguistic Studies in Honour of Arthur Capell.* 1970; viii + 1292 pp.; 25 maps; 1 photograph. Reprinted 1975. ISBN 0 85883 005 1 — $35.50

Articles authored, or co-authored, by:
B.W. Bender, Catherine M. Berndt, R.M. Berndt, H. Bluhme, J.E. Bolt, C.G. von Brandenstein, †C.D. Chrétien, J.R. Cleverly, C. Court, R.M.W. Dixon, W.H. Douglas, T.E. Dutton, I. Dyen, S.H. Elbert, A.P. Elkin, E.H. Flint, K.J. Franklin, Marie Godfrey, G.W. Grace, K. Hale, Joy Harris, A. Healey, H. Hershberger, Ruth Hershberger, W.G. Hoddinot, P.W. Hohepa, N.M. Holmer, B.A. Hooley, Dorothy J. James, H. Kähler, Susan Kaldor, H. Kerr, Jean F. Kirton, D.C. Laycock, Nguyen Dang Liem, K.A. McElhanon, H. McKaughan, G.N. O'Grady, A. Pawley, Eunice V. Pike, R. Pittman, D.J. Prentice, A.J. Schütz, M.C. Sharpe, †W.E. Smythe, A.J. Taylor, D.T. Tryon, E.M. Uhlenbeck, C.F. Voegelin, F.M. Voegelin, C.L. Voorhoeve, S.A. Wurm, J. Z'graggen.

No.14 **GEERTS, P.** *'Āre'āre Dictionary.* 1970; iv + 185 pp.; 1 map. ISBN 0 85883 064 7 — $5.50

No.15 **McELHANON, K.A. and N.A.** *Selepet-English Dictionary.* 1970; xxi + 144 pp. ISBN 0 85883 065 5 — $5.00

PACIFIC LINGUISTICS

Books - *continued*

No.16 **FRANKLIN, K.J.** *A Grammar of Kewa, New Guinea.* 1971; ix + 138 pp. ISBN 0 85883 066 3 — $4.50

No.17 **PARKER, G.J.** *Southeast Ambrym Dictionary.* 1971; xiii + 60 pp. ISBN 0 85883 067 1 — $2.50

No.18 **PRENTICE, D.J.** *The Murut Languages of Sabah.* 1971; xi + 311 pp.; 1 map. ISBN 0 85883 068 X — $9.00

No.19 **Z'GRAGGEN, J.A.** *Classificatory and Typological Studies in Languages of the Madang District.* 1971; viii + 179 pp.; 4 maps. ISBN 0 85883 069 8 — $5.50

No.20 **LANG, Adrianne** *Enga Dictionary with English Index.* 1973; lvi + 219 pp. + 1 map. ISBN 0 85883 093 0 — $10.00

No.21 **PATON, W.F.** *Ambrym (Lonwolwol) Dictionary.* 1973; ix + 337 pp. + 1 map. ISBN 0 85883 092 2 — $11.50

No.22 **LONGACRE, Robert E., ed.** *Philippine Discourse and Paragraph Studies in Memory of Betty McLachlin.* 1971; xv + 366 pp.; 1 photograph. ISBN 0 85883 070 1 — $10.50
Articles authored by: †Betty McLachlin and Barbara Blackburn, Hazel Wrigglesworth, Claudia Whittle, Charles Walton.

No.23 **TRYON, D.T. and M.-J. Dubois** *Nengone Dictionary. Part II: English-Nengone.* 1971; iii + 202 pp. ISBN 0 85883 060 4 and ISBN 0 85883 071 X — $6.00

No.24 **ELBERT, Samuel H.** *Puluwat Dictionary.* 1972; ix + 401 pp. ISBN 0 85883 082 5 — $13.00

No.25 **FOX, Charles E.** *Lau Dictionary*, with English Index. 1974; vi + 260 pp. Reprinted 1976. ISBN 0 85883 101 5 — $9.50

No.26 **FRANKLIN, Karl, ed.** in cooperation with M. Brown, T. Dutton, R. Lloyd, G. McDonald, D. Shaw, C. Voorhoeve, S. Wurm *The Linguistic Situation in the Gulf District and Adjacent Areas, Papua New Guinea.* 1973; x + 597 pp.; 8 maps. ISBN 0 85883 100 7 — $18.00

No.27 **HO-MIN SOHN and B.W. Bender** *A Ulithian Grammar.* 1973; xv + 398 pp.; 2 maps. ISBN 0 85883 098 1 — $13.50

No.28 **HEADLAND, Thomas N. and Janet D.** *A Dumagat (Casiguran) - English Dictionary.* 1974; lxii + 232 pp.; 1 map. ISBN 0 85883 107 4 — $10.50

PACIFIC LINGUISTICS

Books - *continued*

No.29 **DUTTON, T.E., ed.** *Studies in Languages of Central and South-East Papua.* 1975; xviii + 834 pp.; 5 maps. $25.50
ISBN 0 85883 119 8
A collection of illustrative sketches of many hitherto undescribed languages of Central and South-East Papua by J. Austing, R.E. Cooper, T.E. Dutton, J. and C. Farr, R. and S. Garland, J.E. Henderson, J.A. Kolia (formerly Collier), M. Olsen, A. Pawley, E.L. Richert, N.P. Thomson, R. Upia, H. and N. Weimer.

No.30 **LOVING, Richard and Aretta** *Awa Dictionary.* 1975; xliv + 203 pp.; 1 map. ISBN 0 85883 137 6 $9.00

No.31 **NGUYEN DANG LIEM, ed.** *South-East Asian Linguistic Studies,* vol.1. 1974; vii + 213 pp. Reprinted 1978. $9.50
ISBN 0 85883 144 9 and ISBN 0 85883 099 X
Articles authored by: Soenjono Dardjowidjojo, Cesar A. Hidalgo, Arthur G. Crisfield, Philip N. Jenner, Marybeth Clark, Nguyen Dang Liem, Saveros Pou.

No.32 **TRYON, D.T.** *Daly Family Languages, Australia.* 1974; xvii + 303 pp.; 1 map. ISBN 0 85883 106 6 $11.00

No.33 **WURM, S.A. and B. Wilson** *English Finderlist of Reconstructions in Austronesian Languages (post Brandstetter).* 1975; xxxii + 246 pp. ISBN 0 85883 129 5 $10.00

No.34 **GUY, J.B.M.** *Handbook of Bichelamar - Manuel de Bichelamar.* 1974; iii + 256 pp. Reprinted 1975. ISBN 0 85883 109 0 $9.50

No.35 **KEESING, R.M.** *Kwaio Dictionary.* 1975; xxxiv + 296 pp.; 1 map. ISBN 0 85883 120 1 $11.50

No.36 **REID, Lawrence A.** *Bontok-English Dictionary.* 1976; xxiv + 500 pp. ISBN 0 85883 145 7 $16.00

No.37 **RENCK, G.L.** *Yagaria Dictionary with English Index.* 1977; xxx + 327 pp.; 1 map. ISBN 0 85883 161 9 $12.00

No.38 **WURM, S.A., ed.** *Papuan Languages and the New Guinea Linguistic Scene (New Guinea Area Languages and Language Study,* vol.1). 1975; xlvi + 1038 pp.; 28 maps. Reprinted 1977. $32.00
ISBN 0 85883 131 7 and ISBN 0 85883 132 5

No.39 **WURM, S.A., ed.** *Austronesian Languages (New Guinea Area Languages and Language Study,* vol.2). 1976; xxxv + 736 pp.; 21 maps. ISBN 0 85883 131 7 and ISBN 0 85883 155 4 $23.50

PACIFIC LINGUISTICS

Books - *continued*

No.40 **WURM, S.A., ed.** *Language, Culture, Society, and the Modern World (New Guinea Area Languages and Language Study*, vol.3). 1977; lxxxvi + 1449 pp. in two fascicles; 3 maps; 40 photographs. ISBN 0 85883 131 7 and ISBN 0 85883 159 7 — $44.00

No.41 **FLIERL, †W. and H. Strauss, eds** *Kâte Dictionary.* 1977; xxxvi + 499 pp.; 1 map. ISBN 0 85883 149 X — $16.00

No.42 **NGUYEN DANG LIEM, ed.** *South-East Asian Linguistic Studies*, vol.2. 1976; iv + 262 pp.; 2 maps. ISBN 0 85883 144 9 and ISBN 0 85883 143 0 — $10.50

Articles authored by: Eugénie J.A. Henderson, Judith M. Jacob, P.N. Jenner, G. Diffloth, Sidharta (Sie Ing Djiang), T.A. Llamzon, M. Teresita Martin, J.F. Kess, M.W. Mintz, H.L. Shorto, J.U. Wolff, P.K. Benedict, Lili Rabel-Heyman.

No.43 **SMALLEY, W.A., ed.** *Phonemes and Orthography: Language Planning in Ten Minority Languages of Thailand.* 1976; xi + 347 pp. ISBN 0 85883 144 9 — $13.00

Articles authored by: W.A. Smalley, E.R. Hope, P. Wyss, J.R. Cooke, J.E. Hudspith, J.A. Morris, Lois Callaway, C.W. Callaway, D. Filbeck, B.M. Johnston, D. Schlatter, D.W. Hogan.

No.44 **ZORC, R.D.P.** *The Bisayan Dialects of the Philippines: Subgrouping and Reconstruction.* 1977; xxi + 328 pp.; 9 maps. ISBN 0 85883 157 0 — $11.50

No.46 **HEALEY, Phyllis and Alan** *Telefol Dictionary.* 1977; xix + 358 pp. ISBN 0 85883 160 0 — $12.50

No.50 **TRYON, D.T.** *New Hebrides Languages: an Internal Classification.* 1976; v + 545 pp.; 7 maps. ISBN 0 85883 152 X — $17.00

No.51 **GLOVER, W.W., J.R. Glover, and Deu Bahadur Gurung** *Gurung-Nepali-English Dictionary with English-Gurung and Nepali-Gurung Indexes.* 1977; xiii + 316 pp. ISBN 0 85883 147 3 — $11.50

No.55 **LYNCH, John** *Lenakel Dictionary.* 1977; vii + 167 pp. ISBN 0 85883 165 1 — $5.50

In preparation:

No.45 **NGUYEN DANG LIEM, ed.** *South-East Asian Linguistic Studies*, vol.3

No.47 **PEREZ, A.Q., A.O. Santiago, and Nguyen Dang Liem, eds** *Papers from the Conference on the Standardization of Asian Languages, Manila, Philippines, December 16-21, 1974*

PACIFIC LINGUISTICS

Books in preparation - *continued*

No.48 **WURM, S.A., ed.,** with P. Mühlhäusler, D.C. Laycock, and T.E. Dutton *Handbook of New Guinea Pidgin*

No.49 **LAYCOCK, D.C.** *Basic Materials in Buin: Grammar, Texts and Dictionary*

No.52 **MÜHLHÄUSLER, P.** *Growth and Structure of the Lexicon of New Guinea Pidgin*

No.53 **FRANKLIN, Karl J. and Joice Franklin** *Kewa Dictionary (with Supplementary Materials)*

No.54 **THARP, J.A. and Y'Bham Buon-Ya** *A Rhade-English Dictionary with English-Rhade Finder List*

No.56 **CAPELL, A.** *Futuna Dictionary*

No.57 **BAUTISTA, Maria L.S.** *The Filipino Bilingual's Competence: a Model Based on an Analysis of Tagalog-English Code Switching*

SERIES D - SPECIAL PUBLICATIONS
(Bulletins, archival materials and other publications)

No. 1 *Bulletin No.1.* 1964; 9 pp. ISBN 0 85883 072 8 — $0.50

No. 2 *Bulletin No.2.* 1965; 84 pp. ISBN 0 85883 073 6 — $3.00

No. 3 **WURM, S.A.** *New Guinea Highlands Pidgin: Course Materials.* 1971; vii + 175 pp. ISBN 0 85883 074 4 — $5.50

No. 4 **WURM, S.A.** *Language Map of the Eastern, Western and Southern Highlands, Territory of Papua and New Guinea.* In 14 colours. 1961. ISBN 0 85883 075 2 — $1.00

No. 5 **LAYCOCK, Don** *Materials in New Guinea Pidgin (Coastal and Lowlands).* 1970; xxxvii + 62 pp. Reprinted 1974. ISBN 0 85883 076 0 — $3.50

No. 6 **NGUYEN DANG LIEM** *Four-Syllable Idiomatic Expressions in Vietnamese.* 1970; v + 60 pp. ISBN 0 85883 077 9 — $2.50

No. 7 **ELBERT, S.H.** *Three Legends of Puluwat and a Bit of Talk.* 1971; viii + 85 pp.; 1 map; 1 photograph. ISBN 0 85883 078 7 — $3.50

No. 8 **LANG, A., K.E.W. Mather, and M.L. Rose** *Information Storage and Retrieval: a Dictionary Project.* 1973; vii + 151 pp. ISBN 0 85883 087 6 — $5.00

No. 9 *Index to Pacific Linguistics, Series A-D, as at the end of 1970.* 1971; iv + 75 pp. ISBN 0 85883 079 5 — $3.00

PACIFIC LINGUISTICS

Special Publications - *continued*

No.10 **PATON, W.F.** *Tales of Ambrym.* 1971; xiii + 82 pp.; 1 map. $3.50
ISBN 0 85883 080 9

No.12 **DUTTON, T.E.** *Conversational New Guinea Pidgin.* 1973; xviii + 292 pp. Reprinted 1974, 1977. ISBN 0 85883 096 5 $8.50

No.21 **SCHEBECK, B.** *Texts on the Social System of the Atʸnʸamaṯaṉa People. With Grammatical Notes.* 1974; xviii + 278 pp. + 1 photograph. ISBN 0 85883 102 3 $8.50

No.23 **CLYNE, Michael, coll. and ed.** *Australia Talks: Essays on the Sociology of Australian Immigrant and Aboriginal Languages.* 1976; viii + 244 pp. Reprinted 1978. ISBN 0 85883 148 1 $8.00

No.24 **DUTTON, T.E. and C.L. Voorhoeve** *Beginning Hiri Motu.* 1974; xvii + 259 pp. Reprinted 1975. ISBN 0 85883 112 0 $8.00

No.25 **Z'GRAGGEN, J.A.** *Language Map of the Madang District, Papua New Guinea.* 1973. ISBN 0 85883 105 8 $1.00

No.26 **LAYCOCK, D.** *Languages of the Sepik Region, Papua New Guinea* (map). 1975. ISBN 0 85883 136 8 $1.00

No.27 **WURM, S.A.** *Spreading of Languages in the Southwestern Pacific* (map). 1975. ISBN 0 85883 127 9 $1.00

In preparation:

No.11 **PATON, W.F.** *Customs of Ambrym (Texts, Songs, Games and Drawings)*

No.13 **GLOVER, Jessie R. and Deu Bahadur Gurung** *Conversational Gurung*

No.14 **Z'GRAGGEN, J.A.** *A Comparative Word List of the Northern Adelbert Range Languages, Madang District, Papua New Guinea*

No.15 -------------- *A Comparative Word List of the Southern Adelbert Range Languages, Madang District, Papua New Guinea*

No.16 -------------- *A Comparative Word List of the Mabuso Languages, Madang District, Papua New Guinea*

No.17 -------------- *A Comparative Word List of the Rai Coast Languages, Madang District, Papua New Guinea*

No.18 **STANHOPE, J.M.** *The Language of the Rao People, Grengabu, Madang District, Papua New Guinea*

No.19 **STOKHOF, W.A.L.** *Woisika I: an Ethnographic Introduction*

PACIFIC LINGUISTICS

Special Publications in preparation - *continued*

No.20 **CAPELL, A. and J. Layard** *Materials in Aitchin, Malekula: Grammar, Vocabulary and Texts*